The Ethnic Dimension
in American Society

Contributing Editors

Oliver Patterson (Chapter 10)
City College of New York

Stanley Plastrik (Chapter 6)
Staten Island Community College

Joseph W. Wieczerzak (Chapter 5)
Bronx Community College

Salvatore J. LaGumina
Nassau Community College, SUNY

Frank J. Cavaioli
*State University of New York
at Farmingdale*

The Ethnic Dimension in American Society

Holbrook Press, Inc.   Boston

To Julie and Lorraine

Library of Congress Catalog Card Number: 73-87098

Printed in the United States of America.

Contents

Preface

The central theme of this book is that the American experience can be understood through a study of immigrants and ethnic minorities. As logical and as obvious as the theme may be, it is our contention that this reader is a unique effort to fathom the American social fabric through the eyes, ears, travail, and writings of American ethnic groups. The readings are woven into a narrative that explains the reason for inclusion of each article and its place in the nation's historical, social, and political setting.

The following ethnic groups are included: Native Americans, English, Blacks, French, Dutch, Germans, Scots, Welsh, Irish, Norwegians, Swedes, Danes, Chinese, Japanese, Filipinos, Poles, Slavs, Hungarians, Russians, Jews, Ruthenians, Ukrainians, Italians, Greeks, Portuguese, Syrians, Canadians, Mexicans, Puerto Ricans, Cubans, Haitians, and Virgin Islanders. It is to be noted that coverage of certain racial groups, which are the preoccupation of most ethnic books of recent years, is given attention here; however, it is included without disturbing the central theme. The major thrust of the book is on "new immigration" peoples. That is, it concentrates on those ethnic groups that have entered the country since the Civil War and on those people freed by that conflict. Accordingly, coverage of the early colonial and federal periods is limited but is included to demonstrate the continuity of ethnic forces in American life.

Selections used in this volume emanate from a variety of primary and secondary sources, including published and unpublished material. They are borrowed from personal papers, official documents, biographical and autobiographical works, memoirs, newspapers, and periodicals. They provide vibrancy, historical perspective, and societal vision. Above all they are intended to make manifest the intent of the book: that to understand American society is to understand the periphery Americans.

Editors' notes are provided to present the reader with an overview of ethnicity in American life. Also treated is official United States immigration policy as it has reacted to and affected ethnicity. In addition, the authors have formulated a bibliography, appendix, and thought questions to meet certain pedagogical needs of students who use the reader.

The reader is intended for all levels of college students who seek to understand that America's pluralistic society is most functional. Specifically the book can be used most profitably in courses in American history or civilization, American immigration or history of American ethnic group life, and sociology of American minorities.

It is our happy task to mention here the individuals who have helped to make this reader possible: the contributing editors, the library staffs of Nassau Community College, State University at Farmingdale, Plainview-Old Bethpage, and the Center for Migration Studies, our typist Edward Forte, and our students, who have been exposed to some of this material in our courses.

Frank J. Cavaioli, Ph.D.

Salvatore J. LaGumina, Ph.D.

1

Introduction

Diversity in American life is an ever-recurring theme. Whether one speaks about the competition between various immigrant groups in the early period of American History or about contemporary manifestations of racial and ethnic unrest, it is evident that ethnic diversity has played and continues to play a major role in the weaving of the peculiar American social fabric. Blacks and several other minority groups are now extremely aware of their own ethnicity and the need to articulate it. Recent studies only underline the fact that white ethnic Americans are also becoming restive and are looking out for the interests of their distinctive groups. Much of this phenomenon is in the form of reaction against incendiary black militants and other alienated minorities; the average white middle-class American has come to think of himself at times as a member of a besieged minority. These "forgotten Americans," as a recent article reports, want more programs for themselves. Historian John Roche says, "the Irish and the Jews don't want to penalize the Negro but they feel strongly that the rules that they came up with should apply."[1]

While many deplore the negative reaction of ethnic power in the context of competition for jobs, housing, and political power, not enough attention has been given to the positive aspects of ethnicity. The simple fact is that out of the crucible of American pluralism a unique and effective, if somewhat unsteady, unity has resulted. In 1782, J. Hector St. John de Crevecoeur observed, "Here individuals of all nations are melted into a new race of men."[2] Crevecoeur was not entirely accurate in describing the amalgamation of different nationalities into a new breed as already achieved. The great process of national fusion has been a slow phenome-

---

[1] "The Troubled American," *Newsweek*, 6 October 1969, p. 29.

[2] See "The American Farmer—Gallic Style," J. Hector St. Jean de Crèvecoeur, in Oscar Handlin, ed., *This was America* (Harper & Row: New York, 1964), p. 39.

non, attained only in part since that time. An early twentieth-century observation of the same theme found the perceptive Horace Kallen commenting as follows:

> There is a culture in the United States and not an ignoble one. . . .
> It is founded on variations of racial groups and individual character; upon spontaneous differences of social heritage, institutional habit, mental attitude and emotional tone; upon the continuous, free and fruitful crossfertilization of these by one another. Within these Many, gathered upon the American scene from the four corners of the earth and taking root and finding nourishment, growth and integrity upon its soil, lies the American One, as poets, painters, musicians and philosophers feel and utter this One.[3]

Nor did this process necessitate the elimination of cultural differences. As Kallen further observed:

> Democracy involves . . . the perfection and conservation of differences. . . . It involves a give and take between radically different types, and a mutual respect and mutual cooperation based on mutual understanding.[4]

That the United States possesses a pluralistic society is not a novel concept. It has always been thus. Still Americans often delude themselves into believing that whatever their cultural and social differences, newcomers become assimilated or virtually assimilated in a short time. In short, they still believe in the "melting pot" myth. A reexamination of contemporary America reveals, however, that the melting pot concept is far from an accurate description of American society, despite the cessation long since of mass immigration.

Rioting and racial clashes in the 1960's, which called forth much analysis of the movement for power among the nation's blacks, temporarily obscured the force of ethnic feeling among white ethnic groups. Nevertheless, a closer examination of the current civil rights movement and the crusade for social justice and equal opportunity for all Americans reveals sharpened divisions and embittered relations between all our minorities, black and white, and the more entrenched groups in American society, simultaneously with exacerbation of feeling between those ethnic groups that have won their struggle for recognition and those who are continuing their pilgrimage for a meaningful place in our national life. The ethnic factor persists with astonishing tenacity as an important element in American society in spite of seemingly growing assimilation. Indeed nationality groups have reemerged to manifest their brands of

[3] Horace Kallen, *Culture and Democracy in the United States* (New York: Liveright, 1924), pp. 41–42.
[4] Ibid., p. 61.

ethnic power as they vie with blacks for what they allege is the undue attention paid to blacks while the ethnics are neglected.[5]

One of the most recent analyses of ethnicity in American life makes the important observation that white ethnics readily agree that blacks get the worst deal in American life. "But their persistent question is why the gains of the blacks should be solely at their expense. They themselves have so little and feel so terribly constricted."[6] They are not receptive to a kind of moralizing that fails to appreciate the reality of their plight. Nor are they comforted by assertions of "new coalitions" that will dominate American politics and that leave them out of consideration. The human need for identity and self-respect is just as valid for whites as it is for blacks, and it is in this vein that the aspirations of America's ethnic groups must be examined.

Ethnic subcultures appeared as far back as early colonial times as new immigrants attempted to reconstruct replications of the Old World societies from which they emerged. For the most part this endeavor to conserve indigenous systems of accumulated beliefs, styles, solutions, and practices failed, with important exceptions. The record shows that most immigrant groups became acculturated by the second or third generation. Notwithstanding this acculturation, true assimilation often did not follow. As one scholar has recently observed, Americanization of an ethnic group "says little about its social relations with the host society."[7]

In sociological terms an "ethnic group" is defined as a group of people racially and historically related, having a common and distinctive culture. Further, such a group is described as "a foreign-stock segment of the population which preserves in some degree a distinctive way of life, in language, mannerism, habit, loyalty and the like."[8] However, sociologists also acknowledge that some individuals are ethnics even though their attitudes and behavior are indistinguishable from the majority. Nor is birth location a certain indicator or identifier of ethnic group attachment. "The essence of minority group membership has today become not so much observable differences in appearances and behavior . . . as it is the extent to which one's group-identified forebears are held to be socially unacceptable by the majority or other minorities."[9]

Another researcher finds that ethnic stratification is virtually inevitable so long as ethnocentrism, competition, and the power differential are brought into play. Competition provides motivation for stratification, while ethnocentrism channels the competition along ethnic lines, and

[5] Wall Street Journal, 24 April 1969.

[6] Michael Novak, The Rise of the Unmeltable Ethnics (New York: Macmillan, 1972), pp. 13–14.

[7] Michael Parenti, "Ethnic Politics and Ethnic Identification," American Political Science Review 61 (September 1967): 119.

[8] Arnold W. Green, Sociology, 4th ed. (New York: McGraw-Hill, 1964), p. 262.

[9] Ibid., p. 242.

the power differential determines whether one group will be able to subordinate the other.[10]

Statistically, 20 percent of Americans are in the "foreign stock" category, which is defined by the Census Bureau as either foreign born or having at least one foreign-born parent. But by using the widest possible latitude, the term "ethnic" can also be defined as any individual who differs from the white Anglo-Saxon settlers by religion, language, and culture.[11] This would account for 65 percent of the total population and thus further enhance the validity of the assumption that the various ethnic and nationality groups bear studying. As one of the foremost contemporary students of the topic writes:

> Ethnic differences, even in the second half of the twentieth century, proved far more important to men than did differences in philosophy or economic system. Men who would not die for a premise or a dogma or a division of labor would more or less cheerfully die for a difference rooted in ethnic origins.[12]

The existence of ethnicity ought not to be regarded as a remnant of immigration; rather, it must be acknowledged that group differences form an enduring part of social life. This principle was given ringing affirmation in June 1972, as the Congress and the President approved Public Law 92–318, The Ethnic Heritage Studies Act. As Pennsylvania Senator Richard S. Schweiker, sponsor of the bill in the United States Senate, put it:

> America's melting pot has not melted. . . . More and more, we see throughout society a new pluralism in America. I feel this is healthy and constructive. It can help all persons to break down the prejudices and divisiveness of the past, so that communities can begin to work together to solve mutual problems. . . . Now is the time to give equal time to the "many" [ethnic groups] and to recognize that only through cultural diversity can we achieve the harmonious society that the "one" is designed to achieve.
>
> The "new pluralism" is not really a new concept. It is merely a recognition that we have ignored a great American resource: ethnicity and cultural diversity.[13]

If we are to appraise and evaluate the nation in which they form an integral part properly, it behooves us to know more about our various

---

[10] Donald L. Noel, "A Theory of the Origin of Ethnic Stratification," *Social Problems* 16 (Fall 1968): 157.

[11] *The Reacting Americans* (New York: American Jewish Congress, 1969), p. 12.

[12] Ibid.

[13] Richard S. Schweiker, "Ethnic Studies: Toward a New Pluralism in America," in Michael Wenk, Silvan M. Tomasi, and Geno Baroni (eds.), *Pieces of a Dream* (New York: Center for Migration Studies, 1972), pp. 65, 66, 67, 68.

ethnic and nationality groups. We have an urgent obligation to become acquainted with the history and culture of all American peoples and their reaction to the problems of adjustment and accomplishment in American society.

This volume is an effort to understand America's history and development as a nation through the eyes of "periphery Americans." In the sense that we are all ethnics (since, as the readings will show, each group had to come to terms with a new way of life in America), the experience of all groups can be instructive toward the attainment of a greater understanding of American civilization. To the extent that today's problems of vital national concern are racial and ethnic problems, then meaningful studies directed toward the solution of these problems will be indispensable to an interpretation of contemporary society. A study of ethnic group dynamics is of immense importance to a greater appreciation of the problems faced by victims of discrimination. As the United States is the classic country of immigration, it is also the classic ethnic country. It is a land of many and varied cultures that give it the richness of diversity and the danger of divisiveness. Today, as never before, it is imperative that every effort be undertaken to preserve the former and prevent the latter.

This reader is an endeavor to fill a gap in the too-long-neglected area of "ethnic America." It is an appraisal, an observation, and a comment on the growth and development of this nation's history unlike usual readers in the analysis of American Society. Rather than covering the course of America's history by quoting from government documents or from remarks made by political or other leaders by and large associated with the establishment, this reader will focus on selections from those individuals who were on the periphery of American life or who spoke for the periphery Americans or interpreted their experience in America. The emphasis will be the hopes and aspirations, and the laments and disappointments, of representative or typical individuals of various ethnic groups who, although residents of the United States, tended to be looking in on American life from the outside. This will sometimes be seen in the writings of the periphery Americans and sometimes in the writings of those who harbored little good will toward them.

To look at the ethnic constellation is to learn something important about American societal problems. It is also to learn that the melting pot concept not only is inadequate to an understanding of contemporary problems and issues but also has always been, at any period, inaccurate as an explanation of group interrelationships. From the very beginning of recorded American history to our own time, group interests, group power, and group aspirations have affected American society. Although not evenly developed and subject to modification according to local conditions, the responses of different groups, and conflicts between these responses, have been different in given situations.

To emphasize the role of ethnicity in American life is not to make a value judgment. It is not to say that this role is positive or negative. In fact it can be either or both. But even more basic is the recognition of it as a phenomenon making a significant impact on American life. It exists, and that is sufficient reason for studying it.

2

The Factor of Ethnicity: FROM THE COLONIAL PERIOD TO THE CIVIL WAR

In this chapter the pre–Civil War period will be surveyed cursorily to establish the role, the extent, and the impact of ethnic group response to the earliest days of the American experience. The number of nationalities that entered into American life in this period necessarily precludes coverage of each group at this point. Therefore, the groups who were predominant at this time will be given attention here while other ethnic groups will be examined later in the book.

The ethnic groups to be examined in this chapter include Indians, English, blacks, French, Dutch, Germans, Scots, Welsh, and Irish. These people underwent a variety of experiences in this land. In the case of one, the black, the experience of slavery was all-pervasive; in the case of others it may have been the religious experience that was all-encompassing, as with the English Puritans; for still others economics may have played a foremost role. Regardless of the predominant forces in their lives, all of these groups manifested an ethnic consciousness to a greater or lesser degree. For example, while the (French) Huguenots were, of course, strongly aware of their Protestantism, they were also cognizant of the French heritage and culture; and while the poor Welsh miners certainly had deep concern over their condition of poverty, they were also aware of their Welsh identity. And so it was with all groups. It is this thread of identity attached to a language and a tradition unique to one people and not to others that ran through a major portion of their lives in what came to be the United States.

It will be seen that the role of ethnicity was not limited geographically in this period. On the frontier as well as in the South, in the East and in the North, wherever the American character was molded, considerable variety of race and nationality was maintained. Thus, the Indian experience in the Far West and in the Northeast and the black experience in the South found the ethnic element strong. The ethnic identity was part of the experience of emigrants from the British Isles: Englishmen, Welsh-men, and Scots. The fact that widespread use of the Dutch and German language persisted long after the Revolution attests to the staying power of ethnicity within these groups. Likewise, ethnic awareness was manifest in the Irish who constituted a heavy percentage of newcomers in the first half of the nineteenth century. Even where it was short-lived, as in the instance of the French in what came to be the United States, ethnicity made its impact.

THE AMERICAN INDIANS

To describe the Indians as an ethnic group might at first glance seem to be gratuitous, since they do not fall into the traditional image of immi-grant groups. We know that with the exception of the American Indians America is entirely populated by immigrants and their descendants. We also should realize that even the American Indians were at one time immigrants to the American shores. Of a certainty they have been one of the groups most victimized by the distinctions that separate one ethnic group from another. In any case American Indians constitute a unique segment of a nation composed of a variety of cultural, linguistic, racial, and religious strains. As such they can be viewed as an ethnic minority in America's midst. Furthermore, their experiences with the first white settlers form a valuable commentary on the relationship between different ethnic groups. As one studies the phenomenon of ethnic group interaction involving Indians, one becomes increasingly aware that questions encoun-tered in contemporary problems of pluralism are ancient and primitive ones.

It is instructive to note how the Indians appeared to the first Euro-peans who laid eyes on them. Nothing serves the purpose of examining the "first contact" experience better than the narratives that have been bequeathed to us by early explorers. Accordingly we begin with a de-scription of the Indian as an admirable creature, in a writing attributed to Christopher Columbus.[1]

> "I," he says, "in order that they might feel great amity toward us, because I knew that they were a people to be delivered and con-verted to our holy faith rather by love than by force, gave to some among them some red caps and some glass beads, which they hung round their necks, and many other things of little value. At this they were greatly pleased and became so entirely our friends that it was a wonder to see. Afterwards they came swimming to the ships' boats, where we were, and brought us parrots and cotton thread in balls, and spears and many other things, and we ex-

[1] From Clarkson N. Potter, ed., *The Journal of Christopher Columbus* (New York: Crown Publishers, Inc., 1960), pp. 23–24. By permission of Anthony Blond Ltd.

changed for them other things, such as small glass beads and hawks' bells, which we gave to them. In fact, they took all and gave all, such as they had, with good will, but it seemed to me that they were a people very deficient in everything. They all go naked as their mothers bore them, and the women also, although I saw only one very young girl. And all those whom I did see were youths, so that I did not see one who was over thirty years of age; they were very well built, with very handsome bodies and very good faces. Their hair is coarse almost like the hairs of a horse's tail and short; they wear their hair down over their eyebrows, except for a few strands behind, which they wear long and never cut. Some of them are painted black, and they are the colour of the people of the Canaries, neither black nor white, and some of them are painted white and some red and some in any colour that they find. Some of them paint their faces, some their whole bodies, some only the eyes, and some only the nose. They do not bear arms or know them, for I showed to them swords and they took them by the blade and cut themselves through ignorance. They have no iron. Their spears are certain reeds, without iron, and some of these have a fish tooth at the end, while others are pointed in various ways. They are all generally fairly tall, good looking and well proportioned. I saw some who bore marks of wounds on their bodies, and I made signs to them to ask how this came about, and they indicated to me that people came from other islands, which are near, and wished to capture them, and they defended themselves. And I believed and still believe that they come here from the mainland to take them for slaves. They should be good servants and of quick intelligence, since I see that they very soon say all that is said to them, and I believe that they would easily be made Christians, for it appeared to me that they had no creed. Our Lord willing, at the time of my departure I will bring back six of them to Your Highnesses, that they may learn to talk. I saw no beast of any kind in this island, except parrots." All these are the words of the admiral.

One of the best studies on Indian-white relations in seventeenth-century English America is Douglas Edward Leach's *Flintlock and Tomahawk*. Important as a military history of King Philip's War (1675–1676), it is also a social history depicting the impact the Indians had on the English and vice versa.

In appearance as well as in mode of life the Indians differed sharply from the fair-skinned English colonists.[2] Physically well-formed and agile, they possessed a native toughness derived from centuries of wilderness experience. In complexion they were dark, the skin being reddish coppery in color, the eyes black and piercing. . . .
   Whenever the English thought of the possibility of converting and redeeming the savages, it was always in terms of bringing them into conformity with the higher civilization at the expense of

[2] Reprinted from *Flintlock and Tomahawk, New England in King Philip's War*, by Douglas Edward Leach, pp. 2, 6, 20, 21, 22. By permission of W. W. Norton & Company, Inc. Copyright © 1958 by Douglas Edward Leach.

the native way of life, a concept fraught with difficulty and danger. The usual policy of the missionaries was to gather the converts into villages of their own as quickly as possible in order to remove them from the harmful influence of the unconverted heathen. By 1675 there were several thousand "Praying Indians" in New England, many of them living in these special villages which were organized in accordance with colonial patterns and under close colonial supervision.

Ever since the coming of the white men, there had been economic intercourse between Indians and English traders. At first it had seemed that the flourishing trade in furs, tools, cloth, and foodstuffs was as beneficial to the Indians as to the colonists, but as time went on and the English extended their activities the Indians grew more and more dissatisfied with the situation. It became apparent that they were gradually sinking into a position of complete economic subservience. Indian villages which once had enjoyed almost total self-sufficiency were now increasingly dependent upon products of English manufacture. Individual Indians became enmeshed in debt, which degraded them still further in the eyes of the English. The wiser leaders among the Indians saw that if the trend were not reversed, the time would soon come when the natives of New England would be completely stripped of their independence.

In the meantime, some of the Indians were exchanging their forest ways for the security and comfort of English habitations by engaging themselves as servants or laborers to the settlers, whose ambitious expansionism was fostering a continual shortage of labor. This meant that members of the two races were now being brought into frequent contact with each other on the streets of colonial villages, producing still more interracial friction. Furthermore, the migration of individual Indians to the English plantations was disturbing to the other Indians who chose to cling to their old independence, and who saw with dismay the weakening of tribal and family bonds.

In like fashion the efforts of Christian missionaries to convert the natives were viewed by many Indians as a divisive force threatening their own way of life. The sachems feared the loss of their own authority within the tribe, and many of them, including Philip, maintained a generally hostile attitude toward Christianity. Even more obstructive were the powaws, who stood to lose great power and influence if the Indians adopted the white men's religion. Thus the preaching of the gospel tended to divide Indian society, and confirmed the pagan elements in the belief that their own native culture was being undermined by the English.

Even those Indians who resisted all attempts to convert them to Christianity sometimes could not escape its influence entirely, as the colonial authorities imposed upon them a Puritanical code of behavior. In 1646, for example, Massachusetts decreed that Indians as well as colonists could be executed for blasphemy, a crime which was interpreted to include denial or cursing of the true God, and derogation of the Christian religion. At Plymouth the Indians were forbidden to fish, hunt, plant, or carry burdens on the Sabbath. In the spring of 1675 the government of Connecticut sponsored a great meeting of the subject Pequot Indians, at which time the authorities introduced to the assembled natives a new code of laws which they must obey, a code which specifically prohibited such offenses as Sabbath breaking, the practice of heathen rites, adultery, and drunkenness. Interestingly enough, the "Old Queen" of the Narragansetts, Quaiapen, and her council were also present at this meeting. One can easily imagine her secret thoughts as she watched the power of the English exert itself over the docile Pequots.

More and more the Indians as a people were becoming aware of a disagreeable fact, that at every point where their own way of life came into conflict with the white men's civilization the latter always revealed an aggressive and usually predominant strength. . . .

At the same time, the English colonists were being hardened in the conviction that the Indians were a graceless and savage people, dirty and slothful in their personal habits, treacherous in their relations with the superior race. To put it bluntly, they were fit only to be pushed aside and subordinated, so that the land could be occupied and made productive by those for whom it had been destined by God. If the Indians could be made to fit into a humble niche in the edifice of colonial religion, economy, and government, very well, but if not, sooner or later they would have to be driven away or crushed.

The difference in cultures is strikingly illustrated in the following letter by Benjamin Franklin, written in 1753.[3] Notice how the maintenance of distinct ethnic group autonomy among Indians and the English served to preserve mutual ethnocentrism.

The proneness of human Nature to a life of ease, of freedom from care and labour appears strongly in the little success that has hitherto attended every attempt to civilize our American Indians, in their present way of living, almost all their Wants are supplied by the spontaneous Productions of Nature, with the addition of very little labour, if hunting and fishing may indeed be called labour when Game is so plenty, they visit us frequently, and see the advantages that Arts, Sciences, and compact Society procure us, they are not deficient in natural understanding and yet they have never shewn any Inclination to change their manner of life for ours, or to learn any of our Arts; When an Indian Child had been brought up among us, taught our language and habituated to our Customs, yet if he goes to see his relations and make one Indian Ramble with them, there is no persuading him ever to return, and that this is not natural (to them) merely as Indians, but as men, is plain from this, that when white persons of either sex have been taken prisoners young by the Indians, and lived a while among them, tho' ransomed by their Friends, and treated with all imaginable tenderness to prevail with them to stay among the English, yet in a Short time they become disgusted with our manner of life, and the care and pains that are necessary to support it, and take the first good Opportunity of escaping again into the Woods, from whence there is no reclaiming them. One instance I remember to have heard, where the person

[3] Reprinted from Leonard W. Larabee, ed., *The Papers of Benamin Franklin,* vol. 4 (New Haven, Conn.: Yale University Press, 1961), pp. 481–483. By permission of Yale University Press.

was brought home to possess a good Estate; but finding some care necessary to keep it together, he relinquished it to a younger Brother, reserving to himself nothing but a gun and a match-Coat, with which he took his way again to the Wilderness. . . .

The little value Indians set on what we prize so highly under the name of Learning appears from a pleasant passage that happened some years since at a Treaty between one of our Colonies and the Six Nations; when every thing had been settled to the Satisfaction of both sides, and nothing remained but a mutual exchange of civilities, the English Commissioners told the Indians, they had in their Country a College for the instruction of Youth who were there taught various languages, Arts, and Sciences; that there was a particular foundation in favour of the Indians to defray the expense of the Education of any of their sons who should desire to take the Benefit of it. And now if the Indians would accept of the Offer, the English would take half a dozen of their brightest lads and bring them up in the Best manner; The Indians after consulting on the proposal replied that it was remembered some of their Youths had formerly been educated in that College, but it had been observed that for a long time after they returned to their Friends, they were absolutely good for nothing being neither acquainted with the true methods of killing deer, catching Beaver or surprizing an enemy. The Proposition however, they looked on as a mark of the kindness and good will of the English to the Indian Nations which merited a grateful return; and therefore if the English Gentlemen would send a dozen or two of their Children to Onondago the Great Council would take of their Education, bring them up in really what was the best manner and make men of them.

Though white men displaced Indians across the length of the country, it was not without thought or shame. George Catlin, painter and student of American Indians, displayed a sensitivity about Indian life and lamented the inexorable expansion of white culture at the expense of Indian traditions. He also demonstrated the problems encountered when ethnic cultures confront each other, as in the following excerpt.[4]

For the purpose of placing the Indian in a proper light before the world, as I hope to do in many respects, it is of importance to me— it is but justice to the savage—and justice to my readers also, that such points should be cleared up as I proceed; and for the world who enquire for correct and just information, they must take my words for the truth, or else come to this country and look for themselves, into these grotesque circles of never-ending laughter and fun, instead of going to Washington City to gaze on the poor embarrassed Indian who is called there by his "Great Father," to contend with the sophistry of the learned and acquisitive world, in bartering away his lands with the graves and the hunting grounds of his ancestors. There is not the proper place to study the Indian character; yet it is the place where the sycophant and the scribbler

[4] Reprinted from George Catlin, *Letters and Notes of the Manners, Customs and Conditions of the North American Indians* (London: 1841), vol. 1, pp. 85, 86, 102, 103.

go to gaze and frown upon him—to learn his character, and write his history! and because he does not speak, and quaffs the delicious beverage which he receives from white mens' hands, "he's a speechless brute and a drunkard." An Indian is a beggar in Washington City, and a white man is almost equally so in the Mandan village. An Indian in Washington is mute, is dumb and embarrassed; and so is a white man (and for the very same reasons) in this place—he has nobody to talk to.

A wild Indian, to reach the civilized world, must needs travel some thousands of miles in vehicles of conveyance, to which he is unaccustomed—through latitudes and longitudes which are new to him—living on food that he is unused to—stared and gazed at by the thousands and tens of thousands whom he cannot talk to —his heart grieving and his body sickening at the exhibition of white men's wealth and luxuries, which are enjoyed on the land, and over the bones of his ancestors. And at the end of his journey he stands (like a caged animal) to be scanned—to be criticised—to be pitied—and heralded to the world as a mute—as a brute, and a beggar.

A white man, to reach this village, must travel by steam-boat —by canoes—on horseback and on foot; swim rivers—wade quagmires—fight mosquitoes—patch his moccasins, and patch them again and again, and his breeches; live on meat alone—sleep on the ground the whole way, and think and dream of his friends he has left behind; and when he gets here, half-starved, and half-naked, and more than half sick, he finds himself a beggar for a place to sleep, and for something to eat; a mute amongst thousands who flock about him, to look and to criticise, and to laugh at him for his jaded appearance, and to speak of him as they do of all white men (without distinction) as liars. These people are in the habit of seeing no white men in their country but Traders, and know of no other; deeming us all alike, and receiving us all under the presumption that we come to trade or barter; applying to us all, indiscriminately, the epithet of "liars" or Traders.

The reader will therefore see, that we mutually suffer in each other's estimation from the unfortunate ignorance, which distance has chained us in; and (as I can vouch, and the Indian also, who has visited the civilized world) that the historian who would record justly and correctly the character and customs of a people, must go and live among them. . . .

The civilized world look upon a group of Indians, in their classic dress, with their few and simple oddities, all of which have their moral or meaning, and laugh at them excessively, because they are not like ourselves—we ask, "why do the silly creatures wear such great bunches of quills on their heads?—Such loads and streaks of paint upon their bodies—and bear's grease? abominable!" and a thousand other equally silly questions, without ever stopping to think that Nature taught them to do so—and that they all have some definite importance or meaning which an Indian could explain to us at once, if he were asked and felt disposed to do so— that each quill in his head stood, in the eyes of his whole tribe, as the symbols of an enemy who had fallen by his hand—that every streak of red paint covered a wound which he had got in honourable combat—and that the bear's grease with which he carefully anoints his body every morning, from head to foot, cleanses and purifies the body, and protects his skin from the bite of mosquitoes, and at the same time preserves him from colds and coughs which are usually taken through the pores of the skin.

At the same time, an Indian looks among the civilized world, no doubt, with equal, if not much greater, astonishment, at our apparently, as well as really, ridiculous customs and fashions; but he laughs not, nor ridicules, nor questions, —for his natural good sense and good manners forbid him, —until he is reclining about the fireside of his wigwam companions, when he vents forth his just criticisms upon the learned world, who are a rich and just theme for Indian criticism and Indian gossip.

An Indian will not ask a white man the reason why he does not oil his skin with bear's grease, or why he does not paint his body—or why he wears a hat on his head, or why he has buttons on the back of his coat, where they never can be used—or why he wears whiskers, and a shirt collar up to his eyes—or why he sleeps with his head towards the fire instead of his feet—why he walks with his toes out instead of turning them in—or why it is that hundreds of white folks will flock and crowd round a table to see an Indian eat—but he will go home to his wigwam fire-side, and "make the welkin ring" with jokes and fun upon the ignorance and folly of the knowing world.

THE ENGLISH

Among the first peoples that can be surveyed with an eye to ethnic identity are the English. There can be little doubt that the United States of America today has been the recipient of much in the English culture: language, the common law, and architecture are only some of the more easily identifiable proofs of the indelible English imprint. Nevertheless, English emigrants in the opening stage of colonization, as well as contemporary and later observers of English emigration, demonstrated an ethnic consciousness that in some instances indicated uncertainty and apprehension. In other instances this awareness included a great degree of confidence about the English because of their national background.

The first selection includes excerpts from William Bradford, *Of Plymouth Plantation, 1620–1647*. Bradford, first governor of Plymouth colony, the second successful English colony in what is now the United States, was an English yeoman (a freeman farmer below the landed gentry class) who exercised extraordinary perseverance and reasonableness as a colonial leader. His chronicle has become a classic and contains early expressions of English immigrants as ethnically conscious people. For example, although the Pilgrims were prepared to flee England in order to practice their religion without interference, they found it impossible to live in Holland, a neighboring and tolerant country which, nevertheless, proved to be insensitive to the needs of an English ethnic minority. The consequence was emigration to America.

Of Their Departure into Holland and Their Troubles Thereabout, With Some of the Many Difficulties They Found and Met Withal, Anno 1608[5]

Being thus constrained to leave their native soil and country, their lands and livings, and all their friends and familiar acquaintances, it was much; and thought marvelous by many. But to go into a country they knew not but by heresay, where they must learn a new language and get their livings they knew not how it being a dear place and subject to the miseries of war, it was by many thought an adventure almost desperate; a case intolerable and a misery worse than death. . . .

Of Their Setting in Holland, and Their Manner of Living, and Entertainment There

Being now come into the Low Countries, they saw many and goodly fortified cities, strongly walled and guarded with troops of armed men. Also, they heard a strange and uncouth language, and beheld the different manners and customs of the people, with their strange fashions and attires, all so far differing from that of their plain country villages (wherein they were bred and had so long lived) as it seemed they were come into a new world. . . .

Showing the Reasons and Causes of Their Removal

After they had lived in this city about some eleven or twelve years (which is the more observable being the whole time of that famous truce between that state and the Spaniards) and sundry of them were taken away by death and many others began to be well stricken in years (the grave mistress of Experience having taught them many things), those prudent governors with sundry of the sagest members began both deeply to apprehend their present dangers and wisely to foresee the future and think of timely remedy. In the agitation of their thoughts, and much discourse of things hereabout, at length they began to incline to this conclusion: of removal to some other place. Not out of any newfangledness or other such like giddy humor by which men are oftentimes transported to their great hurt and danger, but for sundry weighty and solid reasons, some of the chief of which I will here briefly touch. . . .

As necessity was a taskmaster over them so they were forced to be such, not only to their servants but in a sort to their dearest children, the which as it did not a little wound the tender hearts of many a loving father and mother, so it produced likewise sundry sad and sorrowful effects. For many of their children that were of best dispositions and gracious inclinations, having learned to bear the yoke in their youth and willing to bear part of their parents' burden, were oftentimes so oppressed with their heavy labours that though their minds were free and willing, yet their bodies bowed under the weight of the same, and became decrepit in their early youth, the vigour of nature being consumed in the very bud as it were. But that which was more lamentable, and of all sorrows most heavy to be borne, was that many of their children, by these occasions and the great licentiousness of youth in that country, and the manifold temptations of the place, were drawn away by evil examples into extravagant and dangerous courses, getting the reins off their necks and departing from their parents. Some became soldiers, others took upon them far voyages by sea, and others some worse courses tending to dissoluteness and the danger of their souls, to the great grief of their parents and dishonour of God. So that they saw their posterity would be in danger to degenerate and be corrupted. . . .

Being thus convinced of the undesirability of residence in Holland, the Pilgrims determined to locate in the New World to carry on their distinctive way of life.

Being thus arrived in a good harbor, and brought safe to land, they fell upon their knees and blessed the God of Heaven who had brought them over the vast and furious ocean, and delivered them from all the perils and miseries thereof, again to set their feet on the firm and stable earth, their proper element. . . .

If they looked behind them, there was the mighty ocean which they had passed and was now as a main bar and gulf to separate them from all the civil parts of the world. If it be said they had a ship to succour them, it is true; . . . of these fathers rightly say: "Our fathers were Englishmen which came over this great ocean, and were ready to perish in this wilderness; but they cried unto the Lord, and He heard their voice and looked on their adversity," etc. "Let them therefore praise the Lord, because He is good: and His mercies endure forever."

By the eve of the War of Independence the pluralistic nature of American society had emerged, as settlers included people from many nations. This fact notwithstanding it was apparent that English culture prevailed, especially in language. This point is well illustrated in the following selection from William Eddis, a Crown-appointed surveyor of customs at Annapolis. The Englishman Eddis proved very perceptive about the important developments in the colonies during the Revolutionary era.

[from a letter by Eddis dated June 8, 1770][6]

The colonists are a compound of adventurers, not only from every district of Great Britain and Ireland, but from almost every other European government, where the principles of liberty and commerce have operated with spirit and efficacy. Is it not, therefore, reasonable to suppose that the English language must be greatly corrupted by such a strange intermixture of various nations? The reverse is, however, true. The language of the immediate descen-

[6] Reprinted from William Eddis, *Letters from America, Historical and Descriptive, Comprising Occurrences from 1769 to 1770; inclusive* (London, 1772), pp. 59, 60.

dants of such a promiscuous ancestry is perfectly uniform and un-adulterated. . . .

The American Revolution did not fundamentally change the preferential feeling that most Americans had for the English heritage. Indeed, the priority enjoyed by English culture in early nineteenth-century America was well attested to by Washington Irving in *The Sketchbook*. In a chapter entitled "English Writers On America," Irving responds to the publication of anti-American writers in England by admonishing Americans not to react in kind but to acknowledge that, for Americans, English culture is more worthy of emulation than that of any other people.

There is a general impression in England, that the people of the United States are inimical to the parent country.[7] It is one of the errors which have been diligently propagated by designing writers. There is, doubtless, considerable political hostility, and a general soreness at the illiberality of the English press; but, generally speaking, the prepossessions of the people are strongly in favor of England. Indeed, at one time they amounted, in many parts of the Union, to an absurd degree of bigotry. The bare name of Englishman was a passport to the confidence and hospitality of every family, and too often gave a transient currency to the worthless and the ungrateful. Throughout the country there was something of enthusiasm connected with the idea of England. We looked to it with a hallowed feeling of tenderness and veneration, as the land of our forefathers—the august repository of the monuments and antiquities of our race—the birthplace and mausoleum of the sages and heroes of our paternal history. After our own country, there was none in whose glory we more delighted—none whose good opinion we were more anxious to possess—none toward which our hearts yearned with such throbbings of warm consanguinity. Even during the late war, whenever there was the least opportunity for kind feelings to spring forth, it was the delight of the generous spirits of our country to show that, in the midst of hostilities, they still kept alive the sparks of future friendship.

Is all this to be at an end? Is this golden band of kindred sympathies, so rare between nations, to be broken forever? Perhaps it is for the best—it may dispel an illusion which might have kept us in mental vassalage; which might have interfered occasionally with our true interests, and prevented the growth of proper national pride. But it is hard to give up the kindred tie! and there are feelings dearer than interest—closer to the heart than pride—that will still make us cast back a look of regret as we wander farther and farther from the paternal roof, and lament the waywardness of the parent that would repel the affections of the child. . . .

But above all let us not be influenced by any angry feelings, so far as to shut our eyes to the perception of what is really excellent and amiable in the English character. We are a young people, necessarily an imitative one, and must take our examples and mod-

7 Reprinted from Washington Irving, *The Sketchbook* (Philadelphia: Henry Altemus, 1895), pp. 79, 80, 82.

els, in a great degree, from the existing nations of Europe. There is no country more worthy of our study than England. The spirit of her constitution is most analogous to ours. The manners of her people—their intellectual activity, their freedom of opinion, their habits of thinking on those subjects which concern the dearest interests and most sacred charities of private life—are all congenial to the American character; and, in fact, are all intrinsically excellent: for it is in the moral feeling of the people that the deep foundations of British prosperity are laid; and however the superstructure may be timeworn or overrun by abuses, there must be something solid in the basis, admirable in the materials, and stable in the structure, of an edifice that so long has towered unshaken amidst the tempests of the world.

English immigration provided many settlers for the new nation in the decades following independence. For some Englishmen the American experience was a positive one. The selection from Morris Birkbeck, *Letters from Illinois* (Philadelphia, 1818), which follows is an example: it is a glowing picture of America painted by a well-to-do English farmer who considered settlement near other English immigrants to be among the important advantages he had found. In voicing this view, he revealed an ethnic concern typical of many Englishmen. At the same time Birkbeck found that the distinctive American nationality that was emerging was itself becoming so ethnocentric that even prospective English immigrants were placed in the category of "foreigners."

I am so well satisfied with the election we have made, that I have not for a moment felt a disposition to recede. . . .[8] Society we shall not want, I believe; and with the fear of that want every other fear has vanished. The comforts and luxuries of life we shall obtain with ease and in abundance: pomp and state will follow but too quickly. . . .

I have not for a moment felt despondency, scarcely discouragement, in this happy country, this land of hope! Life here is only *too* valuable, from the wonderful efficiency of every well-directed effort. Such is the field of delightful action lying before me, that I am ready to regret the years wasted in the support of taxes and pauperism, and to grieve that I am growing old now, that a really useful career seems just beginning. I am happier, much happier, in my prospects, I feel that I am doing well for my family: and the privations I anticipated seem to vanish before us.

We shall have some English friends next summer; and a welcome they shall experience. But if not one had the resolution to follow the track we have smoothed before them, he should never wish to retrace it, except perhaps as travellers. As to what are called the comforts of life, I feel that they are much more easily obtainable here than they have ever been to me; and for those who are to succeed me, I look forward with pleasure which can be understood by one who has felt the anxieties of an English father.

[8] Reprinted from Edith Abbott, *Historical Aspects of the Immigration Problem.* Copyright © 1926 by University of Chicago Press. By permission of Arno Press.

I expect to see around me in prosperity many of my old neighbors, whose hard fare has often embittered my own enjoyments. Three of them have already made the effort, and succeeded in getting out to us. This delights us, but we have by no means depended on it; joyful as we are at the prospect of giving them an asylum.

March 24, 1818. . . . We are in a good country, are in no danger of perishing for want of society, and have abundant means of supplying every other want.

But I am sorry to inform you that our plan of colonizing extensively, with a special view to the relief of our suffering countrymen of the lower orders, is not at present successful. A good number may be benefited by the arrangements we are making for their reception on a contracted scale; but the application to Congress, alluded to in my journal, which was calculated principally for the service of that class, has, I fear, proved abortive. I have transmitted to Congress, through the hands of our member for Illinois, the following memorial: *To the Representatives of the United States in Congress assembled, the Memorial of Morris Birkbeck, an English farmer, lately settled in the territory of the Illinois, respectfully states:*

That a number of his countrymen, chiefly yeoman farmers, farming labourers, and rural mechanics, are desirous of removing with their families and their capital into this country, provided that, by having situations prepared for them, they might escape the weariness and expensive travel in quest of a settlement, which has broken the spirits and drained the purses of many of their emigrant brethren, terminating too frequently in disappointment.

Feeling, as does your memorialist, that the people of England and the people of America are of one family, notwithstanding the unhappy political disputes which have divided the two countries, he believes that this recollection will be sufficient to insure, from the representatives of a free people, a favourable issue to his application in behalf of their suffering brethren.

MORRIS BIRKBECK

Other petitions for grants of land in favour of particular descriptions of emigrants have been rejected during this session, for reasons which my friends give me to understand will be fatal to mine. The following I consider to be the tenor of these objections:

That no public lands can be granted or disposed of but according to the general law on that subject, without a special act of legislation.

That although in certain cases such special acts have been made in favour of bodies of foreign emigrants, it has always been on the ground, and in consideration of, a *general public* benefit accruing; such as the introduction of the culture of the vine by the Swiss colony at Vevay, Indiana, and the olive in Louisiana.

The influx of so many inhabitants from England led to the development of programs and advice to prospective immigrants as to the kinds of experiences they might expect in making a journey to America. In the following selection excerpts have been taken from John Knight, *The Immigrants Best Instructor or, The Most Recent and Important Information Respecting the United States of America Selected from the Works of the Latest Travellers in that Country Particularly Brandbury, Hulme, Brown, Birkbeck etc. Containing Information on its Climates and Temperatures, the Manners and Dispositions of its Inhabitants also the Price of the Land, Taxes, and Wages of Labour, Soil, Production etc. Arts, Manufacturers. The English Laws on Emigration and every other information needful to the Emigrant.*

[Instructions to Emigrants][9]

The first step is to procure a certificate, from the Minister of the Church and the Church wardens; countersigned by a resident Magistrate, stating that the person about to emigrate is not nor has been, employed in any of the prohibited trades or manufactures. . . .

The next thing is to provide the necessaries for the voyage: these for both sorts of passengers will consist of a bed and bedding; which may be had at the shops in all the seaports, made up in a suitable manner; may frequently be sold after the voyage for the sum they cost. Flannel waist coat and drawers; should be provided by each passenger; also a small quantity of medicines, such as rhubarb, salts, cream of tartar and magnesia; these may be necessary not only to the preservation of health, but of life; for the change of situation, exercise, diet, air, etc. often produce such changes in the body, or, without a judicious use of these kinds of medicines, might be highly injurious to the health, if not fatal. It would also be well for delicate persons to provide a little preserved fruit, eggs, etc. . . .

On landing at the desired port if the Emigrant has any letters of introduction, he should deliver them immediately: then his friends may probably assist him in finding a proper place where his family may rest a few days. His next care will be to land his baggage, and lodge them in a place of safety—If he has no letter of introduction to anyone in the place where he lands, he ought to be on his guard: for in all American ports, a great number of small stores are established for the sale of spiritous liquors etc. many of these are kept by natives of Great Britain: and some of those who keep them are so selfish, as to induce Emigrants to remain in the city, under various pretenses, but in reality to tempt them to spend their money with them—So many emigrants arrive at all the Principal Ports in the United States, that there is very little chance of procuring employment in them, and most of the distress which has been reported to exist in America, has been suffered by those who have imprudently lingered in the cities, until their money was exhausted. . . .

[advice to prospective farmers]

If a man of this class will work, he has nothing to fear in America: he has the requisites of a farmer, except the skill, and that he may soon acquire. Many farmers have more land than they can well manage: ask them the reason, they reply, they want help.

[9] From John Knight, *The Immigrants Best Instructor* (Manchester, 1818).

Letters from America to friends and relations in England frequently referred to aspirations of Englishmen that could be satisfied in America without damage to their own ethnic attachment. The following letter, written in this vein, is taken from J. Knight, *Important Extracts from Original and Recent Letters Written By Englishmen, in the United States of America, to Their Friends in England* (2nd series, Manchester, 1818).

Carmi, White's Country, Illinois State, North America[10]

25th September, 1818

Dear Mother:

I now sit down in a country, where fortune is within my reach. I suffered a little for want of money, but I now look beyond all that. . . . Lands such as you never saw, which you may use for three years, and then its wants no manure. I have purchased one hundred and sixty acres, on a fine level plain, where there is not a tree to be seen, they are always covered with grass. Coins are sometimes found in sinking wells, a proof it has been inhabited. There are a great many thousand of acres of these lands in these parts. I intend purchasing eighty acres of woodland, then I shall have two hundred and forty acres.

These two hundred and forty acres, sown with Indian corn, will produce from sixty to a hundred bushels per acre, suppose we take the average at seventy, that upon the whole will be sixteen thousand eight hundred, which sells at ¾ of a dollar per bushel, and very scarce at that price. Perhaps you may think this strange, but if you were here you would not think so, for the people will not work; they can live with the greatest ease and don't want to be rich; but they who come here and are industrious, make great fortune in a short time. The inhabitants cultivate very little land, but live principally on hunting, and breeding cattle and hogs; this is done with the greatest ease, they being surrounded by land possessed by no one, where the cattle and hogs feed very fast without trouble or expense. . . .

You will please to notice, that this letter has no reference to the Atlantic States, there, everything is quite reversed: people had better stay at home than go there. I have travelled two thousand miles into the interior of America, where every European must come to do himself good. The people here want me to take the Oath and become an American, but I will not, unless you will come, then I shall have no objection; the people here are very benevolent and obliging to Englishmen. Now my dear mother I want you to send me word that you, my brothers and sister will come after me: [name of the letter writer not provided]

---

[10] From *Immigration, The American Mosaic: From Pilgrims to Modern Refugees,* by Michael Kraus, pp. 123–24. © 1966 by Litton Educational Publishing, Inc. Reprinted by permission of Van Nostrand Reinhold Company.

The celebrated Alexis de Tocqueville discussed the importance of English origins in American society in his impressive and prophetic classic, *Democracy in America.* In the selection below Tocqueville describes the common background of the Anglo-Americans.[11]

> If we carefully examine the social and political state of America, after having studied its history, we shall remain perfectly convinced that not an opinion, not a custom, not a law, I may even say not an event is upon record which the origin of that people will not explain. The readers of this book will find in the present chapter the germ of all that is to follow and the key to almost the whole work.
>
> The emigrants who came at different periods to occupy the territory now covered by the American Union differed from each other in many respects; their aim was not the same, and they governed themselves on different principles.
>
> These men had, however, certain features in common, and they were all placed in an analogous situation. The tie of language is, perhaps, the strongest and the most durable that can unite mankind. All the emigrants spoke the same language; they were all children of the same people. Born in a country which had been agitated for centuries by the struggles of faction, and in which all parties had been obliged in their turn to place themselves under the protection of the laws, their political education had been perfected in this rude school; and they were more conversant with the notions of right and the principles of true freedom than the greater part of their European contemporaries. At the period of the first emigrations the township system, that fruitful germ of free institutions, was deply rooted in the habits of the English; and with it the doctrine of the sovereignty of the people had been introduced into the very bosom of the monarchy of the house of Tudor.

THE BLACKS

The entry of the black man into what is now the United States was different from that of every other ethnic group. He was an involuntary immigrant; he came in chains. Even before the establishment of the first English colony black men were performing as slaves in what is now Florida. Then came the establishment of the English colonies and the planting of slavery in those settlements. It began in Virginia in 1619 and was formally recognized by that colony in 1661. Maryland recognized the institution three years later. Indeed slavery took hold in all the southern colonies, although Georgia forbade it in the early years of its history. The middle colonies soon succumbed to the practice, although their number of slaves was never great. Nevertheless, even Quaker Pennsylvania recognized slavery in 1700. In New England the system met with little success, although it did exist.

[11] Reprinted from Alexis de Tocqueville, *Democracy in America,* vol. 1 (New York: Alfred A. Knopf, 1961), p. 29.

The primary black experience in early America, then, was one of a slave population. From this peripheral position the black man has been viewed and has viewed American society and culture, with the inevitable consequence that black ethnicity has been reinforced. This ethnic identity often manifested itself in slave revolts despite the desperate odds against them. Unsuccessful in these attempts blacks developed a culture within the slave experience. The selections that follow depict aspects of that culture as well as demonstrate distinguishing features between the blacks and other ethnic groups.

Skin color has played a prominent and degrading role in American history. In November 1787, in Philadelphia, the Right Reverend Richard Allen described how this condition led to the forcible expulsion of free blacks from St. George's Church and how the ousted black men formed the African Methodist Episcopal Church. Clearly, skin color differences resulted in distinctive ethnic grouping.

Negroes of Philadelphia Stage a "Kneel In," and Start Their Own Church[12]

(The Right Reverend Richard Allen tells of the incidents leading up to the establishment of the African Methodist Episcopal Church of Philadelphia. The date was a Sunday in November, 1787—only a month after the Constitutional Convention ended.)

A number of us usually attended St. George's Church in Fourth street; and when the colored people began to get numerous in attending the church, they moved us from the seats we usually sat on, and placed us around the wall, and on Sabbath mornings we went to church and the sexton stood at the door, and told us to go in the gallery. He told us to go, and we would see where to sit. We expected to take the seats over the ones we formerly occupied below, not knowing any better. We took those seats. Meeting had begun, and they were nearly done singing, and just as we got to the seats, the elder said, "Let us pray." We had not been long upon our knees before I heard considerable scuffling and low talking. I raised my head up and saw one of the trustees, H____ M____, having hold of the Rev. Absalom Jones, pulling him off his knees, and saying, "You must get up—you must not kneel here." Mr. Jones replied, "Wait until prayer is over." Mr. H____ M____ said, "No, you must get up now, or I will call for aid and force you away." Mr. Jones said, "Wait until prayer is over, and I will get up and trouble you no more." With that he (Mr. H____ M____) beckoned to one of the other trustees, Mr. L____ S____ to come to his assistance. He came, and went to William White to pull him up. By this time prayer was over, and we all went out of the church in a body, and they were nor more plagued with us in the church.

---

12 Reprinted from William L. Katz, *Eyewitness: The Negro in American History* (New York: Pitman Publishing Corporation, 1967), pp. 58–59.

The following brief but poignant protest against slavery by a black emphasizes the paradox of American democracy in 1788.

> *(In 1788 there appeared the first known Negro protest against slavery to be published. Its author, "Othello," has left no history.)*

> In you (whites) the superiority of power produces nothing but a superiority of brutality and barbarism. Weakness, which calls for protection, appears to provoke your inhumanity. Your fine political systems are sullied by the outrages committed against human nature and the divine majesty.
>   When America opposed the pretensions of England, she declared that all men have the same rights. After having manifested her hatred against tyrants, ought she to have abandoned her principles?[13]

Solomon Northup, an upstate New York resident, was an educated freeman, married, and father of three children. At the age of thirty-two years he was enslaved. He was forcibly sold to a slave trader in the District of Columbia, then shipped to New Orleans, where he spent a dozen years in bondage. In 1853 he was rescued from a cotton plantation in Louisiana. Northup vividly described his experiences, which offer a valuable comment on the institution of slavery.

> The existence of Slavery in its most cruel form among them has a tendency to brutalize the humane and finer feelings of their nature.[14] Daily witnesses of human suffering—listening to the agonizing screeches of the slave—beholding him writhing beneath the merciless lash—bitten and torn by dogs—dying without attention, and buried without shroud or coffin—it cannot otherwise be expected, than that they should become brutified and reckless of human life. It is true there are many kind-hearted and good men in the parish of Avoyelles—such men as William Ford—who can look with pity upon the sufferings of a slave, just as they are, over all the world, sensitive and sympathetic spirits, who cannot look with indifference upon the sufferings of any creature which the Almighty has endowed with life. It is not the fault of the slaveholder that he is cruel, so much as it is the fault of the system under which he lives. He cannot withstand the influence of habit and associations that surround him. Taught from earliest childhood, by all that he sees and hears, that the rod is for the slave's back, he will not be apt to change his opinions in maturer years.
>   There may be humane masters, as there certainly are inhuman ones—there may be slaves well-clothed, well-fed, and happy as there are surely those half-clad, half-starved and miserable; nevertheless, the institution that tolerates such wrong and inhumanity as I have witnessed, is a cruel, unjust and barbarous one.

---

[13] Ibid., p. 35.

[14] Reprinted from Solomon Northup, *Twelve Years a Slave,* ed. Sue Eakin and Joseph Logsdon (Baton Rouge: Louisiana State University Press, 1968), pp. 157–58.

Men may write fictions portraying lowly life as it is, or as it is not—may expatiate with owlish gravity upon the bliss of ignorance—discourse flippantly from arm chairs of the pleasures of slave life; but let them toil with him in the field—sleep with him in the cabin—feed with him on husks; let them behold him scourged, hunted, trampled on, and they will come back with another story in their mouths. Let them know the *heart* of the poor slave—learn his secret thoughts—thoughts he dare not utter in the hearing of the white man; let them sit by him in the silent watches of the night—converse with him in trustful confidence, of "life, liberty, and the pursuit of happiness," and they will find that ninety-nine out of every hundred are intelligent enough to understand their situation, and to cherish in their bosoms the love of freedom, as passionately as themselves.

"I believe slaveholding to be a sin against God and man under all circumstances," said Henry Bibb, a self-emancipated slave. Bibb's narrative, published originally in 1849, presents some interesting aspects of the slave system. Having escaped from slavery, he describes the social conditions of the slaves and of the different white classes. He also relates the slave's deep longing for freedom by sensitively recounting its power within his own soul.

In 1833, I had some very serious religious impressions, and there was quite a number of slaves in the neighborhood, who felt very desirous to be taught to read the Bible.[15] There was a Miss Davis, a poor white girl, who offered to teach a Sabbath School for the slaves, notwithstanding public opinion and the law opposed to it. Books were furnished and she commenced the school; but the news soon got to our owners that she was teaching us to read. This caused quite an excitement in the neighborhood. Patrols* were appointed to go and break it up the next Sabbath. They were determined that we should not have a Sabbath School in operation. For slaves this was called an incendiary movement.

The Sabbath is not regarded by a large number of the slaves as a day of rest. They have no schools to go to; no moral nor religious instruction at all in many localities where there are hundreds of slaves. Hence they resort to some kind of amusement. Those who make no profession of religion, resort to the woods in large numbers on that day to gamble, fight, get drunk, and break the Sabbath. This is often encouraged by slaveholders. When they wish to have a little sport of that kind, they go among the slaves and give them whiskey, to see them dance, "pat juber," sing and play on the banjo. Then get them to wrestling, fighting, jumping, running foot races, butting each other like sheep. This is urged on by giving them whiskey; making bets on them; laying chips on one slave's head, and daring another to tip it off with his hand; and if

[15] Reprinted from pp. 68–70 in *Puttin' on Ole Massa, The Slave Narratives of Henry Bibb, William Wells Brown, and Solomon Northup*, edited by Gilbert Osofsky (New York: Harper & Row, 1969).

* Police peculiar to the South

he tipped it off, it would be called an insult, and cause a fight. Before fighting, the parties choose their seconds to stand by them while fighting; a ring or circle is formed to fight in, and no one is allowed to enter the ring while they are fighting, but their seconds, and the white gentlemen. They are not allowed to fight a duel, nor to use weapons of any kind. The blows are made by kicking, knocking, and butting with their heads; they grab each other by their ears, and jam their heads together like sheep. If they are likely to hurt each other very bad, their masters would rap them with their walking canes, and make them stop. After fighting, they make friends, shake hands, and take a dram together, and there is no more of it.

But this is all principally for want of moral instruction. This is where they have no Sabbath Schools; no one to read the Bible to them; no one to preach the gospel who is competent to expound the Scripture, except slaveholders. And the slaves, with but few exceptions, have no confidence at all in their preaching, because they preach a proslavery doctrine. They say, "Servants be obedient to your masters;—and he that knoweth his master's will and doeth it not, shall be beaten with many stripes;—means that God will send them to hell, if they disobey their masters. This kind of preaching has driven thousands into infidelity. They view themselves as suffering unjustly under the lash, without friends, without protection of law or gospel, and the green-eyed monster tyranny staring them in the face. They know that they are destined to die in that wretched condition, unless they are delivered by the arm of Omnipotence. And they cannot believe or trust in such a religion, as above-named.

The poor and loafering class of whites, are about on a par in point of morals with the slaves at the South. They are generally ignorant, intemperate, licentious, and profane. They associate much with the slave; are often found gambling together on the Sabbath; encouraging slaves to steal from their owners, and sell to them, corn, wheat, sheep, chickens, or any thing of the kind which they can well conceal. For such offences there is no law to reach a slave but lynch law. But if both parties are caught in the act by a white person, the slave is punished with the lash, while the white man is often punished with both lynch and common law. But there is another class of poor white people in the South, who, I think would be glad to see slavery abolished in self defence; they despise the institution because it is impoverishing and degrading to them and their children.

The slave holders are generally rich, aristocratic, overbearing; and they look with utter contempt upon a poor laboring man, who earns his bread by the "sweat of his brow," whether he be moral or immoral, honest or dishonest. No matter whether he is white or black; if he performs manual labor for a livelihood, he is looked upon as being inferior to a slaveholder, and but little better off than the slave, who toils without wages under the lash. It is true, that the slaveholder, and non-slaveholder, are living under the same laws in the same State. But the one is rich, the other is poor; one is educated, the other is uneducated; one has houses, land and influence, the other has none. This being the case, that class of the non-slaveholders would be glad to see slavery abolished, but they dare not speak it aloud.

As all the instrumentalities which I as a slave, could bring to bear upon the system, had utterly failed to palliate my sufferings, all hope and consolation fled. I must be a slave for life, and suffer under the lash or die. The influence which this had only tended to make me more unhappy. I resolved that I would be free if running away could make me so. I had heard that Canada was a land of liberty, somewhere in the North; and every wave of trouble that rolled across my breast, caused me to think more and more about Canada, and liberty. But more especially after having been flogged, I have fled to the highest hills of the forest, pressing my way to the North for refuge; but the river Ohio was my limit. To me it was an impassable gulf. I had no rod wherewith to smite the stream, and thereby divide the waters. I had no Moses to go before me and lead the way from bondage to a promised land. Yet I was in far worse state than Egyptian bondage; for they had houses and land; I had none; they had oxen and sheep; I had none; they had a wise counsel, to tell them what to do, and where to go, and even to go with them; I had none. I was surrounded by opposition on every hand. My friends were few and far between. I have often felt when running away as if I had scarcely a friend on earth.

THE FRENCH

French emigration to the United States has never been very large. Of the approximately 700,000 Frenchmen who have migrated to this nation in the course of its history, more than half came prior to 1790. With few exceptions the ethnic trait did not in the long run emerge as a readily identifiable factor as the French were assimilated into the American social fabric. As distinct from the French Canadians, there are scarcely any vestiges of "French-Americans" as an ethnically viable social group today. This fact notwithstanding, ethnic origin shaped the experiences of French emigrants in what is now the United States during the colonial period.

The growth of religious intolerance in France in the latter part of the seventeenth century led to the arrival in the colonies of a group of French Huguenots. It is to be noted that although their Protestantism and their industry removed two of the principal prejudices normally lodged against foreigners, they nevertheless were treated with suspicion and even violence. This ill will probably goes a long way toward explaining their rapid amalgamation.

Although relatively small in number, French Huguenots as an ethnic group exerted a considerable influence. They imparted a high-spirited and aristocratic tone to the colony of South Carolina, for example, yet at the same time quickly adopted the English language and joined the established Anglican Church. The following selection attempts to explain the rapid assimilation that took place over the course of two generations.

The Assimiliation of The Huguenots[16]

The rapid assimilation of the French in Carolina into the Established Church and their intermarriage with other nationalities are remarkable features of their early history. The absorption into the Anglican Church was indirectly coercive, rapid and thorough. The English institutions mastered and overpowered the French. The French became English in language and religion, British in sentiment and policies. The fulcrum by which it was accomplished was economic necessity, the lever was political preferment. We are slow to conclude that the change was made with graceful ease. . . . Only after a conflict, the temper of which is too remote to be easily understood today, did the French Protestants relinquish their church affiliation and embrace Anglicanism. . . .

There seems to have been little effort on the part of the Carolina French Protestants to perpetuate the remembrance of a distinct nationality. Their children, except in the isolated sections, were not encouraged to speak French. Frequent interruptions in the conduct of the French churches, caused by the illness, death and resignations of French pastors, constantly afforded reason for their members to attend the services of churches other than their own. Owing to Dissenter antipathies the step to Anglicanism was sometimes made proportionately easy. By 1706, sufficient time had elapsed since the Revocation to give rise to a younger generation unsatisfied with the adherence to old French forms, a generation adverse to a language not in general use in the province, clamoring for the new and the popular. The rising generation could not be expected to feel the bitterness of the Revocation as did their parents. The children of many of the refugees were even ashamed to bear French names. The idea of remaining foreigners in a land in which they were born and reared was alien to their thought. The establishment of the Church of England by law in the colony in 1700 welded these several links into a chain of necessity. The Bishop of London sagaciously supplied the Huguenots with a ministry of French nativity and Anglican ordination, men proficient in both the French language and the ritual of the Establishment. . . .

But the absorption of the French was more extensive than a mere change in church forms. It extended to proper names, to language, to customs, and even to blood. It has become evident that for several reasons the Huguenots were regarded with disfavor before they were able to rise socially by the accumulation of wealth. However unreasonable that circumstance may have been regarded it was nevertheless a fact and became very unpleasant. Out of it grew the desire to become anglicized. A French name was constantly a bid to disfavor. Therefore some people changed their names completely, others modified them, still others accepted the English equivalent. Jacques Serrurier easily became Smith; for convenience Pasquereau degenerated into Packerow; Villepontoux became Pontoux; Lewis Janvier, a goldsmith, became Louis Jennings; Timothée was anglicized to Timothy. . . .

[16] Reprinted from Arthur Henry Hirsh, *The Huguenots of Colonial South Carolina* (Hamden, Conn.: The Shoe String Press, 1962), pp. 90, 95, 100. By permission of the Duke University Press.

An eighteenth-century observation underscoring the theme of relative indifference to ethnic elements is that of J. Hector St. John de Crevecoeur. His is an overly optimistic evaluation of the American as a "new man." The "melting pot" concept gained an early advocate in Crevecoeur. The selection that follows is from his *Letters from an American Farmer* (Dublin, 1782).[17]

The next wish of this traveler will be to know whence came all these people? They are a mixture of English, Scotch, Irish, French, Dutch, Germans, and Swedes. From this promiscuous breed, that race, now called Americans, have arisen. In this great American asylum the poor of Europe have by some means met together, and in consequence of various causes. To what purpose should they ask one another what countrymen they are? Alas, two-thirds of them had no country. Can a wretch, who wanders about, who works and starves, whose life is a continual scene of sore afflication or pinching penury; can that man call England or any other kingdom his country, a country that had no bread for him, whose fields produced him no harvest; who met with nothing but the frowns of the rich, the severity of the laws, with jails and punishments, who owned not a single foot of the extensive surface of this planet? No! Urged by a variety of motives, here they came. Everything has tended to regenerate them: new laws, a new mode of living, a new social system. Here they are become men. In Europe they were so many useless plants, wanting vegetative mold and refreshing showers. They withered; and were mowed down by want, hunger, and war. But now, by the power of transplantation, like all other plants, they have taken root and flourished! Formerly they were not numbered in any civil lists of their country, except in those of the poor; here they rank as citizens. . . .

What attachment can a poor European emigrant have for a country where he had nothing? The knowledge of the language, the love of a few kindred as poor as himself, were the only cords that tied him. His country is now that which gives him land, bread, protection, and consequence. "Ubi panis ibi patria" is the motto of all emigrants. He is either a European, or the descendant of a European; hence that strange mixture of blood which you will find in no other country. I could point out to you a man whose grandfather was an Englishman, whose wife was Dutch, whose son married a French woman, and whose present four sons have now four wives of different nations. He is an American, who, leaving behind him all his ancient prejudices and manners, receives new ones from the new mode of life he has embraced, the new government he obeys, and the new rank he holds. He becomes an American by being received in the broad lap of our great alma mater. Here individuals of all nations are melted into a new race of men, whose labors and posterity will one day cause great changes in the world. Americans are the western pilgrims who are carrying along with

[17] Reprinted by permission of the publishers from *This Was America*, edited by Oscar Handlin, Cambridge, Mass.: Harvard University Press, Copyright 1949 by the President and Fellows of Harvard College, pp. 38–39.

them that great mass of arts, sciences, vigor, and industry which began long since in the east. They will finish the great circle.

Other students of French emigration were much more critical of the French experience in America than was Crevecoeur. DeMontlezun, author of *Voyage fait dans les années 1816 et 1817, de New-Yorck à la Nouvelle Orleans et de l'Orinoque au Mississippi . . .* (1818), was caustic in his impressions about the United States. But he does give an insight into the thinking of at least many French aristocrats who searched for and rejoiced over the presence of ethnic traits in the French communities in the United States, such as New Orleans.

> On disembarking at New Orleans it is immediately apparent that one is in a French city.[18] The place contains 28,000 to 30,000 souls, of which three-quarters are Negroes or have colored blood. It is heartrending to see in the streets white people whose misery contrasts with the insolent luxury of some colored women. The French inhabitants are mad Bonapartists; there are scarcely a dozen royalists among them. . . .
> The morose habits of the sad American have not won out here. Sunday is a day of pleasures as in France. The balls are attended with an inconceivable avidity. The passion for dancing is at its height. The carnival is about to begin. It is a time for dressing up, for games, for love. The comedy is only a medium for relaxation, for more immediate and more piquant pleasures. The ladies who live in the country come into the city to take part in the gaiety and to contest the prize for beauty, for elegance, and for grace.
> The legislature of the state of Louisiana is now in session. I listened to the House of Representatives yesterday in a little room, bad in appearance, where a dozen or so champions of liberty, equality, and fraternity sat. A French lawyer had the floor when I entered. . . .
> Despite the efforts of the Americans to unite Louisiana with the other states, to amalgamate its population with theirs, and to reshape its laws and customs in the intolerant form of their own hateful mold, nature, stronger, laughs at their vain attempt. French gaiety remains unperturbable. The American is still the stranger in the land; the general spirit still contrasts sharply with his own, and I do not think that he can reasonably flatter himself with the hope that Louisiana will ever be truly American.

In the wake of the great French Revolution, immigration to the United States underwent one of its most fascinating phases. Thousands of French aristocrats came to this country. As a class they were the proudest and most dazzling people to enter this land in the late eighteenth and early nineteenth century. They lived for a time among Americans while simultaneously regarding them with contempt. When they returned to France, as most of them did, they left hardly a trace of their influence

[18] Ibid., pp. 133, 134, 137.

upon American society. Nevertheless, it is of significance to note the extraordinary intermixture of class and ethnic interests in the pockets of French life that they tried to establish in the United States. This phenomenon is described in the narrative of C. F. Volney, "Gallipolis, or the French colony at Scioto," in *A View of the Soil and Climate of the United States of America.*[19]

> On my arrival in America, in October, 1795, I made some enquiry after these people, but could only hear a vague story that they were buried somewhere in the western wilds, and had not prospered. Next summer I shaped my course through Virginia, and after traveling three hundred miles to Staunton, two hundred more over a rugged desert to the Great Kenhawah, and sixty miles down that river, through a scene still more dreary and desolate, to the Ohio, I at last reached a village called Point Pleasant, four miles from Gallipolis; by this splendid appellation (which means French city) the emigrants denominated their settlement. My eagerness to see the face and hear the language of my countrymen, once more, made me hasten thither without delay.
>
> Colonel Lewis, a kinsman of General Washington, facilitated my journey. I went on, but reflecting that I was going to visit Frenchmen disappointed in their dearest hopes, their vanity mortified, and their mortification likely to be aggravated by the sight of one, who had probably foretold their misfortunes to some of them, my impatience was greatly diminished. It was night-fall before I reached the village, and I could perceive nothing but a double row of small white houses, built on the flat top of a bank of the Ohio, which here laves the foot of a cliff fifty feet high. The water being low, I climbed the bank, by a slope formed in its side, and was conducted to a log house called an inn. It was kept by a Frenchman, who asked me but few questions, and his demeanour evinced the truth of all my prognostics.
>
> Next day I took a view of the place, and was struck with its forlorn appearance; with the thin pale faces, sickly looks, and anxious air of its inhabitants. They were shy of conversing with me. Their dwellings, though made externally cheerful by whitewash, were only log huts, patched with clay, and roofed with shingles, consequently damp, unwholesome, and uncomfortable. The village forms an oblong quadrangle of two rows of contiguous buildings, which a spark would consume altogether. . . .
>
> All the labours of clearing and tillage were imposed on the family itself of the proprietor, labourers not being to be hired but at enormous prices. It may easily be imagined how severe a hardship it was, on men brought up in the ease and indolence of Paris, to chop trees, to plough, to sow, to reap, to labour in the field or the barn, in a heat of 85 or 95 degrees. . . .
>
> Such is the condition of the Scioto colony, which does not altogether realize the pictures of the inland paradise given by American farmers, nor the glories of the future capital of the Ohio and its realms, predicted by a certain writer. . . .

[19] From Abbott, *Historical Aspects of Immigration Problem*, pp. 30–36. Copyright © 1926 by University of Chicago Press. By permission of Arno Press.

I wished to leave this settlement with a persuasion that they were doing well and would prosper; but, besides the original and incurable error in the choice of situation, I am afraid that their despondency will never be entirely removed, since there will always be some cause for it, and since the French nation are less qualified for settling a new country than the emigrants from England, Ireland, or Germany. Among fifteen instances of farms, cultivated or formed by Frenchmen, which were mentioned to me in America, only two or three were likely to thrive. As to collecting men in villages, such as Gallipolis, those that have been formed on the frontiers of Louisiana or Canada, and have been left to shift for themselves, have generally dwindled, and sooner or later disappeared; while plain men, from the British Isles or Germany, who have pierced the heart of the forest with their families only, and even ventured alone into the Indian territory, have generally made good their footing, and have prospered and multiplied.

For the most part, however, French emigrants to the United States were ethnically little distinguished, except by their surnames, from English settlers. Even those who colonized the French-named New Rochelle had become well assimilated.

The French Protestants who colonized New Rochelle have chiefly, if not wholly, become mere Americans; in no way distinguishable, except by their surnames, from the descendants of the English Colonists.[20] It is a fact, deserving of notice, that a considerable number of these people have been persons of high respectability, and have been elevated to very honorable stations; and many others have acquired ample fortunes, and sustained very desirable characters in private life. A prophet might attribute their prosperity to a particular blessing of God, who on many occasions has been pleased to shower his favour upon the descendants of those who have been persecuted for their piety.

Of all these classes of Colonists it is to be observed, generally, that they will soon be so entirely amalgamated with those from New England as to be undistinguishable.

THE DUTCH

In the latter part of the sixteenth century, the Dutch entered into a successful movement for independence against their Spanish monarchs which simultaneously predisposed the nation to a remarkable period of expansion. This expansion led to important claims on North America, as the colony of New Netherlands was founded. In the wake of that colony's growth, several thousand Dutch immigrants came to the New World early in the seventeenth century. These Dutchmen remained the predominant strain in the otherwise cosmopolitan character of what later became New York.

[20] Ibid., p. 429.

Promoters of the Dutch colony were intent on establishing a military and economic base in North America. In the process they gave the Hudson Valley region an indelible Dutch stamp. So strong was the Dutch imprint that as late as the American Revolution, Dutch was one of two foreign tongues apparently firmly rooted in American society.

New Netherlands was never to be a Dutch frontier in the same sense that Jamestown and Plymouth were for England. The Dutch government was apathetic about the settlement in America. Nevertheless, the Dutch who emigrated to New Netherlands had a strong attachment to their ethnic roots. In the following extract Arnold Mulder speculates on what might have been in regard to the implanting of Dutch culture in America.

> The folk of New Netherland in terms of the wave of what was their future were far more enlightened than their leaders who tried to govern them with supercilious contempt. An objective examination of the record, honestly allowing for all their faults and weaknesses, shows that they were worthy of becoming the bearers of their country's culture across our continent. The ineptness and short-sightedness of politicians and traders robbed them of that destiny, but their defeat was only partial, as the subsequent story of the life of their nationality in America shows.
>
> There is a footnote to the story of the Dutch colonial episode on the American continent. In less than a decade after the surrender to the English, the Dutch recaptured New York during the war that broke out between England and Holland in 1672. The folk of New Netherland industriously set about restoring their own institutions, even to the extent of wiping out many of the English place names and substituting for them the Dutch words by which they had been known for half a century. It was a last instinctive attempt to impose their culture on America.[21]

One of the first institutions that the Dutch inhabitants of New Netherlands were determined to establish was a schoolhouse. An illustration of their understanding of the value of education, this institution also perpetuated national traits. As the following excerpt shows, after the English replaced the Dutch as rulers of New Netherlands, the Dutch school, taught in the Dutch language and with other concessions to ethnicity, remained.

> Under early English rule the schooling of the Dutch children was little interfered with.[22] They were to be instructed in the "Netherlandisch tongue" as of old, and the schoolmaster was still to be under

[21] Reprinted from Arnold Mulder, *Americans from Holland* (Philadelphia: J. B. Lippincott Company, 1947), p. 57.

[22] Reprinted from Maud Wilder Goodwin et al. (eds.), *Historic New York*, vol. 2 (reprint ed., Port Washington, N.Y.: Ira J. Friedman, Publishers, Kennikat Press, 1969), pp. 341–42.

the supervision of the Consistory. The school hours were fixed from nine to eleven A.M. in summer, from half-past nine to half-past twelve in winter, while the afternoon session the year round lasted from one to five o'clock. The schools were opened and closed with prayer, twice a week the pupils were examined in the catechism and express stipulation was made that teachers should use "none but edifying and orthodox text-books and such as should meet the approbation of the Consistory."

The control of the schools so wisely conceded by the English continued in the hands of the Dutch long enough to stamp the character which endures to this day in the representative school of the Collegiate Reformed Dutch Church of New York, which with its fine buildings and elaborate equipments is the direct successor of the little school gathered together by Adam Roelantsen under the shadow of the old Fort.

Those of us of Dutch blood have a special right to look with pride upon this steady growth of the educational institution planted and fostered by our forefathers and bearing perpetual testimony to their energy and perseverance, their just valuation of "the things of the spirit," their respect for learning, and their determination to "learn the youth the first principles" and to make them men "who may be able to serve their country in Church and State."

Nearly a century after the English conquest of New Netherlands, perceptive observers had little difficulty in recognizing the strength of ethnic feeling among the Dutch inhabitants of New York. The following selection from Peter Kalm, *En Resa Til Norra America pa Kongl* (Stockholm, 1753–1761), makes this manifest. Kalm, a Swedish naturalist, was very uncomplimentary of the Dutch and in this passage he implies that his opinion reflected the view commonly held by other colonists.

In Albany the inhabitants are almost all Dutchmen.[23] They speak Dutch, have Dutch preachers, and the divine service is performed in that language. Their manners are likewise quite Dutch, although their dress is like that of the English. The avarice, selfishness, and immeasurable love of money of the inhabitants of Albany are very well-known throughout all North America. If a real Jew, who understands the art of getting forward perfectly well, should settle amongst them, they would not fail to ruin him. For this reason nobody comes to this place without the most pressing necessity. I found that the judgment which other people formed of the Dutch was not without foundation. For though they seldom see any strangers (except those who go from the British colonies to Canada and back again) and one might therefore expect to find victuals and accommodations for travelers cheaper than in places where they always resort, yet I experienced the contrary. I was obliged to pay for everything twice, thrice, and four times as much as in any part of North America through which I have passed. If I wanted their assistance I was obliged to pay them very well for it, and when I wanted to purchase anything or be helped in some case or other

[23] Reprinted by permission of the publishers from *This Was America*, ed. Handlin, Copyright 1949 by the President and Fellows of Harvard College, p. 33.

I could at once see what kind of blood ran in their veins, for they either fixed exorbitant prices for their services or were very reluctant to assist me.

In the 1840's immigration became epidemic as over 1,700,000 new-comers arrived in America. The Dutch, heretofore not an emigrating people, found a significant minority of their countrymen participating in this movement because of a combination of religious and economic motives. Many of the Dutch immigrants gave evidence of their ethnic loyalties by establishing a number of settlements in Michigan in the 1840's and 1850's and giving them characteristic Dutch names, such as Holland and Zeeland. The following letter records what was perhaps the typical reaction of these immigrants. Leaving his homeland primarily because of religious persecution, the writer sought a place where he could carry on a vigorous and unmolested religious life and earn a livelihood. He found a means of making a living but lamented the apparent loss of religious commitment among the Dutch in America.

Then came a farmer, living five miles from Kalamazoo, to Allegan to get a yoke of oxen.[24] From him Mrs. Ely learned that he could make use of at least two Hollanders. Having been recommended, we decided to accompany him. The next morning, we were told what we were to do, but we could not understand a word of what was said. One of our host's three sons had to show us by example what was expected of us. The sons relieved each other every hour. We had to work pretty hard. It was May. Our breakfast was finished at sunrise, and we had to work all day until evening when the lamp was lit. As our host seemed devout and said grace at table and we were otherwise well treated and, besides, were earning a little, we were hoping for the best and stayed. In the evening when we went to bed we knelt and complained to the Lord about our folly and blindness and ignorance in all things, and begged Him for understanding and wisdom and direction in matters external. The members of our host's family noted something of this and began to respect us. They asked us to go to church with them. We accepted their suggestion but we could not understand the services.

This and other acts made a favorable impression upon the Americans so that they gladly sought to teach us and help us. Although we still wore our ordinary Dutch clothing and adhered to our old customs this did us no harm. They regarded us as religious people and had a good opinion of Dutch immigrants. This impression deepened when they noted that our people generally conducted themselves in this manner. For it happened from time to time that when others with money came from the Kolonie to buy cows and had to sit at table with these farmers they did not hesitate to profess their faith simply and uprightly. They offered prayer

[24] Reprinted from Henry S. Lucas, *Dutch Immigrant Memoirs and Selected Writings*, vol. 1 (Seattle: University of Washington Press, 1955), pp. 88–89. Copyright © 1965 by Kowinklÿ Ke Van Gorcom & Co. N.V. Assen, Netherlands. Reprinted by permission of the University of Washington Press.

at table just as they did at home. This custom caused Americans (like Dominie Isaac Wyckoff in 1848) to speak about our first settlers with much praise. They said that the faith of our people resembled that of the first Christians.

When I reflect upon our spiritual condition in those early days and how we conducted ourselves not only among our people but also among strangers, shame comes to my face as I think of the present. Whenever we came together we talked about our spiritual welfare. We had learned to regard ourselves as lost sinners who were seeking Jesus. We were happy among ourselves and thanked God for his grace shown us and for His faithfulness which we experienced in so many ways.

Alas! how things have changed; but they have not become better. Our fields indeed have been cleared and we have gone foreward in material matters, but we have lost much of our early earnestness and piety. In those first days our conversation often was about the Lord and His worship; today we often talk about the news of the day, which leaves our hearts cold. I have written this account in the hope that it may contribute something to the knowledge of the history of our earliest settlement and to the extension of the praise of God who has helped and blessed us beyond what we could ask in prayer. To Him be all the glory.

THE GERMANS

The German ethnic strain began to penetrate the New World in the latter part of the seventeenth century with the inauguration of the new colony of Pennsylvania. In planning the settlement of his colony, William Penn, the founder, gave serious thought to the downtrodden in Germany, especially in the southwestern regions of that country. Accordingly, in 1683 Francis Pastorius led the first band of German families from the Rhineland to Pennsylvania. Many Germans of even lesser means followed, so that the Germans eventually became one of the largest of all ethnic groups in the United States. As did all others, they came as strangers to the New World. However, they were required to make greater adjustments than most of the immigrants to the colonies because unlike many others, e.g., the English, Welsh, and Scotch-Irish, the Germans differed in language, customs, and religion, being for the most part Lutherans.

Many Germans were faced with the additional problem, upon arrival, of being obliged to work a number of years in a dependent status. A. B. Faust, historian of German emigration to the United States, describes the process by which many became redemptioners. His history also includes a contemporary critical account of the practice by Muhlenberg, as well as some comments regarding Germans who turned the redemption system to their own advantage.

A system was established very early in American colonial history, by which an immigrant could get to the promised land, though not in possession of the means to pay for his passage.[25] He would agree to serve from three to seven years in the colonies until the price of his transportation was paid off to the shipmaster who had advanced it. At the end of his term he was released, given a suit of clothes, sometimes money or land, and awarded all the rights of a free citizen. Hence the term redemptioners (because redeemed) was applied to this class of immigrants, who were also known as "indented servants." At first the system seemed humane and liberal, yielding the poor ultimately the same opportunities as the well-to-do. It had been advocated by Furley, the agent of William Penn, and had been in vogue in Virginia since the first decade of that colony's existence. The system began to be applied extensively to German immigration about 1728. Muhlenberg describes the arrival of a ship in Philadelphia in the following manner:

Before the ship is allowed to cast anchor in the harbor, the immigrants are all examined, as to whether any contagious disease be among them. The next step is to bring all the new arrivals in a procession before the city hall and there compel them to take the oath of allegiance to the king of Great Britain. After that they are brought back to the ship. Those that have paid their passage are released, the others are advertised in the newspapers for sale. The ship becomes the market. The buyers make their choice and bargain with the immigrants for a certain number of years and days, depending upon the price demanded by the ship captain or other 'merchant' who made the outlay for transportation, etc. Colonial governments recognize the written contract, which is then made binding for the redemptioner. The young unmarried people of both sexes are very quickly sold, and their fortunes are either good or bad, according to the character of the buyer. Old married people, widows, and the feeble, are a drug on the market, but if they have sound children, then their transportation charges are added to those of the children, and the latter must serve the longer. This does not save families from being separated in the various towns or even provinces. Again, the healthiest are taken first, and the sick are frequently detained beyond the period of recovery, when a release would frequently have saved them.

Not only tillers of the soil and artisans became serfs for their passage money, students and schoolmasters also were often sold in this labor market. The Reverend Mr. Kunze naively writes, that he had entertained the thought, if ever he became the owner of twenty pounds, of buying the first German student who would land at Philadelphia, put him into his garret, and there with his help begin a Latin school, which he was sure would quickly pay off the outlay. People of rank, who had lost their money, fared no better than the low-born peasant. There was Frederick Helfenstein, probably a lineal descendant of Count Helfenstein and the Emperor Maximilian, who was compelled to sell himself as a redemptioner in Georgia.

[25] Reprinted from Albert B. Faust, *The German Element in the United States*, vol. 1 (New York: Arno Press, Inc., 1969), pp. 66–67, 72.

In the early part of the nineteenth century, the desire to leave Germany for America increased as the "Auswanderung" (emigration) notion spread throughout Germany. This period found large numbers of German people seeking escape from economic, religious, or political difficulties in the homeland. At the same time they wished to maintain their ethnic identity.

> The Auswanderer went to America less to build something new than to regain and conserve something old, which they remembered or thought they did: to till new fields and find new customers, true enough, but ultimately to keep the ways of life they were used to, which the new Europe seemed determined to destroy.[26] In the hearts of the Auswanderer of those years, theirs were not so much acts of radical affirmation as acts of conservative rejection. They wanted to escape rootlessness (or mobility, if you prefer); or rather, they felt their roots being torn up, and sought a place to sink them again, for they could not contemplate living in another way. They were not characterized by "the willingness to break with old traditions . . . to gamble the peace of their families and the security of their heirs on an uncertain future," to quote a typical description. Something like that may have happened to many of them in America, but few intended it when they left. They were rather, I think, people who traveled thousands of grim miles in order to keep their roots, their habits, their united families and the kind of future they wanted for their families. They did not wait passively for their roots to be broken, to be sure; yet they were conservatives, who acted radically in order to preserve, and who journeyed to another world to keep their homes.

Attachment to German customs and language was constant among German immigrants, especially in Pennsylvania. One effect of this attachment was criticism for allegedly being unable to see the value of education. Faust analyzes the problem in the selection below.[27]

> The Pennsylvania Germans have frequently suffered the rebuke of being neglectful in matters of education. It was a charge made during nativistic epochs, and has made by far too strong an impression. The main origin of the charge was the tenacity with which Germans held to their own language and customs. The German settlers brought with them their school-teachers and preachers. Schools were invariably established by them, and sometimes before churches. The schools were, however, rarely separated from the churches, and when a movement began for establishing public schools in their districts, the Germans opposed it. They viewed the movement with suspicion, as if its purpose were to deprive them of their religion, the influence of their preachers, or the use of their language.

[26] Reprinted by permission of the publishers from *Germany and the Emigration, 1816–1885*, by Mack Walker, Cambridge, Mass.: Harvard University Press, Copyright 1964 by the President and Fellows of Harvard College, p. 69.

[27] From Faust, *German Element in the United States*, pp. 146–47.

Along with that went a degree of pride (Bauernstolz) in their ability to pay for the instruction of their children. They did not wish to inflict this burden upon the state, failing altogether to see the benefits derived from a common school system. It was long before the church school could be replaced by a public school in their counties. An attempt was made to train a body of teachers among the German population, giving instruction in the English language and the rudiments of American law and politics, by the establishment of a college. This foundation was located in Lancaster County, in 1787, and was named after Benjamin Franklin. Henry Muhlenberg was chosen the first head of Franklin College. The charge of ignorance against the Pennsylvania Germans was frequently due to their lack of proficiency in the use of the English language. Education in that day did not go beyond the three R's, or the practical necessities of life, and to the native population the first of these necessities seemed, of course, the ability to use the English language.

Sometimes tenacious clinging to German customs and speech brought them into conflict with other ethnic groups. In Virginia, for example, ethnic-based battles between Germans and Irish occurred simultaneously with an assimilative process which tended to ameliorate the strained relations.

Customs and speech the Germans brought with them, into the Valley, and for a time held to them tenaciously.[28] When the Germans and Irish met, there was often friction, such as Kercheval describes, e.g., in the town of Winchester, the capital of Frederick County. Winchester had a mixed population of Germans, Irish, and a few Scotch and English. "It was customary for the Dutch on St. Patrick's Day," says Kercheval, "to exhibit the effigy of the saint, with a string of Irish potatoes around his neck, and his wife, Sheeley, with her apron loaded also with potatoes. This was always followed by a riot. The Irish resented the indignity offered to their saint and his holy spouse, and a battle followed. On St. Michael's Day the Irish would retort, and exhibit the saint with a rope of sauerkraut about the neck. Then the Dutch, like the Yankee, 'felt chock full of fight,' and at it they went, pell-mell, and many a black eye, bloody nose and broken head was the result. The practice was finally put down by the rigor with which the courts of justice punished the rioters." But as the two elements lived longer together, with common interests, they began to appreciate one another. . . .

Transatlantic emigration from Germany reached epidemic proportions in the period 1830–1854. For many, removal and relocation was en masse, in groups rather than as individuals. The American Calvin Colton, in his *Manual for Emigrants to America* (originally published in London in 1832), recounts the phenomenon.

[28] Ibid., pp. 199–200.

The Germans and other nations of the European continent seem to understand the advantage of emigrating in groups, or small colonies by association, better than the English, or the Americans themselves.[29] And they are now annually pouring these associated masses into the Mississippi Valley. I happened in the summer of 1830 to pass, in company with one of these Colonies of Germans, across Lake Erie in a steam-boat. The principal, or Chief, was a well-educated gentleman, of large estate, himself and family evidently accustomed to all the refinements of the best society in Germany. He had himself gone before, made his purchase of land in the State of Ohio, returned to Germany, disposed of his estates there, and was now on his way, with his family, and some scores of the native and hardy German peasantry, under his protection and guidance— himself the patriarch of the interesting and happy group, all looking to him, as their chief and father. Such an association did not leave their home—they carried it with them. There was no breaking up of families—no separation of parents and children. And, notwithstanding their long voyage across the Atlantic and up to this place, they seemed as happy on board of the steamer on the waters of the Lake, as if they had been sitting by their own fire-sides in Germany. And I have no doubt, that they are happy still in their new abode, surrounded with cheering circumstances created by their own hands, and looking forward to the most cheering prospects. And this is doubtless one of the happiest modes of emigration.

In discussing Pennsylvania, Colton affirmed the retention of ethnic flavor among Germans, although he was certain that it would eventually succumb to the pervasive English culture.

Next to the Quakers and even more taking into consideration the whole extent of the state, the Germans constituted a great portion of the society, so much so, that throughout all the German districts, the language of their parent country is almost exclusively used.[30] Their common schools, their pulpit, their newspapers and most of their literature are generally sustained through the medium of the mother tongue—all doomed, however, to the gradual encroachments of the English, which must ultimately supplant the German.

THE SCOTS

In examining emigration from Scotland, it is important to distinguish the Scotch-Irish from the Scots. The Scotch-Irish came from Ulster and were almost exclusively of Lowland Scots blood. They settled on the frontier in the South and in the central Appalachians and played a prominent part in the American Revolution, especially in the colonies of Penn-

---

[29] Reprinted from Calvin Colton, *Manual for Emigrants to America* (New York: Arno Press, 1969), pp. 155–57.

[30] Ibid., p. 67.

sylvania and North Carolina. It is estimated that over 50,000 Scotch-Irish arrived in America in the fifty years preceding the Revolution.

The Scots came from the Highlands of Scotland and followed a different development. The Scots were not frontiersmen; they remained loyal to the King during the American Revolution; and they sought to maintain their ties with the home country. About 25,000 Scots entered America's ports in the third quarter of the eighteenth century.

In spite of their sober views of America, the emigrants from Scotland were generally industrious, frugal, and successful in their endeavors. One Scottish observer criticized his fellow countrymen in 1802 for expressing optimistic hopes of becoming "great or affluent." The Scottish experiences, as pointed out in the following selections, reveal persistent ethnic characteristics: deep religious faith, strict moral code, realistic attitudes, and desire to duplicate life patterns of the Old Country.

Religion left an indelible mark on the Scotch-Irish, as attested to in numerous old church records in the Scotch-Irish settlements. In the following, the Reverend Samuel Wilson, pastor of the Big Spring Church, Cumberland County, Pennsylvania, gives stern moral admonishment in a marriage ceremony around 1800.

> From old church records that have been preserved some idea may be obtained of the thoroughness with which religious instruction was diffused through Scotch-Irish settlements.[31] Big Spring congregation, in the western part of Cumberland County, was organized not later than the spring of 1737, for in June of that year a minister was called. This congregation had a succession of pastors, either natives of Ulster or born of Ulster parents. One of these early pastors was the Rev. Samuel Wilson. He was born in 1754 in Letterkenny township, now included in Franklin County, was graduated from Princeton in 1782, licensed by Donegal Presbytery on October 17, 1786, and was installed pastor of the Big Spring Church, June 20, 1787. Some records of his pastorate have been preserved, and they give an instructive view of the workings of the system, the details showing that Ulster traditions were still vigorous after the lapse of over half a century. He used a form of address in the marriage ceremony which illustrates the plainness and directness of speech then still in vogue. After searching inquiry whether or not objections to the marriage existed Mr. Wilson proceeded to address the couple as follows:

> > The design of marriage is, that fornication may be avoided, and as our race is more dignified than the lower creations, so then, our passions should be regulated by reason and religion. It is likewise intended for producing a legitimate offspring, and a seed for the church. There are duties incumbent upon those who enter this relation, some of them are equally binding upon both parties, some upon one party, some upon the other.

[31] Reprinted from Henry Jones Ford, *The Scotch-Irish in America* (New York: Arno Press, Inc., 1969), pp. 286–88.

First, it is equally binding upon you both to love each other's persons, to avoid freedom with all others which formerly might have been excusable, to keep each other's lawful secrets, fidelity to the marriage bed, and if God shall give you an offspring, it will be mutually binding upon you both, to consult their spiritual, as well as their temporal concerns.

Secondly, it will be particularly binding upon you, Sir, who is to be the head of the family, to maintain the authority which God hath given you. In every society there must be a head, and in families, by divine authority, this is given to the man, but as woman was given to man for an helpmeet and a bosom companion, you are not to treat this woman in a tyrannical manner, much less as a slave, but to love and kindly entreat her, as becomes one so nearly allied to you.

Lastly, it is incumbent upon you, Madam, who is to be the wife, to acknowledge the authority of him who is to be your husband, and for this, you have the example of Sarah, who is commended for calling Abraham, Lord. It seems to be your privilege in matters in which you and he cannot agree, that you advise with him, endeavoring in an easy way by persuasion to gain him to your side; but if you cannot in this way gain your point, it is fit and proper that you submit in matters in which conscience is not concerned. It will be your duty in a particular manner, to use good economy in regard to those things which may be placed in your hands. In a word, you are to be industrious in your place and station.

The Scots were assimilated quite readily when they arrived in America. Yet they insisted that a distinction be made between them and other groups from the British Isles, and they chose to regard themselves as "American Scots." The passage below describes the need for ethnic identification felt by the Scots. Many of the characteristics of Scottish social and cultural life were continued in the United States.

Among the many immigrants to the United States, those who came from Great Britain on the whole assimilated themselves readily to the American nation, mainly because it has always been hard to think of people speaking the same language as being different nationalities, and they were apt to identify themselves with other Americans of British descent as against those of other national origins.[32] The Scots, in particular, had always had a great gift for assimilation, and most of them readily adopted the American idiom and ways of life, though there were always the representatives of the more angular type of Scot who delights in making himself conspicuous. In general, however, while the Scot became an American he became an American Scot, insistent that he was distinct from English, Welsh and Irish, and where there were Scottish communities they carefully fostered—and sometimes exaggerated—what they could preserve of Scottish life and Scottish ways.

Not least significant was the retention of many of the characteristics of Scottish church life. The rigid discipline of the Presby-

[32] Reprinted from Gordon Donaldson, *The Scots Overseas* (London: Robert Hale, 1966), pp. 124–28.

terian system was maintained in the United States at least as long as it lasted at home. Antiquated customs in worship survived, like the practice of 'lining out' the metrical psalms, a practice which meant that the precentor (who led the singing when instrumental music of any kind was abhorred) read each line, after which the congregation sang it. In America as in Scotland, church services were provided in Gaelic for highland congregations. One hears of them at Elmira in Illinois, at Boston and elsewhere, but the last Gaelic sermon in North Carolina is said to have been preached in 1860 and the language is now extinct in that area. . . .

The Protestant Episcopal Church in the United States had peculiarly close associations with the Scottish Episcopal Church. In 1784 its first bishop, Samuel Seabury, was consecrated by Scottish bishops in Aberdeen, and an undertaking was given that the American Communion service would follow the pattern of the Scottish Liturgy. Scottish Episcopalians who went to America therefore felt themselves at home, and Scottish immigrants provided some clergy for the American Church: James Bonner, for instance, born in Edinburgh in 1810, was a teacher in Scotland before he emigrated in 1835 to America, where he took orders and ministered in a succession of churches in Pennsylvania, New York, Ohio and Maryland.

In the secular sphere, Scots kept up their festivities at Hogmanay (New Year's Eve) and New Year's Day, and also the traditional 'guising' and other customs connected with Hallowe'en. St. Andrew's Day was observed in the United States in generations when it was almost forgotten in Scotland—a curious example of the triumph of national sentiment over ecclesiastical standards which had at the Reformation renounced the observance of saints' days. Another anniversary which came to be of even greater importance was the birthday of Robert Burns (25th January), which was celebrated in the United States at least as early as 1820, with a banquet in New York. The first Burns Club in America was established in in New York in 1847, and now one finds Burns Clubs in places like Akron (Ohio), Atlanta (Georgia), Buffalo (New York), Charlotte (North Carolina), Flint (Michigan) and St. Louis (Missouri). No other Scottish author captured the imagination to quite the same degree, but Sir Walter Scott was not forgotten on the centenary of his birth in 1871. . . .

THE WELSH

Welsh immigrants were among the early colonists, first arriving in large numbers late in the seventeenth century, as Baptists and Quakers settled in Massachusetts, Pennsylvania, and Delaware. Welsh Anglicans and Presbyterians followed later. Immigration figures show that no steady flow of immigrants from Wales was maintained. Nevertheless, in the pre-Civil War period there were enough Welshmen in Pennsylvania who sought to retain their own ethnicity to justify printing some books in Welsh.

The Welsh helped to lay the foundation for the United States during the colonial period by making significant contributions in all fields of endeavor. Welsh-Americans contributed their share to the success of the American Revolution. For example, five signers of the Declaration of Independence were of Welsh stock: Francis Lewis, Lewis Morris, Thomas Jefferson, William Floyd, and Button Gwinnett.

After the American Revolution economic conditions in Wales became so critical that the lure of free land and a new life drew more Welshmen to the United States. Overcoming problems of social and economic adjustment, they sent letters back to the home country that generally extolled the advantages of living in America, especially in the agricultural areas.

The selections that follow reveal a strong awareness of ethnic identification. Living together, aiding each other, and retaining the old patterns of life gave comfort and security to Welshmen in an alien land.

The religious upheavals sweeping Europe in the seventeenth century penetrated Wales and resulted in strained relations between Welsh religious reformers and the Anglican Church. The Baptists and the Quakers were the first two separatist sects that sent Welsh group settlements to the American colonies. The first selection below describes Welsh Quakers seeking to establish a religious refuge in Pennsylvania and simultaneously attempting to "maintain a community of their own with their distinctive Welsh language and institutions." The selection also summarizes their many achievements during the colonial and revolutionary periods. Note the ethnic pride and awareness of the author, himself the son of a Welsh-born, Welsh-speaking mother from Pennsylvania. The extract relates how the Welsh became a substantial group of Quakers in seventeenth-century Pennsylvania.

> The Friends made their greatest conquest when they converted the noted William Penn to their beliefs, for it was the latter who furnished them a refuge in America where they might propagate their religion in peace.[33] Penn, so tradition held, was the grandson of a Welshman, John Tudor, who was called Pen-mynydd (of the hilltop) and who took the name Penn when he removed from Wales to Ireland. William's father had been a noted admiral in the English Navy and had loaned King Charles II a considerable sum of money while the latter had been in exile. . . .
>
> Penn's plans for a Quaker refuge became known to the Welsh Friends. They viewed them with enthusiasm as a means of escaping the then current persecution. Furthermore they believed that in the new colony they could purchase a large tract of land and to settle there in a body so that they could maintain a community of their own with their distinctive Welsh language and institutions. Many of them were gentry of considerable means and could meet the liberal terms of purchase offered by Penn. Then, too, the fact that Penn was both a Quaker and a Welshman (so they believed) made the plan ever more attractive. Accordingly, the Welsh Quakers were

[33] Reprinted from Edward G. Hartmann, *Americans from Wales* (North Quincy, Mass.: The Christopher Publishing House, 1967), pp. 43–44, 54–55.

among the first to take advantage of Penn's liberal terms. A group of prominence among them, led by John ap John, went to London in 1681 to start negotiations with Penn for the proposed purchase. An agreement was later worked out with Penn whereby 40,000 acres in the new colony were purchased by the Welsh Quakers with the oral understanding that the plot would be set aside as a separate "barony" within which the Welsh would have full rights of self-government in order to protect their distinctive language and institutions. Unfortunately, this latter part of the agreement was verbal on Penn's part and was never put into writing. It was to become a cause of controversy between Penn and the Welsh later on.

A special committee of the Welsh Quakers had consummated the purchase, but since considerable time might elapse before the land could be disposed of to settlers, leaders of the enterprise were made trustees for 30,000 acres of the tract and took out patents in their own names with the understanding that they would sell their holdings to other Welsh Quakers. The leaders formed self-constituted heads of seven companies for the division and sale of the land.

The so-called "Welsh Barony" was eventually located on the west side of Schuylkill River to the northwest of Philadelphia. It included what became the townships of Upper Merion, Lower Merion, Haverford, Radnor, Tredyffrin, East Whiteland, West Whiteland, East Goshen, West Goshen, Willistown, East Town, and part of West Town, in the present counties of Montgomery, Chester, and Delaware. It was situated in a magnificently fertile territory and was admirably suited to meet the desires of the Welsh. The "Barony" was not surveyed until 1684, and its exact boundaries were not determined until 1687. . . .

Thus by the end of the colonial period, Welsh immigrants and their descendants were to be found not only scattered throughout the thirteen colonies, but also in compact numbers in various key areas. In the north was the smallest of these Welsh settlements, that of Swansea, Massachusetts, consisting of some two hundred settlers. Farther to the south were the extensive Pennsylvania settlements, comprising the so-called Welsh Barony and adjacent Great Valley settlements to the west of the Schuylkill River, the Gwynedd settlement to the north of the city of Philadelphia, the small Lancaster and Berks counties settlements, and a considerable proportion of the inhabitants of the Pennsylvania metropolis itself. It has been estimated that the number of Welsh settlers in these areas amounted to some 6,000. Over the provincial line lay the Delaware Welsh Tract in Newcastle County with a Welsh population estimated around 1,000. Then far to the south were to be found the North Carolina Black River colony of unknown strength and the Welsh Neck settlement of South Carolina with an estimated Welsh population of some 500.

As one might expect, it was in Philadelphia and Pennsylvania that the Welsh exerted a very strong influence socially and politically for here they were most numerous. For over a century, men of Welsh blood occupied prominent positions in the life of the city, and inasmuch as the city and its surrounding counties dominated the life of the province, the Welsh played an equally prominent part in the life of the Pennsylvania province itself. A large proportion of the early city fathers, including mayors, Edward Roberts and Robert Wharton, were Welsh. Such, too, was the case in respect to the fields of justice, the arts, science, business and commerce. For the first quarter of the century, 1682–1730, almost all the physicians were Welshmen including Dr. Thomas Wynne, who attended William Penn during his first voyage to America. Many of the eminent religious leaders, too, as we have seen were Welshmen.

Here in early Philadelphia were published two monumental books in the Welsh language. The first *Annerch i'r Cymru* (Salutation to the Welsh), was the pietistic work of Ellis Pugh, a humble stonemason and Quaker preacher, who willed the manuscript to the Gwynedd Quaker Meeting. The latter had it printed by Andrew Bradford in 1721. It was subsequently translated and issued in an English version. The other, *Cyd-gordiad Egwyddorawl o'r Scrythurau* (Alphabetical Concordance of the Scriptures), was the work of Abel Morgan, the noted Baptist divine, and was the first real Welsh concordance of the Bible. It was published in 1730 by Samuel Keimer and Dafydd Harry, a Welshman, eight years after Morgan's death. Both books rate among the rarest of Americana.

Two other works in Welsh were also published in Philadelphia during these early years. The firm of Benjamin Franklin and Hugh Meredydd published a Welsh translation of an English book by Benjamin Wallin, *Y Dull a Fedyddio a Dwfr* (The Manner of Baptizing with Water), in 1730. Meredydd, a Welshman, later aided Franklin in publishing the noted *Pennsylvania Gazette*. The other work in Welsh entitled simply, *A Welsh Pamphlet*, was a reprint of a British original printed by Andrew Bradford in 1735. It dealt with moral reflections on death, judgment, Heaven and Hell.

It was in Philadelphia that the oldest Welsh-American society was founded in 1729 for the purpose of honoring St. David, the patron saint of Wales. It developed eventually into a benevolent society aiding newly arrived immigrants from Wales, dispensing charity when necessary, and sponsoring interest in Welsh culture. The Welsh Society of Philadelphia is still in existence today, a monument to the durability of self-consciousness of the little ethnic group that made its weight felt so strongly in the early life of the city. It claims the honor of being the oldest existing society of Philadelphia.

The Welsh settlers in America who engaged in farming experienced great success. After extensive description of the soil and the climate, the following letter, written in 1800 by a group of Welsh settlers in Cambria, Pennsylvania, to the home country, generously praises the numerous rich resources of America. Within this context, there emerges evidence of a strong desire by the Welsh to retain their distinct ethnicity.

Our end in establishing this settlement was for the general good of the Welch, particularly that they may have the privilege of hearing the gospel in their own language.[34] There are in Cambria preachers of different denominations, living together in peace and amity. We have three or four Welch sermons every first day in the

[34] From Abbott, *Historical Aspects of Immigration Problem*, pp. 29–30. Copyright © 1926 by University of Chicago Press. By permission of Arno Press.

week, and there are English preachers in Beula. There are 350 lots in (and some near) the town given to support a school; more than 1,000 books have been purchased for a general library, and 200 acres of land for the support of the preachers, not of any one particular sect or party, but such as esteemed worthy, of every denomination, and profess that Jesus is the Son of God, and Saviour of Men. We do not mention the above privileges to allure you into this neighbourhood, if you can do better in any other. . . .

Though having met with many difficulties, as it is natural to expect the first years, we now increase our stock every year. Within the last four years, upwards of 100 families have come to our neighborhood, and 100 more may get a comfortable livelihood here. Should any of you be disposed to come over here, we would advise you to consult the captain of the vessel with respect to victuals that will be necessary for your voyage, with a sufficient quantity of bread, water, salt, meat, potatoes, oatmeal, and malt liquor.

After landing in America, many sorts of people will be met with; some will say this is the best place, and some another. All who are acquainted with our nation know it is easy to impose upon a Welchman; therefore, we would advise them to be upon their guard. They who have families would do well to get a waggon immediately after their landing, and remove all their goods out of the ship into in, and convey them to the place of their destination without delay. If they come hither (though they abide not), it will be cheaper for them to leave their families with us until they can find a place to their satisfaction, than in the cities, which in the summer are unhealthy to strangers, but the country round is as healthy as any part of Wales. Should any of the poor be disposed to come, and not able to bear the expense of their voyage, if their friends be able to assist them, and can depend on their faithfulness, they will not be long here before they are repaid with thankfulness. . . .

> (Signed) THEOPHILUS REES
> WILLIAM JENKINS
> REES LLOYD
> SIMON JAMES, etc.

As with other ethnic groups in America, the Welsh tended to settle together. The following selection speaks favorably of the tolerant atmosphere, despite mention of the intolerant Native American Party. The writer advises formation of a Welsh society to assist in the acquisition of land and to look for cheap and fertile soil in the Mississippi region.

FROM RICHARD EDWARDS IN NEW YORK TO ED.[35]

March 4, 1844

IT IS true that those called Protestants in this country do not fight with each other as they do in Wales as the difference between them

---

[35] Reprinted from Conway, Alan, ed. *The Welsh in America: Letters from the Immigrants,* p. 68, University of Minnesota Press, Minneapolis, © 1961 by University of Minnesota.

is not so great. This can be attributed to the free and independent spirit that fills the Americans. They teach their children in the first place, that they have a mind and that it is their duty to use it and judge things for themselves and not to think or do anything because others do so in matters of judgment and conscience.

There is a political party here calling themselves Native Americans, their chief purpose being to deny votes to emigrants until they have lived here for at least twenty-one years. Anyone coming to this country can have a vote in five years if he wants one.

A word to emigrants. You know that almost all the Welsh smallholders who have emigrated to this country have settled in Oneida County, somewhere between Utica and Steubenville. In these districts, there are churches and Welsh sermons. The land has become dearer than usual. I am not against the Welsh living together in a Welsh settlement in this country and I am not against them settling in mountainous districts where the land is covered with snow for five months of the year, when the fertile lands of the Mississippi are much cheaper and have a more pleasant climate. Other nations send over first their agents who know their job and who find out the best part of the country for settlement. The Welsh in this city intend founding a society, if you cooperate with us, for this purpose. This can do our nation a great deal of good in the future, as the western and southern states are sure to gain a great deal of the trade and population of the states shortly. I would very much like the Welsh to be more thoughtful when coming over. All that they seem to think about is buying land and they spend all they have on this without thinking that it is better to have a little land, well cultivated, than a great amount in the barren wilderness. Many here have borrowed money to buy land and the profit is not enough to pay the interest. It is obvious that they need some organization.

The author of the following letter to the home country praises America as "vast in extent, mighty in resources, and destined, ere long, to be at the head of all the nations of the earth." He advises his ex-countrymen to come to America to enjoy its opportunities; the land is cheap, the need for labor great, and the wages high.

FROM LEWIS HOWELL, JR., IN NEW YORK, TO ED.
FOR THE BENEFIT OF HIS ACQUAINTANCES IN THE
OLD COUNTRY[36]

August 27, 1844

I HAVE allowed myself a couple of hours to afford, as far as I am able, the wavering, hard-pressed, half-starved laborers of Wales an opportunity of judging which country is the best and of deciding the very important question, "Which is best, to go or not to go?" and to advise as to the preparation for the voyage and above all to give particular warning to avoid the Liverpool and New York lodging-house keepers, or, to give them their due, emigrant-plunderers—a set of lazy, ravenous scamps who watch the arrival

[36] Ibid., pp. 69–70.

of the shipping, pounce upon the poor, unsuspecting "greens" (as they call them), fleece them, and finally get clear of them by kicking them out of doors.

But to the task. America, little known, greatly abused and mighty America—vast in extent, mighty in resources, and destined, ere long, to be the head of all the nations of the earth. To a stranger just landed from Europe, the first objects which attract his attention are its people, all so neatly and comfortably clad—the expression of happiness depicted upon every countenance. The stranger is involuntarily led to inquire where are the working classes, the tattered and half-fed miserable-looking starvelings whom his eye was wont to rest upon whilst crossing the streets of his native land. He enters their neat and cleanly dwellings and beholds their tables loaded not only with the necessities, but also a good deal of the luxuries of life. Here he concludes that America is infinitely superior to the Old Country and heartily wishes all the hard-pressed of his native country to come and take their abode in this land of Canaan.

Land can be procured at all times and, generally speaking, in all places—cleared, partly cleared, and uncleared—the prices of which vary from one dollar (4s. English) to twenty dollars an acre. When the means allow, a partly cleared farm is always preferable; for the difficulties of a first settlement on an uncleared piece of ground are very great, in fact, of a very serious nature, for let all remember, that they will see a country consisting of dreary forests, interspersed with settlements on the rudest scale, that the roads are generally in a very bad condition, and, above all, that everyone must work hard with his own hands. Even amidst the rudeness and wildness that surrounds the poor American farmer, he is perfectly happy and in a fair way of realizing a happy independence— whereas the poor Welsh farmer is continually poor and has no hope but the grave to extricate him from his miserable poverty.

Almost every trade is in great request and the rates of wages very nearly double those of the Old Country. Bricklayers, masons, and stone-cutters are in great request, especially the first, owing to the general taste for brick structures—wages in these trades average from $10 to $14 per week. Painters, plumbers, and plasterers are first-rate businesses; painters not only obtain the highest rate of wages but a certainty of constant work.

The large influx of Catholic immigrants caused the Welsh much concern. Beginning in the 1830's, and continuing for the next several decades, non-Protestant elements settled in the United States. The most important were the Irish whose ethnicity, particularly religion, was quite different from the older immigration. The following letter, written in 1835 by Ezekiel Hughes of Ebensburg, Pennsylvania, to an acquaintance in Wales, sees a papal plot behind the number of priests and money being sent to the United States. Complete assimilation in the American culture appears to be an accepted fact by the letter's author, a former Welshman, and measures must be taken to guard against the threat of an alien influence. (Alan Conway, editor, *The Welsh in America*, University of Minnesota Press, Minneapolis, 1961, pp. 73–74.)

OUR country abounds with everything necessary for the support of man—the laws, the variety of climate and soil, and the extent of our territory, all of which are calculated to move and do move people to emigrate to this country from every quarter of the globe. The valley of the Mississippi River, perhaps the most fertile and extensive in the world is settling with astonishing rapidity. Papal Europe is well aware of its importance and is pouring in its Jesuits and money by thousands into the western part of our country. It has been lately ascertained that from six to eight hundred Roman Catholic priests have come into the different ports of this country clandestinely during the year 1834. I have been also informed that regular societies have been lately formed in different parts of Southern Europe for the purpose of procuring priests and nuns and money to establish the papal throne in this land of liberty. Large donations are also made by the pope to their different churches in our own neighborhood. The money sent from Europe is expended either in building churches or to buy large tracts of land in the West which they can buy now very low and which they will sell again only to the members of their own church. Thus they intend, in course of time, to become possessed of very large portions of the western valley, which if they succeed will be a source of large profit and greatly augment their power and thereby may at some future day bring this country under the trammels of popery.

Protestants have been roused by sense of duty and the impending danger and are making great exertions to establish Sunday Schools in every part of the Union and thereby diffuse a general knowledge of the scriptures, which the Roman Catholics rigidly deny.

Here will in a few years be undoubtedly the abode of countless millions of human beings. Ministers of the gospel are much wanted in this country as many thriving settlements in the West are entirely destitute. I candidly think that a faithful minister could do more good here perhaps than in any other part of the world, and as we have claims on our native land we will expect not to be forgotten.

Your friend and fellow traveler to eternity.

THE IRISH

No official records of immigration statistics were kept before 1820; however, it is estimated that about 15,000 Irish entered this country before that date, most of them settling in Maryland and Pennsylvania. The great flow of Irish immigrants occurred from 1830 to 1860 and was primarily motivated by British oppression and economic hardships at home. In the 1830's the Irish constituted 44 percent of the total immigration, and this figure increased to 49 percent in the 1840's. The immigration peak topped 221,253 in 1851, the famine of 1846 serving as the catalyst that drove the Irish from their homeland.

Protestant America overreacted to the "alien" culture. The Irish were Roman Catholic, anti-British, and generally uneducated and unskilled. The most violent Native American movement developed in the 1830's and produced an inglorious record of intolerance. "No Irish need apply" appeared in advertisements in Boston and other cities. A convent was burned in Charlestown, Massachusetts, in 1831; a mob attacked a Catholic church in Philadelphia in 1846.

The Irish saw America against this background of flourishing bigotry. The selections in this section illustrate Irish efforts to accommodate to the situation by retaining a high degree of ethnicity. Irishmen expressed their disappointment at the American experience, while contemporaries criticized them for being clannish and "noisy, turbulent, and intolerant."

The early Irish who came to America engaged in the most menial tasks. In this narrative, the Irish actor Tyrone Power, an ancestor of the Tyrone Power of motion picture fame, relates with awe, pride, and respect the conditions under which his fellow countrymen worked on a canal connecting Lake Ponchartrain with New Orleans.

> I only wish that the wise men at home who cooly charge the present conditions of Ireland upon the inherent lazyness of her population could be transported to this spot, to look upon the hundreds of fine fellows labouring beneath a sun that at this winter season was insufferably fierce, and amidst a pestilential swamp whose exhalations were fetid to a degree scarcely endurable for a few moments; wading amidst stumps of trees, mid-deep in black mud, clearing the spaces pumped out by powerful steam engines; wheeling, digging, hewing, or bearing burdens it made one's shoulders ache to look upon; exposed meantime to every change of temperature in log huts laid down in the very swamps, on a foundation of newly-felled trees, having the waters lying stagnant between the floor-logs, whose interstices, together with those of the side-walls, are open, pervious alike to sun, wind or snow.[37] Here they subsist on the coarsest fare, holding life on a tenure as uncertain as does the leader of a forlorn hope; excluded from all the advantages of civilization; often at the mercy of a hard contractor, who wrings his profits from their blood; and all this for a pittance that merely enables him to exist, with little power to save, or a hope beyond the continuance of the like exertion.

Francis Leiber was a Prussian who had been twice imprisoned for his political views. As political conditions worsened, he fled to England and then to the United States. In the following selection, Leiber draws upon the Irish experience in examining the problems of assimilation in America. Critical of the Irish attitude, he upbraids them for exploiting ethnicity to their own advantage.

> The Irish—in spite of what I have said above of their facility in assimilating with the Americans—clan more together than the emigrants of any other nation.[38] They, in fact, openly retain their name,

---

[37] Reprinted from Tyrone Power, "Irish Workmen Build a Canal near New Orleans," in Rhoda Hoff, *America's Immigrants* (New York: Henry Z. Walck, 1967), p. 22.

[38] From Abbott, *Historical Aspects of Immigration Problem*, pp. 438–39. Copyright © 1926 by University of Chicago Press. By permission of Arno Press.

and often, in the very moment that they make use of the highest privileges of citizenship which any country can bestow, they do it under the banner of Irishmen. There is no election in any of the large cities without some previous calls upon the "true-born sons of Ireland," to vote so or so. On the election day itself banners are seen floating from the windows of taverns, some of which, you may be certain, are ornamented with mottos having reference to the Irish alone. They do farther, sometimes; they will bring forward their own candidate, if they feel strong enough. All this is, to speak guardedly, at least impolite towards the natives, who receive the foreigner with a degree of national hospitality unequalled by any other nation. Every career on the wide field of enterprise which is open to the natural citizens of this republic, is equally open to the naturalized. After the brief period of five years' residence, any alien may take the citizen's oath, and this done, he enjoys every privilege of which a free-born American can boast, an unstinted citizenship, with the single exception that he cannot become a president of the United States. The least that could be expected, in return for such a boon, it should be supposed, would be the frankest and most heartfelt union, in every thing, with the nation which so hospitably makes no difference between its own sons and the new comers. But the Irish are desirous of becoming Americans and yet remaining Irish, and this serving of two masters will not do. Whatever the innermost feelings of an emigrant toward his native country may be, and with every generous heart will be, as a citizen of America, he should be American and American only, or let him remain alien. As the latter, he is protected as much by the law of the land as is a citizen; there is no necessity whatever for his becoming naturalized. It is, therefore, with great concern, that a good citizen must observe that disturbances at elections are not infrequently caused by those who do not enjoy their citizenship by birthright, sometimes by those who do not enjoy it at all.

What are the reasons that the Irish in this country can clan more together than the emigrants of any other nation? I believe they are three-fold. First, more Irish than people of other countries come to the United States, and, as I think I have observed in a previous letter, they have a predilection for large cities, so that they remain in greater numbers together. Secondly, the Irish feel that they have been wronged in their country; they have, in a degree, been driven from it; the feelings with which they look back to it are, therefore, of a more intense character than they would otherwise be; or, if this be not the case, they feel among themselves the strong tie of bearing one common wrong. Thirdly, they are encouraged to this clanship by party men; their Irish feelings are flattered and excited, in order to win them; they are called upon as Irish in order to gain their votes, which become, in some quarters of large cities, or, indeed in some whole counties, at times, very important, when, otherwise, the parties might be nearly balanced.

Let me throw in, here, the remark, though it be not quite in its place, that the common language of the English, Scotch, Irish, and Americans, causes the last, unconsciously to themselves, to consider emigrants of the three first nations, when settled among them, nearer akin than those of other countries. There are many Irish in congress, of whom it is hardly known that they are strangers by birth. I have been told a story, which I feel inclined to believe. A German offered himself for a professorship of one of the colleges in the middle states; he was unsuccessful in his application; and it was pretty generally understood that a native would be preferred; but a short time after, an Irish gentleman obtained the chair, certainly not on account of his superiority. This, however, is not always the course of things; for instance, in Cambridge, Massachusetts, there are two Germans who hold prominent professorships. But if you glance over the list of officers of the United States, you will find very many Irish; nor does any difficulty arise at the appointment of one of that people, while the contrary would, probably, be the case were a German, or a Frenchman by birth, to offer himself for a place, which easily might be filled by some one else. This, I think, is not quite fair; the Irish emigrants do by no means deserve more confidence, than those of other countries; and though the existence of a common language may naturally lead the Americans not to feel so strongly the difference between themselves and the Irish, they ought to be careful not to act upon this feeling.

The early Irish-American was poor and uneducated. Thomas D'Arcy McGee, editor and publisher of the New York *Nation,* an Irish-American newspaper, fought hard for the establishment of educational facilities to aid the Irish immigrants. In an 1848 editorial entitled "What Irishmen Can Do," McGee urged the establishment of adult schools for immigrant education, giving as his reason:

> In a country where every native can write and read a letter, it is painful to see good and trusty men shut out from the reward of their fidelity and industry for lack of that easily acquired art. They might nearly as well want the right hand as be unable to hold a pen in it.[39]

In 1850 a Joseph Brenan expressed disillusionment over the true condition and treatment of the Irish in the United States. He wrote back to Dublin as follows:

> It is time to speak of ourselves. I have been much disheartened since my arrival here by the unfortunate condition of my countrymen. I came with high hopes and sanguine expectations, and I have realized my disappointment. . . . Religious bigotry and party feuds have crossed the Atlantic with our people. Our nature has not changed with the clime. . . . What I state of the Irish in America is fact, and it is foolish or criminal to conceal it. Their position is not what it is represented to be at home—far different; it is one of shame and poverty. They are shunned and despised. The name of Irish politics is anathema, and Ireland is as much a subject of contempt as of pity. "My master is a great tyrant," said a negro lately, "he treats me as badly as if I was a common Irishman."[40]

[39] Reprinted from Florence Elizabeth Gibson, *The Attitude of the New York Irish toward State and National Affairs, 1848–1892* (New York: Columbia University Press, 1954), p. 15. Reprinted by permission of the publisher.
[40] Ibid.

A surprisingly moderate view toward the Know-Nothing movement in 1854 is presented in the selection that follows. The writer exhorts Irish-Americans to reform their behavior in order to evoke favor among the more tolerant and democratic elements in the United States, thereby presaging victory over bigotry.

An Irish View of "Know-Nothingism"[41]

We have at all times been averse to the course taken by those who fled from Ireland, within the last six years, without taking time to consider maturely the prospects before them, and the dangers and difficulties they would meet with in a strange land. They rushed headlong from their native country, instead of battling for land and life, and flung themselves amongst a people who are proverbial for their love of gain, and who welcomed the Irish, not because they sympathized with their sufferings, but because they required them to build their railroads, dig their canals, clear their forests, till their fields, and work in their factories.

We are told now that Jonathan has got more of the Irish than he requires, and lest the Celt should become his master, that he desires to oppress him as the Egyptians oppressed the Israelites in Egypt. A storm of Know-Nothing persecution rages against the Irish and their religion in America, the object of which is to deprive them of many of their civil rights, and if possible make it penal to profess their faith openly.

We cannot believe that this persecution will continue very long. We believe that the good sense of the country will again return, and that the bastard policy of the Know-Nothings will speedily die out. But while censuring the outrageous conduct of the Know-Nothings, let us be impartial and just. Has this persecution been unprovoked? Have all the Irish conducted themselves, as citizens of the Great Republic, in that sober, orderly, and prudent manner becoming a persecuted people who fled from the lash of tyrants and found a home and a refuge in America?

We fear that some of them have been a noisy, turbulent, and intolerant class, who did no credit to the character of their native country, and were of little benefit to the land of their adoption. We fear, too, that some of the ultra-Catholic journals went far beyond the bounds of prudence in writing on religious subjects.

We do not make these remarks to palliate the conduct of the native despots, who assign and malign the Irish. We merely allude to the matter for the purpose of stating that the conduct of some of the Irish emigrants is not what it ought to be, and to counsel them to give up their intemperate habits, their rows, their faction fights, and act in such a manner as to earn the respect of their bitterest enemies.

If they do this they will at once disarm the Know-Nothings, and bring to their aid every good citizen in the United States, those glorious spirits who subscribe to the tolerant views of Washington, Jefferson, and the other illustrious fathers of the Republic. But if by

[41] From Abbott, *Historical Aspects of Immigration Problem*, pp. 817–819. Copyright © 1926 by University of Chicago Press. By permission of Arno Press.

their follies they disgrace themselves, can it be wondered at if the Americans declare that such a people are unworthy to share with them the freedom and blessings guaranteed by the constitution of their country?

What, we ask, would the Irish people say, if two millions of Russians, Prussians, or Greeks should come amongst them, and by their conduct set us all by the ears, commence rows in our streets, faction fights on our railways; and in their journals assail our creed, and evince little willingness to respect our best institutions? Would not the native population begin to think it right to exclude them from public offices, and declare them dangerous foes to the country?

We still consider the United States a better home for the Irish emigrant than any colony belonging to despotic England. . . . The Irish Catholics can maintain the freedom of their faith in the States, if they only act prudently, and warn their newspaper writers to be less intolerant on religious topics. What good can they effect for the faith by calling Protestants hard names? No man ever made a convert by such means as that; on the contrary, it is by showing themselves good Christians, full of charity, benevolence, and kindness to their neighbors, that they will prove the superiority of their religion, and attract persons differing from them to inquire into its dogmas, and in the end submit to its teaching.

These are our views. . . . We have no doubt that many of the Irish in America are not faultless, and that they are not what they ought to be. Let those turbulent characters reform themselves and persecution will soon die a natural death. The good sense of the American people will revolt against it; and remembering how the Irish bled in the struggle for independence, Jonathan will clasp them to his breast, and both united will make the Republic of the West the enemy of slavery and despotism, the refuge of the persecuted, and "the home of the brave, and the land of the free."

KEY QUESTIONS

1. Did the white man and the Indian suffer in their estimations of each other? Discuss this by reference to the selections on Indians.

2. The American Revolution notwithstanding, could it be said that ethnic affinity between the English and many Americans still persisted in the generation following independence?

3. The primary black experience in the early period of American history was a slave experience. In what ways could it be described as an ethnic experience?

4. Despite the conversion of blacks to Christianity, they were still required to fashion an ethnic type of Church, e.g., the African Methodist Episcopal Church. Explain this development.

5. How strongly did French Huguenots consciously strive to assert their distinctive national traits?

6. Despite the persistence of Dutch ethnicity in the United States, some of the more sensitive Dutch migrants lamented the loss of religious fervor. Comment on this by reference to the Lucas selection.

7. Describe the tenacity with which the German-Americans held onto their language and customs by citing the behavior of Pennsylvania Germans as an example.

8. Describe how tenacious preservation of ethnicity entered into inter-ethnic conflict between German-Americans and Irish-Americans.

9. Discuss the situation of the Scots, who, although having no major problems in assimilating, nevertheless continued their ethnic identification.

10. Did relative success in farming tend to lead to rapid erosion of ethnic interest among Welsh in America?

11. To what degree did the Irish in America manifest clannishness in the pre–Civil War period?

3

The Period After 1865: THE NORTH-WESTERN EUROPEAN CHARACTER— SCANDINAVIAN, IRISH, DUTCH, GERMAN, ENGLISH

For two decades following the conclusion of the Civil War the character of immigration to the United States remained essentially as it had been prior to the internecine conflict. That is, immigrants continued to come almost exclusively from the countries of northern and western Europe. Marcus L. Hansen, whose works on immigration proved to be seminal, described it in racial terms: "This exodus was Teutonic in blood, in institutions, and in the basis of its language, forming the most homogenous of all the migrations to America."[1] Scandinavians, Irishmen, Dutchmen, Germans, and Englishmen formed the heart of this massive movement.

Substantial Scandinavian immigration began in the pre–Civil War era; however, it was in the post–Civil War period (1868–1882) that it reached its peak. In all, the Scandinavian countries (Norway, Sweden, Denmark) have accounted for 2½ million immigrants to the United States. These people were impelled to remove from their homelands largely because of economic causes, such as crop failures and decline in fishing and the maritime industries, although in the pre–Civil War era a small number came for religious reasons.

THE NORWEGIANS

A high proportion of Scandinavians settled in rural communities because of the abundant quantities of land still available, either free or at very low cost, and because not a few Norwegian immigrants possessed the capital necessary to embark on farming. Their experiences in and writings about America afford us an opportunity to examine American society from the viewpoint of people who spoke a different language but

[1] Marcus Lee Hansen, *The Atlantic Migration 1607–1860* (New York: Harper Torchbooks, 1961), p. 10.

were otherwise similar to the predominant ethnic backgrounds of Teutonic lineage and Protestant (in this case Lutheran) religion. The selection below is from Ole Munch Raeder, *The Forties and the Letters of Ole Munch Raeder* (Minneapolis, 1929), who comments on the tenacious quality of ethnic residues that he found during his travels through the centers of Norwegian-American settlements.

As you know, I cannot convince myself that all these countrymen of ours, as they leave our own country, are to be regarded as completely lost and as strangers to us.[2] Let them become Americans, as is the duty of holders of American soil, but this need not prevent them from remaining Norwegian for a long time to come. The American character is not yet so fixed and established that it excludes all others.

There are even now, so many of our people out here in the West that they already appear as a group and thereby are protected against influences foreign to themselves, because their relationship to one another is stronger than their relationship to other races. But if this condition is to be at all lasting, there must be more intelligence among them; they must realize that this instinct of theirs is quite consistent with good sense and honor; they must learn to appreciate their own nationality more than they do and to cause others to respect it, too. For these reasons the establishment of a press among them is undoubtedly of the greatest importance.

I have already suggested how desirable it would be for the Norwegians to see their language frequently in somewhat pure form, not only in their religious literature, but otherwise as well. I had in mind particularly the great ease with which they learn the English language and, unfortunately, the equal facility they have in forgetting their own as soon as they cease to use it every day. . . . They do not bother about keeping the two languages separate, so that they speak Norwegian to their countrymen and English to others; instead, they eliminate one word after the other from their Norwegian and substitute English words in such a way that the Norwegian will soon be completely forgotten.

Such a practice, to be sure, is rather common among uneducated people who emigrate to a foreign country, but the Norwegians seem to have a special knack at it. . . .

It is, on the whole, quite remarkable how quickly our farm girls improve when they are among strangers. Their English is quite correct, but as soon as they start to speak their mother tongue, it generally sounds broad and clumsy enough. No matter how much patriotic love you may profess to feel for the various dialects of our language, you cannot deny or at any rate avoid the feeling that the harmony is broken, even if the unfortunate expression comes from the fairest mouth or is animated by the friendliest smile. I believe that most of them are not conscious of the peculiar impression made by their way of speaking Norwegian; at any rate, they are too good-hearted and too happy in the recollection of their native land to be bothered by such a trifle. One can scarcely say as much for the

[2] Reprinted from Blegen, Theodore C., ed. *Land of Their Choice*, pp. 208–210, University of Minnesota Press, Minneapolis, © 1955, University of Minnesota.

Norwegian boys; at any rate, I have heard the opinion expressed that as soon as they have learned "to guess" and "to calculate," they at once become strangers to their less fortunate countrymen and are very loath to admit their Norwegian origin.

Emigrant songs and poems were mediums through which Norwegians debated the benefits and disadvantages of migrating to America. Although the major concerns emphasized were economic, social, and class issues, ethnic considerations were also important. Some of these poems and songs emerged in the pre–Civil War period and became more and more familiar to Norwegians in the post–Civil War period.

One of the earliest Norwegian emigrant songs was that composed by Ole Rynning and sung in 1837:

> The cliffs of Norway lie hidden now behind the waters, but our longings go out to those shores, with their dim and ancient oak-forests, where the sloughing of the pines and the thunder of the glaciers are music to Norway's son.
> And although Destiny should bid him pitch his tent where once Bjorn and Leif pitched theirs, he will cherish always the mountains of old Mother Norway, and yearn with pious longing to see his beloved home once more.[3]

Emigrant farewells help one to understand the poignancy of the leave-taking. A dialect poet of Telemarken sings:

> And now farewell to all my folk and parish, for I am going to America, to seek a happier life in the new world. There is no help for it, I must cross the sea. Life has become too hard here for poor folk.[4]

Songs and poems were also mediums for the emigration debate that raged in Norway in the forties, fifties, and sixties. Thus M. B. Landstad, a noted divine, spoke to the people in 1842:

> My brothers hear a word of counsel: remain at home here in the friendly North! From a sorrowful heart I beg you to stay here at home; do not sail over yonder. Little do you know what it is you are doing, nor the bitter disillusioning that may be yours. For when you are buried over there in the deep forests or the wilderness, a restless longing will shatter your peace, and you will remember then what now you forget.[5]

The Norwegian-American novelist Ole Rolvaag, in *Giants in the Earth*, wrote one of the most poignant of all novels concerning immigrants

[3] Reprinted from Theodore C. Blegen, *Norwegian Migration to America 1825–1860* (Northfield, Minn.: Norwegian-American Historical Association, 1931), pp. 308–310.

[4] Ibid.

[5] Ibid.

in America. A truly epic story of Norwegian pioneers struggling for an existence in the Dakota country of the 1870's and 1880's, it chronicles as does no other book on the topic the combination of physical and spiritual experiences which formed the texture of this people's westward journey. This movement is regarded not as a conquest but as an instance of the earth's defeating man. The excerpts below depict the fear that seized settlers on a lonely plain, the resurgence of ethnicity when loneliness was broken, and the immigrant's examination of his own soul as he pondered the value of emigrating.

> They had been here four months now; to her it seemed like so many generations; in all this time they had seen no strangers except the Indians—nor would they be likely to see any others. . . .[6]
>
> People had never dwelt here, people would never come; never could they find home in this vast, wind-swept void. . . .
>
> Yes, they were the only ones who had been bewitched into straying out here! . . . Thus it was with the erring sons of men; they were lost before they knew it; they went astray without being aware; only others could see them as they were. Some were saved, and returned from their wanderings, changed into different people; others never came back! . . . God pity them: others never came back! . . .
>
> At last he grew impatient, because he was unable to follow the conversation as well as he wished; he grasped Tonseten by the arm and pinched it so hard that he turned around angrily; but the next second he was talking again.
>
> "What sort of people are they?"
>
> "Germans. . . . Don't bother me now!"
>
> "You must tell them not to stop. . . . We want only Norwegians here, you know!" . . .
>
> Then Store-Hans came galloping in, and told a story so strange that all were lost in amazement.
>
> "They are Norskies!" he shouted as he pulled up.
>
> "What's that you say?" exclaimed Tonseten.
>
> "Yes, Norskies, every single one, I tell you! A whole shoal of them—and they are coming right here! They talk Norwegian, too."
>
> "Are you crazy!" shouted Tonseten. . . . At once he began to assume a great dignity and authority; he ordered Kjersti indoors to put on the coffeepot, and sent the other women to help her. . . . "Don't you hear Hans say that they are Norskies! Decent folks must get a decent reception!"
>
> And now he took Sam with him, and did like the patriarch of old: he went out to meet the strangers, entreating them to enter in under his humble roof. . . .
>
> "There isn't much to say about such things," Per Hansa began. "She has never felt at home here in America. . . . There are some people, I know now, who never should emigrate, because, you see, they can't take pleasure in that which is to come—they simply can't

[6] Abridged from pp. 127, 129, 159, 385 in *Giants in the Earth* by O. E. Rolvaag. Copyright © 1927 by Harper & Row, Publishers, Inc.; renewed, 1955 by Jennie Marie Berdahl Rolvaag.

see it! . . . And yet, she has never reproached me. And in spite of everything, we got along fairly well up to the time when our last child was born. . . . Yes, the one you baptized to-day. . . . Then she took a notion that she was going to die—but I didn't understand it at the time. . . . She has never had the habit of fault-finding. . . . She struggled hard when the child was born, and we all thought she wouldn't survive—or him, either. That's why we had to baptize him at once.

Born in Stavanger, Norway, Birger Osland left for the United States in 1888, settled in Chicago, and proceeded to become thoroughly familiar with the Norwegian-American community. For several years he had a position with *Scandinavian,* one of the leading Norwegian-American newspapers in the United States. Most of its subscribers were farmers in the Northwest: Wisconsin, Minnesota, Iowa, Illinois, the Dakotas, Nebraska, Montana, Oregon, Idaho, and Washington. He also became the American correspondent for a newspaper in Norway. Active in numerous Norwegian-American clubs in the Chicago area, he became a principal figure in the creation of the Norwegian-American steamship line and was also an important figure in the Norwegian-American Historical Association. Thus he was both a student of and active participant in life in the Norwegian communities in the United States and thereby well versed in the ethnic attitudes of these people.

The following excerpts cover such important aspects of ethnicity as dependency on native language, activities of Norwegian-American clubs, loyalty to the fatherland, and Norwegian influence in the Chicago area.

The Norwegian immigrants who homesteaded in the West in the 1880's did not have much opportunity to become proficient in English.[7] Hence they not only subscribed to Norwegian-language newspapers, but they also read Norwegian books almost exclusively. . . .

Among immigrant farmers, laborers, and others to whom complete mastery of the English language and wider social and business contacts were not essential to material success, the foreign-language papers in the United States have been a blessing and a practical necessity. To all those who emigrated after school age and who had not studied English in their native land, the foreign-language newspaper was an open, easily read, and fully understood book, which brought them, besides news from the homeland, information about the daily happenings, political developments, laws, customs of their adopted land. Except for this source of information, the immigrants would have remained strangers much longer than they did and their isolation in things spiritual would have been more complete. Of the old Norwegian, Swedish, Danish, and German papers in America which I used to read, I know of none which was not thoroughly loyal to the United States, and most of them maintained as high ethical standards as our good American newspapers.

[7] Reprinted from Birger Osland, *A Long Pull from Stavanger, The Reminiscences of a Norwegian Immigrant* (Northfield, Minn.: Norwegian-American Historical Association, 1945), pp. 16, 17, 46, 47, 58, 59, 210, 211.

The language question—whether English or Norwegian should be the official language of the club—has at times been the cause of heated discussion. . . .

During my period of service as president, the language question flared up. Many of the club's new members were born in the United States and insisted on at least full equality for the two languages. We sent to all members a circular letter, favoring English, and designating December 20, 1917, as the date for a meeting when they would be able to vote upon the issue.

But the letter did not work. The opposition was stirred as never before, and it had enough votes at the meeting to prevent the two-thirds majority required for the change.

On June 7, 1905, the Norwegian Storting, or parliament, notified King Oscar II of Norway and Sweden that the elected representatives of the Norwegian people considered the union with Sweden dissolved. This step aroused great interest and some anxiety all over the civilized world, especially among Norwegian-Americans. Outwardly, at least, our Swedish-American fellow citizens took it calmly and in general showed no ill feeling. To all Norwegians this was a fateful day, fraught with great anxiety but also with promise, for it pointed to the restoration of that complete independence which, over four hundred years earlier, had slipped away from Norway, unnoticed and without a struggle. Many young Norwegian-Americans were ready to join the colors at once.

In presenting the resolution, I made a few introductory remarks which concluded thus, "The message which we now are about to adopt and send to the Norwegian government is an assurance to our native land of our firm purpose to render her all support within our means, should her independence and liberty be placed in danger."

Simultaneously with our attempt to create a Norwegian-American exhibit, strong efforts were made to secure participation in the exposition by our motherland, Norway. In July 1930, an address in Norwegian was sent "To the King and People of Norway."

Chicago knows that many of the people of America have Norse roots, and that Norway and the other northern European commonwealths have much in common with the United States in their view of life, system of government, political ideals, culture, and morals. The grandest of all the boulevards of the city along the lake has been given Leif Ericson's name; the dramas of Ibsen are played in the theaters of Chicago, and the later Norwegian authors have numerous readers; the great part played by Norway in arctic explorations and research is known and recognized; the flag of Norway often waves in the harbor of our city, and the forward trend in Norway, politically and commercially and in the life of its people, is valued according to merit in the progressive metropolis on the shore of Lake Michigan. Chicago expects to see Norway seated among its honored guests at the exposition.

The Norwegian part of the population of Chicago join in this wish, feeling confident that the homeland will participate in a worthy manner at the coming world meet. The Norwegians are not one of the largest national groups in Chicago,

but they are one of the oldest and one of those who proportionally have made very valuable contributions to the development and progress of the city, both commercially and
socially. . . .

The life story of Laurence M. Larson affords another example of
ethnicity among Norwegian-Americans. Born in Norway in 1868, Larson
was brought to the United States when his family emigrated in 1870. He
was raised in the Norwegian-American social, religious, and cultural
milieu of the American Middle West and went on to fame and honors
in his chosen profession of history, ultimately becoming president of the
American Historical Association. His autobiography excellently records
his own growth and experience against the background of race and tradition, section and nation. And so in the excerpts that follow we become
familiar with the customs of the Norwegian-American home, the problems of language, attachment to affairs of the native land, the importance
of the foreign-language press, the Norwegian church in America, feelings
of inferiority before the "Yankees," political compensation in ethnicity,
the Americanizing influence of the common school, and the influence of
higher education.

In many respects our community was a bit of the Old World transplanted to the richer soil of the Northwest.[8] It was a garden almost
entirely filled with plants of a foreign culture. These did not all
flourish in the new environment, but some of them throve exceed-
ingly well. This condition was not peculiar to our township or
county; all through the Middle West and the Northwest similar
communities had been established or were in the process of formation.

But we lived in America, not in Norway, and the physical and
social environments cannot fail to be of great significance, even in
such alien communities. Furthermore, we were American citizens; at
least we enjoyed all the rights that could be conferred by naturalization. My father was naturalized in 1876, just in time to vote for
Hayes and Wheeler. I became a citizen by the same declaration.
But, though we were in a sense Americans, we lived as Norwegians,
or as nearly so as conditions would permit.

There was first the matter of speech. English was recognized
as the language of the land and was acknowledged to be of first
importance. Adult immigrants were not, however, so very keen about
learning to speak or read this language. My father and my uncles
attended the public school, such as it was. . . . He came in the
course of time to speak English fairly well, though with a marked
accent and with a pleasant disregard for grammatical usage. He
could write English after a fashion. . . .

My mother spoke a form of the language that her friends

[8] Reprinted from Laurence Marcellus Larson, *The Log Book of a Young Immigrant*
(Northfield, Minn.: Norwegian-American Historical Association, 1939), pp. 47–49,
50, 52–53, 67, 68, 69, 100, 108, 114, 301–302.

could understand but which never failed to mystify a stranger. My grandparents were wholly innocent of English. In fact very few of the adult immigrants in our neighborhood were able to get very far toward the mastery of the national idiom.

There was, for that matter, only small incentive to learn to use this language. Nearly all our business transactions could be (and frequently were) carried out in Norwegian. The merchants at the county seat soon found it expedient to provide themselves with Norwegian clerks and salesmen. When there was no such help available, the next best was an interpreter. There were Norse in Forest City who pocketed many welcome fees an interpreters, especially at the sessions of the public court.

The details of local administration and to an extent the business of the county itself were often discussed in the alien tongue. My father was frequently called into jury service and it sometimes happened that every juror in a given case was a Norsemen. In such cases the deliberations in the jury room were carried on in the language that all knew. . . .

The most serious difficulty would arise when one of the older immigrants found that he needed the services of a physician. The doctor usually finds it necessary to get some information from his patient, and the latter on his part needs to understand the doctor's instructions. In such difficulties the interpreter might be of little help; his vocabulary might fail, as it no doubt often did. I recall the case of a German, for instance, who sent a friend to town to procure medicine for a sick child but found when the messenger had returned that the doctor had prescribed for a totally different ailment than the one that he had tried to describe.

The immigrant, like the native, was interested in the doings of the country in which he lived; but he was interested still more in what was going on in the land from which he had come. In his view a good paper was one that had much news from Norway. Even today the Norwegian-American press finds it expedient to devote a considerable part of its space to happenings over the sea. Next in importance was the news from the Norwegian settlements. Many were also keenly interested in what was happening in the church, that is, in their own branch of Lutheranism. . . .

From the viewpoint of the native citizen, the foreign-language newspaper was an evil thing, since it delayed the process of Americanization. However, it also had much to say about affairs in this country and was therefore a very useful institution, inasmuch as it helped to inform the immigrant as to the constitutional forms and habits of the land in which he had come to live.

Of the Norsemen who came to find homes in the Northwest the vast majority had great reverence for the national church. So far as possible they wished to reproduce its institutions in the new land. The Norwegian establishment is Lutheran in doctrine and Episcopal in polity, though the bishops are by no means so highly clothed with power as their fellows in the English church. The local pastors, however, are men of prominent position and authority. Usually they are able men, carefully educated, trained to leadership, and jealous of their rights and privileges. In all the affairs of the parishes they have always played the leading part; in secular activities, too, their will and counsel are not to be ignored. . . .

Another matter of contention was the ritual, which some wished to employ in its complete Norwegian form, while others sought to reduce the ceremonial to a scant minimum.

Those who wished to conserve as much as possible of the old establishment and rebuild it on western soil found their leaders in an able and aggressive group of young university graduates. . . . These men formed their churches into a compact body commonly called the Norwegian Synod. In this body the authority of the priesthood received a decided emphasis. Ministerial robes were regarded as the only decent garb for an officiating clergyman; and parts of the ritual had to be chanted, as the rule was in Norway. . . .

The immigrant is often and quite naturally afflicted with a sense of inferiority. As a rule, the Norwegian settler came from a little hut in the old country and found his home in a humble log cabin in the new land. Neither here nor abroad had he ever enjoyed the comforts of a prosperous life. His substance on his new farm was continuously increasing in value as well as in quantity, but notes and mortgages blinded his eyes to the fact of material advancement. He felt that his burden was heavy and that only his poverty was evident to his neighbors.

At the county seat he saw men and women who lived in houses that looked palatial to his hungering soul. They wore what he regarded as fine clothes and there could be no doubt that they ate good food. They were believed to have an easy time; they held nearly all the public offices, from which they pocketed large salaries; at least, so the alien believed. They controlled the affairs of the county and the alien was sure that through this control they were able to lay exorbitant taxes on the poor farmers' land.

The Yankees were "smart" and the immigrant had a lurking fear that he himself was not smart in the same way. Of course, he was handicapped all around; his ignorance of English put him at a disadvantage in all sorts of business transactions. It is therefore not strange that he came to believe that he was being exploited by the native businessmen, and often too the belief was well founded. Usury was a practice of which farmers complained most bitterly; in one case a helpless immigrant paid interest at the rate of fifty-five percent. In their resentment the farmers sought out the traders and businessmen who spoke their own idiom. They felt safer with them; at least they could make them understand what they thought of men whom they suspected of dishonest dealings.

It might seem likely that the propinquity of the two peoples would lead to an early fusion by intermarriage; but there was little of this in the seventies. American parents frowned on any union with young men or women of the invading race. On the other side the Norse farmers regarded marriage into an American family as something very much like treason to their own nationality. Young Norwegian girls occasionally took husbands of the native stock; but the young men as a rule sought and found their wives among their own people. Time came when all this was to change. . . .

Complete isolation of life and thought, such as the immigrant leaders favored in those early days, could not, of course, be maintained for any length of time, and gradually the situation became more tolerable. With better acquaintance the two peoples came to respect each other and even to hold each other in high regard. The older and cruder methods of trade were soon a thing of the past. More and more the Norwegians found it convenient to transact business with their American fellow citizens. In addition there was the need for help from professional men, which in this case would mean lawyers and doctors. And of these practically all had come from the native stock. . . .

The importance of the common school as an Americanizing influence can scarcely receive too much emphasis. There have been many communities, however, where this institution has not been able to exert its full measure of influence, having to compete with parochial schools where most of the instruction was, in earlier days, at least, given and received in languages other than English. Our community was loyal to the common school; but even there its influence was closely limited. We learned much about the American people but we did not learn to know them. The chasm between the races was not easily bridged. Each lived in its own world of thoughts and ideas and made little effort to understand the inner life of the other. There was no active hostility; but the old antipathy continued to influence our lives and conduct. Until this was removed the process of Americanization could not proceed very far.

The most difficult subject that the immigrant has to master in the study of English is spelling. From his point of view the appearance of the English word is often ludicrous and sometimes even grotesque. One can, of course, present what is believed to be a satisfactory argument for the strange forms from long past history; but of this the learner knows nothing. Spelling makes particular trouble for adults; but children, too, who, like myself, learned a completely phonetic system before taking up the new language, find English spelling troublesome. Nor is it always so easily mastered by the native himself. Hence it has become necessary to prepare spelling books, which in most languages seem not to be known. . . .

In the process of Americanization, politics was a highly important factor. It brought the alien group into contact with the institutional arrangements of the nation. In that field all sympathetic interest in a foreign system was wholly ruled out. It also brought the leaders of the naturalized contingents into close touch with some of the keenest minds in the native element. In this way their appreciation of the republic and its institutions in the abstract became practical knowledge of a working government in its more concrete forms.

The Norseman is a born politician. Since the dawn of history the farmers in Old Norway have, in a large degree, managed the affairs of their political units. For centuries they were engaged in fighting the petty tyrants of local officialdom and were never wholly daunted by failure or defeat. They had therefore long been trained in practical politics and in the simpler forms of administration. The American system in its larger outline met their immediate approval. Here was a form of popular government that extended to the uttermost limits of authority with no hereditary monarch and no governing class. All this was as it should be, and the new citizens could not be happy until their hands had touched the levers of political power and control. . . .

My development in the direction of a more complete Americanism, though seemingly slow, had indeed been swift and thorough. It may be said with much truth that in the course of my life I have gone through a process of change and education that normally requires two or even three generations.

But I have not forgotten my past. The knowledge of things Norwegian, new and old, which came to me in early life is a heritage that I prize most highly and should be loath to lose even in the slightest measure. As the years have come and gone, my interest in all those mighty forces that shaped the culture and the civilization into which I was born has, if anything, become deeper and more intense, possibly because their significance has come out into clear light. Nor can I deny that it is a matter of real pride to me that my cradle stood in that stern and rugged but grandly beautiful country whence so much of human strength has gone forth into all the western world.

For more than sixty years I have shared in the citizenship of the great Republic. I owe no allegiance, political or spiritual, to any other land; but my past is a fact and a vital fact that I cannot ignore. Between an active loyalty to a land and a system into which one has been received and an honest recognition of the values that inhere in a culture out of which one has come, there need be no conflict. America herself has a European past, from the long experience of which she has drawn knowledge and wisdom and power. And the individual citizen no more than the nation itself can escape the implications of his past.

THE SWEDISH

Gustaf Unonius was a Swedish immigrant who became an Episcopalian clergyman; consequently he was at variance with many of his countrymen who professed adherence to the Lutheran Church. His autobiography is, therefore, a defensive apology for a seventeen-year period during which he administered to the spiritual and physical needs of Swedes and Norwegians in what was then considered the Northwest. Often critical of his own countrymen, he made numerous observations that revealed an ethnic awareness reigning alongside his predominant religious interest. The following passage describes the ethnic considerations bearing on his decision to become a minister, the conflict of class traits, and ethnic attempts to solve problems.[9]

In these qualities the Swedish immigrant may be behind the Norwegian, who is inclined to excel in that kind of independence, but the manners of even the Swedish immigrants often try the patience of those who come in close touch with them. Both groups have been accustomed to a subordinate position in the old country. Perhaps they have been too much repressed there and overlooked

[9] Reprinted from Backlund, Jonas Oscar, trans. *A Pioneer in North America, 1841–1858: The Memoirs of Gustaf Unonius*, ed. by Nils William Olsson, University of Minnesota Press, Minneapolis, pp. 116–117, 191, 201. © 1960 by the Swedish Pioneer Historical Society.

by those in high position; even here they are inclined at first to show too much servility and to cringe before those who seem to be above them in wealth and social standing. But just give them time enough to get a notion of republican freedom and equality, and they soon reveal what conception they have of it. From being too humble and subservient, they soon grow discourteous, impertinent, and insolent toward those who are their superiors in culture and wealth, in order to prove that they knew their rights and that in America one man is as good as another. Many a time it happened that I found it difficult to make an immigrant keep his hat on his head when talking with me in the street, and a few days later I had still more trouble to persuade him to remove it when he came to call on me in my home. . . . Many cultivated Americans who were used to the characteristics of the lower classes of their own people, which were adduced as proof of their lack of good breeding, often remarked, and justly, that in regard to courtesy and breeding, as well as personal neatness, my beloved Scandinavian fellow nationals had nothing to boast of when placed side by side with the comparable class of Americans. . . .

The cholera spread further and further, and raged with great violence among the poorer population. . . . The Swedish immigrants who arrived that year in greater numbers than ever before were attacked by the disease and succumbed to it in masses. And how could it be otherwise? Packed together in the immigrant ships during the long ocean journey, unaccustomed to idleness, often eating spoiled and unwholesome food, living in filth and dirt, they were predisposed to the disease even before arriving in Chicago. Here many of them had to seek employment to earn their daily bread. Lodged in miserable hovels, often hungry, and avidly gorging themselves with foods to which they were as little accustomed as to the climate, and furthermore paying no attention to the usual symptoms of the disease, it was natural that in most cases medical treatment proved unavailing. The misery of those poor people cannot be described. More than half of those who remained in Chicago succumbed. Entire families died within the space of a few weeks. The same conditions prevailed among the Norwegians, though they were generally better off than the Swedes and were able to continue their journey inland, where the mortality was lower. . . .

In connection with what I have told of the charity shown our poor Swedish immigrants, I cannot refrain from telling, though reluctantly, how some of them availed themselves in an improper manner of this benevolence and made use of it even when they did not need it. Their begging went beyond all bounds. Americans, since they were accustomed to find a measure of cleanliness and neatness even in the home of a poor laborer, took for granted that when these qualities were lacking in the homes of the Swedes, it meant poverty and want. When the Americans entered these homes —in general no worse and sometimes considerably better than the huts the immigrants had left in Sweden—and saw the filthy beds, the unappetizing food dished out in bowls and jars of earthenware and served on the lids of chests (especially was the coarse bread, the remnants of their traveling supply, looked upon as a great curiosity); when they saw adults as well as children in rough, dirty clothes which not even the humblest laborers in their country would wear, they were moved to compassion and gave the unfortunates money and other gifts. . . .

Unonius also discusses different views regarding Swedish migration to the United States.[10]

On only one or two minor points am I inclined to disagree. . . . that the emigrants unite in one company before leaving the homeland and later, upon their arrival, settle in one section. That may be true as far as it concerns the early social relations in the new country, and without a doubt the settlers can be of great help to each other. . . . If the aim is temporal progress, and that is no doubt the principal purpose of emigration in most cases, then it is undoubtedly gained more quickly by coming in closer touch with the Americans. Thus the immigrant is more rapidly made familiar with various conditions in the new country and gains more insight into the occupation he has selected. Even if his chosen occupation is not new to him, there are nevertheless many phases of it he is likely to be unfamiliar with, and if he is to make a real success of it he will need to get into the American go-ahead system. Furthermore, if one has once decided to emigrate it is far better for both oneself and for one's posterity to become fully naturalized, and the sooner the better. . . .

Finally, the following brief account of his work as a minister of a national church is a telling picture of the hardships faced by the less lucky immigrants.[11]

To indicate further how my time as well as that of most other clergymen was occupied and, furthermore, to illustrate the special conditions within my own church, I wish to quote from one of my diaries, that of 1854, which I have opened at random.

January 30, Carl Gustafson called. He had just left the poorhouse, along with his wife, who is about to be confined. At present they are without a roof over their heads. Their bedclothes were lost on the journey. They say that some of their other clothes were stolen from them in the poorhouse and that they themselves were ill-treated by the Irish who were in the majority there. Must call on the superintendent and find out about this. In the meantime I supplied them with an order on the aid society.

Called on Sven Knudsen. The husband is sick abed; the wife has yellow jaundice; one of the children idiotic. I can see no way but to send them to the poorhouse.

Called on Gustaf Pettersson, 3 La Salle Street. The husband has been sick in bed for a long time; has probably contracted consumption. No heater in the room; temperature—18 degrees. He and his wife seem to be good Christian people. Had prayer with them. Must try to get help for them.

[10] Ibid., p. 222.
[11] Ibid., p. 294.

One manifestation of ethnicity is the exercise of political power. In this the Swedes were no exception, as they strove to gain their share of political recognition in an amount proportional to their numbers.

A study of the census of the United States and the distribution of immigrants clearly indicates a correlation between the numbers in the national groups and their representation in politics—a factor which, with rapid Americanization, will become even more evident.[12] In 1930 there were, in the United States, approximately 1,562,700 persons of Swedish descent of the first and second generations. In Minnesota the Swedes constituted almost 11 per cent of the total population. . . . The geographical distribution of the Swedes may be more effectively represented by saying that about one-third of the Swedes in America are to be found in Minnesota and Illinois. The Swedes thus constitute a very small percentage of the entire population in the United States. . . .

Further, it must be stated that only a comparatively small number of Swedes arrived in America before the Civil War. Participation in the war and membership in the military order of the Grand Army of the Republic were almost a prerequisite, after the war, for a successful political career in the North, just as an enlistment in the Confederate Army was a prerequisite for political preferment in the South during the age of hate that followed the war. . . .

But soon the Swedes began to clamor for political recognition, though as yet they were unwilling, or unable, to change their own environment. At election time they organized their own "Republican Clubs" as "Lincoln Clubs," "Grant Clubs," and, by 1880, the Swedish-American press was loud in its insistence that Swedes should assert themselves more in politics. Though this press severely criticized the political parties for not selecting Swedes for either elective or appointive offices, the truth hardly justified their outcry. Most of the Swedes, even if some had had university training in Sweden, had few of the qualifications required for political preferment. They were too exclusive; few had mastered the language; few had a legal training. Swedes of even the second generation were taught Swedish before they were taught English. Their colleges and other educational institutions were looked upon as essentially schools for training ministers; and often the very existence of these institutions was precarious. In view of these facts, one is amazed to find that even prior to 1900 a large number of Swedes had been favored with political appointments or elective offices, thus probably causing Professor H. H. Boyesen of Columbia University to write in the nineties that the Scandinavians "take as naturally to politics as goslings do to water."

The best-known Swede in American politics before 1900 was John Lind. He was born in Sweden and was the first Swede to be elected to Congress. He was elected in 1886, and reelected in 1888 and 1890. In 1896 he was the Fusion party nominee for Governor of Minnesota, and in 1898 he was elected, serving as Governor

---

[12] Reprinted from Adolph B. Benson and Naboth Hedin (eds.), *Swedes in America, 1638–1938* (New Haven: Yale University Press, 1938), pp. 322–24. Copyright © 1938 by the Swedish American Tercentenary Association, Inc.

from 1899 to 1901. He was also the first Swede to hold this important office, but the Swedes of strong Republican sentiments never really appreciated Lind, because he had deserted their own party.

Although the population of Americans of Swedish descent is heaviest in northern midwestern states like Minnesota, Illinois, North Dakota, Kansas, and Nebraska, the resurgence of ethnicity among Swedes from other states is also interesting. Thus a Swedish consciousness was clearly discernible in New Jersey in the latter part of the nineteenth century as many Swedish-Americans exhibited an ethnic sensitivity to the role of Swedes in the colonial period of American history.

The year 1874 marks a turning point in Swedish consciousness in the East, for it was then that Israel Acrelius' *History of New Sweden* was first translated into English and published in the United States.[13] The Centennial of American Independence, celebrated two years later, helped to awaken interest in all phases of American history and served to make Swedish-Americans sensitive to their nation's part in the development of America. As historical and genealogical societies became more important, gradually more and more information was revealed about the half-forgotten role of Sweden in the New World. . . .

Interest in the history of New Sweden reached a climax in 1909 with the founding of the Swedish Colonial Society at Philadelphia. On its rolls were immediately found the names of many Swedish families which recalled the original voyages up the creeks of New Jersey.

Constant intermarriage gradually obliterated the physical characteristics of the Swedes and Finns, and by the twentieth century they were virtually indistinguishable from the other nationalities in South Jersey. The Anglicization of names had continued, although often the Swedish origin was apparent. For example, Bengston changed to Banks, Kyn to Keen, Bonde to Boon, Svenson to Swanson, Whiler to Wheeler, Hopman to Hoffman, and Joneson to Jones. Given names were similarly altered, Per to Peter, Lars to Lawrence, Nils to Nicholas, and Olave to William.

Place names in Southern New Jersey, however, retained a strong Swedish cast. The old New Stockholm Township now includes the three towns of Bridgeport, Gibbstown and Nortonville; Finnstown has changed to Finns Point, but there survive Repaupo, Rambo Station, Dalbo's Landing, Helm's Cove, Elsinborough Township, and Swedesboro itself. As noted earlier, Eric Mullica and James Steelman left their names over a wide area of the coastal region. A few Swedish names are even of comparatively recent origin, as in the case of New Sweden Crossroad in Gloucester County and Swedes Run in both Burlington and Salem Counties.

Yet in the southern part of the State persons of Swedish descent are no longer concentrated in the historically Swedish regions. Gloucester and Salem Counties were the eighteenth century strongholds of the Swedes. According to the 1930 census, these

[13] Reprinted from the Federal Writers' Project, *The Swedes and Finns in New Jersey* (Bayonne, N.J.: Works Projects Administration (WPA), 1938), pp. 105–107.

two counties contain only one-seventh of the Swedes in southern New Jersey. Atlantic and Cape May Counties, once sparsely settled with Swedes, now have more than one-third of the South Jersey total.

The descendants of the Swedes of Colonial times are still concentrated in Camden, Gloucester and Salem Counties. Town and city directories in these sections are studded with names transplanted from abroad while New Sweden was still a political entity in the Delaware Valley. Among them are Hanson, Tallman, Mecum, Steelman, Dalbow, Helms, Erickson, Sinnickson, Hendrickson, Vannaman and Lock. These Swedish-Americans, as well as later Swedes in the area, follow generally the custom of the earlier Swedes by crossing the Delaware for the continued observance of Swedish ways. They attend Swedish Lutheran Churches in and around Philadelphia and belong to the Swedish Colonial Society. Many have joined the Swedish singing societies in Philadelphia.

Economic factors in the homeland—which included an expanding population, limited cultivable land, a low death rate, and crop failures—conspired with an efficient system of cargo ships to account for large-scale Swedish emigration. In addition, some dissenting religious groups gave added impetus to the removal of many Swedes from their mother country. Ballads and poems expressed the variety of views and observations that became part of the emigration experience. In songs of justification as in songs of disillusionment one can detect the ethnic dimension.

The Unlucky Emigrant[14]

I am a stranger in the New World

I am a stranger in the New World
Far away from home,
I loved pleasure and sought only frivolity
And I found them.
But they are only deceitful,
And I saw that too late.

I am far away from my native land,
To groaning brought.
I have not listened to good advice
Which people gave me
To them I seem a wretch here,
Like a wreck cast up by fate.

I thought only to reap wealth's harvest
Which fortune gave.
Instead I got a heavier burden,
A beggar's staff.
I could have been without it.
To relatives and family I want to return.

[14] Reprinted from *Swedish Emigrant Ballads* by Robert L. Wright, pp. 97, 98, by permission of University of Nebraska Press. Copyright © 1966 by University of Nebraska Press.

My youth which is now past,
Have I no more.
Against the new days I push on in time,
Like many others.
As the fugitive from his calm shore
By the storm is driven to an unknown island.

Oh, when I think of days gone by,
Of mother and father,
Then my conscience accuses me.
Each time I have acted
Against my parents' will,
Disobedient I have been as I should not.

Yes, my family and my childhood friends,
They are not here.
Here almost no one knows me
As they did there.
For my disobedience have I understood
That I must reap what I have sown.

My dear home place and childhood home
I lack here,
Where so often I played in the evening.
Yes, and where as well
My childhood's school in which I learned
That which for me is so dear and so beloved.

I want to go home, if only I had money.
Now I cannot
For an hour be counted among the happy ones.
Oh no, oh no!
O home, you are my greatest wealth,
That which before I valued not.

Goodbye to valleys, mountains, woods,
To tiny brooks,
Where I have had so many happy days.
I cannot go
To father's house in Sweden's land
To squeeze the hands of family and friends.

THE DANES

Jacob August Riis was one of the most famous of the Danish immigrants.
He came to the United States in 1870 at the age of twenty-one and gained
fame as a newspaper reporter and social reformer. His many years of work
in slum and immigrant neighborhoods led him to develop ideas for social
improvement that spread throughout the land. Nevertheless, Riis could
not forget his Danish roots and culture, and he found it possible to be
both a useful United States citizen and one who was conscious of his
non-American ethnic lineage.

I was back in the harness of the carpenter-shop when, in the middle of July, the news struck down in our quiet community like a bombshell that France had declared war on Prussia; also that Denmark was expected to join her forces to those of her old ally and take revenge for the great robbery of 1864.[15] I dropped my tools the moment I heard it, and flew rather than ran to the company's office to demand my time; thence to our boarding-house to pack. Adler (a German worker) reasoned and entreated, called it an insane notion, but when he saw that nothing would stop me, lent a hand in stuffing my trunk, praying pathetically between pulls that his countrymen would make short work of me, as they certainly would of France. I heeded nothing. All the hot blood of youth was surging through me. I remembered the defeat, the humiliation of the flag I loved,—aye! and love yet, for there is no flag like the flag of my fathers, save only that of my children and of my manhood. . . .

In the midnight hour we walked into the Church Street police station and asked for lodging. The rain was still pouring in torrents. The sergeant spied the dog under my tattered coat and gruffly told me to put it out, if I wanted to sleep there. I pleaded for it in vain. There was no choice. To stay in the street was to perish. So I left my dog out on the stoop, where it curled up to wait for me. Poor little friend! It was its last watch. The lodging-room was jammed with a foul and stewing crowd of tramps. A loud-mouthed German was holding forth about the war in Europe, and crowding me on my plank. Cold and hunger had not sufficed to put out the patriotic spark within me. It was promptly fanned into flame, and I told him what I thought of him and his crew. Some Irishmen cheered and fomented trouble, and the doorman came in threatening to lock us all up. I smothered my disgust at the place as well as I could, and slept, wearied nearly to death. . . .

With angry tears I went up and complained to the sergeant that I had been robbed. He scowled at me over the blotter, called me a thief, and said that he had a good mind to lock me up. How should I, a tramp boy, have come by a gold locket? He had heard, he added, that I had said in the lodging-room that I wished the French would win, and he would only be giving me what I deserved if he sent me to the Island. I heard and understood. He was himself a German. All the suffering rose up before me, all the bitterness of my soul poured itself out upon him. I do not know what I said. I remember that he told the doorman to put me out. I remember that he told me and threw me out of the door, coming after to kick me down the stoop. . . .

It was when I went home to mother that I met King Christian last. They had told me the right way to approach the King, the proper number of bows and all that, and I meant to faithfully observe it all. I saw a tired and lonely old man, to whom my heart went out on the instant, and I went right up and shook hands, and told him how much I thought of him and how sorry I was for his losing his wife, the Queen Louise, whom everybody loved. He looked surprised a moment; then such a friendly look came into his

[15] Reprinted from Jacob A. Riis, *The Making of an American* (New York: MacMillan, 1901), pp. 46, 47, 71, 72, 428, 429.

face, and I thought him the handsomest King that ever was. He asked about the Danes in America, and I told him they were good citizens, better for not forgetting their motherland and him in his age and loss. He patted my hand with a glad little laugh, and bade me tell them how much he appreciated it, and how kindly his thoughts were of them all. As I made to go, after a long talk, he stopped me and, touching the little silver cross on my coat lapel, asked what it was.

THE GERMANS

German immigrants to America may be placed in one of three periods. The first period (1815–1855) was an attempt by the settlers to transplant Germanism into their new surroundings. The second period (1855–1914) has been described as the failure of the "New Germany" idea, a time during which Germans lived in the United States but were consciously German-Americans. The third period followed World War I, and in this last era anti-German-American sentiment, resulting from World War I and the Hitler period, shook the hyphen completely out of the Germans in America.

Thus, up until the final period, German settlers in the United States exhibited certain social, economic, and political peculiarities which made assimilation difficult at times and brought them into conflict with the ideas and practices of earlier comers. Their resistance to the Americanizing tendency was attributable also to a pride in their own culture and language which tended to leave German-American communities apart, German islands in a sea of Americanism.

In the nineteenth century Germany continued to supply more immigrants to the United States than any other country. In large measure the characteristics of German immigration of the pre–Civil War period persisted in the post–Civil War era. Yet there were some important differences, as more men of culture and more refugees from political oppression and espionage migrated. A comparison of the differences in periods is contained in Albert B. Faust, *The German Element in the United States.*

There were three periods.[16] Immigration No. 1, attracted by such books as Duden's, turned to Missouri and other Western states, and devoted themselves to agriculture. Laborers and peasants, without any high standard of life and accustomed to hard work, found the situation to their satisfaction and gradually but steadily became prosperous. The better educated, sometimes even in spite of strenuous efforts, frequently died in the struggle. . . .

The immigration No. 2 was heartily welcomed by the first immigration, but the former were not well satisfied with their

[16] Reprinted from Albert B. Faust, *The German Element in the United States,* vol. 1 (New York: Arno Press, Inc., 1969), pp. 588–89.

countrymen in America. They did not like the backwoods condition of the earlier immigration. . . . Most of them went into the cities as merchants, manufacturers, or brain-workers of various kinds. . . .

The third immigration came after the period of 1866. They were mostly of the working class, with far better schooling than the same class of thirty years before. In comparison with the earlier immigrations they were overbearing, dissatisfied with conditions as they found them in the new country, and too well impressed with those they left at home. As a rule they would not do the work of an inferior class, and as a result frequently found all desirable positions occupied. . . .

Concern with the retention of the native language in American schools is the subject of the next extract.

The school question, that is, the introduction of the German language into the public schools, was also a cause for which the Germans in various localities brought pressure to bear at the polls.[17] The Germans in Ohio, having given powerful support to the Democratic Party in the election of 1836, began to feel that the party owed them some recognition. The preservation of the German language in the next generation has always been a fond aim of the German immigrant; so it was in Cincinnati. Though there existed a Presbyterian school and a Catholic institution in which German instruction was given, nevertheless a more general opportunity was desired. Since they had paid taxes for the support of the public schools, the Germans considered it their right to exercise some influence on the course of study. According to their idea, English was not to be excluded, but German was to be taught, parallel with the language of the country, in the public schools. The German element turned to the legislature of Ohio, and the latter in 1838 passed a law by which the German language might be taught in the public schools in those districts where there was a large German population and the people desired it. The law was expected to be enforced by the school board, who, however, interpreted the law as advisory and not compulsory. In the succeeding election of 1839 pledges were taken from the candidates that the wording of the law should be revised so as to prevent any possibility of loopholes. Accordingly the law was changed in 1840, which marks the date of the introduction of German-English public schools in Cincinnati and Ohio. . . .

Within the last decades the Germans have made a successful attempt at uniting all the German clubs of the United States, whether social, musical, gymnastic, military, or political, into one large national organization. The movement began in the original home of Germanism, the state of Pennsylvania, and in its ancient stronghold, Philadelphia, where a union of all the German societies of the states was effected in the year 1899. Since then the organization has grown into the so-called "National German-American Alliance," which includes societies of every city, state, and territory of the United States where there is a German population. The mem-

[17] Ibid., pp. 150–51.

bership is about a million and a half. . . . The object on the whole is to preserve and unite what is best in German culture and character, and devote it to the best interests of the adopted country. The principle, therefore, which Carl Schurz and Friedrich Muench announced for the Germans in America—namely, that they become American citizens as quickly as possible, without, however, losing their culture and character—has won in our own day.

Carl Schurz was the epitome of the educated, urbane German immigrant to the United States. A storied romantic fighter against tyranny, he was in the forefront of virtually every reform movement of his era. A towering spokesman of progressive American ideals, he was far ahead of most German-Americans of his time; nevertheless, he too felt an ethnic sympathy with his Germanic past. In the selections that follow, he champions German-American patriotism and defends as a positive good the persistence of many ethnic features, such as the use of foreign language and the foreign press. He also describes the role of ethnicity in his campaign for a senate seat against Senator Drake.

I have as much personal experience of the German-born population of the United States, its character, its aspirations, and its American patriotism, as any person now living; and this experience enables me to affirm that the prejudice against the German-American press is groundless.[18] On the contrary, that press does the country a necessary and very important service. In the first place, it fills a real and very urgent want. That want will exist so long as there is a large number of German-born citizens in this republic. There will always be many among them, especially persons of mature years who arrived on American soil without any knowledge of the English language, who may be able to acquire enough of it to serve them in their daily walk, but not enough to enable them to understand newspaper articles on political or similar subjects. Such persons must receive the necessary information about current events, questions to be considered and duties to be performed, from journals published in the language they understand, or they will not have it at all. The suppression of the German-American press would, therefore, be equivalent to the cultivation of political ignorance among a large and highly estimable class of citizens.

It is argued that the existence of the German newspaper is apt to render the German immigrant less sensible of the necessity of learning English. This is the case only to a very limited extent. A large majority of the German immigrants of mature age, being farmers or industrial laborers, do not acquire their knowledge of English in this country through regular linguistic instruction, or by reading books or newspapers, but from conversation or attempts at conversation with their neighbors who do not speak German, and that knowledge will, of necessity, remain very imperfect. . . .

The charge that the existence of the German-American press promotes the use of the German language in this country and thus

18 Reprinted from Carl Schurz, *The Reminiscences of Carl Schurz*, vol. 3 (New York: The McClure Co., 1908), pp. 258–62, 298–99.

impedes the development of a healthy American patriotism among the population concerned, can be entertained only by those who do not know the German-Americans. I speak from a large personal experience when I say that their love of their new home and their devotion to this republic does not at all depend upon their knowledge of the English language. . . .

The same may be said of the inhabitants of German settlements of more recent date who have come with the bona fide intention to make this country their permanent home. Among them German may long remain the language of social and business intercourse, they may be slow in acquiring easy familiarity with the English tongue, but even if they have come here for the mere purpose of bettering their fortunes, they are as a rule not slow in appreciating the benefits conferred upon them by American conditions, and in conceiving an attachment to this republic which before long ripens into genuine devotion. . . .

That the existence of the German press tells for the preservation in this country of the German language as a language of social and business intercourse is to a limited extent true. But what harm is there in this? While it is of great use to the older immigrants, it does not keep their children from learning English, even in settlements which are preponderatingly German, for such settlements are no longer isolated as the original German settlements in Pennsylvania were. But it does give the younger generation the advantage of knowing two languages. That kind of American patriotism which takes umbrage at an American citizen's knowledge of a foreign tongue besides the English—a sort of patriotism I have here and there met with—is certainly too narrow-minded, not to say too silly, to be seriously considered. No educated, nay, no sound-minded person, will deny, that the knowledge of more than one language tends to widen our mental horizons, to facilitate the acquisition of useful intelligence, and thus to broaden education. . . .

The career of Richard Bartholdt is still another story of a German immigrant who, having become a success in his newly adopted land, yet steadfastly retained a strong attachment to the cultural values of his original nationality. A newspaperman, Bartholdt went on to serve in Congress for over two decades, spanning the years 1893 to 1915. Throughout his career he found himself championing and defending the cultural and social values of his ethnic group. In the excerpts that follow, he judges the prohibition movement as an obvious example of race prejudice, is critical of the effort to Anglo-Saxonize everyone, and deals with the issue of allegiance during the First World War.

As to the prohibition movement it was not difficult to demonstrate that one of its underlying motives, too, was race prejudice because it aimed to undermine the social life of the Germans and to bankrupt the richest men among them.[19] In fact, it is claimed by shrewd observers that the prohibition fire would have died aborning but

[19] Reprinted from Richard Bartholdt, *From Steerage to Congress, Reminiscences and Reflections* (Philadelphia: Dorrance, 1930), pp. 82, 84, 86, 88, 89, 90.

for the fuel with which race prejudice constantly fed it. The fact that the crusade of professional drys is directed more viciously against the harmless beverage of the Germans than against ardent spirits seems fully to confirm that assertion. . . .

In my editorial opposition to the different fads invented to torment the German element, I believed that I was on solid American ground. My opinion was and is that the form of worship, the customs and racial aspirations of our adopted citizens, as long as they do not conflict with the laws of the land, should be given free play in a democracy. If this be true, then every attempt to make them conform to the social habits, dress, mannerisms, ways of thinking and all other peculiarities of one particular element, even if it be numerically the strongest, must be adjudged undemocratic and un-American and is, therefore, intolerable. And I went even further by venturing the assertion that any man incapable of freeing himself from race prejudice which manifests itself in self-exaltation and a domineering attitude toward others, is by nature disqualified from being a real American. . . .

The public mind is now sufficiently composed, I believe, to realize what a cruel outrage was committed against American citizens of German blood by the propaganda press using them as scape-goats to kindle the war passions of the nation. It was done, too, against the better judgment of their assailants, because the latter know them full well and have never, at any other time, so studiedly misunderstood and misjudged them. These same self-styled one hundred percenters were perfectly aware that the hyphen was used innocently, and merely as a racial designation, but they purposely imputed an objectionable meaning to it at a time when they had the ear of the public and when every word of defense was lost in the fury of the storm.

To the Englishman, the Scotchman, the Irishman we habitually do concede the right of devotion to ancient traditions and of affection for the ancestral home. Why not the German? Is it because he speaks a different tongue? God save the mark! If that were the reason, the world's conscience would push us from the high pedestal we occupy, and adjudge such narrow-mindedness a national disgrace. Or is it because his old Fatherland was one of the great powers, hence a world factor? Well, I have already shown that the native country of nearly nine-tenths of our citizens of German stock is America. And the last tenth? Suppose they do sing German songs and cherish, because most conversant with them, German literature, art, science, music and philosophy, what on earth has that to do with official Germany? As one who knows whereof he speaks I assert that not even in the innermost recesses of their hearts is a trace to be found of their old political allegiance. . . . Affection for the old home, after all, is only a sentiment, an emotion of the heart, while loyalty to the new is a matter of conscience, and no instance is known in history in which men of German blood ever failed to respond to the voice of conscience or the call of duty. Double allegiance? Why, in its only possible meaning, namely in a political sense, it does not exist in America. . . .

The severest test was the one to which the American Germans were put during the last years of the World War. Have they stood it? For an answer I refer to the "rolls of honor," the casualty lists, the records of the War, Treasury and all other departments of the government. Their loyalty to the flag, tried and tested in every crisis, is founded not alone on their innate love of freedom and their honest fealty to democratic institutions, but also on a sacred oath, an oath of whose sanctity they believe heaven itself to be the guardian.

Only a short while ago this whole discussion would probably have been denounced as "German Propaganda." Be it so. Propaganda for the truth is a highly meritorious effort and should be welcomed by every honest man. Fortunately, the public has sufficiently recovered to open its eyes and ears to the truth. Therefore, I shall venture a prediction. It is that no danger will ever come to our country, its liberty, security, prosperity and independence, from so-called "German Propaganda" which, as we shall see later, is largely a myth. . . .

John A. Hawgood is one of the more perceptive observers of German life in American history. He has described the numerous instances of ethnic persistence and how this ethnic soul finally began to weaken and stagnate in the twentieth century. In the extracts that follow, he shows how, despite German-American resolution, the debilitating effects of assimilation, together with unpopularity during the World War I period, began to erode the ethnic fiber.

The German language press in the United States began, with the turn of the century, to stagnate, despite all its own efforts in a contrary direction.[20] It was complained that as fast as the old people, who had been the original settlers, died, their children and grandchildren discontinued the family subscription to the local German language newspaper, and confined themselves to the English language papers, which had, of course, already found their way into all but the most strict of German-American homes. In the state of Texas not a single fresh German language newspaper was founded after the year 1904, and very few appeared elsewhere after the turn of the century.

The German language, that greatest weapon of Deutschtum, came to be less used, even in the strongest of German-American circles. The first Lutheran service ever conducted in English in St. Louis, came in the nineties, and though as late as 1905 even some of the negroes and native-stock Americans in Belleville, Illinois, still spoke German. . . .

Long before the war of 1914 cracks in the once solid structure of German-America had appeared, and though efforts were made to paper them over, they widened rather than diminished during those placid pre-war days. The fight of the German schools, newspapers and churches continued; the German Empire, by occasional interest through her diplomatic representatives and publicists, gave benevolent pats on the back to such efforts; the "German-American National Alliance" whose war-time activities were later to

[20] Reprinted by permission of G. P. Putnam's Sons from *The Tragedy of German-America* by John A. Hawgood, pp. 290–91, 292, 293, 296, 297, 301.

receive such a blaze of unwelcome publicity, was founded; the further prolongation of the German-American era was obviously still ardently desired by many Germans in America. . . .

Then came the war between the central and the entente powers, and to the Germans in America this was a crisis even greater than that of the fifties. Not only was the position of Germany in the struggle, even before America's participation, a source of very great embarrassment to the German-Americans, but the emotional tenseness and the propagandist needs of the war caused a nativist movement to rear its head. "One-hundred-percent Americanism" was born, and the hyphen was stigmatized as "un-American" by these new nativists.

The immediate effect of the outbreak of the war in Europe was to draw the Germans in America (or all of those who had not gone over completely into Americanism) closer together again, just as they had been drawn closer together in the fifties. The breakup of German-America, which had been steadily becoming more imminent in the pre-war days, was temporarily checked, but only temporarily. . . .

From 1914 to 1917, and particularly after the Lusitania incident and the adoption of less and less restricted, and finally unrestricted submarine warfare by Germany, had embittered American opinion and given the entente cause magnificent opportunities for propaganda, which were used to the full, the German-Americans were fighting with their backs to the wall. Their elaborate stockade composed of the various defences of Deutschtum was stormed, but right up to America's entry into the war they continued their forlorn struggle. . . .

The fully Americanized Germans and their descendants inclined to lean backwards in their adherence to Americanism. . . .

It is not surprising in the circumstances that the reaction against all things German went even further among the American people as a whole, further in fact than in any allied country of Europe. The teaching of German was not only discontinued by legislative action in the schools and colleges of some states, but in one state at least, and a state with a large population of German stock, it was not reintroduced until the year 1929, eleven years after the war had ended. . . ..

By 1930 the German-American era appeared to be definitely over, and hardly likely to return. Memories of it were still vivid and bitter, and the experiment of hyphenation seemed to have been in every way too disastrous, for those who had tried it, for any similar experiment to be attempted in the future.

The most recent survey of Germans in America is Richard O'Connor's *The German-Americans, An Informal History*. O'Connor concludes that the German-Americans have been so thoroughly assimilated that they no longer feel a need to create protective organizations to defend themselves against slurs, as is the case with other ethnic groups. He finds that while German influence in the United States is readily seen in virtually every aspect of life, Germans have become all but invisible as an ethnic group. If this assessment is largely, although not completely, true, it was not always so. Indeed, well into the twentieth century the Germans exhibited ethnic traits in varying degrees. In the selection that follows, O'Connor discusses some examples of the ethnic flavor as exemplified by the beer saloon and other clearly Germanic customs.

German-Americans, in particular, seemed to regulate their lives by the ebb and flow of the beer seasons.[21] Many came from South Germany, where beer was as indigenous as mother's milk. Those from the wine-growing provinces of the Rhineland naturally favored Moselle and other wines, while Prussians and others from North Germany clung to the more potent schnapps, a quarrelsome brother to whiskey.

In the German sections of St. Louis, towheaded children raced for the nearest beer saloons Easter Sunday morning for the first of the bock, which "hailed the Risen Lord and the end of the Lenten season." Each child carried a bucket and a chip, which cost four cents. At Hermann Klein's the proprietor was so exhilarated by the bock season that he would order his pet rooster, named Hindenburg, to march on command for the children "just like I used to march in the guard back in Baden." The German beer saloon was as respectable a place, as family-oriented, as the corner grocery. . . .

O'Connor also discusses the role ethnicity played in the German struggle for power in the American Catholic Church.

A Battle For The "Rooftop Of The Church"[22]

Among those "desirable fields of expansion" which caught the German eye in the latter part of the nineteenth century was the hierarchy of the Catholic Church. Almost half of all German-Americans were Roman Catholics, and in the 1880's it occurred to many of them that they did not exert an influence on its affairs in proportion to their numbers. "The Germans are a pillar of the Church in America," as Sir Shane Leslie wrote, "but the Irish have always held the rooftop."

Politically, the Irish had blocked German aspirations with consummate ease by staying in the Democratic party and capturing the leadership of its big-city vote. And in the Church, Irish immigrants soon swept aside the dominant French influence which had preceded them, then proceeded to hold its highest places against the influx of German clergy. . . .

Early in the 1880's, when John Cardinal McCloskey of New York was the titular head of American Catholicism, it became alarmingly apparent to the Irish that while they still held the "rooftop," the hierarchy, the Germans were burrowing away at the

[21] Reprinted from *The German-Americans* by Richard O'Connor, p. 293, by permission of Little, Brown and Co. Copyright © 1968 by Richard O'Connor.

[22] Ibid., pp. 349, 352, 353.

foundations. It was possible that the Irish might wear the red hats while in many of the parishes they would find "German Spoken Here" signs all over the place. The Roman Catholic Church had already become, in effect, the Irish Catholic Church. Would it soon become the German Catholic Church?

The Irish archbishops were being made increasingly aware of the fact that their German coreligionists were displeased at being kept out of the places of power. In the number of communicants the Irish had only a slight edge over the Germans, yet the Irish had a noticeable monopoly on the episcopal offices. Of the sixty-nine American bishops in 1886, thirty-five were Irish, only fifteen were Germanic (including the Swiss and Austrians), eleven were French, five English, and the Dutch, Scotch and Spanish had one bishop each. . . .

The Irish resented the fact that the Germans clung to their mother tongue. "Wherever they settled in any numbers the familiar pattern of church, parish school, parish clubs and the German language newspaper soon appeared." Many American Catholics "became more sensitive about their German coreligionists' holding on to their native language, for with good reason did they remember that the charge of 'foreignism' was one of the constant refrains against Catholics in former times." In addition, there were personality conflicts between the Germans and the Irish inevitable in people of their often opposed temperaments. The temperamental difference was so apparent that "for several generations American vaudeville and variety stage audiences were entertained by exaggerated versions of the contrasting characteristics of the stage Irishman and the 'Dutch' comedian. To the phlegmatic German his mercurial Irish neighbor appeared fickle and unstable, while the somewhat volatile Irishman viewed the somber and plodding German as a respectable but generally dull companion. . . .

Finally, he examines German-American ways in recent history.

The visible and physical Germanic influences on American life have now all but disappeared or been homogenized—gone with the little German bands that played on street corners, the German butchers in their sawed-off straw hats and white aprons, the beer gardens, the summer-night festivals, the May wine parades.[23] From each national migration American culture has taken much, adapted it to its own purposes, and left only the faintest individual stamp to be imprinted for more than a generation or two on the ethnic group itself. The Fourth Rome—ours—has dicovered and perfected to an almost unimaginable degree the process of absorption which the earlier struggled and failed to formulate. . . .

They are now generally regarded as being part of the conservative element, for the most part, who leaned toward McCarthyism in the early Fifties, who are isolationist except when it comes to confronting international Communism, who are inclined to hang back on open housing and other civil rights issues.

[23] Ibid., pp. 453, 458.

THE BRITISH

British immigrants continued to come to the United States in the period following the Civil War. While some of them were farmers, a high proportion were industrial workers transplanting the skills acquired in the world's pioneer industrial nation. As skilled miners and millhands they played an indispensable part in accelerating this country's industrial development.

Economically well off in comparison with other foreigners and not generally subjected to ostracism because of their cultural traits, British immigrants nevertheless reacted to the American experience with the same sense of ethnic consciousness as did other newcomers. Thus, like other ethnic groups they tried to carry on their old ways in the new country. They published their own newspapers, organized their own societies and churches, and introduced their own sports, activities which in and of themselves brought into question the inference that British immigrants merged imperceptibly with the native population.

These points are well investigated and examined by Rowland Tappan Berthoff in *British Immigrants in Industrial America, 1790–1950*. In the extracts given here, he discusses a degree of Anglophobia still prevalent in the post–Civil War period, although the British were not really thought of as foreigners in the same sense that others were; he analyzes the belittling of American culture on the part of British immigrants who held on to their own culture tenaciously; he mentions ethnic friction with the Irish; and he explores the question of assimilation.

> Englishmen were disconcerted, of course, to find that in Yankee breasts a family grudge rankled against the old mother country.[24] "The instant they find you are English they immediately drop all other topics of conversation to refer to the time 'we licked you badly,' or to discuss the degeneracy of the House of Lords, or some other topic which they think will be of interest to you." (Welshmen thus accosted were likely to startle Americans by most heartily seconding the indictment of England!) American Anglophobia had many sources: old wars against redcoats, the Irish bias of the press, manufacturers' dread of free trade, free-silverites' fear of London bankers, and behind all a lingering sense of colonial inferiority. During the 1860's an English-American warned against ruffling this tuft in the Yankee plumage:
>
>> I would advise new settlers not to meddle with politics, nor to speak with disparagement of either the people or their country; never give their own country the least advantage when comparing it with America; never tell their neighbors that they neither like America nor her institutions—or that they

[24] Reprinted by permission of the publishers from *British Immigrants in Industrial America, 1790–1950* by Rowland T. Berthoff, Cambridge, Mass.: Harvard University Press, Copyright 1953 by the President and Fellows of Harvard College.

wish themselves at home again. The American people are ex-
ceedingly sensitive, about both themselves and their favoured
land, and they are seldom troubled with anything like squeam-
ishness in thinking aloud in the presence of strangers. Englishmen in particular would do well not to brag about the
"Flag that's braved a thousand years," nor of the land where
the great Charter of the Constitution acknowledges every
man's house his castle; neither should they boast of England
being the birthplace and the cradle of social liberty!

But those British who settled among the Americans passed almost
unnoticed. They hardly seemed to be "immigrants" in the usual
condescending sense of the word. The "immigrant problem" had
nothing to do with prosaic English, Scots, and Canadians, or even
the more clannish and foreign-speaking Welsh.

Thus the British escaped the usual American ridicule of foreigners, and they themselves saw nothing ludicrous in their place
in American society. On the vaudeville stage the caricature of the
Irishman, German, Jew, or Italian was an exaggeration of an actual
lower-class type which any immigrant or city-bred American could
recognize. The "stage Englishman," however, was a titled fop, "vul-
garly overdressed, almost invariably wearing white spats over his
boots, with a single eye-glass, with a walking stick, and silk hat.
Whatever his class in life he uses no h's and repeatedly exclaims,
'Don't you know,' 'deucedly clever,' and the word 'blooming' in
every other sentence." This incongruous dandy hardly represented
anyone's notion—except for the "h's"—of the miners and mill hands
who settled in America.

In fact, in all things but money and quick promotion, British-
Americans thought the United States a debased copy of their homeland. Many seemingly familiar customs and institutions had lost
their British essence. "The Land of Slipshod," one immigrant in
1885 called the country, its language not English but "a silly idiotic
jargon—a mere jumble of German idioms and popular solecisms,
savored by a few Irish blunders," the enforcement of its basically
English legal code "totally farcical," and its children half-educated,
spoiled, and unruly. . . .

Many returned home discontented with "the manners and
habits of the people." Only memories of America's high wages and
full dinner tables could draw them back there again. . . .

Although as the years passed the immigrants' personal ties
came to be in America rather than in Britain, their fondness for and
pride in the old country waxed. British travelers found them everywhere, "British in heart and memory, . . . always with a touch of
the exile, eager to see an English face and to hear an English
voice!" . . .

Love of the homeland was of course not peculiar to British
immigrants. But they suffered no economic and psychological buf-
feting such as sharpened most other nationalities' nostalgia. Their
wages were the highest; no artificial barriers kept wealth and recognition from them; Americans accepted them as equals. Yet they too
clung to old loyalties. The bond was not merely sentimental or figu-
rative. British-Americans were sure to answer the cries of British
soldiers wounded in the Crimean War or of victims of a Welsh

mine disaster or a Lancashire or Highland depression by raising relief funds of several thousand dollars.

Most significantly, even after years in the United States subjects of the Queen disliked to renounce their old allegiance and to become American citizens. When war between the two countries threatened in 1842, even British sailors who had served several years in the Yankee navy departed for Liverpool. During the 1860's an English-American observed of his countrymen generally, "They are patriotic John Bulls. They take British papers, frequent British beer-houses, drink British ale, and are proud and happy to call themselves "British residents." And after 1870, when an Anglo-American naturalization treaty was finally adopted, they could no longer continue to claim British citizenship once they had taken out American papers.

Among workingmen job rivalry sharpened this ill will. When Irishmen crossed the Irish Sea to find work, wages fell—or seemed to—in England and Scotland. English agricultural laborers and Scottish, English, Welsh, and Cornish miners often came to blows with the Paddies. Religious prejudice deepened the grudge; in Lancashire towns during the 1850's the cry of "No Popery" was good for a three-day riot. In the United States the skilled and well-paid British and the unskilled and ill-paid Irishmen renewed this strife. During the early years of Michigan copper mining Cornish and Irish mobs—"Pasties" and "Codfish"—waged pitched battles. The Fall River Irish accused the English of a secret pact to keep them out of the skilled trade of loom-fixing.

In the anthracite valleys of Pennsylvania brawls began as soon as British and Irish mineworkers appeared in the late 1820's. At Carbondale a few years later, Irish resentment over the Welsh and Scots' working the best chambers kept the two factions on the brink of riot. "Welsh miners carried ammunition, while others had to be kept on watch night and day," an old Welshman later recalled. Matters were worst during the 1860's and 1870's, the era of the Molly Maguires. The history of this secret Irish band, linked in some way with the loyal lodges of the Ancient Order of Hibernians, is still vague; men tended to blame it for any mysterious murder. Since most of the victims were colliery foreman and superintendents, many were British. Thus national hatreds tinged the labor disorders along the Susquehanna. The murder of a Scottish mine superintendent in western Maryland at once was ascribed to the Mollies. Nor were mine bosses the only British to offend the Irish. As in the old country, Irish mine laborers resented the Welsh and English near monopoly of skilled jobs, while the Welsh blamed Irish blacklegiaeth for the weakness of their unions. Here, too, religious passions fed the fire; at Edwardsville in 1869 Irish Catholics broke up Welsh Congregationalist services.

Would the earlier immigrants' children fill the place left empty for lack of newcomers? British-American societies did their best to welcome the American-born generation; some even established juvenile sections from which young men would pass into the adult lodges. Children of other immigrant nationalities carried on the parents' societies, but despite British pride in the culture of England, Wales, or Scotland and of Great Britain, the children usually abandoned the organizations founded to preserve it. A few might have the habit of referring to their parents' native land as "home." But with no old-country memories of their own and, unlike many foreigners' children, finding that what they did retain of their foreign heritage was no bar to success among old-stock Americans, they easily cut loose from the British-American community. The second generation usually did not even follow their parents' skilled occupations, as they would have been likely to do in the old country. Perhaps most of those who did were the less enterprising individuals. In many trades they earned wages lower than men trained in Britain itself. But the second generation was apt to take up the more promising pursuits that attracted the run of Americans.

Thus in a sense the British-American had no "second generation," no ill-adjusted class, like the children of less fortunate foreigners, without firm roots in either the old or the new culture. In effect their children were simply Americans, neither better nor worse adapted to the normal life of the country than were the children of old-stock parents. They seldom thought of themselves as anything but Americans. To an Englishman who had lived in the United States it seemed in 1895, "The children born in America of English parents out-herod Herod and are the most decided partisans of the America for the Americans policy." The young son of a Chicago Yorkshireman bragged to his father after a school lesson on the Revolution, "You had the king's army, and we were only a lot of farmers, but we thrashed you!"

THE IRISH

The rate of Irish immigration in the postwar years continued to be high. It had the consequence of making the Irish one of the largest ethnic groups in the country, faced with numerous problems of adjustment and assimilation similar to those experienced by pre–Civil War Irish immigrants. Despite the hostility they encountered, they gradually became esteemed in the eyes of American citizens.

John Francis Maguire's *The Irish in America,* originally published in 1868, is an extensive personal account by an Irish Member of Parliament. One of Maguire's concerns was for the Irish crowded together in the cities on the eastern seaboard, a condition which he deplored as a great evil, especially for a people so passionately attached to the soil.

> . . . But there is no excuse whatever for his remaining in the cities of America, crowding and blocking them up, when there are at this hour as many opportunities for his getting on in the country—that is, making a home and independence for himself and his children— as there were for the millions of all nationalities who went before him, and who now constitute the strength and glory of the Republic.[25]

[25] Reprinted from John Francis Maguire, *The Irish in America* (reprint ed., New York: Arno Press, 1969), p. 236.

By contrast, he observed with satisfaction Irish attraction to the West, to the mining region, and to land cultivation.

> ... With the pick and the shovel they were a match for any workers under the sun, and their luck was on the average as fortunate as that of others. It was a fair start, and no favour—just what best suits the true Irishman: and the result at this moment is, that one-half, or nearly one-half, of the entire mining property of the country is in the hands of Irishmen or the sons of Irishmen.
> ... Employment was to be had in every direction by those who were willing to work; and none were more willing than the Irish. Everything had to be built up, literally created—cities and towns as well as communities. . . . Happily, the cities and towns did not seduce the Irish from their legitimate sphere, and the dollars made in the mine, or in ditching and digging, or in hard toil of various kinds, were converted into land. . . .[26]

Maguire was also interested in the religious welfare of Irish Catholics.

> Whatever religious indifferentism there may be in other parts of America, there is none in San Francisco among its Irish Catholic population. In their hard struggle for the good things of this life they did not forget their interests in the next. . . . Giving Catholics of other nationalities full credit for their liberality, and allowing for the generous assistance afforded by those of different denominations, it is admitted that three-fourths of what has been done for the Church in the city and county of San Francisco has been done by the Irish. In fact, without them little could have been done; but with them everything was possible. . . .[27]

He suggested encouraging further immigration on the part of the Irish.

> As this sheet was going through the press, my attention was attracted by an article in the Monitor of San Francisco, from which I quote the concluding passage, written, as I believe, in the right spirit:—
>
> > It is our interest to have as many of our countrymen here as possible. . . . Why cannot the Irishmen of this city form a society for diffusing a knowledge of California's resources among our countrymen, and communicating with employers throughout the State, for securing immediate employment on their arrival? We almost feel a scruple about encouraging emigration from poor depopulated Ireland, where the fortunes of our race have yet to be retrieved; but in England and Scotland there are nearly a million of Irishmen from whose ranks we could easily obtain an annual immigration of many

[26] Ibid., pp. 270, 271.
[27] Ibid., p. 277.

thousands by a system such as that we have just proposed. We know by experience the state of feeling existing among our countrymen in Europe, and we believe that by a plan such as we have described, an immense Irish population could be drawn here, to both their own and our advantage. The Irish of California are wealthy and liberal, and surely such a society as the one we have proposed could be easily started among them. We hope our suggestions may turn the attention of some of them to the practical development of Irish immigration from England and the Eastern cities.[28]

Maguire made some meaningful observations on the reasons for and effects of drinking among the Irish.

Were I asked to say what I believed to be the most serious obstacle to the advancement of the Irish in America I would unhesitatingly answer—Drink;[29] meaning thereby the excessive use, or abuse, of that which, when taken in excess, intoxicates, deprives man of his reason, interferes with his industry, injures his health, damages his position, compromises his respectability, renders him unfit for the successful exercise of his trade, profession, or employment—which leads to quarrel, turbulence, violence, crime. . . . Were this belief, as to the tendency of the Irish to excess in the use of stimulants, based on the testimony of Americans, who might probably be somewhat prejudiced, and therefore inclined to judge unfavorably, or pronounce unsparingly, I should not venture to record it; but it was impressed upon me by Irishmen of every rank, class, and condition of life, wherever I went, North or South, East or West.

This prevailing custom or habit springs more from a spirit of kindness than from a craving for sensual gratification. Invitations to drink are universal, as to rank and station, time and place, hour and circumstance; they literally rain upon you. . . . To the generous, company-loving Irishman there is something like treason to friendship and death to good-fellowship in refusing these kindly-meant invitations; but woe to the impulsive Irishman who becomes the victim of this custom of the country! The Americans drink, the Germans drink, the Scotch drink, the English drink—all drink with more or less injury to their health or circumstances; but whatever the injury to these, or any of these, is far greater to the mercurial and light-hearted Irish than to races of hard head and lethargic temperament.

The 'liquor business' is most pernicious, either directly or indirectly, to the Irish. Requiring little capital, at least to commence with, the Irish rush into it; and the temptation to excess which it offers is often more than the virtue of the proprietor of the business can withstand. If the evil were confined to the individual himself, the result would be a matter of comparatively trifling consequence; but the Irishman attracts the Irishman to his saloon or his bar, and so the evil spreads. Almost invariably the lowest class of groggery or liquor-store—that which supplies the most villainous and de-

[28] Ibid., p. 280.
[29] Ibid., pp. 281, 283, 286.

structive mixtures to its unfortunate customers—is planted right in the centre of the densely-crowded Irish quarter of a great city; while too often the name on the sign-board acts as a fatal lure to those who quaff ruin or death in the maddening bowl. . . . The bad liquor of the native American or the Dutchman is far less perilous to poor Pat than what is sold by the bar-keeper whose name has in it a flavour of the shamrock. A feeling of clanship, if not a spirit of nationality, operates as an additional inducement to the Irishman, who probably requires little incentive to excess, beyond his own craving for momentary enjoyment and dangerous excitement.

Maguire spoke eloquently of how the Irish were doing in America, his feelings regarding the Scotch-Irish, and, finally, Irish-Catholic problems.

And here I answer a question which is in every Irishman's mind, on the tip of every Irishman's tongue,—how are the Irish doing in America?—have they bettered their condition, or the contrary?—are they improving or going back? . . .[30]

The result, then, of every observation I could make, of every inquiry I instituted, of every information I received, is this,—that while, in some places, there are evils to deplore, but evils which are being remedied, and while many are not doing what they ought or could do for their advancement, on the whole, and dealing with them in mass, the Irish in America are steadily rising, steadily advancing, steadily improving in circumstances and in position; and that, as a rule, they have enormously benefited their condition by having left the old country for the new. . . . Where, as must necessarily be the case, the Irish constitute a large proportion of the working population of a great city, they may be looked down upon by the prejudiced or the superfine—those who dislike their religion, or despise homely manners or rude employment; but the toiling, hard-working mass of the Irish are nevertheless rising day by day, not only to greater comfort, but to a fuller appreciation of their duties and their destiny as citizens of America.

On the whole, then, and making due allowance for the causes and motives at which I have glanced, the Irish do stand well in the public esteem of America; and in many places in which I have been I know they are not only generally esteemed, but are highly popular. . . .

But there is one class of whom, neither from Irishmen nor Americans, is much said in praise. 'Whole-souled' and 'high-toned' would sound as a sarcasm and a mockery if applied to those Irish, or sons of Irish, who style themselves 'Scotch-Irish'—a title or designation so unworthy and so unnatural as to excite the derision of every man of large heart and generous spirit. . . .

Scotch-Irish are those Irish, or descendants of Irishmen, who are ashamed of their country, and represent themselves to Americans as other than what they really are. Not only are they ashamed of their country, but, so far as this false feeling influences them,

[30] Ibid., pp. 304–305, 308, 309, 547.

they are its shame. Detested by every true Irishman, they are despised by every genuine American. . . .

Let it be distinctly borne in mind, that the Irish Catholic had everything against him, nothing in his favour. With the Irish Protestant, of whatever denomination, the case was totally different. The Irish Protestant practically knew nothing of the difficulties by which the Irish Catholic was surrounded, nothing of the trials and temptations to which the Catholic and the family of the Catholic were subjected or exposed. Wherever the Irish Protestant turned his face, there he found a congregation and a church, nay even the people and the very atmosphere to suit him. If he had not, convenient to his dwelling, a church or a congregation of his immediate denomination, there was some kindred church which opened its doors to welcome him, some sect to sympathize with his belief, and receive him in the spirit of religious fraternity. Not so with the Catholic. The multitude of denominations was to him of little avail. There was no friendly sect or kindred communion to receive or sympathize with him. He had to stand alone and aloof, for with none could he amalgamate, or, as Protestant sects might, fuse down in one grand accord every minor difference. Thus, alone and aloof, the Irish Catholic, without church or pastor, had to keep the faith alive in his own breast, and foster it by every parental influence in the breasts of his children. . . .

Residence in a new country did not mean an abandonment of the culture of the old country. Many Irishmen in America deliberately chose to perpetuate their ancient heritage. This aspect of ethnic identification is clearly evident in the following poem by T. D. Sullivan.

The Irish-American[31]

1

Columbia the free is the land of my birth
And my paths have been all on American earth
But my birth is as Irish as any can be,
And my heart is with Erin afar o'er the sea.

2

My father, and mother, and friends all around.
Are daughters and sons of the sacred old ground;
They rambled its bright plains and mountains among,
And filled its fair valleys with laugh and with song.

3

But I sing their sweet music; and often they own
It is true to old Ireland in style and in tone;

[31] Reprinted from Edith Abbott, *Historical Aspects of the Immigration Problem,* pp. 530–31. Copyright © 1926 by University of Chicago Press. By permission of Arno Press.

I dance their gay dances, and hear them with glee
Say each touch tells of Erin afar o'er the sea. . . .

8

Dear home of my fathers! I'd hold thee to blame
And my cheeks would at times take the crimson of shame,
Did thy sad tale not show, in each sorrow-stained line,
That the might of thy tryant was greater than thine.

Abbott's collection also contains the views of Philip H. Bagenal, an Englishman who presents a picture of the Irish as they struggled to achieve a place for themselves in America. He stresses the function and value of politics as the vehicle through which the Irish gained respectability. Concomitantly, he recounts the deadening experience of Irish existence in the tenements of New York City.

Position of the Irish in America: An English View[32]

Since the final issue of the American war of Rebellion, the position of the Irish in America has in every way changed. They have been acknowledged as a power in politics, in religion, and society. They have not increased in popularity as a section of the American population, principally because they have always persisted, against their own interests, in keeping up their distinctiveness of race and religion in a manner antagonistic to the great mass of the American people. Their bands, their societies, their newspapers, and their foreign politics, all very well when unobtrusive, have from time immemorial been distasteful to the undemonstrative and more Puritanic or native American.

The Irishman has long been taught to look upon America as the refuge of his race, the home of his kindred. His feelings towards her are those of love and loyalty. But when he lands, his great expectations are sometimes checked. He often finds himself slighted as a man, and his people despised as a race, and this not by any means directly, but indirectly. Then he throws himself with all the fervour of his race into party politics, determined to show he is as good as the best. Five years' probation (sometimes less) in electioneering tactics makes him an able auxiliary at the poll, and soon the fierce zeal with which he enters political strife excites the jealousy and dislike of the native American. The most sober and tolerant cannot endure the boisterous patriotism of the newly-fledged citizens, nor feel at ease in seeing those who were a few years ago despised subjects of England acquire per saltum an equality of right with the offspring of home-born Republicans. It is this survival of Native-Americanism which makes the Irish question in America a delicate one from a political point of view. And when the fate of a Presidential election depends upon the votes of a single state, and that state is New York, the empire state of the Union, which is governed almost entirely by the Irish vote, we then see how bitter may be the thoughts of old-fashioned Americans

[32] Ibid., pp. 532–33, 535.

when they find the election of a President virtually in the hands of a race whom for years they had looked upon as alien and inferior.

The more modern Americans, however, have accepted facts, and, with the well-known ingenuity of the race, have turned the Irish population to good advantage. They manipulate Irish nationality, flatter Irish pride, and "scoop" the Irish vote with the same aptness that they corner wheat in Chicago or "utilize the margin" on the New York Stock Exchange. But if the Americans are still jealous of the political power of the Irish race that is planted in their midst, there is also in some quarters a religious-born fear and distrust of the Catholic Church which has been built up by means of the Irish population to its present position of wealth and influence. . . .

I was not surprised at the statistics I have quoted when I visited the tenement houses in New York where the Irish population dwell.

The effect produced upon the mind by an inspection of these human rookeries is a vehement desire to pull down and raze to the ground the vast system which holds in bondage thousands and thousands of men, women, and children. These high brick houses tower up to heaven, each flat holding from five to ten families, and one building numbering frequently a population of six hundred souls. To their credit, be it said, the condition of the Irish is by no means the worst, but the atmosphere of the place is death, morally and physically. Crowded into one small room a whole family lives, a unit among a dozen other such families. Can such a place be called a house? Most assuredly not. There is a high rent to be paid —but no one dares in New York to say with Michael Davitt that such a rent is an "immoral tax." The street below is dirty and ill kept. In the basement is a beer saloon, where crime and want jostle each other, and curses fill the air. On the other side is an Italian tenement reeking with dirt and rags. Close by is a Chinese quarter, or a Polish-Jew colony. Everywhere the moral atmosphere is one of degradation and human demoralization. Gross sensuality prevails. The sense of shame, if ever known, is early stifled. Domestic morals are too often abandoned and simple manners are things of the past. There is no family life possible in such surroundings; no noble traditions can descend from father to son. The fireside is hired by the week, the inmate is a hireling, and his family are most probably chained as hirelings also in some great neighbouring factory or mill. . . .

Still another interesting Irish experience in the second half of the nineteenth century was that of labor violence. An admixture of ethnicity, politics, labor, and violence characterized the Molly Maguires, who were active in the anthracite region of Pennsylvania.

[In Ireland] the political sufferer who met a felon's death was considered a martyr and a hero, whilst the "informer" was regarded with a feeling of utter detestation, as a traitor not only to the traditions of his race, to his country's honor and his country's future, but also to his family, his religion, and his God.[33] When it is taken

[33] Ibid., pp. 672, 673, 677, 681.

into consideration that they regarded their position as one of subjugation, the rulers of England as usurpers, the laws made without
authority, and the lands held by illegal tenure, it may be regretted,
but cannot be a matter of great wonder, that the detestation of an
"informer," with which an ignorant, prejudiced, and romantic
people were imbued, should extend to an informer of any kind.
Such, unfortunately, has been the case: to inform of a crime had in
many instances come to be considered as great a wrong as the crime
itself, and to such an extent has this feeling developed that it has
become a part of the Irish character, and is universal in its
application. . . .

By reason of this feeling the Molly Maguire has held "high
carnival" in crime, both in Ireland and in the anthracite coal regions
of Pennsylvania; and this feeling must be thoroughly appreciated in
order to understand how it is that a people of kindly, generous, and
just impulses may in a civilized land keep the murderer and assassin
among them, known, feared, and detested, and yet the crimes be
concealed and the offenders allowed to defy the law and the
authorities. . . .

The order is composed entirely of Irishmen and the sons of
Irishmen, professing the Roman Catholic faith, and yet their crimes
are regarded with intense horror by the body of the Irish people,
and against the order the church has hurled its fiercest anathemas,
denouncing its members as outlaws, and denying them Christian
burial. That despite such sentiment of the people and such action
on the part of the church the society should grow and flourish is to
be accounted for, as before stated, in a romantic and perverted
exercise of impulses founded on virtues.

It was by means of this organization, through which unity of
action was attainable, that a political influence was acquired that
for a time seemed to render the Molly Maguire omnipotent for
evil. That the society has existed in some form and under various
names as far back as 1855, or perhaps before, there is little doubt,
but prior to 1862 or 1863 it was confined to particular localities,
and, although the instrument of much evil, had not reached the
degree of arrogant confidence attained in after-years, and only now
shaken by the terrible revelation in regard to its true objects and
character.

Hostility to Irish immigrants was not the preserve of the native
Americans alone. The excerpt below leaves the impression that Swedish-
Americans had little love for the Irish. Unonius was a rather intolerant
Protestant clergyman whose dislike of the Irish was due as much to the
difference in religion as to the difference in nationality.

Several owners of lots on which such uninvited guests had made
themselves at home without anyone's permission had been put to a
good deal of trouble and expense in getting rid of them.[34] As long
as the owners did not need to use their land they did not care if

[34] From Backlund, trans. *Pioneer in North America,* ed. by Olsson, pp. 286–87. ©
1960 by the Swedish Pioneer Historical Society.

a few squatters settled on it, but later their compliance was to cost them dearly. Some, to be sure, sought to prevent the encroachment by fencing in the lots. If anyone built a shanty in a fenced area he could be legally driven off. This was not so if the ground was unfenced. Even keeping a watchman on the land to prevent such building was not enough. And once the Irishman had built his shanty and moved in with his family it was no easy matter to get rid of the vermin. To put up those dwellings (which could as properly be called pigsties—for four-footed creatures lived there on a family basis with those on two feet) presented few difficulties and could be accomplished in very short time. The man who had been sent to watch the place might leave the land clear and unoccupied in the evening, but when he returned there the next evening, he would find a house built or rather carried onto the lot. It might lack both floor and windows and nevertheless be occupied by half a dozen big and little Paddies with the potato pot boiling; a pig grunting under the bed; the horse, for which no shed had been provided, grazing at the side of the street; and the well-pleased squatter taking his tenth drink from his whiskey bottle. By then it was too late to drive away the invaders; they had got a firm foothold on the land, and the owner of the lot who was preparing to build a house for himself would be able to regain possession of his legal property only after much trouble and inconvenience. . . .

For several years we had trouble with the squatters and oftentimes feared for our persons and property. No sooner had windows been fitted into the church before a number of panes were broken. This happened again and again. Finally we caught the perpetrators, and I was happy, by means of threats of legal prosecution, to prevent that kind of vandalism in the future. The Irish are generally as cowardly as they are sly, and before a son of Erin has bared his sheath knife it is easy for a courageous person to knock it out of his hand.

The unwillingness of the American community to accept great contingents of foreign people or to make significant changes in its own cultural features is well illustrated by Oscar Handlin in *Boston's Immigrants*. His study of Boston society in the nineteenth century stresses the role of group consciousness and group conflict as a result of the Irish impact on a particular society. It can be seen that the Irish experience in Boston intensified consciousness of ethnic affinity among the Irish while it contributed to a greater delineation of ethnic distinction on the part of the older "Yankee" stock. First, evidence of group consciousness among the Irish institutions is examined; then Irish distinctiveness in Boston, which persisted long after the Know-Nothing period of the 1850's, is covered.

The flourishing growth of Irish institutions was an accurate reflection of their consciousness of group identity.[35] These autonomous

[35] Reprinted by permission of the publishers from *Boston's Immigrants*, Rev. Ed., by Oscar Handlin, Cambridge, Mass.: The Belknap Press of Harvard University Press, pp. 215–16, 219. Copyright © 1941, 1959 by the President and Fellows of Harvard College; 1969 by Oscar Handlin.

activities had no counterpart in the Old World where the community was a unified whole, adequately satisfying all the social desires of its members. Independent societies developed among immigrants only in Boston in response to the inadequacy of the city as it was to fill their needs. Since the non-Irish foreigners felt differences only at occasional particular points, they diverged from native social organizations infrequently, in localized activities of diminishing vitality. . . . Unable to participate in the normal associational affairs of the community, the Irish felt obliged to erect a society within a society, to act together in their own way. In every contact therefore the group, acting apart from other sections of the community, became intensely aware of its peculiar and exclusive identity.

The degree of intermarriage at once reflected and buttressed the distinction between the Irish and all others. Among the Irish, religious and social considerations reenforced the natural tendency to mate with their own kind. As Catholics, they were repeatedly warned that union with Protestants was tantamount to loss of faith; while the great majority of non-Irish in the city considered marriage with them degrading. As a result, the percentage of Irish intermarriage was lower than that of any other group including the Negroes, 12 per cent of whose marriages were with whites.

Group consciousness in the newcomers provoked a secondary reaction in native Bostonians, almost nonexistent in the eighteenth and early nineteenth centuries, when French Huguenots, Jews, Scots, Scotch-Irish and Irishmen had had no difficulty in assimilating with the older stock. Americans now became more conscious of their own identity. They began to distinguish themselves, the Anglo-Saxons, from the Irish "Kelts." The old society felt a sense of malaise because newcomers did not fit into its categories, and resentment, because they threatened its stability. Uneasy, it attempted to avoid contact by withdrawing ever farther into a solid, coherent, and circumscribed group of its own, until in the fifties it evolved the true Brahmin who believed, with Holmes, that a man of family required "four or five generations of gentlemen and gentlewomen" behind him.

For though the Irish acquired a secure place in the community, they remained distinct as a group. Prejudice against them lingered for many year. Not until 1879, for instance, did Catholic chaplains secure the right to officiate in state institutions. They never merged with the other elements in the city and consistently retained the characteristics originally segregating them from other Bostonians. Even while supporting the Union, their opposition to reform, their dislike of Lincoln, and their hatred of the Negroes, abolition, and emancipation proclamation, shown in the draft riot of 1863, demonstrated that the basic divergence emanating from the nature of their adjustment to Boston society still existed.

The mass of Irishmen continued to occupy the low places in society they had earlier held. Their wives and daughters performed most of the city's domestic service; and men and boys of Irish ancestry constituted the bulk of unskilled workers. . . .

There was more mobility in the second generation, members of which found increased opportunities for apprenticeship and training. Many entered upon semiskilled occupations as longshoremen, teamsters, and draymen. Not a few also advanced to the skilled crafts in the building and furniture trades. But it remained difficult for the sons of Irishmen to move upward into clerical and professional occupations. In those spheres, they faced the barriers of prejudice and of lack of capital. They were also handicapped by their limited access to the facilities for education.

The concern with status created by the presence of the Irish immigrants and their offspring affected every group in the city. No man now could think of his place in society simply in terms of occupation or income level. It was necessary also ever to consider ethnic affiliation.

Most of the non-Irish foreign-born groups tried with some success to adapt themselves to the ideals and patterns of the society around them. They faced relatively little difficulty in doing so. The old Boston community offered them a ready model for emulation. Yet, at the same time, such people as the Germans and the Jews understood that their own separateness was the product of the recency of their arrival and compensated for it through creation of their own social institutions.

KEY QUESTIONS

1. Compare and contrast the role of language in the retention of ethnicity among Scandinavians.

2. According to the experience of the Scandinavian population, was it possible to remain isolated in an ethnic community beyond the first generation?

3. In its attempt to unite its people into groups, was the German-American experience different from that of the Irish?

4. Comment on the phenomenon of Catholic immigrant groups' entering into ethnic discord although possessing the same religious creed.

5. Was the British experience in America in the nineteenth century exceptional or similar to that of other ethnic groups? Substantiate your response by comparing the British-American experience with that of the Irish, German-Americans, or Scandinavian-Americans.

4

The Orientals

The record of American treatment of Asiatics within the country has been marked by three periods: acceptance, opposition, and assimilation. The middle period of opposition was the longest, extending from approximately the Civil War to about 1950. The Asiatics, specifically the Chinese, Japanese, and Filipinos, have experienced nearly insurmountable obstacles in their attempt to move from the periphery to the center of American society. In grappling with the question of race and nationality, Henry Pratt Fairchild provides an answer to the cause of prejudice:[1]

> But group feeling is not based solely on characteristics of individuals. Like all true race and nationality matters it has a mass aspect. There is undoubtedly a definite quantitative factor involved in it. An increase in the numbers of strangers does not merely intensify the antipathy proportionately, it may even cause an actual reversal of sentiment. The first two or three representatives of a foreign type frequently arouse no actual antagonism whatever. They are regarded as interesting, quaint, exotic.

This evolution of feeling applied to the Asiatics in the United States, especially on the West Coast. At first the Chinese were warmly received, but as their numbers increased and as they developed their own communities and provided economic rivalry, they incurred American resentment and antagonism.[2] The same pattern was true in the case of the Japanese and the Filipinos.

Anti-Chinese sentiment on the West Coast increased to fever pitch during the 1870's, highlighted by the Sandlot Riots in San Francisco in 1877. Altogether there were numerous examples of segregation and physi-

[1] Reprinted from Henry Pratt Fairchild, *Race and Nationality* (New York: Ronald Press, 1947), p. 91.

[2] Recently this interpretation has been challenged by Stuart Creighton Miller, *The Unwelcome Immigrant* (Berkeley: University of California Press, 1969).

cal violence. All of this culminated in the Exclusion Act of 1882, which prohibited the entry of Chinese laborers. The exclusion principle was to be renewed on several more occasions, extending its legality to 1943, when it was eliminated. The 1970 census reported 435,000 Chinese-Americans living in the United States.

Japanese immigration began in large numbers after 1890. By the Gentleman's Agreement of 1907, Japan agreed to prohibit emigration of laborers to the United States. In 1924 a new arrangement excluded Japanese as "aliens ineligible to citizenship." In 1952 the McCarran-Walter Act ended both the policy of denial of citizenship to Japanese residents and racial discrimination in immigration. The 1965 immigration law eliminated the discriminatory national quota provisions. According to the 1970 census, 591,000 Japanese-Americans were residing in this country.

One of the most unsavory incidents in the treatment of an ethnic group occurred after the attack on Pearl Harbor, when 110,000 Japanese-Americans, two-thirds of them American citizens, were taken from their homes on the West Coast and placed in ten "relocation centers." Bolstered by the anger from the sudden attack on Pearl Harbor, coupled with the deep-seated animosity against the Japanese, the Western Defense Command, the President, Congress, and the Supreme Court all sanctioned the Japanese internment. The German-Americans and Italian-Americans received no such treatment. Nevertheless, the Japanese-Americans remained loyal to the American cause during the war. After World War II the United States Government compensated the Japanese-Americans who were forcibly relocated, although the matter was never satisfactorily resolved.

The Filipinos first started to come to the United States around 1906, but as late as 1920 they numbered only about 5,000. A large influx arrived in the 1920's as a consequence of the need for workers on the West Coast and the exclusion of the Filipinos from the newly adopted quota system. In fact, the Filipinos were the only Oriental people not restricted from immigrating. However, the Exclusion Act of 1924 prohibited the Filipinos from becoming citizens, although they were not regarded as aliens. Their unique status resulted from the fact that the United States owned the Philippine Islands. They were considered nationals but were not subject to the quota system. As a result of anti-Filipino agitation on the Pacific Coast, however, demands for exclusion grew. Finally, the Philippines Independence Act of 1934 provided for an annual quota of fifty immigrants to the Hawaiian Islands and complete exclusion from the continental United States when independence should become a reality. Although the great depression halted immigration, when independence was proclaimed in 1946, immigration was accelerated. Today there are about 343,000 Filipinos in the United States.

Contributing to the Filipinos' confused status was their Spanish heritage. The Filipinos did not consider themselves Orientals, but local officials in the western states, interpreting their ethnicity according to local tradition, looked on them as Asians. On the West Coast they were discriminated against; if seen on the street in the evenings, they were stopped by police; states passed laws prohibiting marriage between Caucasians and Orientals.

When it became evident that hostility would not completely subside, the Filipinos organized the Filipino Federation of America in 1925 in Stockton, California. The Stockton center was bombed in the 1930's and rebuilt in 1962, a decidedly less hostile period.

The Bureau of the Census applies a color classification to divide the population into two groups: white and nonwhite. The nonwhite group includes Negroes, American Indians, Japanese, Chinese, Filipinos, Koreans, Hawaiians, Asian Indians, Mayans, Aleuts, etc. The racial categories of the Japanese, Chinese, and Filipinos are based largely on the country or area of origin, not necessarily on biological stock.

THE CHINESE

The Chinese have undergone a wide variety of ethnic experiences in the United States. After the Civil War, an increase in Chinese immigration paved the way for discriminatory treatment by Californians. This prejudice, strong at the turn of the century, is illustrated by the unsuccessful attempt of a prominent Presbyterian and editor of a Chinese daily newspaper to move out of Chinatown to a white neighborhood.

> The story of the attempts of one Chinaman to find a place to live outside of Chinatown, in order that he might bring up his children as Christians and good Americans, will serve better than any abstract statement, to illustrate the difficulties produced by anti-Chinese prejudice.[3] The writer of this story is a prominent member of a Presbyterian Church and the Editor of a Chinese Daily paper. He and his family speak excellent English, dress in American clothes and his children are being educated carefully after the manner of well-to-do Americans:
>
> > In the summer of 1901 I proposed to bring my family from Los Angeles to San Francisco. I tried many times to find a suitable house outside of Chinatown so that my children might be properly brought up in the ways of the Americans, that in the years to come they may perform the duties of American citizenship.
> >
> > I found a good flat with five rooms and bath and and the rent was within my ability to pay. The landlady was willing also to rent the house to me after having heard the explanation I made regarding myself. The rent was paid and preparation

[3] Reprinted from Mary Roberts Coolidge, *Chinese Immigration* (reprint ed., New York: Arno Press, 1969), pp. 438–39.

was made for moving in, but after two days the landlady came to my office and returned the money to me and explained the situation: the whole neighborhood had risen in arms against the idea of having a Chinese family in their midst, and since the landlady would not give up the house to me it was out of the question to move in, so my first attempt to find a home outside of the district where my own people live was a flat failure.

A few weeks later I again tried my luck, and in the course of an afternoon, I found two houses which I thought would be suitable to me, since they were not far from Chinatown and rent was not exorbitant. The agents kindly made arrangements to rent the premises to me but when the landlords were apprised of the nationality of their prospective tenants all arrangements were annulled.

After all these failures, I was not yet dismayed, I resolved, to try again and hoped for better results. Accordingly one ideal afternoon, after having gone through the rush of business, I sallied forth putting aside the memory of all previous defeats from my mind. I found a flat on Mason Street near Sacramento, which I thought was the ideal place for a home. The landlord was a good-natured Frenchman. He had no race prejudice in his mind and what he had there was only dollars and cents. So he agreed to rent the place to me provided his other tenants would not object and that he would let me know one way or the other in two days. At the end of the two days I called at his house and he told me that it was out of the question to rent me the house since the other tenants objected strenuously to renting the flat to a Chinese family. I was greatly disappointed but not the least surprised. I had the temerity to ask him what family objected to my living there, and he replied that it was a family of negroes. That was the last straw that broke the back of my buoyancy of hope. I then repeated again and again to myself saying, if negroes even object to my getting a house outside of Chinatown, how can I ever succeed in getting a place where no one objects. From that time on I never made another move. The proverbial Chinese perseverance seemed to have left me for good.

Despite the strong prejudice against the Chinese and against the Chinatowns that developed in the major cities they inhabited, there is much evidence to indicate that the Chinese became Americanized quite rapidly. In her excellent study, Mary Roberts Coolidge dramatizes the desire of the Chinese to adopt American life patterns.

The Chinaman is above all, a lover of home and children and if married men were allowed to bring in their wives freely the conditions of life of the Chinese entitled to live in this country would become much more normal.[4] In no one respect have the Chinese in America altered more than in their ideas about women. Wives have a far greater amount of freedom in America than in China; daugh-

[4] Ibid., pp. 440–43.

ters are no longer unwelcome. The Chinese have repeatedly tried to adopt white children and half-bloods of other races from the asylums, but the anti-Chinese prejudice is so strong as to make it impossible. It has often been rumored that the Chinese sell children in San Francisco. This idea probably arose from their custom of binding any bargain with a money payment. The contract of adoption is made final among them by the payment of a small sum of money.

On account of the difficulty and expense of bringing in Chinese wives, there have been a number of marriages between the laboring Chinese and women of the darker foreign-blood—Indian and Mexican and even Europeans. A number of native-born Chinese have married American women, and the children, so far from being the "monstrosities" predicted by early Californians, are superior, both physically and mentally. In the Southwest, the offspring of marriages between Chinese and Mexican women are conspicuously superior; but the prejudice against the mixture of North-European whites and Chinese is extreme and has resulted in an amendment adding the word Mongolians, to the law prohibiting intermarriage of white persons and negroes, in several states and territories.

It was assumed for many years that the Chinese were unassimilable and their clannishness, the slowness with which they adopted American dress and the English language lent color to the assumption. But a comparison of the Chinese with other aliens, particularly with the Italians, Mexicans and Greeks in San Francisco, discloses the fact that they are being Americanized quite as rapidly, and in some respects, make better citizens because of their superior intellectual capacity. At the time of the first Restriction act very few Chinese had cut their queues and adopted American clothes, and they chiefly because they were converts to Christianity; but since 1900 the movement in this direction has been very rapid. Only about one boy in six in the graded school wears a queue and there are now four barbers in Chinatown itself who advertise to do queue-cutting. Those who still wear the queue do so because they mean to return to China to live or to visit their parents. One very much Americanized Chinamen said that his aged mother in China would be so shocked to see him without it that he would not have it cut till he returned from the visit home which would probably be his last.

The majority of Chinese immigrants some time ago exchanged their baggy pantaloons for American trousers, but like many other foreigners they have not yet compassed the idea that the cut of them must be changed frequently to be truly in the American fashion. Nor have they yet generally adopted in place of the soft cotton or silk shirt the starched garment, nor in place of the loose linen or wadded silk tunic the conventional tailor-made vest and coat; although a considerable number of the educated Chinese now wear the conventional business man's dress; and the native-born Chinese of the second generation are extremely American in their clothing.

To an Oriental the mastery of English is necessarily much more difficult than to a European, but it may be set down that every Chinaman who has cut his queue and every Christian Chinaman, speaks English, and many others speak it a little. Some who speak badly have nevertheless learned to read the American papers. Just as in the case of other foreigners, if the Chinaman came to the United States when he was a little boy or if he has a wife and children here, he speaks English and is Americanized to a considerable degree; and the native-born boys are, almost without exception, fully Americanized in speech as well as in dress.

Among the few hundred men who have families in' this country not many care to vote themselves, but all of them are proud of the fact that their sons can vote. One old Chinaman said: "I no care much about vote—my son, I make him vote." The older Chinese are sensitive about the denial of naturalization because it is a discrimination against their race, and the native-born are proportionately proud of the privilege. More than a hundred native-born Chinese registered in San Francisco as voters in 1904; and in that campaign the anomalous spectacle was presented of a Union-Labor candidate for Mayor making election speeches in Chinatown. There is abundant evidence that the Chinese of the second generation mean to claim their citizenship. In the smaller towns of California and in some other states they show strong patriotism, marching in Fourth of July parades and even drilling and volunteering for the army.

The next author engages in a friendly criticism of American civilization. No-Yong Park, a Harvard Ph.D., admits to being a "Chinese recipient of American kindness and hospitality." Yet he presents a frank evaluation of various aspects of American life: the fast-paced pattern of behavior, the moral standards, materialism, commercialism, race prejudice, "boostmanship," and the press. No-Yong Park's observations get to the substance of American life styles.

Take another illustration: the Americans "rush."[5] Look at them; how they hurry! They rush all the way from the maternity hospital to the graveyard. . . . Undoubtedly it is the machine which makes the speedy Americans speedier, but their rush is too much rush. They burn up their energy, life and all in the "pursuit of happiness" but never have time to enjoy happiness itself. But what one would say if the Americans were extremely slow and inactive and, like the classical Chinese scholars, sought contentment in all things, including "cold water to drink and coarse rice to eat"! . . .

"American materialism" is probably the strongest case against the United States. In taking up this point, however, I must admit frankly that it is not a proper time for us Chinese to condemn American materialism, for what we need in China today is American science, American industry, and many other things which might be branded as American materialism. But, as a citizen of the world at large, I cannot help feeling that American civilization is too materialistic to be described as an ideal civilization. . . . Man is more or less materialistic, but the American is too much so. If the ancient Chinese philosophers have gone to one extreme by condemning everything that is materialistic, the modern American has gone to

[5] Reprinted from No-Yong Park, *An Oriental View of American Civilization* (Boston: Hale, Cushman & Flint, 1934), pp. 14–15, 28–30, 34–35, 38–40, 110–111, 114–115.

the opposite extreme. He has abandoned cultural and spiritual values, and has given himself up to the gods of materialism and commercialism. He has let the blind forces of materialism and commercialism dominate himself and his institutions, and control every move he makes. He can hardly listen to the radio three minutes without being interrupted by the voice of commercialism. He can hardly travel a mile on the highway without being confronted by the sticky hands of commercialism. He can hardly sleep at night without being haunted by the ghost of commercialism, hovering over his head and peeking into his purse. Thus the inevitable commercialism manifests itself in everything in America.

Money, money, money,—that is the alpha and omega in America; it is the master of all things and the measure of all values. Money does not exist for man, man exists for money. He works, toils and struggles for money and more of it. He conquers the sky, levels the mountains and wrecks the earth, for money. He exploits his woman, makes her smoke, makes her wear all sorts of laughable clothes year after year, all for the purpose of making money. Money is his strength; it is his weakness, too. To the God of Gold he offers for sale all his morals, his character, his culture and his life itself. . . .

Race prejudice is probably one of the ugliest scars on American civilization. Nowhere in the world is it more outspoken and more deeply rooted than in America, perhaps with the exception of Hitler's Germany. Truly, this land of the free deserves the appellation "a land of race prejudice." A little sense of preference for one's own race is not only harmless, but would be considered desirable. How tragic would it be if we all treated unknown strangers as our wives or sisters! How dangerous would it be if we treated tigers and serpents as our brethren! We should have kinder feelings for our relatives and friends, our own nationals and races, than we have for others. But American race prejudice has gone a little too far. This prejudice is most strongly manifested against the Jews, the Negroes and the Orientals. Their ostracism of the Jews, their condemnation of the Negroes and their discrimination against the Orientals make it difficult for the Americans to laugh at the Indians for their caste system. . . .

With such a pride and optimism and ever-progressive frame of mind, the American cannot help being a "booster." . . . He will tell you that his people are the most civilized and his country the best in the world. He will also tell you that his state is the best in the Union and his town is the best in the state. You will hear the same statement in every state and in every town, hence all the states and all the towns in America are the best. In a small town in North Dakota, I was talking to an undertaker. Even that undertaker was boosting his town before me. He said that his town was the best in the state, business was better than in other towns, and more people died there than in any other town in the state! The booster looks at times very childish, and often foolish. . . .

The American does not stop with boosting. He works, works and works. I have never seen any one who likes to work more than he. To him work is his religion, his recreation and his life. You take work away from him, and you will kill him. He is born to work, he lives to work, and he dies for his work. He works when he has something to do; he works when he has nothing to do. He builds up when he can and he tears down when he has nothing to build. He has no time to be graceful, polite and stylish. He is always on the go. He runs, jumps and hops back and forth like a rabbit. Speed! Speed! Speed! It gets on one's nerves. But that is better than being lazy, idle and mischievous. . . .

In the following two selections, Betty Lee Sung points out the changing pattern of Chinese-American life in contemporary society. The security and companionship formerly obtained in Chinatowns are now gone because there is little or no discrimination against the Chinese-American's choice of residence. The author states that only a small percentage of Chinese-Americans live in Chinatowns today.

Family circles now provide the companionship and warmth formerly sought in Chinatown.[6] Financial improvement and more knowledge of English enable the Chinese to seek entertainment elsewhere. Cars, once an unknown luxury among Chinese families, are now commonplace. Spacious houses and suburban dwellings make possible entertainment in the homes. Diversion can be found outside of Chinatown.

Segregation is no longer a factor in the perpetuation of Chinatowns. The social climate and the general attitude toward the Chinese have changed so rapidly in recent years that the Chinese actually encounter little or no discrimination in their choice of a place to live. In fact, only a small percentage of the Chinese in the United States live in Chinatowns, and the old-time residents have practically all moved away.

I am personally acquainted with a woman who brought up her brood of seven children in a four-room apartment on Bayard Street in New York's Chinatown. For thirty years, she occupied the same apartment and stubbornly refused to move to larger and more comfortable quarters elsewhere.

Money was not the problem. Her husband was a successful jeweler and could well afford a large house. The family definitely needed more room and privacy, but the mother felt comfortable in her old surroundings. Her friends were there. Her husband's business was there. It was convenient for her to shop. Knowing her, I thought she would be the last person to leave Chinatown. But in 1961, with most of her children grown up, married, and living in the suburbs, she, too, succumbed and bought a home in the suburbs near her children. . . .

Chinatowns have been a colorful landmark on the American scene. Cities with one have always used it as a tourist attraction. To heighten curiosity and make Chinatowns seem more exciting, a great many stories have been fabricated about these places. Even today, the tendency is to associate all Chinese in the United States with Chinatowns and to presume that whatever occurs in Chinatown may be taken to apply to all the Chinese in the United States at large. In actuality, only a small percentage of the Chinese now live in Chinatowns. Most have successfully found their niches in the larger American society. Those who live there are essentially newcomers, people with businesses or restaurants in the area, and old-timers who have not broken away.

In population and area, the larger Chinatowns have expanded, swelled by the increased numbers of immigrants within the past two decades. But the new Chinatowns are not like the old. Nor will they ever be unless we turn back the clock of history and re-create the conditions of yesteryears. The bonds that held the early Chinese together in Chinatowns are gone. Communal organizations have lost their leadership and their functions. The new Chinatowns will be characterized more as loosely knit ethnic neighborhoods with an artificially contrived Oriental atmosphere mainly for the sake of the tourist trade. Behind this facade, however, the true essence of Chinatowns will be found in the sense of identity and belonging they impart to the Chinese living beyond as well as within their borders.

THE JAPANESE

"No immigrant group encountered higher walls of prejudice and discrimination than did the Japanese." Edwin O. Reischauer's assessment in the foreword to *Nisei* by Bill Hosokawa points up the extreme ethnic difficulties experienced by the Japanese-Americans. The thread of hostility toward the Japanese minority runs continuously from the time they arrived in large numbers around the turn of the twentieth century to the end of World War II.

The pressure against the Japanese in California mounted to an intolerable degree at the beginning of this century. Physical attacks on the San Francisco Issei (the first-generation Japanese, born in Japan) became a regular occurrence in 1906, and the assaults were motivated by racial hostility and instigated by newspaper accounts. The following are accounts by Japanese-Americans.

> I am proprietor of Sunset City Laundry.[7] Soon after the earthquake the persecutions became intolerable. My drivers were constantly attacked on the highways, my place of business defiled by rotten eggs and fruit; windows were smashed several times. . . . The miscreants are generally young men, 17 or 18 years old. Whenever newspapers attack the Japanese these roughs renew their misdeeds with redoubled energy.

Japanese pedestrians were not safe either. M. Sugawa, a shoemaker stated:

[7] Reprinted from Roger Daniels, *The Politics of Prejudice* (New York: Atheneum, 1968), p. 84. Originally published by the University of California Press; reprinted by permission of The Regents of the University of California.

As I was passing on Sutter, near Scott, three boys, 21 or 22 years of age, attacked my person.[8] I nearly fainted. Upon rising to my feet they again assaulted me. This time they smashed my nose. I grabbed the coat of one of the trio, and after having my nose dressed at one of the nearby hospitals, I went home. The next day, a policeman came requesting me to give up the coat. I at first refused, but finally, upon his reassuring me that it would be deposited at the police station, I gave it up. I reported the matter to the police. When the case came up for trial the youngster was dismissed on the plea of insufficiency of evidence.

The World War I years were especially difficult for Japanese-Americans on the West Coast. A leading spokesman for the Japanese in this period, Kiyoshi Karl Kawakami, stated that he witnessed the "best, as well as the worst, elements of the American people in California." As a result, he had ceased to regard the United States as the apotheosis of justice and humanity. Kawakami critically appraised the California newspapers in the following account. He offered examples to dramatize the prejudice against the Japanese.

Perhaps the least harmless of the common tricks of California papers is either to ignore completely news or statements favorable to the Japanese or to bury them in an obscure corner or in the body of a long article, playing up unfavorable news in blazing headlines, often broad bands of huge type streaming across the front pages. . . .[9]

Somewhere in the Sacramento Valley lived a gentleman who wanted to be a state legislator. He talked a lot about the Japanese menace, and repeatedly stated that the Japanese had leased 10,000,000 acres of land in the upper end of the Sutter Basin. That was great news and the man got all the publicity he wanted. But remember that the Sutter Basin has only 60,000 acres in all. How any one can lease 10,000,000 acres just in the upper end of it, when the entire basin comprises only 60,000 acres, is beyond the comprehension of a sane man. Yet this wild statement was published in newspapers all over California, and perhaps in other States. If any intelligent man tried to get the correct statement in the press, it was of no avail because it was not news. . . .

Shortly before the November election last year almost all California newspapers published the most ridiculous yet most malicious story of a Los Angeles "society woman" having been made the victim of a Japanese "murder plot." "There was placed in her food," so the story went, "a dozen small pieces of sharp bamboo splinters, each enclosed within a binding gut." And the good lady swallowed these bamboo pieces put in her food by her Japanese cook. Of course she never masticated her food! The good woman is to-day as healthy as ever. The whole thing was so baseless and utterly foolish. Both the reporters who wrote the story and the editors who printed it knew it was a foolish lie, for I take them to be normal human beings. Yet

[8] Ibid., p. 34.

[9] Reprinted from Kiyoshi Karl Kawakami, *The Real Japanese Question* (New York: Macmillan, 1921), pp. 135–41.

they did not hesitate to publish such stories under big headlines on the front pages. And Mr. Phelan, then candidate for reelection to the United States Senate, went the newspaper one better, freely exploiting the above story in his campaign speeches! Verily, this revolving planet of ours is full of picturesque folks.

Enough has been written to show the idiosyncrasies of the California press. But may I add just one more story, a happy story in which I was made a hero.

On July 19, 1920, I appeared before the Congressional Committee on Immigration and Naturalization which was holding hearings in San Francisco. The committee asked me miscellaneous questions, some sensible, some absurd, some congressman-like. One was whether I knew a Japanese girl who was employed in the censor's office of the San Francisco Post Office. I replied, "Yes." Then they asked me whether she told me about her work, and whether I got any information from her. I said, "No."

To my great delight I saw my name adorning the front pages of the newspapers that evening and the "morning after." One paper had this headline in letters, each as big as a fist: "KAWAKAMI SAYS WOMAN CENSOR GAVE INFORMATION." Other papers had much the same headlines, and the story was copied by almost every paper in California.

At last my lifelong ambition to have my name in big headlines on the front pages of newspapers was gratified. But Representative Albert Johnson, Chairman of the Immigration Committee, thought I was getting unmerited distinction and wrote a letter scolding me for accepting it and admonishing the press for being over-generous.

The Japanese attack on Pearl Harbor on December 7, 1941, reverberated with frightening intensity in the United States. Fear of a Japanese invasion on the West Coast gripped the American people. But how would the attack on Pearl Harbor affect the Issei (or first-generation Japanese) and the Nisei (or second-generation Japanese) in the United States? Though the transferring of the Japanese-Americans to relocation centers is not predicted in the following reading, it details some of the crisis-packed events immediately following announcement of the sudden attack.

On December 7, 1941, the Reverend Donald Toriumi, the first Japanese-American Presbyterian minister in the United States, was in Long Beach, California, assisting at a church service.[10] A graduate of the San Francisco Theological Seminary, he was a youth worker in four Japanese churches in Southern California. On that Sunday morning following the service, a boy came running into the church to say he had just heard on his car radio that Japan had bombed Pearl Harbor. . . .

The American Japanese stood in the quiet sun-drenched street, two thousand miles from where a peaceful island had been turned into a battlefield. They stared at each other in disbelief. For years

[10] Reprinted with permission of The Macmillan Company from *The Great Betrayal* by Audrie Girdner and Anne Loftis, pp. 1–2. Copyright © 1969 by Audrie Girdner and Anne Loftis.

there had been talk about war between Japan and the United States. In the last few days the newspaper headlines had blazed with news of the crisis in the Pacific. The Secretary of State was at that moment discussing peace terms with the Japanese envoys in Washington. This news of an attack might be a false rumor. But the incredible report was verified when it was learned that President Roosevelt was telephoning members of his cabinet. There was no mistaking the reality of the crisis. Reverend Toriumi turned away, stunned and shaken. He wondered how the war would affect the people of Japanese ancestry living on the West Coast, two-thirds of whom were, like him, Nisei (second generation), born in America.

Later, while he was at lunch at the home of a church member, Mr. Toriumi was called to the telephone. The pastor of the First Presbyterian Church in Long Beach proposed that the two congregations hold a joint service at his church that evening. At eight o'clock Nisei and Caucasian youth marched down the aisle and sat together as a testimony to their friendship. Symbolically, they declared that they were all Americans, that the war would not divide them. Still moved by this experience, Mr. Toriumi was standing later that night on a street corner waiting to catch an electric train back to Los Angeles when an FBI man walked up to him, flashed a badge, and asked for his identification. The young minister, an American citizen, was startled. "It gave me a funny feeling, a very uneasy feeling."

David Sakai, a student at San Jose State College, spent the day with his roommate and three other Nisei students. "The news hit us like a bomb. We never left that radio the rest of the day. We were really shocked. We wondered what was going to happen to everybody, to friends and relatives in Japan."

Masao Hamamura was a high school student in Gonzales near Salinas. His initial reaction was like that of most Nisei: "They are attacking us." His mother was not surprised, however. She had recently visited Japan and thought that was likely.

Monica Sone's father, a first-generation immigrant who ran a waterfront hotel in Seattle, would not believe in the attack until he heard the words in his own language on a short-wave broadcast from Japan. Like the rest of the nation, the American Japanese spent the afternoon of Sunday, December 7, trying to dispel but only increasing their anxiety by listening to reports on the radio.

Interspersed with the news that the President was calling an emergency meeting of members of his cabinet and congressional leaders for eight-thirty that evening, came special bulletins from state governors and the mayors of large cities across the nation. Hawaii's governor announced that the islands were under martial law. In all West Coast cities extra guards were posted around harbors, airports, and defense installations. Telephone switchboards were jammed with calls from people wanting to talk to friends and relatives. Citizens rushed out to sign up for civil defense work. In Seattle a Marine Corps recruiting station was opened by demand at 6 p.m. and by nine o'clock, seventy-eight men had enlisted. Military personnel were ordered back to their bases.

San Francisco's mayor, Angelo J. Rossi, proclaimed a state of emergency and dispatched extra police to block off traffic in the Japanese sector of the city. Many Japanese-owned stores remained open, but in the residential area shades were drawn and people stayed indoors. . . .

The War Relocation Authority was established by President Franklin D. Roosevelt in 1942 for the purpose of ensuring the welfare of the evacuated Japanese-Americans. Throughout most of that year the WRA people worked at setting up living quarters, hospitals, schools, farms, and other businesses in the relocation centers for the evacuees. The Manzanar Relocation Center in southern California, from which the following extract is taken, was one of the ten centers, all west of the Mississippi. The account is an actual transcription from a Nisei (American-born children of immigrant Japanese) who refused to swear an oath of allegiance to the United States. It describes vividly the firsthand experiences and impressions of a Nisei's evacuation.

Hearing Board Member: I see you have always lived in this country.[11]
Nisei: Yes.
HBM: Are you a dual citizen?
Nisei: No, I am an American citizen only.
HBM: In February, during the army registration, you said "No" to Question 28 according to our record. Did you understand the question?
Nisei: I guess I did understand the question.
HBM: And do you want to change the answer or do you want the "No" to stand?
Nisei: I'll keep it "No."
HBM: What does that mean?
(The boy stands there. His lips are quivering but he does not speak.)
HBM: Do you want to talk about it? Something is bothering you.
Nisei: What is bothering me could not be answered by any one person in particular.
HBM: Don't you want to tell us? Perhaps there is something that we can do. If you say "No," you are giving away your American citizenship. Is that what you want to do? Feel free to talk. We're not here to argue with you but we want to help you.
Nisei: What I was thinking. I thought that since there is a war on between Japan and America, since the people of this country have to be geared up to fight against Japan, they are taught to hate us. So they don't accept us. First I wanted to help this country, but they evacuated us instead of giving us a chance. Then I wanted to be neutral, but now that you force a decision, I have to say this. We have a Japanese face. Even if I try to be American I won't be entirely accepted.
HBM: What is this about "the Japanese face" deal? Up to today we haven't heard this expression, and today we hear it all over this block. Have you been reading Mary Oyama's article in *Liberty?*

[11] Reprinted from "A Nisei Who Said 'No'," in *War Relocation Authority*, Community Analysis Notes No. 1, January 15, 1944, pp. 1–9.

Nisei: I read Mary's article. It doesn't say much. It just tells about the conditions of leaving our homes, about the hardships we suffered and how well we took them. But that was just the beginning. A great deal has happened since then that she says nothing about.

HBM: What do you plan to do?

Nisei: I planned to stay in this country before the war. I planned to be a farmer.

HBM: What about your folks?

Nisei: They figure they'll stay here if I do or they'll go to Tule Lake if I do.

HBM: Is it that some of your friends are going to Tule Lake? Are you being influenced by the talk of friends?

Nisei: No, my best friend is going to stay here.

HBM: Then what is at the bottom of this?

Nisei: If I would say "Yes," I'd be expected to say that I'd give up my life for this country. I don't think I could say that because this country has not treated me as a citizen. I could go three-quarters of the way but not all the way after what has happened.

HBM: Would you be willing to be drafted?

Nisei: No, I couldn't do that.

HBM: That's all. I see that you have thought about it and that your mind is made up. (Nisei goes out.)

HBM: I feel sorry for that boy. Some of them I don't feel sorry for.

Later I contacted this young man and asked him for a fuller statement of his views. The following is what he told me:

I'm just a fellow who has always worked as a farmer. I've never met the real community yet. When I was at home, I thought about this hearing and how to explain my feelings. But you come before a board like this. I'm not used to it. I couldn't say it the way I meant it.

Back home, before evacuation, when fellows were drafted for the United States Army, that was good. The Japanese gave a party for them, a big sendoff. It was not a party for them all together but for each one individually. There were fifty people or more at the bus to see each one of them off. You saw the white American boys there who were going too. In most cases no one would be there to see them off but the immediate family. We were glad to serve in the American Army then. We thought it was right because we lived here.

Before evacuation, all our parents thought that since they were aliens they would probably have to go to a camp. That was only natural—they were enemy aliens. But they never thought that it would come to the place where their sons, who were born in America and were American citizens would be evacuated. We citizens had hopes of staying there because President Roosevelt and Attorney General Biddle said it was not a military necessity to evacuate American citizens of Japanese ancestry.

So we went ahead and planted our crops. If anyone didn't believe it and didn't plant, everyone said it was sabotage. So we lost a lot of money that we wouldn't have had to lose if we had not put the crop in and had been told in the first place that we were going to be evacuated. Then we came up to Manzanar. It was just the same whether you were alien or citizen. When they asked for people to go on furlough, it was not only the citizen but the alien who could go out if he wanted to.

At first when we got here, when people thought we were dangerous, that should have been the time where we should have been guarded. But it was about a half a year afterwards that they thought those things up. Then they put up the fence and the towers. When we first came here, if you had business to do you could go to Lone Pine or Independence. But afterwards you couldn't go anywhere, even with a military guard.

By the way, what is this for, why do you want to know all this? We've had so much trouble, we've been lied about so much that we hate to tell anything to anybody any more. Look at the papers. At first some people said: "Don't buy the *Examiner*, buy the *Los Angeles Times*, it is more fair to the Japanese." Now it has changed and is as bad as the other. They can say anything and we have no way of answering back. We hate to say anything or to do anything because everything we do is twisted. If someone lies about us it is put on the first page in big print. There are lies and misinformation and then action. Action against us always comes before investigation. If the American government is honest, if the American people are honest, why don't they investigate what is said before acting? By the time the truth is known something has been done to us. We never know what is coming next. We have no peace of mind. Every few months it is something else.

When we were put here we thought that we'd be here just a few weeks and then would be allowed to go out. When we found out that that wasn't so and that we were all going to be treated like enemy aliens, we thought that we would be allowed to stay here in peace as neutrals during the war. We didn't expect all this haggling with the government. We didn't expect that the people would be split and bothered by one request and proposition after another. We didn't expect fights over self-government, registration, volunteering, relocation, and now segregation. Haven't these people been tortured enough. Do you know how many are going to Tule Lake to put an end to this once and for all, to get a little peace of mind?

I don't know Japan. I'm not interested in Japan. That's another thing that worries me. I don't know what will become of me and people like me if we have to go to Japan. The only thing that might save us is that most of us have our old parents still alive. If we were third generation and were entirely cut off from Japan we might not be able to make it. But if they are still alive we can go with our old parents. In Japan they respect the old people and, therefore, for their sake they may treat us well. There isn't much for our family in Japan but at least there is something. My father was a younger son.

When his father died and the family estate was divided, his share was small. Rather than take it he left it with his older brother and came away. That's why he came to America. But his share is still there and it's the only thing in the world he has left. Naturally he thinks of returning to Japan after the war now and thinks that his brother can help him. He doesn't tell me what to do but I know what he wants me to do about this answer. I can sense it from the way he talks.

My dad is 58 years old now. He has been here 30 years at least. He came to this country with nothing but a bed roll. He worked on the railroads and he worked in the sugar beet fields. If I told you the hardships he had you wouldn't believe me. I owe a lot to my father. Everything I am I owe to him. All through his life he was working for me. During these last years he was happy because he thought he was coming to the place where his son would have a good life. I am the only son. I have to carry on the family name. You white people have some feeling like this but with us it is greatly exaggerated.

I tell you this because it has something to do with my answer about that draft question. We are taught that if you go out to war you should go out with the idea that you are never coming back. That's the Japanese way of looking at it. Of course many in the Japanese armies come back after the war, just like in all armies, but the men go out prepared to die. If they live through it, that's their good luck. I listen to white American boys talk. They look at it differently. They all take the stand that they are coming back, no matter who dies. It's a different mental attitude.

In order to go out prepared and willing to die, expecting to die, you have to believe in what you are fighting for. If I am going to end the family line, if my father is going to lose his only son, it should be for some cause we respect. I believe in democracy as I was taught in school. I would have been willing to go out forever before evacuation. It's not that I'm a coward or afraid to die. My father would have been willing to see me go out at one time. But my father can't feel the same after this evacuation and I can't either.

I suppose you know that if there is one thing the Japanese respects, it is integrity. I have to tell the truth. If these questions were just man-to-man talk, it might be all right to say "yes." But if it is put down as a record, I want it to be just what I feel. If I feel one per cent different I don't want to say "yes." That's how hard it is for us to answer that question.

This integrity in the main thing to me. I want to know where I stand. In Japan if a man is peaceful and cooperates, if he does not bother his neighbors, they let him alone. Even if he is a little queer, they let him alone. But when a man disturbs the peace, and refuses to cooperate, when he interferes with his neighbors, they really get after him. The whole village rises against him and they have no place for him. That's what these people cannot understand. They were behaving themselves; they were cooperating with others. Yet the American people have turned against them. Even if they were a little different in some ways, there was no cause for it. The people don't understand it. These Japanese would have been the most peaceful group in the country and the most cooperative if they had been left alone instead of being badgered in this way.

I have thought about this. I worry a lot. My father does not worry much; I worry for both of us. I thought I would tell some of this to the board. But I have never met people like that before. I can't find the words. They are busy and have many cases. And me I did just what all the others do—I just gave the surface, not what's deep underneath. But because we don't talk about it much doesn't mean that we haven't been worrying about it; I'm sick right now. Right now while I've been talking to you I've had a cramp in the pit of my stomach.

There has been nothing but trouble and division of these people from the beginning as a result of evacuation. This segregation is only carrying it farther. In December we had serious trouble. It had nothing to do with the anniversary of Pearl Harbor or with sympathy for Japan as the papers said. It was about supplies for the people of this camp which were being stolen. When someone found it out they tried to push him around. His friends stuck by him and there was a real explosion. How did Tanaka and these fellows associated with the J.A.C.L. get mixed up in it? When a mob forms they'll go after anyone they've got a grudge against. You can't control them. They had plenty against Tanaka, Slocum, and that bunch. They say that they were the ones who led the people to these camps; who advised them to believe all the promises that were made. Some said they were paid by the government to do this. After they got the people here they were accused of being stooges for the government, of being informers. How true all this is I don't know; I'm just telling you what people believed. I do know that this bunch was the first to agree to evacuation and told the people to trust the government and come to places like this. When the people realized what evacuation meant to them, they turned against this bunch and all their bitterness and resentment came out on them.

This evacuation and the way we live here causes trouble in the family too, and trouble between parents and children. Before, if a boy liked a girl he would try to see her once in a while. Even if a boy and girl were just about engaged he probably would not see her more than four times a week. Now if a boy gets interested in a girl he sees her all the time. He eats every meal with her. He hangs around the place where she works. The two don't think of anything else. The old people don't like this; they feel that conditions like these break down morals and proper behavior but they have no control over the situation. I'd like to marry; I get lonely. And I don't want to go around wolving like some of those fellows either. But the future is too uncertain. I'm not going to do anything until I see where I'm going to be, and what the future is going to be like.

In religion our family is Buddhist. I don't make too much of this. I believe that when you get down to the central part every religion stands for much the same thing. But they say this about those who change from Buddhism to Christianity lately and I notice that it is true. The ones who do something wrong, who get into trouble, are the ones who change. They become Christians and then they say that the past is all wiped out and they don't have to worry about what they did in the past. There is one part of the Bible they depend on, the part that says "Forgive the transgressors." They take this literally and hang on to it, but they don't pay much attention to the rest of the Bible.

I appreciate this talk with you. But my mind is made up. I know my father is planning to return to Japan. I know he expects me to say "No" so there will be no possibility that the family will be separated. There isn't much I can do for my father any more; I can't work for him the way I used to. But I can at least quiet his mind on this.

The following extract is taken from a report on life in the Tule Lake Relocation Center in northern California, as prepared by the Community Analysis staff there. Its basic thrust is disillusionment, loneliness, lack of wholesome community activities, and factional conflicts among the Nisei residents at Lake Tule.

When the news of segregation to Tule Lake first broke, many Nisei took this as good news, a welcome change from the old camp.[12] Of course, those with fond attachments were reluctant to leave, but on the whole the idea of a new camp was novel. The trip was even eagerly awaited.

The name, Tule Lake, itself lent a note of enchantment, especially to those in the arid desert camps of Arizona. Visions of a watery vastness where swimming, fishing, and other water sports could be enjoyed boosted the morale of many Nisei. And then there were the winter sports! Those with friends in Tule Lake received glowing letters about the camp, ice skating, skiing, and sledding. The weather was described as ideal and similar to that of a Californian coastal town. Another intriguing point was that Tule had no mud, for the soil soaked up the rain immediately. Photographs displayed by the Social Welfare Department added much to the attractiveness of Tule Lake; the shot of a mixed group of Nisei enjoying sledding down a snow-covered slope was particularly appealing.

Counteracting this propaganda to some extent were rumors that soldiers patrolled each block and that each block was fenced in with a ten-foot barbed-wire fence. But these rumors were discounted as having been started by the Caucasian personnel to encourage the borderline "double no's"* to change their answers.

---

* Editor's note: Evacuees were asked during registration whether (1) they promised allegiance to the United States, and (2) would serve in the armed forces wherever sent. Those who answered "no" to both questions are popularly referred to as the "No-no's."

12 Reprinted from "Nisei Report on Their Adjustment to Tule Lake," in *War Relocation Authority*, Community Analysis Notes No. 7, December 20, 1944, pp. 1–3.

The actual change to Tule Lake itself was disappointing and disillusioning. The first impression was that the entire camp in spite of its thousands of inhabitants looked gray and desolate. The absence of trees or shrubs of any kind added to the feeling of loneliness created by the appearance of the camp. This was especially noticeable to the segregants from the camps in Arizona and Arkansas where trees, greenery, and neatly kept gardens were the rule rather than the exception. The barracks looked filthy and dirty. The patchwork construction of the many ramshackle porches recalled a shanty town.

The rooms also were disappointing. Double floors and plaster-board walls sounded like heaven to the Postonians who were accustomed to bare walls and no ceiling. The walls and ceiling, however, were smudgy and the floors full of splinters. In mopping, one would end up with half the mop-head sticking to various places in the floor.

Former Tuleans seemed indifferent and even bitter toward the new segregants. With people from each center located helter-skelter throughout Tule Lake, the period of readjustment was a long one.

Why did Americans react so furiously against the Issei and Nisei Japanese while manifesting only a relatively mild degree of feeling against German-Americans and Italian-Americans? Bill Hosokawa, himself the son of Japanese immigrants, explores the answer to this pertinent question in the following selection. Hosokawa gets to the root of the ethnic problem of the Oriental in America.

In seeking to analyze the reason why reaction against Japanese Americans was so intense, some observers have noted that Germany had Hitler and Italy had Mussolini, both figures that were easy to hate and easy to caricature.[13] These caricatures could not be linked with German Americans or Italo Americans. But there were no such handy targets in Japan for America's patriotic ire. Tojo and Hirohito were virtually unknown to the American public. They had not appeared larger-than-life on American newsreel screens, ranting and posturing in front of phalanxes of uniformed henchmen. So an old stereotype was dusted off and the Japanese enemy pictured as a buck-toothed, bespectacled, monkey-faced sneak, a hateful racial canard that was easily applicable to the Issei and Nisei. Their racial homogeneity ("They all look alike to me," two generations of whites had complained without really trying to see individuals) made them perfect subjects for stereotyping. The physical characteristics of the Japanese made it simple to segregate them, just as with the Negroes. And in the stereotype mold, a Nisei instantly became a "Jap," no matter how many generations his family had been separated from the old country, no matter how wide the cultural and ideological gap that had been opened between him and his ancestral land. The

[13] Reprinted by permission of William Morrow & Company, Inc., from *Nisei: The Quiet Americans* by Bill Hosokawa, pp. 247–49. Copyright © 1969 by Bill Hosokawa.

caricature of the Japanese enemy was identifiable as the schoolboy, the vegetable farmer, the gardener and corner grocer in military uniform. Not so with Germans and Italians. Like other elements of the racial potpourri that is America, they came in many shades of white, in many suit sizes, their noses hooked or straight with their hair ranging from blond to darkest brunette. In the melting pot they quickly became indistinguishable. Morton Grodzins points out additionally that the German enemy (Nazi) and Italian enemy (Fascist) would be distinguished verbally from Germans and Italians in the United States, "but no such convenient nomenclature existed for the Japanese. In most public discussions both citizens and enemies were 'Japs.'"

Caught napping and humiliated at Pearl Harbor, albeit by a dishonorable act, it was only human for Americans to point the finger of righteous anger at the treachery of the Jap in an effort to lighten the weight of their own culpability. And in an environment where anti-Oriental racism had been a seldom-questioned tradition —comparable to the Deep South's attitude toward Negroes—and a way of successful political life, it was inevitable that the racial stereotype should be projected onto the Issei and Nisei and their loyalty loudly challenged. On the West Coast this was as predictable as a knee-jerk is to the stimulus of a rap with a rubber hammer. There were whites who honestly believed they were helping to win the war by throwing a brick through the window of a Japanese grocery store or firing a shot from a speeding car into the home of a Japanese farmer; their mentality was little different from the sheeted and hooded night riders in the Deep South. After Pearl Harbor the Issei who had experienced the West Coast's racism feared the worst. The Nisei, too young as a group to be aware of the past, were less disturbed by the darkening clouds.

Their youth and immaturity was another key factor in the inability of the Nisei to stand up and be recognized as loyal Americans. Their parents for many reasons had kept largely to themselves and were little known outside their segregated communities. The Nisei had gone to school with white children, played ball with them, visited in their homes, but they were still strangers to the men in positions of authority and influence. There were too few Nisei like Tom Yatabe. Literally and figuratively, the Nisei had no Joe DiMaggio whose baseball brilliance all but obliterated the fact of his Italian immigrant heritage. No one would dream of suspecting Joe DiMaggio's father, much less the great Yankee Clipper himself, of disloyalty toward the United States even though the elder DiMaggio was an alien. (One small but significant point needs to be made: Unlike the Issei, the elder DiMaggio had the privilege of naturalization. Up to 1941 he had not chosen to exercise it.) Yet the vast preponderance of Issei and Nisei were no less loyal than the DiMaggios, father and son.

Social psychologist Harry H. L. Kitano of the University of California in Los Angeles has studied the Japanese-American subculture in the context of American civilization. He based many of his conclusions on personal interviews with Japanese-Americans. The following account describes the discrimination against and eventual acceptance of a Nisei in the teaching profession.

> Today the Japanese have made rapid progress in the teaching field.[14] A successful Nisei teacher told us:
>
>> When I came to UCLA (1936) I had to pick a college major so I chose elementary education. I always wanted to be a teacher, so even when they told me there would never be a job for me, I went ahead to work for my teacher's certificate. Actually, some of the other girls were in sociology, or economics and they'd never be able to get a job either. So I guess you can say we were all even.
>>
>> After I got my degree in 1940, I didn't even look for a job in teaching since there were no openings for Japanese. Soon after, I was evacuated. While in camp, they needed teachers very badly and somehow or other, they knew I had teacher training and the state sent over a teaching certificate. So I taught for several years in camp—when I relocated to Idaho, that state kept after me to teach.
>>
>> I came back to California in 1946 and tried to find a teaching job. It was still discouraging but I stuck to it and finally landed a position. I still remember that first day . . . as I was walking into the teachers' lunchroom, one of the teachers said in a voice loud enough so that I could hear, "Look who we're hiring now, we really must be hard up."
>>
>> It wasn't a pleasant situation but I knew I could teach and my experiences in camp helped out. Now that I look back on it, I always wanted to teach, I finally got the opportunity, and I'm glad I stuck it out.

From his own private interviews with Japanese-Americans, Professor Kitano found that the Sansei (third-generation Japanese born in the United States) faced the real problem of alienation simultaneously with their acceptance into the larger community. A Sansei high school student on the West Coast expressed the social gap between the oriental and western cultures.

> The loneliest time for some of us is the Easter recess.[15] We're pretty well accepted in the classroom and some of the social and athletic groups. But it gets kind of hard at Easter; most of the guys and gals (white) take off for Newport or some place like that. . . . There are two problems. One is I don't know whether my parents will let me go. But the main problem is what would happen if I went. One Sansei went with a (non-Japanese) group last year and he told me he felt left out on certain things. . . . He didn't have a good time so he's not going this year. . . . But, I don't want to go out with an all-Japanese group either.

[14] Reprinted from Harry H. L. Kitano, *Japanese Americans: The Evolution of a Subculture*, © 1969, p. 56. Reprinted by permission of Prentice-Hall, Inc., Englewood Cliffs, N.J.

[15] Ibid., p. 97.

THE FILIPINOS

Compared to the Chinese and Japanese, the Filipinos were late arrivals to the United States. But the pattern of treatment they received was essentially the same, complicated only by their Spanish origins and United States' possession of the Philippine Islands. The following descriptions of their ethnic experiences touch upon the following: the position of Filipinos in the United States; state laws forbidding marriage between Filipinos and Caucasians during World War II; mistreatment by police; the high caliber of work performed by Filipino workers; and Americans' tolerant attitude toward and treatment of Filipinos after World War II.

The demand by various labor organizations, patriotic groups such as the American Legion, and finally the California state legislature for exclusion of Filipino immigration prompted a study of this ethnic group from the Pacific. Bruno Lasker collected extensive firsthand data while analyzing the status of the Filipino immigrants on the American mainland. Below, Lasker summarizes the many problems experienced by the Filipinos.

No attempt has been made in the preceding pages to depict those problems which all immigrant groups, in their first phase of contact with the special conditions of a new country, have to meet.[16] Whether due to the lack of facilities in virgin territory or to the necessity of adjustment to a fully developed civilization, these problems are inherent in the circumstances and readily recognized by those who have studied the history of migrations. But there are several novelties in this latest large-scale influx. One of them is precisely that it is the latest, that it inherits all the defenses which a people has built up in its institutions and in its attitudes after a period of enormous population mixture from which it is only just emerging into an era of difficult assimilation. As the latest comer, the Filipino encounters checks in national and state laws, in the precedents of discriminatory treatment set by custom, in the prejudices built up by previous race contacts of the dominant group. Thus, a comparison of the Filipino influx with the earlier Japanese wave of immigration is misleading unless one remembers that while the earlier Japanese immigrants, welcomed to this country, were able by their competency to establish a high degree of prosperity which later became an important factor in fortifying the position of the larger group, the Filipinos were not privileged to establish such a pioneer colony that might later take up the advancement and protection of the national group as a whole. The result is a lack of responsible, economically anchored leadership, which constitutes one of the greatest concrete obstacles to the success of the Filipino group in America as a whole.

The Filipino immigrant is further handicapped by the distance

[16] Reprinted from Bruno Lasker, *Filipino Immigration to Continental United States and to Hawaii*, pp. 333–36. Copyright © 1931 by Edward Clark Carter. By permission of the University of Chicago Press.

of his homeland, which necessitates considerable sacrifice, on his own part or that of his family, before he can make the expensive trip, and usually lands him at his goal without further resources. This distance also makes impossible a rapid adaptation of the current of emigration to the employment conditions in the receiving country and prevents the return of those who, either for personal reasons or because of a choked labor market, find it difficult to make a living.

The limitations of the Filipino are partly physical and partly cultural. His smallness of stature makes him unsuitable in the eyes of employers for work requiring hard muscular exertion. Bad dietary habits often render him much weaker than organically he need be. Overcrowding, the frequenting of smoke-filled poolrooms and insufficient sleep also impair his physical efficiency. Mentally, the Filipino worker is alert enough to take his place beside other national groups; but his vocabulary usually is limited and, unless a Filipino foremanship should grow up from among the more experienced workers, employers have difficulty in handling this class of foreigners.

Against the Filipino's chances in competition for work are further his temperament (sometimes) and his reputation. While as an individual the Filipino is considered docile, he often finds himself barred from employment because of the assumption that, as a group, Filipinos are temperamental, prone to take offense easily and to walk out on an employer at small provocation, quarrelsome among themselves and revengeful when considering themselves injured. Moreover, employers, especially in small and rural communities, are influenced more largely by non-economic motivations than in large cities and industrial plants: It is sometimes considered unwise to employ Filipinos where there are women around or where their work may be regarded as in competition with that of white Americans, even when there are no complaints on either score. Again, in the hotel and restaurant trades and retail business, employers are obliged to consider the prejudices of their patrons; and Filipinos find themselves debarred from promotion to positions as waiters or salesmen even when their own employer would consider them qualified and desirable.

Like other newcomers, Filipinos find themselves the victims of many forms of exploitation—by labor agents and contractors, by foremen and straw bosses, by venders of goods and of transportation, by gamblers and racketeers. Ignorance of work opportunities, of their rights when employed, of means to gain legal redress, of prices and charges, of the functions and duties of officials, of American customs; often a childlike faith in the printed word or misplaced confidence in a countryman, romantic hero-worship, inability to resist argument when couched in flamboyant terms—all these handicaps make it difficult for the Filipino immigrant worker to prosper and to realize his economic ambitions on coming to the American mainland. Moreover, he does not know how to avail himself of such protection as American community organization and state legislation afford.

But there are other difficulties not shared by earlier immigrant groups. The permanent settlement of the Filipinos is feared; and this fear reacts against them. In vain do they point out that they have not come here to stay and settle. Just because they are ever conscious of the temporary nature of their stay, they find it harder than those who come for permanent residence to make those adjustments of habits and tastes that would ensure a rapid assimilation.

This statement may seem contradicted by the actual ease with which Filipinos seem to adopt American ideas; but observation here is often at fault: The tastes and notions which the Filipino immigrant endeavors to express through his mode of living are those of his own country with its long history of Spanish cultural domination, modified, to be sure, by an aggressive North American impact during the last thirty years. A bird of passage, the Filipino in his attitude to American life is comparable with other transients rather than with those who come here to settle and throw in their fortunes with native Americans. This makes for a certain aloofness which is only partially disguised by the Filipino's desire for social recognition and the company of American men and women. He wishes to learn from these contacts, not to become one of us.

Closely linked with these conditions, there is the Filipino's youthfulness—, or, if you will, immaturity. This is not merely a matter of age composition of the Filipino group, which is lower than that of any other wave of immigration this country has ever had. Employers, college deans, social workers and public officials frequently comment upon the seeming inability of Filipinos, well in the higher twenties and in the thirties, to take a responsible attitude toward their obligations to others. More specifically we have found, in the preceding pages, as militating against the Filipino's success as an immigrant the absence of a normal home life, the excessive mobility that prevents the formation of close ties within a community, even within his own national group.

Bad housing conditions, limitation of vocational opportunities, exposure to unscrupulous profiteers, especially of their own nationality, ignorance of their legal rights and obligations, the general neglect of the community—these are evils which every newly arriving group of immigrants has had to face. In the case of the Filipinos they are aggravated by lack of experience and the absence of those checks which a normal age- and sex-composition place upon individual recklessness. The very adventurousness which makes it possible·to suffer temporary misfortune, in the case of the Filipinos, is producing an unusual crop of evils; it encourages an instability which stands in the way of those opportunities which only the growth of a reputation for sustained effort opens to newcomers. Thus criticism by employers and by teachers helps to give substance to the inevitable popular verdict that the newcomers are "undesirable."

The Filipinos as an ethnic group were subjected to many indignities by the police in California during the 1930's. If they were seen on the streets at night, they were immediately under suspicion; police stopped them, questioned them, and often jailed them for no concrete reason. Manuel Buaken, a Filipino who came to the United States as a divinity student, describes these degrading experiences in the following extract from his book, *I Have Lived with the American People.*

It was 1935, and the hot California summer night registered the high temperature of ninety degrees and felt as if it was one hundred.[17] I had just gone out to escape the smothering heat in Dr. A. F. Ryan's apartment, where I worked as a houseboy. I was strolling along back of the house when a police car entered the alley at the south side, pulled to a stop, and the two policemen grabbed me by the arms, "Hey, what are you doing here?" queried one burly officer.

"Why I am taking a stroll, after I got through working. I live at the house with my boss, Dr. A. F. Ryan," I answered.

"Where, what house?" demanded the stubborn officer.

"This house at number 624 South New Hampshire. My boss is at home. I am sure it is not bad to take a walk. I have worked for him for eleven years. Go and inquire of him if you are not satisfied," I once more answered.

"Well, move along, you appear like a questionable and suspicious character," he snarled at me.

A week later, I was out again in the same alley taking a walk, and again two policemen, different men this time, accosted me. And again I had to go into the same tedious questioning and exonerating as I had under the same insinuations as previously.

That night when I returned home to my room I told my employer of the incident. He got so angry that he called the police captain and told him how rude the policemen were to me. He said he was going to do something about it, if those policemen ever tried to pull the same trick again. "I live in a respectable neighborhood, and the boy working for me goes to college," Dr. Ryan informed the police captain.

Near Loews' State Theatre, Seventh and Broadway, Los Angeles

It was 1936. I had just emerged from the Loews' State Theatre at Seventh and Broadway, after seeing a late picture show. It was 1:00 A.M., and I was standing at the corner waiting for a streetcar, when two policemen came up, asked why I was out so late, and tried to arrest me. "I work until 9:00 P.M., and when I went to the theater it was already 10:00 P.M. The picture I had just seen was a double feature and both were long, so when I came out it was already 1:00 A.M.," I said in a humble and controlled voice. Not yet satisfied, with my story, the officers searched me all over. They took my pocketbook and emptied its contents. They searched my pockets. All they found was a five-dollar bill and thirty cents in loose change, a student-body card, a church-membership card, and the half of the fifty-five cent ticket, which the theater usher gave me.

"Well, all right, come on, move along," they said. I was very lucky they did not club me in the head, or take me to jail.

Buaken then disputes the canard that Filipinos threatened the economic security of American workers. The low wages they accepted for menial tasks which the usual American worker refused enabled them to

[17] Reprinted from Manuel Buaken, *I Have Lived with the American People,* Caldwell, Idaho—The Caxton Printers, Ltd., pp. 89–90.

perform essential tasks conscientiously while earning the respect of their fellow employees.

A personal experience shows quite clearly how true it is that Filipinos are no competition to white labor.[18] It happened in the year 1930, when white workers haunted the employment agencies of Los Angeles, saying they were desperate for "any honest work."

I sat in an employment agency located on Broadway in .downtown Los Angeles—I sat in a corner and observed. On the blackboard in front of me were written all kinds of jobs—from dishwashing to cooking—jobs calling for help. I listened as the phone rang, and heard at least fifteen calls for a dishwasher, ten for bus boys, three for porters, five for pantrymen, and two for cooks. The agency dealt with both Americans and Filipinos. And I saw that Americans were willing to take cooking jobs with wages of fifty dollars a week, and that they left to the Filipinos the dishwashing, bus boy and porter jobs, where wages averaged about eighteen dollars a week, with board only. Throughout the day, the businesses which needed help kept calling for the agency to send, "as soon as possible," a dishwasher, bus boy or porter. Throughout the day I heard the white applicants for work, at least two hundred of them, turn down these jobs. They didn't even like the cooking jobs if they paid only twenty-five dollars a week. None of these people who were desperate for work would accept a dishwasher, bus boy or porter job at those wages.

I, too, wanted a job that paid living wages. But at length I took what I could get—a dishwasher job.

So I have seen the ways in which selfishness and discrimination have sinned against the ideals of American democracy and of equal opportunity for equal work—those ideals that were such wonderful promises when America came to the Philippines.

In apartment work, Filipino labor is also preferred by employers as against Mexican, Negro or white workers. The reason for this is well told by a typical apartment manager, Mrs. Gaffney, who has ably conducted the Lynwood Apartments for eleven years. She said, "I would never use any Mexican in apartment work for they are not very clean; the Negroes are all right, but they cannot be relied upon and trusted, and the whites just never will work steadily. I always employ Filipinos, for I have found that they are better adapted to this type of work than any other group." . . .

Mrs. Rhea, manager of the Coffield Manor, Los Angeles, a fine, big, fashionable place, says: "The longest time a white janitor ever worked for me was six months. A Negro a year. I don't want to try Chinese or Japanese. Libby, the first Filipino who ever worked for me, is still in my employ, has been here now for nine years. And the other helper, George, has been with me for seven years. Since I have had Libby working for me, I have never employed anyone but Filipinos."

Mrs. Rhea is a lovely, kind lady. She told me that after Libby, short for Liberato, had worked for her three years, he told her he was quitting to go home to the Philippines. She was glad to

[18] Ibid., pp. 189–91.

release him for such a reason. But after a year or so, someone told her he was still in the city. Libby, himself, had wanted to quit to find a job with better pay, and to avoid hurting the feelings of Mrs. Rhea, had made up a fictitious reason—this is the instinctive way of a Filipino—to take a way that is courteous, even though the truth may be stretched a little. So she went to the length of contacting the members of the Apartment Managers' Association, and asking them to locate Libby for her. When they did, she asked him to come back to work for her, and this time in an easier job with a raise of fifteen dollars a month. Libby took the offer and has been there for many years now, realizing that Mrs. Rhea has been exceptionally considerate and good to him, and he expects to repay her by continuing there indefinitely, circumstances allowing.

The laws of the western states that prohibited marriage between Filipinos and Caucasians pointed up one of the cruelest ironies in American history. During World War II the Philippine Islands was a staunch ally much praised in the popular media for its loyalty to the American cause. But certain states restricted Filipino marriages, thereby denying these people their equal rights before the law, to say nothing of making them suffer humiliation. Mrs. Iris B. Buaken, an American Caucasian married to the Filipino Manuel Buaken, relates a poignant account of these restrictive marriage laws, their meaning, attempts to get them changed, and their relation to American democracy.

> Have you heard what the Catholic Chaplain said to the Governor of California?[19] Do you know of the deadlock that has existed for years in California in which thousands of men have been denied the right to marry and told to resort to prostitution? Did you know that of all Christians on the Pacific Coast, only Catholic priests have lifted their voices in defense of the right of Filipinos to have a normal home and family life?
>
> It is a deadlock that has poisoned democracy and Christianity for years. On one side are the Filipinos of the United States— young, loyal Christians brought to this country by the glowing legend of the land of opportunity and equality—in search of education in the modern Christian way. They were not accompanied by Filipino women. The Immigration Service has made that nearly impossible. There is in the Philippines a tradition of inter-marriage. The great leaders of the country have been men of mixed blood— the late President Quezon, Sergio Osmena, President of the Philippines, are good representatives of the vigorous, socially-honored mestizo class. The Filipinos of the U.S. have been firm in their determination to marry here, for economic and social conditions have generally made it impossible for them to return to the Philippines. They are determined not to go home without the training they came here for, and the path of education for Filipinos in the U.S. has

[19] Reprinted from Iris B. Buaken, "You Can't Marry a Filipino," *Commonweal* 41 (March 16, 1945): 534–35. Reprinted by permission of Commonweal Publishing Co., Inc.

been strewn with thorns. Many educational institutions have raised tuitional and other barriers against Filipinos, in specific race discrimination. Filipinos have been determined to marry and enjoy the companionship of decent women. They brought high ideals and Christian up-bringing. They have been attracted to and have attracted many fine white girls.

But California had a race marriage law that prevents the marriage of Filipinos to "Caucasians" on the ground that Filipinos are Mongolians. Resourceful Salvador Roldan successfully disputed this myth in 1933, and forced the state of California to give him a license to marry his white wife.

Immediately the legislature of California passed a law specifically forbidding the marriage of whites and Filipinos.

There has been also great economic discrimination. Filipinos have not been allowed to practice law or medicine in California, or to belong to the majority of unions, or to have skilled industrial employment. They have not been allowed to buy real property so that they could own homes; they have been required to rent in slum districts.

This combination squeeze play has prevented many Filipinos from taking the trip necessary for marriage. So if they are able to win and keep the love of white girls who become their wives, in affection and faithfulness, till death do them part, they have to do so without benefit of clergy or county.

We were among these couples, Manuel and I. My husband is a person of high moral standards, of keenly logical mind, of charm and humor. Sadly for us, we have no children. If we had, we would have made the desperate sacrifice required to get to a state where we could be "married." But "marriage" as a ceremony becomes cynical double-talk and a farcical specimen of legal quibbling under our state regime.

Prostitution, of course, has had no such legal persecution. Organized vice has sent its armies cruising through regions where Filipinos, denied homes and marriage, have been herded together in labor camps. Venereal disease came hand in hand with this state sponsored prostitution.

Our church had nothing to say about all this. Corporal Manuel Buaken, my husband, is son of a Methodist minister. I am a graduate of a Methodist university. The church had for us only ineffectual glares, or angry, or embarrassed stares. One ray of hope! We heard that some Catholic priests were performing Filipino-white marriages in California, that for Catholics they would "go to bat" with the license bureau. But we aren't Catholics, and anyway, we doubted the legal validity of such marriages.

War came. But first came November, 1941, when Filipinos were required to register as aliens, in spite of their years of unwavering loyalty to the U.S. and its ideals, in spite of their status as "nationals" of a country under the jurisdiction of the U.S., in spite of all the golden promises that America took to the Philippines.

Within a few months, Selective Service took them in. This was the achievement of Bataan! In April, 1942, the First Filipino Infantry was activated. Later a second all-Filipino regiment was organized. These Filipino members of the United States Army were made citizens in mass ceremonies. It was a belated legal recognition of what had been true in fact—that they were and are loyal Americans. . . .

Many Filipinos thought citizenship meant equality before the law. They were bitterly disappointed. They were still denied the right to marry, and their right to real property is still in doubt. The Army had their services, their lives to use, but the Army could not give them the service of family allowances or insurance for wives or children. California, Arizona, Utah, Nevada and Wyoming are the saboteur states of this region, refusing the right to marry.

Then Chaplain Eugene C. Noury became the regimental chaplain of the First Filipino Infantry. Its commanding officer is Colonel Robert H. Offley, a man born and raised in the Philippines, a man who feels himself truly a brother of the Filipinos. Finally there was Mr. E. W. Zueger, a Red Cross worker assigned to the First Filipino Infantry—a man to whom the Filipinos demonstrated their eager loyalty by establishing a national record for per capita contributions to the Red Cross, being leaders among all the soldiers of the U.S. Army in this field.

Mr. Zueger began to receive calls for emergency aid to families of Filipino soldiers denied family allowances. At Colonel Offley's request, he made a survey to determine the number of such cases—of unlegalized though true marriages—and found them to be extremely numerous. He learned of the heavy burden of unnecessary worry, of cynicism and of despair, of democracy and Christianity borne by these loyal American soldiers—these Filipinos of the United States Army. So the Red Cross, under the sponsorship of the Army, began its effort to make it possible for Filipino soldiers to make the long trip to some other state—Washington, or New Mexico, to be "married" to their white wives. The Red Cross made loans for funds needed, and asked the Army for emergency furloughs for such Filipino soldiers. My husband and I were among these couples, and we are very grateful to those loyal Americans who made it possible for us.

World War II had a profound effect on the attitude in the United States toward various ethnic groups. Americans realized that the ideals for which they fought had not been carried out at home, and American treatment of the Filipinos, and other ethnic minorities, underwent dramatic change. A noticeable improvement in the treatment of Filipinos after World War II is recounted in the following.

The change of attitude toward the Filipinos in the Philippines is a dramatic story brought forth by this war.[20] Likewise in America there took place the same change of attitude of the American people toward the Filipinos in the United States.

The war has promoted a new justice in treatment of the Filipinos in both the negative and positive happenings.

In the negative happenings—there is a complete stoppage of

[20] From M. Buaken, *I Have Lived with the American People,* pp. 322–24.

publicity that sneers at and ridicules us. No more merchants of hate parade their stuff in big weeklies. No more learned sociological studies purporting to show the great superiority of other racial groups, such as the Japanese over the Filipinos as components of American life, as candidates for citizenship. In fact I can't cite you an example of race-hatred inciting publicity directed against Filipinos since Pearl Harbor, where there used to be floods of such to plague and torment and destroy us, and to destroy American democracy.

In the positive happenings, there is something intangible in the air that says that America has learned to respect us. No longer on the streetcar do I feel myself in the presence of my enemies. We Filipinos are the same—it is Americans that have changed in their recognition of us. We always wanted nothing more than to learn from America, to become good Americans. We have developed no great banks here in the United States—our savings have gone into American banks. We have patronized American stores—not stores devoted to the selling of products from across the seas. We have striven to learn English, not to perpetuate foreign language schools and to teach foreign ideas to our children.

Signs of America's new respect for us are many. The radio has been open to us—various programs have featured Filipino speakers—something they never did before. Women's clubs and civic organizations have invited Filipinos to be their guest speakers. They never did that before. Mrs. Pilar Lim, wife of Brigadier General Lim, the Filipino general under MacArthur, is kept busy explaining to Americans the Filipino point of view in this present crisis. Maria Dayoan, a young Filipina missionary worker from the Philippines and a refugee from the Japs in northern Luzon has a weekly speaking engagement in the various churches in the west coast. Manuel Buaken received four invitations to speak in men's civic organizations after he spoke at the Jonathan Breakfast Club, Los Angeles. Similar events all over the United States are taking place, with Resident Commissioner Joaquin Elizalde filling numerous speaking engagements in New York, Chicago, and Philadelphia.

The interest in the press for Filipinos is something new in the experience of Filipinos in America today. Just as the Japs invaded the Philippines, the Los Angeles Daily News asked me to cover certain aspects of the war in the Philippines. I wrote five articles for this paper. The *Christian Science Monitor* asked me for three articles which I wrote for this publication. I have also received numerous requests to write articles from other magazines.

Streams of articles, stories, in practically all American magazines and newspapers, explaining, admiring, and interpreting things Filipino.

The beginning of the change in discriminatory laws against Filipinos has come. In the land laws, the Filipinos can now buy farms and become farmers, without jealousy of their white neighbors. And today in the Imperial County alone there are five hundred Filipino farmers stopping on the vacated farms of the Japs.

Agitation for citizenship of Filipinos is being carried on now by Americans, whose sense of justice has finally come on to play this subject.

The employment of Filipinos in offices of the Federal government is a decided change from our former status of being excluded from all such skilled work by being excluded from citizenship.

"Yes, sir, we Filipinos will win this war," exclaimed Dr. Glenn Dayton, when a group of distinguished doctors had expressed fears and doubts about the chances of America in the Pacific theater of war.

KEY QUESTIONS

1. Was there any difference between the acceptance and treatment of the Chinese and that of the Japanese when they originally entered the United States?

2. No-Yong Park stated in 1934: "Race prejudice is probably one of the ugliest scars on American civilization." Do you agree? What evidence does he provide?

3. Define the following: Issei, Nisei, Sansei.

4. Why were Japanese-American citizens placed in internment camps at the beginning of World War II? Can such action be justified militarily and constitutionally?

5. Cite the basic ethnic experiences the Filipinos encountered in the United States.

5

East Central Europeans— New Immigrants

As far as significant numbers are concerned, the story of the immigration to America of the Slavic, Magyar, Lithuanian, and Jewish groups from East Central Europe and the Russian Empire begins at about the year 1865. Accuracy, however, also demands at least a brief mention of their existence on the American scene long before that year. Almost as soon as the Colonial Period opens, there are indications of the presence of people from Europe's eastern borderlands among the vast majority originating in its western parts.

. For example, there were some Polish craftsmen and artisans at Jamestown. The records also show that when the franchise was extended to the colonists in 1619 it was at first not extended to the Polish inhabitants, who protested until it was. Among the so-called "Pennsylvania Dutch" and others who belonged to the small sects which had fled persecution in the Old World, there were Czechs and Moravians, as there were Slavic Protestant refugees in New Sweden and New Amsterdam. Almost all settled permanently, many intermarried, and a number changed their names or had them changed, perhaps never again to be identified with their original homelands.

East Central Europe supplied a share of the foreigners who served the American Continental cause during the Revolutionary War. Often these were adventurer-exiles, such as the Polish Count Casimir Pulaski and his assorted cavalrymen, with such names among them as Kovacs (clearly Hungarian) and Zielinski (also Polish), and his engineer compatriot, Thaddeus Kosciuszko. Their contributions to the American victory were far from minimal, despite a tendency in some historical quarters to heap praise on Lafayette and Steuben and relegate other foreigners to the category of troublesome mercenaries.

In the decades following the birth of the United States, the Eastern and East Central Europeans made up a mere trickle in the stream of trans-Atlantic migration. There were occasional clergymen and a small number of others. In the early 1800's a few Polish veterans of Napoleon Bonaparte's abortive campaign against the Haitians arrived. In 1834 two Austrian vessels arrived in New York and literally dumped on American shores 234 Poles who were veterans of an unsuccessful revolution against Russian rule in 1830 to 1831 and who constituted a potential threat to the Metternich regime in Austria, as well as to other absolute powers in Europe. Other unsuccessful revolutions, climaxed by those of 1848, added immigrants. Quite a number of Czechs, Hungarians, and Poles intermingled with the German "Forty-Eighters" and were "adopted" by them and their later historians.

From their own correspondence, printed in European journals of the time, it is evident that many, if not most, of the exrevolutionaries considered themselves temporary exiles, not immigrants. Their first hopes were of an early return on the heels of new European revolutions. For them, adaptation to the natural and social ruggedness of Jacksonian America was difficult. A few dreamed of setting up enclaves on the American frontier—New Polands, New Bohemias, New Hungaries, and so forth —where their ethnic integrity would be maintained in isolation for succeeding generations. Such dreams hardly ever materialized in the slightest. Eventually they were set aside for more practical things— fraternal organizations and newspapers. The Czechs, who tended to gravitate toward the Midwest with the Germans, pioneered. They had organizations and journals in the 1850's. The Poles, although they tried organizing as early as 1842 (and, to some extent, even before), were less successful. Factionalism carried over from Europe and a general scattering of the Polish population throughout the United States contributed to their failure. The first Polish language newspaper in America began publication in 1863.

Some of these immigrants found careers in medicine, engineering, surveying, cartography, and other fields which required technical skills. Others entered teaching (especially of languages), the arts, and government service. They maintained their individual ethnicity and kept in touch with each other and with exrevolutionaries from other nationalities in America and Europe. Yet, many married American women and raised their offspring in the American liberal Protestant milieu. Several, such as Turchin (a Russian), Krzyzanowski and Karge (Poles), Schoepf (part Hungarian, part Pole), and D'Utassy (a Hungarian), attained at least field grade rank during the Civil War.

Ironically, it was during the Civil War that American-Russian friendship reached its closest point ever. Alone of all major European governments, the czarist regime, for reasons of self-interest, was kindly disposed to Lincoln's Union. In this same period, that part of Poland which Russia ruled erupted in another insurrection that was to be mercilessly put down in 1864. Some of the "foreigners" who were in the Union's service were among those who vainly attempted to defend the Polish cause before an almost totally deafened American public. When a Polish seaman who had deserted a visiting Russian warship and had enlisted in the Union Army was returned to the Russian authorities, Czechs and Poles united and marched on New York's City Hall in protest. There were even suggestions for the formation of a permanent Slavic bloc to participate in American politics and to begin by supporting General John C. Fremont, Lincoln's potential opponent in the 1864 elections. The fire of militancy soon died down, and a Slav unity on American soil was never to be consummated. The individuals who had been thus involved, however, became a link between the American community-at-large and the thousands of their fellow countrymen who were to arrive soon in its midst. A number of them became elder statesmen of the Slavic community who helped the newcomers in their adjustment to America.

Agricultural-populational crises in the homelands and industrialization in the United States accelerated as Eastern and East Central European flow into the tide of post–Civil War immigration. Those who made it up, with the significant exception of the Jews, were mainly peasants repelled by poverty and attracted by economic promise. They arrived with their own linguistic and cultural-religious identities, but not with the political awareness and sophistication of nationalism. They were mainly semiliterate, from submerged nationalities under the rule of the Russian, Austrian, or Prussian Empire.

Austria claimed the lion's share of them: Hungarians (who became political partners of the German Austrians starting in 1867), Czechs, Slovaks (who were distinct as a nationality from the Czechs and who, together with a number of Croats and Rumanians, were directly under Hungarian rule), Poles from the region called Galicia, which also had a Ukrainian (Ruthenian) populace, Serbs, Slovenians, and other South Slavic peoples. Other Poles, Byelo- or "White" Russians, Ukrainians, and Lithuanians were under Russian rule. Still other Poles, as well as such long-absorbed Slavic nationalities as the Wends, Sorbs, and Lusatians, lived within the boundaries of Prussia, which became the nucleus of a united Germany. Together these peoples constituted a complex folk patchwork. The unfortunate Jews, with their own religion and Yiddish culture, were interspersed all over the patchwork; deliberate overcrowding and anti-Semitism, often fostered by the imperial regimes, made them candidates for emigration along with the others.

A pithy summarization of the motives behind the "new" immigration is contained in the expression "after bread," common to almost all Eastern and East Central European vocabularies. As a rule, freedom took second place, and it was usually freedom *from* something, such as military conscription and immobility imposed by social discrimination, rather than freedom *of* such things as religion and expression. They did not feel themselves to be exiles as did their predecessors, but a foremost thought in the minds of many (excluding the Jews) was that of saving enough money to return to the homeland and buy a piece of land on which to settle permanently. The overwhelming majority of the hundreds of thousands of them never did return. Most were fated to spend the rest of their lives in ethnic communities around mills, factories, or mines. Many got their wish of land ownership when they paid off mortgages on homes in such communities. Some began or returned to farming. A small fraction went into business, mainly as tavern owners, undertakers, or owners of small grocery stores; rarely did they venture anything bigger.

The Eastern and East Central European nationality patchwork was virtually recreated on American soil by the immigrants themselves. On the whole, with the exception of a few craftsmen and artisans, mainly Czech, they were unskilled laborers who ended up *en masse* in low positions in industry or in the mines. They then became neighbors to each other, principally because of this factor rather than because of the similarity of their languages, cultures, or customs. Indeed, as soon as they could, they set up their own nationality parishes, organizations, and meeting places. Fusion or amalgamation into permanent multi-ethnic groupings (e.g., Polish-Lithuanian, Slovak-Ukrainian) was rare, rarer than intermarriage. It was more likely to occur in labor organizations than in any other forms of organization. And yet through real or feigned ignorance, native-born Americans, as well as representatives of older immigrant groups often lumped all the newcomers together as if they were nondifferentiable. This tendency was to be reflected in the free use of such terms as "Slavish (pronounced "Sla*h*vish") and "Slavonian" and such epithets as "Bohunk" and "Hunky," which were used to cover all except the Jews, for whom other epithets were reserved.

Since each of the Eastern and East Central European ethnic groups not only had an innate uniqueness but was to develop further in its own way—or at least with unique "twists"—in America, any full study of them would require giving each separate and equal treatment. However, several factors loom as obstacles. One is that some groups are just beginning now to tell their own stories and bring out their own primary documents in English translations. Second, sometimes those who wrote about these peoples earlier in English, treating them either as a "peril" or as "new neighbors," tended to treat them collectively. In this book there are necessary limitations on space. It is hoped, however, that the samplings chosen will give the reader the essence of some of the key common problems faced by the "new" immigrants: their initial shocks, their economic difficulties, the prejudices which they faced, and their organizational and loyalty dilemmas. Of course, it is also hoped that some will give the reader a picture of how they lived their everyday lives.[1]

[1] Generally, see Theresita Poltzin, *The Polish American: Whence and Whither?* (Pulaski, Wisconsin: Franciscan Press, 1973).

A classic among firsthand accounts of the beginnings of the "new immigration" is contained among the journalistic writings of the Polish author and eventual Nobel laureate, Henryk Sienkiewicz. In 1876, Sienkiewicz, who was then 30 years old, came to the United States on a two-year visit. In addition to becoming involved in an experiment in utopian colonization in California, he traveled widely and recorded his impressions in the form of "letters" which he sent to Polish journals. In them, he frequently dealt with the phenomenon of ethnicity in America and expressed pleasant amazement at its seemingly successful existence in American society. For many years, the letters were known only among those who read Polish. In 1959 they were translated, edited, and published. Of particular interest is the thirteenth "letter." It begins with Sienkiewicz's vivid description of typical ocean crossings in steerage. It follows the immigrant's first steps on American soil, notes his puzzlement at his new environment, and decries his exploitation by greedy boarding-house owners. Sienkiewicz summarized the plight of his newly arrived compatriots.

> Their lot is a severe and terrifying one and whoever would depict it accurately would create an epic of human misery.[2] To write or to hear of the days without a morsel of bread when hunger tears one's insides with an iron hand, of the nights spent on the docks under the open heavens, and of the dreams interrupted by the humming of mosquitoes in summer or the howling of the wind in winter, it is easier to feel or to experience these things yourself. Is there anyone whose hand is not against them? Their early history is a tale of misery, loneliness, painful despair and humiliation. Do not think, however, that I am narrating the history of some particular group of Polish immigrants. Not at all! Almost a hundred thousand peasants sent by our land across the ocean have gone through such a Dantean inferno—in search of a better life. The Polish immigrants in America have nothing in common with those living in France or in Switzerland. The latter are political exiles, expelled by revolutionary storms. In American there are practically no Polish political *emigrés*. They are primarily peasants and workers who have come in quest of bread. Thus you will easily understand that in a country inhabited by a people who are not all sentimental, but rather energetic, industrious, and whose competition it is difficult to survive, the fate of these newcomers, poorly educated, unfamiliar with American conditions, ignorant of the language, uncertain how to proceed, must truly be lamentable.

After digressing on the value to America of European immigration and describing the "immigrant homes" where newcomers could stay but

[2] Reprinted from Henryk Sienkiewicz, *Portrait of America, Letters of Henryk Sienkiewicz*, ed. and trans. Charles Morley (New York: Columbia University Press, 1959), pp. 272–273. Reprinted by permission of the publisher.

which the unduly frightened Polish peasants avoided because of their institutional appearance, Sienkiewicz resumed:

And yet, is there nothing that our peasants bring to the New World that might guarantee them a peaceful life and a secure livelihood?[3] Of course there is! They bring with them the habit of being content with little, true peasant endurance, patience and an iron constitution. . . . He does not even comprehend the need for various comforts that the German and French immigrant regard as necessities of life. Sun does not burn him; snow and wind do not chill him. In cold Wisconsin and Minnesota he is not perturbed by the snow drifts; in semitropical Texas, once he throws off the fever, he works in the scorching heat like a Negro. Perhaps he may be less skillful than others, but he has greater endurance and he is a humble and quiet worker.

In a country where areas as vast as the German Empire and France combined still stand vacant, where limitless mineral and agricultural resources merely await exploitation by human hands, where labor is as costly as it is hard to find, our settlers should be assured of success. Unfortunately, they often find the road to success as agonizing as the road to the Cross. . . The Western states, those on the other side of the Mississippi, are still uninhabited. Here there would be room for the population of the whole of Central Europe and from the agricultural and mineral wealth another such civilization could be created. . . . On these frontiers everyone may become a landowner. But our peasant undergoes much suffering before he understands the advice tossed at him so casually in the East: "Go to the Far West and there you will find land and work."

Aside from the fact that one must know of the existence of the Far West in order to go there—and our newly arrived immigrant has no such knowledge—getting there is not easy. The railroad fare alone from New York to Chicago, even by immigrant coach, costs more than the passage from Hamburg to New York. Once having reached the unoccupied land, the peasant needs a plow, ax, scythe, wagon, horse, mule, gun, to protect him from wild animals, seed for sowing—in short, a complete supply of settler's effects. But our peasant, whose last penny was squeezed from him in New York, either cannot go to the Far West, or if he gets there, finds himself solitary and defenseless in the midst of a wilderness. . . . And yet under threat of death by starvation most of the immigrants must leave the overpopulated Atlantic seaboard and move into the interior of the country. . . .

Nowadays the newcomer is better off than formerly. Polish newspapers are now published in the United States that can give publicity to adversity. Organizations exist which have relief funds at their disposal for unexpected disasters. But even today success comes slowly. Before the immigrant is able to earn a decent livelihood, he frequently experiences pain and bitter tears. . . .

As I have indicated, nearly everyone undergoes a similar series of experiences. There is a saying in the United States that he who comes here is critical during the first year, begins to understand

[3] Ibid., pp. 274–79.

the country in the second year, and falls in love with it the third year. I have myself experienced the truth of this saying. As for the Poles who have long resided in the United States, I have only this comment: to an emigrant living in France or in Switzerland you may say what you please about these countries, but it would be dangerous to speak disparagingly of the United States to any Pole residing here. He does not cease to love his former fatherland, but after Poland he loves most the United States.

There is nothing strange about this. A Pole in France remains always an immigrant, while this vast land recognizes him immediately as her own. The new arrival appears before a federal judge and declares that he wishes to become a citizen. . . . The judge reads a declaration on the strength of which the newcomer renounces his former allegiance and any noble privileges he may have possessed—and the whole affair is finished. From this moment forward he is under the protection of the Star-Spangled Banner; he is now at home; he is no longer in a foreign country, but in his own. . . .

Since the cities along the shores of the Great Lakes were undergoing industrial expansion and needed workers, it was principally here that Polish laborers settled. Buffalo, Detroit, Chicago, and Milwaukee are full of them. The chief Polish center is Chicago. . . . In this city of almost a half-million inhabitants there are said to be about 20,000 of our compatriots. The small area occupied by them in the city—a sector sneeringly referred to by the Germans as *Polakei*—leads me to think that this figure is somewhat exaggerated. Most Poles reside along Milwaukee Avenue where they have purchased homes. When I arrived in Chicago at daybreak and visited this part of the city, it seemed at times as though I were in Poland. The morning sun rising from the waters of Lake Michigan illuminated Polish inscriptions and names on the buildings. . . . Doors and windows began to open and . . . the first words I heard were uttered in Polish. A few minutes later I caught sight of the Church of St. Stanislaus Kostka. . . . About eight o'clock in the morning flocks of children began to swarm here on the way to the school maintained by the priests and situated beside the church. Their childish chirping made a strange impression upon me, for despite the fact that these children were studying in a Polish school, an English influence was clearly perceptible in their speech. . . .

The Poles of Chicago are united through Polish societies whose aims are to assist new arrivals, to protect their members from foreign influences, and to preserve their national spirit. There are nine such societies, but seven are purely religious in character. . . . Unfortunately, all of these groups do not always work together, following in this respect, the example of their newspapers, the *Polish Catholic Gazette* and the *Chicago Polish Gazette*. At election time this disunity is harmful to Polish candidates and diminishes the influence that the Poles in Illinois might have in view of their numbers.

Another center where numerous Poles have congregated is Milwaukee, Wisconsin. . . . The number of Poles residing here is supposed to be equal to that of Chicago. Being an older settlement, the Poles of Milwaukee are better off than those living in other towns. They have both an elementary and secondary school. All of their organizations are associated with the Church. . . .

In New York City there are about eight thousand Poles. . . . In addition, Poles in varying numbers reside in all of the larger cities. If they belong primarily to the intelligentsia, they combine in secular societies; if they are peasants and laborers, they unite in church-parish organizations.

Exclusively Polish settlements are to be found at Radom, Illinois; Krakow, Missouri; Polonia, Wisconsin; and Panna Maria, Texas. These are small agricultural towns of several hundred families, possessing their own schools, churches, and local government in the American pattern. Their character is so typically Polish that they scarcely differ from similar towns in Poland itself. Even Jews are to be found in these communities, but not in the same numbers as in Poland, for here they are attracted to the large commercial centers.

At this point, Sienkiewicz digressed on the Polish Jews in America. He found them "generally quite wealthy" and contended that a Polish Jew would "arrive in New York on Sunday . . . open a small business on Monday, and already by Tuesday he will lead into the field the most cunning American who tries to cheat him." Furthermore, he saw the Polish Jew, with his "acuteness, knowledge of the German language, and business initiative," as a daring type who, unlike the peasant, ventured out even to the gold-mining areas where American merchants would hesitate to open shop and by "courtesy, kind words, and, above all, extension of credit" won over the most dangerous of desperadoes. Predicting that within a few years some of the Jews would become millionaires and maintaining that emigration from Poland was more beneficial for them than for the peasants, he returned to the latter and discussed the economics of their existence in America.

Such Polish colonies as Radom and Panna Maria are not purely commercial towns.[4] Their inhabitants occupy themselves chiefly with cattle raising and agriculture. In Illinois, Wisconsin, and Indiana they plant potatoes and sow wheat as in Poland; in hot Texas, they grow corn and even cotton. Although their condition is far from opulent, in fact, rather modest, they are able to satisfy their needs and their earnings are sufficient to build churches, establish schools, and defray municipal expenditures. The older settlers, if they are thrifty, are comparatively well off. A certain degree of prosperity is achieved most easily by those having many children, for in the United States where labor is costly, children are a real blessing for the settler.

In the cities a considerable portion of the Polish population are workers who live on daily wages earned in the factories. They are much poorer than the American, German, English or Scottish workers. When there is prosperity in the United States, however, they earn a better livelihood than they knew in Poland, and the more thrifty among them even achieve some measure of security.

[4] Ibid., pp. 280–81.

In many Polish workers' homes I saw floors completely covered with carpeting as in the American fashion. In the so-called "parlor" or drawing room, there was no shortage of rocking chairs; at dinner beefsteak or meat pudding and beer were served. . . .

The forces linking the immigrants were Sienkiewicz's next topic of discussion. He noted that although there were societies, newspapers, and publications,

> . . . the main force . . . which maintains some degree of moral unity among the Poles is the Church and Polish priests.[5] The Church gathers around itself the leading workers or peasants and is constantly creating new parishes. The priest marries, baptizes, and buries, but above all, teaches. Not only do these functions provide a source of income for the priest, but they also enable him to wield political influence for he controls the votes of his flock. That such a state of affairs may be displeasing to some does not prevent its existence. It is even possible that this preponderance of purely clerical influence engenders a certain exclusiveness and diminishes the size of the Polish-American community by excluding, for example, the Protestants of whom there are many among the Prussian Silesians and Mazurians. On the other hand, one must admit that the Church brings together the Polish masses, creates from them a social entity, does not allow them to become scattered and to disappear among foreign elements, and, finally, the Church provides the only refuge for those new arrivals whose fate I described at the beginning of this sketch. . . .

Sienkiewicz complained that, in spite of the efforts of the clergy, the Poles in the United States were insufficiently organized; they were so scattered that one "colony" knew little about another. Statistics on their exact numbers were either unavailable or frequently padded by newspaper editors who did this either to sell more advertising space or to give themselves political importance at election time.

Sienkiewicz noted that several of his compatriots in Europe had suggested that American Poles be brought into a single territory, but that the American Poles themselves realized that such an objective would be unrealistic. Even the organization of a kind of ethnic parliament to give them unity in public life proved to be an impractical idea. Then, he prognosticated:

> In my opinion, despite the most noble endeavors on the part of their leaders, American Poles will sooner or later become denationalized and be completely assimilated.[6] Stronger elements than the Polish have been unable to resist the influence of the Anglo-Saxon

[5] Ibid., p. 282.
[6] Ibid., p. 288.

language and civilization. No one attempts to Americanize you or force anything upon you. . . .

And yet the American influence is irresistible. Foreigners who come to America and who obtain citizenship live under American laws, take part in public life, and sooner or later transform themselves into Americans in spirit. After that, it is only a matter of time before the acceptance of the English language becomes an inexorable necessity. . . .

Finally, assuring his readers that "emigration fever" would only be transitory with the Poles, Sienkiewicz concluded:

As the number of Polish immigrants in the United States declines, the denationalization of those who came earlier will gain momentum.[7] Furthermore, all immigrant groups are composed primarily of men who, unable to find enough women of their own nationality, take wives from among the local inhabitants. Thus, I am unacquainted with a single Pole, married to an American woman, whose children know the Polish language. I do not exclude even the intelligentsia. This is inevitable. But even if they learn Polish, it will no longer be their mother tongue. Exclusively Polish settlements . . . and especially those founded on the prairie far removed from large cities . . . will hold out longer, perhaps even very much longer, but with the passage of years even these will succumb to the common fate. It should be added that people who are poor invariably come under the influence of those who are rich and the native Americans are richer than the Poles. Thus everything conspires against the best intentions of the Poles. This small segment of the Polish nation will sooner or later by the irresistible force of circumstances became absorbed within the foreign element. A shoot grafted on another trunk is transformed into another kind of tree. . . .

But what of the second, third and fourth generations? What of the children born of German, Irish, or American mothers? Sooner or later they will forget. They will change everything, even their names, which English teeth find too difficult to chew and which interfere with business. How long this will take is difficult to say. . . .

Circumstances were to delay fulfillment of Sienkiewicz's prophecy. For almost four decades following his visit, the supply of first-generation Polish Americans was constantly replenished. Polish neighborhoods remained, solidified, and grew. Attempts were made to unify the entire "emigration" under the umbrella of a national organization. In 1880, mainly at the behest of political exiles, the Polish National Alliance was organized. It was secularly controlled and committed to activism on behalf of Polish independence. Its main attraction for membership lay in the burial insurance which it provided. The Alliance's combination of nationalism and progressivism may be seen in the editorial which appeared in the first issue of its official journal *Zgoda* (Harmony):

[7] Ibid., pp. 290–91.

What Awaits the Poles in America?[8]

Posing this question, we have in mind the many thousands of the Polish people scattered throughout the area of the New World without a link among themselves.

One fact strikes the eye: From amid such a numerous Polish emigration, not only has not a single strong personality emerged to shine forth but also its level has not even reached that of the most oppressed of European people, of the Irish nation.

Thus it is a matter of concern as to the dignity with which the Poles will wear on their temple the crown of American citizenship. Whether they will remain behind the Irish and become mere "voting cattle," whether they will forever crush rocks, dig in the mines, fell timber, drive mules, etc., or whether they will stand on a par with the Germans, Frenchmen and Englishmen in higher callings, in journalism, commerce, politics and the crafts.

The field here is open to all, the most talented will triumph, whatever is incapable, unenlightened and infirm, remains at the bottom, behind. This cannot be helped, it is the necessary result of republican freedom.

Therefore, the answer to the above questions will depend upon the influence which the varied and many Polish organizations in this country will have on the totality of the emigration, for, so long as the emigration does not have command of the English language, they will be the only school in which the Poles arriving here will be able to educate themselves.

But then, we can say that if our emigration will fall under the influence of obscurantism as up to now, under the influence of those who for ages kept our people in blindness, it will never rise above the level of the Irish, and the Polish name will shine with no gleam on this land.

It is necessary first of all that associations of Poles which already exist, bind themselves together into one national whole. Secondly, that the Polish National Alliance use the strength of its great organization to support an organ, a progressive journal, which would enlighten and educate the emigration. It is necessary that every group set up a Polish reading room where more enlightened compatriots would conduct lectures for their brethren. Let past and current Polish affairs be discussed at national commemorations; through such means not only will our emigration uplift its spirit and rise above the unenlightened masses, but it will also fulfill its mission towards Poland to which our free voice will reach, with which our thoughts will meet and join. Through oceans, through thousands of miles, we will send our brothers in the homeland the ideals of freedom and equality of the New World, that will awaken new life within them. They, in turn, will send us the sparks of that holy fire of patriotism, which does not burn out in their hearts but merely smoulders covered with ashes.

The Alliance was challenged soon after its creation by a revived clerically dominated organization, the Polish Roman Catholic Union.

---

[8] *Zgoda,* 21 November 1881.

Instead of being "unified," the American Polish community became polarized. Leaders of the Alliance were given such labels as "nonbelievers," "Masons," and "socialists." In return, politically conservative priests who ran the Union were called "sellouts" or "collaborators" by Alliance spokesmen. In some parishes, readers of pro-Alliance newspapers were threatened with excommunication or denial of sacraments. In one instance, in the Green Bay, Wisconsin, diocese, the excommunicating clergy had the backing of the bishop, who happened to be of German birth. Alliance supporters capitalized on this, likening him to the German chancellor Bismarck and his action to Bismarck's policy of oppression of Poles under German rule.

In some Polish-American quarters the analogy was to be extended to the entire American hierarchy of the Roman Catholic Church. The decree of the 1884 Baltimore Council, which gave bishops title to all property in their dioceses, coupled with the policy of "Americanization" of the church[9] at a time when one out of every eight of the faithful was likely to be either a Polish immigrant or the child of Polish immigrants and when many hundreds of churches and parochial schools had been built by Polish immigrants, provided the fuel for a number of flareups. There were fears of "denationalization" (*wynarodowienie*) and of forced elimination of ethnoreligious customs and traditions brought over from the old country. Sometimes—especially when there was the added disillusionment of an unpopular, heavyhanded pastor—parts of congregations would even secede from episcopal jurisdiction and become "independent."

By the 1890's, some of the "independent" parishes that managed to survive began to form movements. On the appeal of truly owning their churches, allowing a democratic lay voice in governance, and, last but not least, having the only Polish bishops in the United States, the movements made some headway. While condemning the "independents" in the strongest language, the Catholic clergy of the American Polish community were in a tight predicament. The policy of patience urged by the most moderate among them seemed to go unrewarded. Finally they met in their own congresses and delegated representatives to go directly to Rome with petitions for a Polish bishop. Their leading spokesman was the young Father Waclaw Kruszka. Father Kruszka made his debut as an activist with an article which to him seemed to embody a most logical principle. In the New York Catholic *Freeman's Journal* of August 3, 1901, he called for "polyglot bishops for polyglot dioceses," advocating the cre-

[9] They hoped to bring all of their faithful into the same mold, especially as far as language was concerned, so that all would end up using English throughout. Some wanted to go further and eliminate religious customs and traditions brought over from the old country. The bishops advocating "Americanism" were usually trying to erase the stigma of foreignness that American Protestants often leveled against the Catholic Church.

ation of vicars-general to serve particular ethnic groups in dioceses where the proportion of such groups warranted it. His article immediately stirred up severe criticism. Perhaps the epitome of it was expressed in the weekly *Michigan Catholic* of January 16, 1902: "When the time comes that there are Polish-American bishops they will be chosen, not because they represent a single race extraction, but because of their learning, their piety and their true Americanism."

Embittered at this, Father Kruszka became more fiery. In comments to Polish-speaking audiences he spoke of a vicious alliance between chauvinist Masons (the Protestant-owned *Chicago Tribune* had advised the Poles to learn English so that they would not be able to say that "their bishops cannot talk with them") and the Irish, who were able to cloak the church in "Americanism" while running it as their own monopoly. In the comments that he made in English there was less sting but, nevertheless, a frankness which made him a controversial figure. A sample of this is contained in a letter written September 8, 1905, to the editor of the *Milwaukee Sentinel*:

> It is an undeniable fact that although the Irish form only about one-third of the Catholic population, of the hundred Catholic bishops in the United States, almost all are of Irish nationality, a few German bishops being only a drop in the sea.[10] This is a fact, and against a fact there is no argument. From this fact one can easily deduct the conclusion that the Irish want a certain priest for a bishop, just because he is Irish; but how in the world can you show me a single fact that the Poles want the same.
>
> What the Poles in their movement for a Polish bishop want is this: To have bishops from any nationality, and not only from one exclusively as it is practiced at this time. The Irish, as facts prove, presented always and still present candidates of Irish extraction, to the exclusion of other nationalities, as if they alone had the monopoly of wisdom and sanctity and episcopal dignity. Now it is wrong to want a certain Polish, Bohemian, etc., priest for a bishop, just because he is a Pole, Bohemian, etc. It is not even wrong to exclude him from the list of candidates just because he is a Pole, Bohemian. But why do the Irish mostly succeed in Rome? Simply by persuading the Roman authorities that the Irish nationality is the only American nationality—all others are "foreign" nationalities. Of course, one must be narrow-minded to call Americans only those who speak exclusively English, and consider others as "foreigners" just because they, besides English, know how to express their thoughts also in other human languages. The Poles, Bohemians, etc., adopted the language and customs of this country. . . . The Poles, Bohemians, etc., are not worse Americans, therefore, than the Irish. . . .
>
> Starting to immigrate in 1831, already since 1854 the Poles built every year churches, schools, asylums, colleges, etc., paid always faithfully their church taxes . . . in a word, they did their duty

[10] *Milwaukee Sentinel,* 8 September 1905.

as Catholics . . . and during this long period never enjoyed any rights and privileges in the church, never had any representation in the hierarchy. This is evidently unjust and un-American! And now, when we make a just complaint, they say to us that there was not as yet any Bohemian, Polish, etc., priest worthy to become a bishop but as soon as they will find one they will make one. I need not say that this is a poor excuse, and an uncharitable one, not worthy of a true Christian. It is an open insult to the whole Polish, Bohemian, etc., clergy. Were so long the Irish and the few Germans the only worthy [ones] upon whom the Holy Ghost deigned to descend? One must be arrogant to assert this. Indeed, to this privileging of one and the disregarding of other nationalities, we safely ascribe the fact, that there was in the United States no gain but a loss of millions of Catholics. The Independent Polish sect says: "If the Pope allows the organization in the United States of an Irish national hierarchy, why does he not allow the formation of a Polish national hierarchy?" And even pure Americans, I mean those of no denomination, either religious or national, I have heard asking: "Where is the mark of catholicity in your church? Is it not predominantly Irish Catholic?" . . .

The petitions which the Polish-American delegates brought before the papal throne were sidetracked. Their hopes for a champion when the Polish Cardinal Miecislaus Ledochowski became the Prefect of the Propaganda, a position which gave him direct guidance over the technically still-missionary American church, proved fruitless. Indeed, it is probable that the papacy moved cautiously in regard to its American bishops lest they threaten revolt.

Both the bishops and the Polish-American clergy used the "Independents" in their arguments. The bishops could claim that the Poles were by nature troublesome and rebellious, while the clergy could claim that the consecration of bishops from the ranks of the Independents would stir up trouble and rebellion. As the arguing continued, there was a consolidation in the rebel ranks. It occurred under the leadership of Father Francis Hodur, a young priest in the Scranton, Pennsylvania, area. Hodur, unlike Kruszka, defied the authority of a bishop to a point where he and his rebellious parishioners suffered excommunication. Peasant-born himself, Hodur developed a movement with strong appeal for the laboring immigrant who felt especially sensitive to exploitation and injustice. His message was often social and nationalistic as well as religious. It was invariably simple. In his hierarchy of figures to be emulated he included, along with canonized Catholic saints, such pre-Reformation heroes as Hus, Wycliffe, and Savonarola and added Polish patriots and "Messianic" poets who had prophesied Poland's resurrection, among them Adam Mickiewicz and Juliusz Slowacki. He also included George Washington and Abraham Lincoln.

The framework of the new movement was essentially Catholic, but modifications were to be made. Besides abolishing auricular confession for adults and making "the word of God as preached by the Church" a sacrament, the movement accepted the use of Polish rather than Latin in the Mass. The translation was done by Father Hodur himself. Added to the movement's hymnology were several well-known Polish patriotic melodies with new emotion-stirring words written by Hodur.

In 1904, representatives from various "independent" parishes met in Scranton and elected Father Hodur bishop of what was called the Polish National Catholic Church. In 1907, he traveled to Holland, where he was consecrated by bishops of the Old Catholic Church. By virtue of the consecration he could claim apostolic succession in a line going back to the first days of Christianity. One year later, Father Paul Rhode was consecrated the Roman Catholic auxiliary bishop of Chicago. At last, and probably not by mere coincidence in the wake of Bishop Hodur's consecration, a priest from the Polish ethnic group attained a place in the American clerical hierarchy. Others were to follow, but never did their number approach a proportional representation.

Other Eastern and East Central European immigrants also had their share of religious troubles on American soil. Much of it was caused by internecine quarrels over administration (this was especially so in the case of members of various Orthodox denominations). The Ukrainians, Ruthenians, and others who belonged to the Uniate or Greek Catholic rite of Roman Catholicism had some initial struggles with the American bishops to maintain the same autonomy which their rite enjoyed in Europe. The bishops were sometimes averse to their unique practices, especially to their having a married priesthood. Lithuanian Catholics sometimes had three fronts for friction: within their own ranks, with the Roman Catholic hierarchy, and with Polish pastors who were grudging about recognizing their ethnic uniqueness. Eventually, most split off into separate parishes. Where this was made impossible or where internecine quarreling went unresolved, they, too, went "independent," and there was also a separate Lithuanian National Catholic movement.

Just as the Slavs and Lithuanians faced turmoil on American soil on other issues, they were to become involved in some of the most violent labor strife that broke out in the United States in the late nineteenth and early twentieth centuries. The labor area in which they saw some of the bloodiest combat was anthracite coal mining. Already by the 1880's their number in the anthracite region of Pennsylvania was significant enough for them not only to be noticed but to have become at the same time objects of prejudice and potential recruits for union organizers.

The story of the Slavs in anthracite mining, set in the small Pennsylvania "patch," has been reconstructed from a number of sources by Victor R. Greene and incorporated into the opening chapters of his work *The Slavic Community on Strike.* Greene begins:

The typical greenhorn would have alighted from the immigrant train in the Pennsylvania hard-coal region undoubtedly apprehensive if he had not yet met his correspondent.[11] With luck, one or both had a photograph to aid in recognizing the other. Otherwise, the weary traveler at the depot asked or shouted the name of his sponsor. One can imagine the tears of joy on both sides when to the immigrant's call his countryman responded, and their relief was expressed in a demonstrative embrace. . . .

The sponsor then led his charge to a group of shacks usually at the edge of town. This ghetto was separated from the rest of the populace, just as in other places in America where the East Europeans lived. Here in the coal country inhabitants termed the foreign nest the Slavic mining "patch." If he arrived at night, the bundle-laden traveler would have to grope through the darkness, as no street illumination, paved roads or signs (even if he could have read them) facilitated this last, short trip.

Entering one of the houses, the arrival found it in some respects like the peasant cottage in Poland. Although mean, it provided both ethnic comfort and economic security. A countryman and his wife managed the crowded household, which ordinarily included other male boarders as well as the rest of the owner's family. And the newcomer felt even more at home when he discovered that this nucleus of the Slavic-American community even represented specific geographic sectors of the old country. In fact, a similar housing arrangement flourished among all Slavs everywhere. Poles, Lithuanians, and others, who wanted an economical place to live— "trzymanie bortnikow," the boardinghouse system. . . .

The appearance of a patch was not very pleasant. Most of the structures, standing ten feet high and twenty-five feet square, were huddled together on small plots. The grey scrap wood was unpainted, as was the ever-present outhouse a short distance away. The peasants were no architects, and the conglomeration looked like a huge dump rather than a settlement. The hovels had roofs slanting in all directions, with eaves and without, sides of different lengths, and windows of various sizes appearing helter-skelter in the walls. Uneven, fenced enclosures and doors of varying lengths finished the jumble. The shacks not only looked like a large dump but also smelled like one. All about lay mounds of garbage and alley offal. . . .

The appearance of the huts probably gave the non-Slav the picture of chronic poverty. But the inhabitants were not poor; they accepted such conditions for maximum income. . . . The immigrant mineworker spent little of his income on furnishings. Many quarters had neither ceilings nor floors. Like those in the old country, the normal household was spare, with at most a stove, table, chests, and benches. Crowded everywhere were beds, protruding from the walls and giving the impression of a dilapidated dormitory. . . .

The room-and-board costs for new immigrants were universally low. The common method of payment evolved with the growth of the shanty itself. Generally after getting a job, the boarder would give the landlord a certain amount for supplying his bed, food and other services.

In the beginning tenants slept on the floor, contributed funds to a common store, and designated one to buy supplies, do house-

[11] Reprinted from Victor R. Greene, The Slavic Community on Strike (Notre Dame: University of Notre Dame Press, 1968), pp. 40–49. By permission of the publisher.

hold chores, and serve as cook. That arrangement at best was unsatisfactory, but throughout the late 1800's this all-male living existed in the newer settlements. As the communities matured, the growing number of Slavic women considerably eased life for the men. The wife of the boardinghouse landlord aided her mate as a hard-working housekeeper, and she added much to keeping the living expense low for all. . . .

Unfortunately, the fanatic drive to economize forced the immigrant woman into a tragic role; she served her male companions almost as a slave. While her husband collected rent, she cooked, washed and kept house for the tenants, and in addition to these tasks had her own large family to raise. . . .

Part of the reason for desiring many children was the economical help they offered. When very young, they assisted the exhausted mother with chores; and when older, they went out to work. Girls usually got jobs in the local textile mills, while the boys had to labor at the mines. Of course, on payday all Polish American youth were expected to pool their earnings with those of the rest of the family.

Food costs were also kept to a minimum. The meals which the wife prepared cost much less than those of ordinary Americans. The fare had improved over that in Europe, but it was still cheap and monotonous. Cereals and starches, potatoes and bread provided the chief staples; meat appeared on the table often, but the immigrants bought the cheapest cuts and scraps for boiling with perhaps a "green" shoulder of pork. Black bread, coffee, and oily fish completed their menu. Without vegetables in their diet, except for cabbage, they suffered occasionally from deficient nutrition, and scurvy at times swept through their settlements.

One store in Schuylkill County showed the average expense for Slavs to be $2.86 per capita per month, while the Anglo-Saxon paid almost twice that ($5.48). Also, buying at stores run by proprietors of their own nationality may have helped, at least by the turn of the century.

The providential Slav had ways of obtaining food and fuel without paying for them. The former peasants did not hesitate to grow their own food. Despite the small land parcels on which the dwellings stood, almost every East European . . . worked a plot into a vegetable garden. . . . The immigrant also raised livestock, perhaps a cow, a few chickens, or a goat, just as in the old country. . . .

The total cost of living, then, for single Slavs in the anthracite region was undoubtedly low in the last years of the century. About 1890, for example, the average boarder could exist on approximately ten dollars a month.

Of course the Poles, Lithuanians and Slovaks also expended some of their money on other, culturally necessary items, their churches and their saloons. In fact, in a strange land the former peasant first sought security with his fellows by supporting self-help societies. It was these mutual aid groups which organized the parish. . . .

While the earlier arrivals perhaps were most devoted, for all the church remained an object of awe and love. A long walk, perhaps even miles, for the anthracite-area Poles to hear Mass was not uncommon. For the parish was more than a place of worship; it was the center of Polonia, the Polish community . . . and the force that perpetuated *polskosc* (Polishness). Perhaps more than for any other ethnic group, nationality and religion were synonymous; to be Polish meant to be Catholic.

The Poles regarded the individual who symbolized religious-ness, the priest, with profound respect and humility. The authority of this leader in the old country extended far, and both Poles and outsiders reemphasized his power over his flock. The cleric was not just a religious director but a teacher, adviser, and mediator as well. However, if the situation in the anthracite region is any criterion, one priest's influence in nonclerical matters, as labor unrest, was not decisive.

The American parish alone could not replace the primary, self-contained village entirely. There were important differences. Church members came from a broader geographic area than in the old country, and undoubtedly even included non-Poles. In addition, a new force, mutual self-help, had built the parish and was main-taining it in a country which separated Church and state. Still an-other institution was needed to bind the several Slavic nationalities and parishes in a freer social atmosphere, and the saloon filled this need.

Upon leaving church on a Sunday, the Pole may well have gone to this other mainstay of the community. The former peasant, indeed, loved his liquor, and Anglo-Americans did not always ap-preciate his thirst. . . .

But the saloons and the nationality stores served a less obvious function: exchange centers for the ethnic settlements. The proprie-tors, usually German Poles, had been the earliest arrivals, and, see-ing the need for a neighborhood center, they invested in a local establishment. They and their saloons did provide necessary ser-vices, such as holding the immigrants' earnings—the so-called "im-migrant banks"—notarizing papers, forwarding money orders home, acting as transportation agents; affording accommodations, inter-preting and translating, giving generous credit to countrymen, and even writing letters for the illiterate. Their business hours were convenient, and the interested parties conducted negotiations over lager. . . .

The most important function of the anthracite district saloon was as a labor exchange. If the immigrant arrived unsponsored or was just looking for employment, he went to the neighborhood pub-lic house. It was here that foremen and employers knew they could get the eager, unskilled labor they desired.

Greene goes on to detail the working conditions which prevailed among the anthracite miners. He paints a picture whose tones are con-sistently gray:

On the novice's first day of work in the mine fields the housewife would have been up long before the town arose to the six o'clock whistle at the mine.[12] In addition to preparing the breakfast, she usually packed the dinner pails for everyone. She also dressed and fed her children, some of whom themselves may have worked at the mine. If the men were lucky, the railroad company provided free

[12] Ibid., pp. 49–52.

rail or trolley service from the settlement to the workplace. Or it may have charged a small fee. Otherwise the workers walked the two or three miles to get to the mine before seven.

The sight of so many children employed in mining along with their fathers appalled many Americans. The Slav would give a ready answer when accused of practising child labor—economic necessity. Popular American abhorrence of the evil forced through minimum age laws, but to little avail, as parents and employers violated them with rare penalty. Some child labor reformers announced that they had found boys as young as six working at the mines; nine or ten was probably the actual minimum. A leading reformer sympathized with the East European youngster as the "helpless victim of the frugality, ignorance, and industrial instincts of his parents." The value placed by Americans on educating the young little interested the Slav, for the valuable child was the working one. Above a minimum, education was useless, and the pressing need for income forced sons into the pits at or before their teens.

At the mines the littlest ones worked in the huge eighty-foot breaker, the "nursery" some named it. This structure in operation presented a terrifying sight to the uninitiated. The coal rushing down the chutes made a deafening roar and sent up clouds of coal dust everywhere. Once the visitor accustomed himself to the haze, he would have to peer through the greyness to see the inmates, young boys seated on boards bent over chutes. From time to time they operated a shutter which regulated the flow, and then they picked out slate to separate it from the coal. The air at times would grow to a choking thickness, but the boys would work on while their supervisor, leaning on a switch, stood above them. In this nursery, too, strangely enough, one could find old men working alongside the youths. They had spent their manhood underground, and, broken and worn out, they had now returned to the surface for the rest of their days. So the breaker could have been termed a home for the elderly as well. All of the workers here, men and boys, labored the normal ten-hour, six-day week, when at full time.

The Slav in the prime of life conducted his work below ground in the mine itself. The former Slavic plowboy going down in the elevator for the first time was surely upset by the rapid descent into utter darkness. Alighting at the bottom and walking toward his chamber, he could just make out headlamp flashes and flitting shadows. He may well have noticed youngsters not much older than the breaker boys accompanying him along the gangway.

Increasingly, then, the total mining operation for the worker took on the appearance of a "school." From the surface at about twelve years of age, boys in their mid-teens graduated underground to tending doors along the gangway which regulated ventilation. Older teenagers moved on to the position of mule leaders and keepers, then drivers hauling coal, until at maturity they, like most average Slavs, worked as miners' helpers. If lucky, some Poles became "miners," but a required examination after 1889 restricted them somewhat. . . .

When the day drew to a close, the laborer would likely find himself alone in the underground room. Since the miner pulled down the black rock faster than his assistants could load it, he frequently went home long before the loading was done. It was the rare miner who labored the full ten hours. He usually departed no later than three or four, to leave the assistant to do the remaining tasks, complete the loading, clear the refuse to the side, and prepare the area for the next day's work. The weary Slavic mineworkers trudged home after sunset, keeping their headlamps lit to find their way. Each completed his day at home with a good bath to restore his skin to its natural color.

Greene goes into the economics of the Slavic anthracite laborer's existence. He describes the practice of subcontracting whereby the salary would go to the "miner" who would then pay his Slavic assistants. He notes that in spite of legislation to the contrary, payment was made on a monthly basis, often necessitating the contraction of credit from local or company stores and loans from the "miner" himself. Then he notes that average wages in the anthracite region drifted downward from about 1870 to the end of the century. And yet, he presents statistics which indicate that the Poles, as well as other Eastern and East Central European immigrants, managed to *save* money even in such times. Most invested their savings in real estate. They purchased homes in the mining towns and took steps to make their lives and the lives of their children more tolerable. They also contributed to the building of churches, church schools, meeting halls, and other public structures, which gave them a good measure of pride. They even managed to send funds to the old country and thereby helped to improve living conditions in their home villages or to bring over new immigrants to replenish the anthracite labor supply.

Greene asks whether the Slavic mine workers would have been "willing to sacrifice income temporarily in strikes and respond to the exhortations of union missionaries." The material he presents in the remainder of *The Slavic Community on Strike* supports a strongly affirmative answer. The Slavic mine workers proved to be patient but not passive. They felt injustice keenly enough to join the union movement. Sometimes they formed their own locals, where meetings were conducted in their own languages. They struck against the mine owners and "bosses" and attacked strikebreaking "scabs," even if the scabs happened to be their compatriots. Newspaper accounts of some of the bloodiest, most violent confrontations were filled with Slavic, Lithuanian, and Hungarian names among those who were arrested or who fell while battling in union ranks. When the strike became prolonged, their thriftiness and resourcefulness paid off, for they, better than other groups, could subsist on what they had. The old-line Anglo-Saxon and Irish union men who most feared the "Slavic peril" of cheap labor threatening their job security and standard of living were thus to realize that their fears had been unfounded.

Nativism, which is as old as the United States itself, reared its ugly head anew against the Slavic immigrants. It provided an outlet for the economic fears of the American workers. Much of it was channeled through newspapers and periodicals, as in the following article.

Between 1880 and 1914, a segment of the periodical press directed its condemnations upon the Poles, South Italians, Czechs, Slovaks, Croats and Hungarians who were arriving in the United States in large numbers during the period.[13] Many writers attacked them because of their high degree of criminality. One frightened American believed that the nation was "draining off the criminals and defectives of Europe," and the country was "charitably" carrying on its "shoulders the burden of their maintenance." Another writer lamented that the new groups were a "bad lot," and the contrast between them and the earlier immigrants was "very marked." A reverend, violating the sanctity of his office, declared that the Slavs and Italians came from the "lowest grades of society." They were "illiterate, ignorant, brutal and filthy—the riffraff and the refuse of European nations." One observer classified the South Italians, Bohemians, Poles and Russian Jews together as "the miserable, the broken, the corrupt, (and) the abject. . . ." He concluded that the Republic would ultimately collapse "from an invasion in comparison with which the invasions under which Rome fell were no more than a series of excursion parties." This pessimistic view was expressed by another commentator who maintained that the immigrant groups before 1860 were civilized while the newer ones were "semi-barbarous."

Some writers labeled the Slavs and Italians a political liability. In a furious rage bordering on insanity, a woman bellowed that the immigrants were spreading "noxious imported vices" and were "fungous growths" upon American political institutions. She concluded that America's "priceless" possession, the vote, suffered from the "base contingent from foreign shores" because the immigrants were "citizens for revenue only." In the *Political Science Quarterly,* a commentator declared that the immigrants were a "heavy strain" on the American political system because the so-called foreign vote, which has never existed, appeared to him "solid, interested and sometimes mercenary."

Mondello noted that W. E. Chandler, the chairman of the Senate committee investigating the immigration question, in 1893 introduced two novel and extreme reasons for curbing the new immigration: (1) It carried the germs of diseases; (2) it would spoil the Chicago World's Fair, since wealthier Europeans would not travel in vessels with "swarms" of immigrants. The senator's views were printed in the respectable *North American Review.*

Further, Mondello calls attention to articles which singled out the Poles for special attack. One, printed in *Lippincott's Magazine,* was written by a Texan who gave a most unflattering account of a Polish wedding to which he had been invited. Among other things, the writer lamented that he could not find "one handsome person,—few, indeed, who attained a degree above positive ugliness." He maintained that the guests could not enjoy themselves without the "excitation of whiskey"

[13] Reprinted from Salvatore Mondello, "America's Polish Heritage as Viewed by Miecislaus Haiman and the Periodical Press," *The Polish Review* 4 (Winter-Spring 1959), pp. 107–18. By permission of Salvatore Mondello and *The Polish Review.*

and saw the women as lacking feminine characteristics and virtues. His conclusion: There was no hope for the eventual rise of the Poles in the United States. A New Englander, also on the basis of observing a wedding, which he described as a drunken orgy ending in a knife-fight, came to the conclusion that Poles were drunkards and criminally inclined. He added a "glimpse" of the Polish farmer in New England, whom he saw as resembling an animal with a stolid, stupid face.

Finally, Mondello turns to those elements of the periodical press which presented the other side of the coin, to articles written by such sympathetic authors as Wellesley Professor and Nobel prize winner Emily Greene Balch, Edward Steiner, and Henry Hoyt Moore, which called attention to the Slavic immigrant's industriousness, thriftiness, and persistence. Some of the articles also called attention to the overcrowding of the immigrants and their children in urban areas and even called for help from charitable institutions. However, Mondello comments that the Poles (and this could well be said for the others) "did rise in the United States not because of the work of charitable institutions but because they possessed basic traits which made their rise 'irresistible'."

World War I stemmed the flow of the new immigration. It also brought about changes in the map of Europe which saw most of the homelands of the "New Immigrants" become independent states. Poland was reborn. The Czechs, Slovaks, and Moravians were to live within the boundaries of a Czechoslovakia. Serbs, Croats, Slovenians, Bosnians, Herzegovinians, Montenegrans, and some Macedonians were enclosed within the borders of a Southern Slav State—Yugoslavia. The Lithuanians had a small spot on the map. Even the Hungarians, though "punished" by loss of considerable territory, were at last completely independent of Austria.

The transformation of the immigrant within one lifetime was a phenomenon to behold. In *Americans from Hungary* Emil Lengyel describes the process of transformation. From peasant backgrounds, lovers of the soil, they came to be strong mineworkers who with frugality managed to save some money and achieve a degree of economic independence. Simultaneously with their efforts to improve their lot in America, Hungarians attempted to develop "Little Hungaries" and, with more success, ethnic-oriented fraternal and social organizations.

> Once the Hungarian immigrant left home he underwent a remarkable sea change.[14] At home he had been a peasant, hopelessly in love with the soil which refused to yield herself to him. He was a peasant not merely as an occupation but also as a profession of faith. He was a Catholic or Protestant, but in his heart of hearts he was a

[14] From the book *Americans from Hungary* by Emil Lengyel, pp. 127, 128, 158, 159. Copyright © 1948 by Emil Lengyel. Reprinted by permission of J. B. Lippincott Company.

nature-worshiper, faithful to only one soil, his own, that of his own village, his own very limited horizon. But when he reached America he never thought of going to work on a farm. He, the thoroughbred peasant, turned his back on the soil and turned toward the mine and the blast furnace. He did this possibly because he remained true to his own soil. In the mine and in the shop he would make money quickly. According to our city standards of today, his wages were small, but looking at them from his own point of view, they grow to gigantic proportions. Then he would return home with his vast treasure of hundreds, perhaps even thousands of dollars, and there he would show his love for the only soil he knew. Moreover, as Geza Hoffman has shown: "The former peasant, who had never left his hamlet at home, would wander tirelessly from city to city. Formerly tied down to the soil, he would become a migratory factory worker. This would take place without transition. In America he would become his own antithesis."

What did the ex-peasants find in the United States? A former resident of County Komaron wrote home: "Here a man is paid for his labors and I am certainly not sorry that I am here. I work from six in the morning until seven at night and get $10–11 a week. Just now it's hot. When it gets cooler I'll make more money, perhaps double, then I'll work only eleven hours. There are 10,000 workers in this shop and my wife is working here too. She makes $9.50 a week. At home I made that much money in a whole month and people thought my job was very good. Here I am sewing dresses on a machine. In America there is no difference between one man and another. If you're a millionaire you are called a Mister just the same, and your wife is Missis." Here is another testimony, contained in an interview: "In Hungary I had a wife, two children, house, six acres of land, two horses, a cow, two pigs and a few poultry. That was my fortune. This same land that afforded existence to my father and grandfather could not support us any longer. Taxes and cost of living in the last few years advanced so greatly that the expenses could not be covered from what a small farm can yield. Things became worse, an early spring storm killed my crops, and I had to buy bread for money. My horses were killed from disease. I had to sell my cow to buy winter clothes for the family. There was no money to work the land and without horses and work the land will not produce. I had to mortgage my home. . . . As a farm laborer in Hungary, one can earn only enough for bread and water. How is one to pay taxes and living expenses? There was but one hope, America. . . . We will never go back to Hungary. It only deprived us of our home and land, while in America the soil covers our child. We have a home, money, and business, everything acquired in America. We lost everything in Hungary. We love Hungary as our native land, but never wish to live in it again."

The Hungarian immigrants settled in the neighborhood of mines and steel furnaces. They settled everywhere the industrial molochs needed unskilled workers, ready to perform the least desirable types of chores. The hardest industrial job was easy in comparison with peasants' work; the working day was short, not more than ten to twelve hours a day. Most of the Hungarians settled in four States: Ohio, New York, New Jersey, and Pennsylvania. Large groups settled also in Illinois, Indiana and West Virginia. New York

City became the "third largest 'Hungarian' city in the world," with a population of 76,575 in 1920. Relatively, Cleveland's population was larger—42,134 in that year, while the Hungarian populations of Chicago and Detroit were fewer than twenty thousand each.

We can judge their success by the size of their remittances to the Old Country. At the height of the immigration they sent home sometimes as much as one hundred to two hundred million kronen a year. It is estimated that the highest annual remittance was a quarter of a billion kronen—the equivalent of $50,000,000. . . .

He went into the mine or the steel mill, the hazards of which were great. He was alone as yet, with no kin to help him in times of stress. The fraternal sick benefit and funeral organizations met his most urgent needs. They were the first organizations the Hungarian immigrant in America developed and he has remained true to them throughout. They became the very lifeblood of American-Hungarian life.

The first such organization among the Hungarians came into existence when the first wave of Kossuth's immigrant followers reached the United States. The Hungarian Sick Benefit Society of New York was nursed into life by Charles Kornis Tothvarady, the founder of the first Hungarian-language newspaper in this country, and was short-lived. There were not enough Hungarian immigrants in those days, contrary to Tothvarady's expectations.

Shortly after the Civil War Hungarian organizations with a little more staying power came into being. The first of these was the *Erster Ungarischer Kranken-Unterstuetzungsverein,* founded by Hungarian immigrants of Jewish faith. The official language of this First Hungarian Sickness Benefit Association was German. It was followed by the *New Yorki Magyar Noegylet* (New York Hungarian Women's Association), which also transacted its business in German. Cleveland residents of northern Hungarian Jews founded the *Cleveland Magyar Betegsegelyzo Egylet.* Its official language was German, too.

The New York Hungarians felt the need of a social organization and so the *New Yorki Magyar Egylet* (New York Hungarian Association) was founded. Its first president was the revolutionary hero, Colonel Miklos Perczel, and one of its leading spirits was Michael Heilprin.

The Association rented a couple of rickety rooms at 319 Bowery. It had an ambitious program, holding meetings three times a week, at which much music was played. Some years later, it branched out into a choral society, *New Yorki Magyar Dalkor,* and into a Hungarian Sickness Benefit Society. The stated object of the Association was to foster the fraternal spirit among the members, awaken sympathy for Hungary, study American institutions and endeavor to popularize them in Hungary, and to stimulate the industrial, scientific and mercantile work of Hungarians here.

The Association struck a keynote which may be summed up in one word: Nationalism. Strong Hungarian national sentiment characterized the American-Hungarian organizations. Paradoxically, the nationalistic feeling increased, rather than declined, as a result of transplantation to the alien soil. The immigrant could not participate in American life and therefore he attempted to create a situation here in which he could participate. He wanted to improve the status of the Hungarians, so that his own status might be improved in American eyes. Home became a much sweeter place when it was no longer his. In America, the immigrant's eyes were opened to the real nature of nationalism. Also he was free to talk and act. He wanted to help in the struggle for self-determination at home. He also may have wanted to gain recognition at home preparatory to his return.

As the tidal wave of Hungarian immigration set in, the fraternal insurance companies came into existence. One of the first of these was a sickness benefit and funeral association named after Count Lajos Batthyany, martyred Premier of the abortive 1848 revolutionary government. The story of its origin casts a vital light on conditions in American Hungary then.

In Cleveland, the largest inland "Hungarian" city of the United States, an unknown Hungarian lived in a boarding house, alone and friendless, and there he died. The landlord was in a great hurry to rent the dead man's bed. He called the police to remove the body. The police came at a late hour and took the body away. Word spread among the Hungarians of the East Side and they made a search for the dead man, but could find nothing. This is precisely the sort of thing the peasant, Hungarian or not Hungarian, dreads. Little Hungary was aroused. Several Hungarians of Cleveland got together and founded the Association named, characteristically, after the executed Premier. Similar societies came into existence in other Hungarian settlements of the East, especially in Pennsylvania coal towns.

KEY QUESTIONS

1. What characteristics would you ascribe to the new immigrants from Eastern and East Central Europe?

2. In light of the readings, how would you evaluate the new immigrants from Eastern and East Central Europe in regard to their alleged foreign "nationalism" and their attitudes toward their new country?

3. Discuss the social institutions which seemed most significant to the new immigrants after their arrival in the United States.

4. In what respects was there discrimination against the new immigrants from Eastern and East Central Europe in the United States? Discuss fully.

5. What role did religion play in the lives of the immigrants from Eastern and East Central Europe?

6

New Immigration from 1865:
EASTERN EUROPE—RUSSIANS, JEWS, RUTHENIANS, UKRAINIANS

As a pilgrim father that missed th' first boats, I must raise me claryon voice again' th' invasion iv this fair land be th' paupers an' arnychists iv effete Europe. Ye bet I must—because I'm here first.

MR. DOOLEY ON IMMIGRATION[1]

Much has been made of the distinction between "old" and "new" immigrants in most conventional studies of American immigration history. The impression is frequently given that at a particular moment in post–Civil War history—the specific year is open to variation—a dramatic shift in the nature of immigration took place, marked by a sudden and equally dramatic geographic shift from Western and Northern Europe to Southern, Central, and Eastern Europe. The white, Anglo-Saxon or Nordic, largely urbanized, and relatively skilled immigrant is buried under an avalanche of swarthy-skinned peasants and poor, erupting out of Italy (including Sicily), the plains of Central Europe (Czechs, Slovaks, Bohemians, Hungarians, and so forth), and the steppes and swamplands of Western Russia (Poles, Jews, Ukrainians, Ruthenians). Belonging to so-called inferior races of mankind, desperately poor, speaking one of a variety of barbaric tongues (Czech, Yiddish, Russian, or some rich peasant dialect of Southern Europe), this new immigrant threatened to engulf America and apparently brought with him more problems than the New World was capable of resolving.

While the distinction between "new" and "old" immigrations is not a completely false notion, it is open to exaggeration. What occurs after 1865 is best described as the gradual tapering off of the "old" immigration and, beginning with the 1880's, the slow building up of the "new" immigration until, shortly after the coming of the twentieth century, it turns into an overwhelming flood of Hungarians, Czechs, Poles, Russians, Jews, Balkan peoples, Italians, Sicilians, and many others.

---

[1] Reprinted from Peter Dunne, *Mr. Dooley: Now and Forever,* ed. Louis Filler (Stanford, CA: Academic Reprints, 1954), p. 173.

By 1907 the old immigration had declined in both an absolute and a relative sense, yet the coming of this shift lasted many decades and was . slower than usually imagined. The year 1882, true enough, marked a kind of watershed between "old" and "new" immigration. After this year, in which almost 650,000 Europeans passed through American ports, the peak annual figure for the entire nineteenth century, the number of Germans, Scandinavians, and English who entered the country began a serious downward trend. But not until 1896 did the actual volume of so-called new immigrants surpass that of the old. The real disparity came only after the turn of the century, as indicated in the following set of figures derived from the annual immigration bureau reports:[2]

1882	788,000 total immigration	87 percent "old" immigration (German, Irish, British, Scandinavian); 13 percent "new" immigration
1907	1,285,000 total immigration	19 percent "old" immigration; 81 percent "new" immigration (Eastern, Southern, and Central European)

It has been calculated that, up to 1880, immigrants from Russia and the Baltic countries alone averaged about 8,000 a year; from 1880 over the next twenty years (1900), the pace grew and expanded many times to 81,500 immigrants per year; then, up to 1902, an average of 100,000 was attained. But in the fifteen great years of 1900 to 1914, a grand total of 2½ million Eastern Europeans (out of a total immigration of 9½ million) came pouring in at an annual rate of close to 170,000.

THE RUSSIAN IMMIGRATION

It is estimated that over four million immigrants came to the New World from Czarist Russia between the years 1883 and the beginning of the First World War in 1914. The vast majority came after the failed Revolution of 1905. This fantastic emigration included so-called Great Russians (out of the region expanded from the medieval Duchy of Moscovy), White Russians from the western regions bordering on Poland, Little Russians from the Ukraine, and Russian Jews from the famous Pale of Russia. Other national minority groups and ethnic peoples—Poles, Lithuanians, Estonians, Letts, Finns, all assembled together in the "prison house of the peoples" known as the Russian Empire—formed part of this exodus, but in considerably smaller numbers. The gates of the Czarist regime were wide open at all times, and the inhabitants of its vast world were encouraged to take the road to exile, never to return!

[2] Maldwyn Allen Jones, *American Immigration* (Chicago: University of Chicago Press, 1960), p. 179.

Up to and including the decade of the 1870's, however, the mass of Russians were largely unaware of the possibility of immigration abroad, let alone of the existence of the United States. The first group of Russians to take the path of immigration consisted of Russian Germans inhabiting the regions of the lower Volga and Don Rivers. As Germans, they had originally been welcomed to settle in Russia by Catherine the Great in the second half of the eighteenth century. Intensely religious, they had embraced the doctrine of the Mennonites, a Christian sect which, among other things, was strongly antiwar and believed in religious tolerance. The Russian Mennonites held fast to their German language and customs in addition to their orthodoxy, which clashed sharply with the established Russian Orthodox Church.

In the mid 1870's, when the Czar began his campaign to "Russianize" the Mennonites by imposing the Russian language and culture upon them and inducting their men into the army, the exodus of the persecuted began. These people, along with other non-Mennonite German groups located along the Volga and the Don, set themselves up against the Imperial Government and set out for the United States in organized groups. Between 1874 and 1894 they formed a trickle of approximately two to three hundred families per year; between 1898 and 1914 this grew to approximately one thousand families annually. Farmers and artisans, quite similar to the German peasantry from Westphalia, Baden, and other parts of Rhineland Germany, their destination was the great open spaces of the New World: Nebraska, Oklahoma, Kansas, Wisconsin, the Dakotas, and Minnesota. Russian Mennonite migration did not last for long, but their contribution to American agriculture, as the following document indicates, was inestimable.

> Among the many interesting features of the Mennonite economic development which might be discussed, most noteworthy is that of their introduction of the Turkey wheat into America.[3] Thoughtful as they were of what might grow in the new country, these German colonists took with them various seeds, among others also hard winter wheat, the so-called Turkey wheat, a fact which was to become of high significance not only for their own farming, but for the whole wheat production in the United States. . . .
>
> Reference need only be made to the statement of the United States government authorities in order to see the relation between the development of the Turkey wheat in the United States, and the German immigration from Russia.
>
> "The history of hard winter wheat in the United States is closely associated with the movement of the Russian Mennonite immigrants to the middle Great Plains. These people originally went from West Prussia to Southern Russia about 1770 because of certain land grants and civil privileges offered by the government

[3] Reprinted from George Leibbrandt, "The Emigration of the German Mennonites from Russia to the United States and Canada, 1873–1880," Part II, *The Mennonite Quarterly Review* 7 (January 1933):36–37; with an extract from U.S., Department of Agriculture, *Classification of American Wheat Varieties*, Bulletin No. 1074, 1922.

under Empress Catherine. Over one hundred years later their descendants, desiring further advantages to be obtained in America, emigrated to the middle Great Plains and settled principally in Kansas. . . .

"The good qualities of the Turkey wheat were not generally appreciated much before the close of the last century, twenty-five years after its introduction by the Mennonites. At the Kansas experiment station its superiority came to light about 1897, though it had been under experiment for some time. . . . As early as 1901 hard winter wheat at New York was quoted at a fairly good price. All recent prices (1914) at the important markets show a decided but gradual change in attitude toward hard winter wheat, so that it is now ranked, where it should be, among the first class wheats. It has 'won its way' through difficulties in accordance with the motto of the state where its production is greatest . . . and is now more generally in favor in this country than any other winter wheat. In California, where it is not adopted, a third to a half of all wheat annually used by the mills is imported from the middle Great Plains. It has encroached upon the hard spring wheat area to the northward in Iowa and Nebraska and upon the area of softer wheats to the westward in the Rocky Mountain States, and has made Montana a wheat state . . . making in all 350,000,000 bushels as the approximate average annual hard wheat production in this country. This is about a half of the average total wheat production in this country."

Russian immigration reached its peak strength in the years 1910–1914. First came individual Russian males, followed within a few years by their large families. A few were educated, some were political refugees from one or another of the numerous radical opposition organizations within Czarist Russia (all illegal and underground), but the vast majority were ordinary Russians, lacking in the most rudimentary education and illiterate in the full sense of the word. Workers and peasants, they possessed a high degree of physical stamina and an even higher degree of personal courage and determination. Once in the United States, they joined and swelled the ranks of the unskilled, toiling away at hard labor. Coal miners, steelworkers, factory hands, farm laborers—they concentrated in the eastern and midwestern industrialized states of America.

That the Russian immigrant factory and mine worker was at the bottom of the ladder in terms of human exploitation seems beyond question. There is a considerable body of evidence indicating that the Russians did not hesitate to complain or to express their feelings, often indicating great bitterness with respect to their adopted land. Below are excerpts from a document circulated by the Russian Orthodox Church in America.

All the factories are the selfsame ichor which poisons the worker's soul and body.[4] Capital is a cruel master; workers are his slaves

---

[4] Reprinted from Jerome Davis, *The Russian Immigrant* (New York: Macmillan, 1922), pp. 98, 99.

foredoomed to death. Each working day shortens the worker's life for a few months, saps the living juice out of him, dries out the heart, dampens the noblest aspirations of the soul; transforms a living man into a sort of machine, embitters the whole life. The ragged soul and body of the worker bring forth to the world half sick children, paralytic, idiotic—therefore the factory's poison kills not merely the unfortunate workers, but also whole generations. It kills invisibly, imperceptibly, in such a manner that the workers themselves—the voluntary slaves of capital—fail to see the whole frightfulness of their own situation. . . .

In Russia, more attention is paid to the man. There, they say: "Men are not cattle"; "Men are not made of iron"; "Work and rest." The mining of gold and silver and iron is called in our land "sing-sing work" (hard labor) which is done by the most hopeless of criminals, not by thieves but by cut-throats—soul-killers or traitors to the State; whereas in America any work is sing-sing (hard labor), and the workers are galley slaves although they call themselves free citizens.

The Russian immigrants were forced by circumstances to live under particularly harsh conditions in the slums of the large cities they inhabited.* Insufficiently numerous either to expand or to organize themselves in a show of strength, they were probably at the bottom of the heap in terms of living standards and health conditions. Dr. Edward T. Devine, a social worker of the time, summarized their situation in terms of its effects upon their children.[5]

Parental neglect, congestion of population, dirty milk, indigestible food, uncleaned streets, with the resulting contaminated atmosphere, the prevalence of infectious diseases, multiplied temptations to break the law, and ordinances regarding the use of the streets for lack of other playground—let them be followed by employment in dead-end occupations in which there are no educational elements, no serious motives to progress and application, and we make assurance doubly sure that we shall have sub-normal adult workers. Add a twelve-hour day, and a seven-day week, irregular, casual employment, sub-standard wages, speeding processes which have no regard to human capacities or nervous strains for which the system is unprepared, indecent housing, insanitary conditions both in home and factory, and we have an explanation amply adequate to account for sub-normal wage earners.

Until either the Russian worker or his children (a native-born second generation) rose out of the factory working class and thus managed

---

* In 1918, the distribution of Russians in America was estimated as follows: By states— 60,000 in New York; 50,000 in Illinois; 40,000 in Massachusetts; 35,000 in Pennsylvania; 45,000 in Ohio; 36,000 in Michigan; 35,000 in New Jersey, and 20,000 in Connecticut. By cities—New York, 25,000; Detroit, 17,000; Chicago, 20,000; San Francisco, 15,000; and scattered thousands in Pittsburgh, Philadelphia, Newark, Jersey City, Cleveland, and others. (Source: Davis, *The Russians*, pp. 22–23)

[5] Reprinted from Edward T. Devine, "Family and Social Work," in Jerome Davis, *The Russians and Ruthenians in America* (New York: Doran, 1922), p. 32.

to shift to easier lines of work, harsh exploitation would be his lot. In the end, relief came primarily in the 1930's, when the Committee for Industrial Organization (CIO) under the leadership of the flamboyant miners' union chief, John L. Lewis, began the formidable task of organizing the millions of unskilled in the country's basic industries. Until then, the descriptive excerpt that follows tells the story of life in the mill.

It is true that some of the Russians draw a distinction between the squad foreman who works with them and the boss foreman.[6] The former shares in their labor and is often friendly, but they consider the latter as almost invariably bad, feeling that he deliberately makes them do work that is too difficult. For example, a Russian in Philadelphia said, "The boss makes two of us carry steel which should require four. If I refuse, I lose my job. Lots of weeks the work is so heavy I get pains in my back and have to lay off three days out of seven." Or again, in a mill in Pittsburgh, the boss, Pete, according to the testimony of a Russian, is a giant who can do the work of two ordinary men. In somewhat exaggerated language more clearly to convey his meaning, he said: "The boss can lift two tons himself. He will watch us straining to lift a two-ton iron and will laugh at us and yell, 'You —— —— Polack, push.' We will break our backs trying and he will not lift a finger to help us." . . .

The Inter-Church Report summarizes what it considers the grievances in the life of the Russian immigrant steel worker as follows:

Nine times out of ten he is a peasant, taking an industrial job for the first time. At the start, only as wages fail to keep him and his family as he wants them to be kept, or the hours break down his health, does he care much about "controlling" either wages or hours. What matters most to him is that if the mill is shut down, he is the first to be laid off; if the job is unusually hot, greasy, or heavy, he is the first to be set to it. He is the most arbitrarily, often brutally, shifted and ordered about; if he takes a lay-off, he is the most likely to be heavily docked, and he is the most likely to be kept beyond his hour with no additional pay. If there is sickness in his home or he is otherwise kept away, his excuses get the shortest shrift. If he is the butt of unusual prejudice in either his foreman or some fellow worker evinced in profanity or the penalties of always the nastier task, he knows least where to go for redress or how to speak it.

Yet the writer is convinced that aside from the fact that the Russian is usually the marginal worker, most of these grievances arise directly from his relations with the boss who to the worker typifies the industry.

For his Master's thesis at Chicago University, J. S. Cole made a careful study of 112 single Russians, the majority of whom were either employed in the stock yards of Chicago or in stables, or were temporarily out of work. He reported that they were very bitter against the boss, their attitude summed up in the following remarks:

[6] From Davis, *Russian Immigrant*, pp. 33–35.

"Before war, very good; but now all, no matter what nationality, laid off on least excuse. If horse no can pull wagon, put on another horse. If man no can pull truck, lay him off."

"Foreman very severe; sometimes lay off day for being minute late. Rush so at work that you almost faint. Treatment worse now since it is very easy to replace men."

"Boss very hard. Fired one man, he was in his place two minutes before whistle blew to enter shop."

"Bosses very unreasonable. One man left truck to get drink and boss fired him. Have to bribe boss to keep job."

"Too strict about time; if one minute late, dock one-half hour. Getting worse all the time. Often work so hard get weak and when tell foreman he says we are drunk."

"Treat Russian like dog."

THE JEWS OF RUSSIA

It is generally agreed that Jewish immigration to the United States from Czarist Russia in the early part of the twentieth century forms one of the most complex and significant episodes in our entire immigration history. This is true both from the standpoint of the numbers of immigrants involved (within a twelve-year period from 1899 to 1910, a total of 1,074,442 Jews were admitted to America from all over Eastern Europe, or an average of 90,000 per year) and from that of the importance of the contribution of these people to American life.

The Jews of Russia lived in a region known officially as the "Pale of Settlement" and popularly and simply as the Pale. The Pale at its largest consisted of some fifteen provinces extending 1,500 miles along the border of Germany and the Austro-Hungarian Empire at an approximate average width of 240 miles; even lands wrested at one time from the Turks were included in this region. It included areas in the Ukraine, parts of ancient Slavic Poland, and regions, tributaries, and stretches of Russia, such as Lithuania, Volkynia, Bessarabia, Galicia, and Roumania.

The Jewish population already present in the United States—mainly German-Jewish—was completely unprepared either to help or to assimilate the great surge of Russian Jews about to flood the New World. The extract below summarizes the problems that faced the Jewish immigrant upon his arrival.

In the ten years covered by our record of the arrival of Jewish immigrants, there has been added to the Jewish population of America, through the port of New York alone, the enormous number of 313,035 foreign Jews, of whom 242,199 were Russians and Roumanians, and 57,818 were Austrians.[7] To this number must be

[7] Reprinted from United Hebrew Charities, *Twentieth Annual Report* (1886), pp. 16–17.

added the Russians who came to America between 1880 and 1884, who certainly numbered 80,000. In viewing our problem, it has not been the practice heretofore to consider Austrian immigration as material. But it should be remembered that the bulk of it is received from the province of Galicia, and that most of the inhabitants of this province are strongly akin to the Russians in all the respects that make the Russians difficult to deal with.

Of the foreign arrivals, by far the larger percentage, safely estimated at seventy-five, remained in New York. In the beginning of the movement to America, the percentage requiring assistance was small, but it has grown constantly until the large expenditure of the year 1891–92 was called for. That the heavy immigration has greatly added to our burden may be understood from the fact that of the $1,850,000 expended by the United Hebrew Charities since its organization, twenty years ago, upwards of $1,000,000 has been expended in the past five years.

Were no other influence than immigration to be taken into account an appalling problem would still confront us when considering how to deal adequately with our poor. But there were evils awaiting the foreigner in New York which, in the nature of things, he himself intensified, and which have rendered efforts to make an impression upon the whole seem well-nigh fruitless. First, and perhaps as important as any of these evils, are the tenement houses. For years the public [officials] of New York have inveighed against the tenement house, yet it exists to-day in all its virulence, despite public disapproval, rigid sanitary laws and inspection, and the attempts of noble men and women to remove the poor from their vile surroundings. The assertion has been made repeatedly that the amount of illness, especially of a zymotic nature, is hardly greater in the tenement houses than in the better portions of the city. This is probably true, but it should not delude us into believing that therefore the tenement does not complicate our problem. The worst result of tenement-house life is an under-vitalization of tenement dwellers both mentally and physically, and they who have searched carefully into the homes of the poor have found also a moral degradation as serious as the mental and physical deterioration. Without a sound body, a sound mind, and sound morals as a base, how shall we be able to raise the standard of the submerged tenth?

The second evil lies in the wage question. It will be remembered that the bulk of the immigrants especially those from Russia and Galicia are unable to perform outdoor work. This caused the larger percentage to secure in-door employment which they found almost entirely in the garment manufacturing trades. Unscrupulous sweaters and middle-men seized upon the poverty of these unfortunates and, finding an opportunity to hire men and women at prices reduced to the starvation point by unwholesome competition, forced thousands into a method of living literally from hand to mouth. The major part of their wages is absorbed by rent for dwellings that are inadequate and unsanitary, their clothing is insufficient, their food the most meagre, and savings are absolutely impossible. The last year has brought home to us in all its horror the result of this form of what might almost be called slavery. Stagnation in commercial circles stopped manufacturing. The thousands thrown out of work had nothing to fall back upon but a few articles of value brought from the Old World. Money raised upon these in the pawn shops, frugally expended, that it might last to the uttermost, reduced still further the standard of living. Scanty food, added to former long hours of labor in unwholesome shops, and hours of rest in vile dwellings, caused many to succumb to chronic disease and, after all resources were exhausted, chronics filled our hospitals and homes, orphans crowded the institutions provided for such unfortunates, and those who were able to be about were forced to come to us or to beg from individuals, and to begin a career whose seeds were sown in the Old World, a career the worst known to civic life, the career of pauperism.

In his statistical study of Russian Jewish immigration,[8] Samuel Joseph offers information summarized in the following: In the thirty years between 1881 and 1910, slightly over one million Jewish refugees arrived in the United States; then, between the years 1910 and 1914, when the war disrupted all immigration, another 200,000 to 300,000 came, constituting the largest single group of all groups. In a more detailed statistical study,[9] Mark Wischnitzer calculated that of a total of 23,722,453 individuals entering the United States from the year 1881 to 1920, the Jews constituted 8.6 percent or 2,064,673. The Jewish percentage of the entire annual immigration varied from .9 percent to a peak of 13.5 percent in the year 1906 (the year after the crushing of the Russian Revolution of 1905). The following chart,[10] taken in part from the same study, gives some idea of the raw statistics involved in an annual calculation:

Year	Jewish Immigration
1881 (start of new wave of Jews)	5,692
1882	13,202
1883	8,731
1885	16,862
1890	28,639
1891	51,398
1900	60,764
1903	76,203
1904	106,236
1905	129,910
1906 (peak year)	153,748
1907	149,182
1913	101,330
1914	138,051
1915	26,497
1916	15,108
1920	65,000

[8] Samuel Joseph, *Jewish Immigration to the United States from 1881 to 1910* (New York: Columbia University, 1914).

[9] Mark Wischnitzer, *Visas to Freedom*, prepared by the Hebrew Immigration Assistance Society (Cleveland: World, 1956), cf. p. 32.

[10] Ibid., cf. p. 32. By permission of World Publishing Co.

Nearly all of the immigrant Jews settled in the cities of the American east coastal region; some families, not considerable in number, went to the West. The percentage of skilled artisans (see below) was considerable: tailors, furriers, and jewelers, for example, quickly constituted a major element of the skilled labor force required in such industries as the manufacture of garments, millinery, the fur industry, and so forth. Manufacturing, wholesale and retail businesses, peddlers whose successful activities led to the opening of retail stores in many regions of the United States, all of these became familiar byproducts of the great Jewish migration. Finally, as the good word spread to Slavic Russia, the wave of non-Jewish Russians previously described began to build up from the 1890's onward as the pull to cross the Atlantic became irresistible.

What, if anything, distinguished the Jewish immigration from other immigrant groups? According to L. Hersch, who closely studied statistical material of the U.S. Immigration Service, the outstanding feature of migrant Russian Jewry was its high proportion of active professionals and skilled people.[11] A significant number of Jews who came to America were skilled workers, with almost 400,000 skilled Jewish workers entering the United States in the years 1899–1910. This was an almost unprecedented contribution to the skilled manpower pool of the United States, and its significance cannot be measured. Out of forty-nine professions and skills listed in American immigration statistics for these years, the Jews had an absolute or relative majority in twenty-five, including hatmakers, furriers, tailors, clockmakers, and jewelers, among others.

Migration was, of course, a familiar part of the history and tradition of the Jews. But this time there was a significant factor in their favor. Word of their persecution in Czarist Russia had reached America and was known to the general population. Hence, public opinion was not favorable to traditional forms of Jew-baiting and anti-Semitism when Jews began to arrive in large numbers. It is not difficult to grasp the grateful excitement and the sense of exalted liberation of these hundreds of thousands in the excerpts that follow from a novel by the popular Jewish authoress, Anzia Yezierska.

Mostly About Myself[12]

I feel like a starved man who is so bewildered by the first sight of food that he wants to grab and devour the ice-cream, the roast, and the entree all in one gulp. For ages and ages, my people in Russia had no more voice than the broomstick in the corner. The poor had no more chance to say what they thought or felt than the dirt under their feet.

[11] L. Hersch, Le Juit Errant d'Aujord'hui (Paris: M. Giard and E. Briese, 1913), p. 130 et seq.

[12] Reprinted from Anzia Yezierska, Children of Loneliness (New York: Funk & Wagnalls, 1923), pp. 17–18.

And here, in America, a miracle has happened to them. They can lift up their heads like real people. After centuries of suppression, they are allowed to speak. Is it a wonder that I am too excited to know where to begin?

I'm too much on fire to wait till I understand what I see and feel. My hands rush out to seize a word from the end, a phrase from the middle, or a sentence from the beginning. I jot down any fragment of a thought that I can get hold of. And then I gather these fragments, words, phrases, sentences, and I paste them together with my own blood.

Think of the toil it takes to wade through a dozen pages that you must cut down into one paragraph. Sometimes, the vivisection I must commit on myself to create one little living sentence leaves me spent for days.

Now I no longer live in a lonely hall-room in a tenement. I have won many friends. I am invited out to teas and dinners and social affairs. And, I wonder, is my insatiable hunger for people so great because for so many centuries my race has been isolated in Ghettos, shut out of contact with others? Here in America races, classes, and creeds are free to meet and mingle on planes as high and wide as all humanity and its problems. And I am aching to touch all the different races, classes, and creeds at all possible points of contact, and I never seem to have enough of people.

By the year 1900 America had the largest community of free Jews in the world. The growth in the capacity of the Jewish community to take care of its own newcomers had reached the point where the case of the helpless Jewish immigrant was practically unknown. However, a so-called Jewish Problem had reentered the picture in the sense that the influx of Russian Jews destroyed all possibility of completion of the assimilation process which the older Jewish groups (Portuguese, Spanish —also known as Sephardic; German—also known as Ashkenazi) were on the brink of achieving. A counterpart to the revival of insistence upon a Jewish identity was the rise of an active Zionist movement (opposed by Jews of Western European origin) and the birth of a strong Jewish working class and trade union movement of socialist persuasion.

According to the *American Jewish Yearbook*, the number of Jews in the city of Chicago had grown to 75,000 by 1904. This is under 5 percent of Chicago's then population of 1,600,000, but more interesting is the division of Jews into the following national categories: 50,000 Russian Jews, 20,000 German Jews, and a balance of 5,000 of those of other national origins. This proportion would be repeated elsewhere, indicating that the older Jewish groups had already been swamped by the influx of arrivals from the Pale. With their strong sense of organization and association, the 75,000 Jews of Chicago were already divided · ɔ 50 religious congregations, 39 charitable societies, 60 lodges, 13 loan associations, 11 social clubs, and 4 active Zionist societies!

In the life of the ghetto Jew, religion played a particularly important role. In Judaism, learning and education are of vital concern to the religious practitioner in the sense that education is, for him, an essentially religious activity. Both the spirit and practice of the great, orthodox centers of learning in eastern Poland and the Russian Pale were transferred successfully to the New World, thanks to the scholarly rabbis who made the trip. Under their leadership, the synagogue was all-powerful in the Jewish community, its influence going far beyond the usual boundaries of religion. One may grasp the reality of life in the ghetto and its culture by putting together three basic elements: *Yiddish,* the spoken language common to all; the *Landsmannschaft,* or association, which brought together in the same place and organization all those emanating from the same village back in the "old country"; and the *chevra,* or the entire religious community and entity. A strict and orthodox brand of Hebraicism, built upon the traditions of thousands of years, prevailed over the challenging conservative and liberal-reform versions. Centers of religious orthodoxy, built upon particular synagogues and located within the Jewish ghettos, could match in wealth, prestige, and influence the great orthodox centers of learning left in the Old World. Little wonder that the first serious controversy in which the American Jewish community became embroiled was the issue of permitting Jewish stores to be open on Sundays, since the Hebrew Sabbath was, of course, on a Saturday.

The specific role of the Russian Jewish synagogue is partly described in the passage that follows.

The Russian Jew brings with him the quaint customs of a religion full of poetry and of the sources of good citizenship.[13] The orthodox synagogue is not merely a house of prayer; it is an intellectual centre, a mutual aid society, a fountain of self-denying altruism, and a literary club, no less than a place of worship. The study-rooms of the hundreds of synagogues, where the good old people of the Ghetto come to read and discuss "words of law" as well as the events of the day, are crowded every evening in the week with poor street peddlers and with those gray-haired misunderstood sweat-shop hands of whom the public hears every time a tailor strike is declared. So few are the joys which this world has to spare for these overworked, enfeebled victims of "the inferno of modern times" that their religion is to many of them the only thing which makes life worth living. In the fervor of prayer or the abandon of religious study they forget the grinding poverty of their homes. Between the walls of the synagogue, on the top floor of some ramshackle tenement house, they sing beautiful melodies, some of them composed in the caves and forests of Spain, where the wandering people worshiped the God of their fathers at the risk of their lives; and these and the sighs and sobs of the Days of Awe, the thrill that passes through the heartbroken talith-covered congregation when the shofar blows, the mirth which fills the house of God and the tenement homes upon the Rejoicing of the Law, the tearful greet-

13 Reprinted from Edmund Jane James (ed.), *The Immigrant Jew in America* (New York, 1907), p. 40.

ings and humbled peace-makings on Atonement Eve, the mysterious light of the Chanuccah (a festival in memory of the Restoration of the Temple in the time of Maccabeans), candles, the gifts and charities of Purim, a festival commemorating the events in the time of Esther, the joys and kingly solemnities of Passover—all these pervade the atmosphere of the Ghetto with a beauty and a charm without which the life of its older residents would often be one of unrelieved misery.

Jews entered American professions on a large scale, soon becoming physicians, druggists, dentists, lawyers, and educators. Energetic and creative, they left their mark everywhere. Irving Howe, the literary critic, has written about Abraham Cahan—long editor of the *Forward*, author of the famous novel, *The Rise of David Levinsky*, Yiddish critic and publicist, and political leader of socialist persuasion—as characteristic of the successful Jewish professional. Cahan came to America in 1882, after the pogroms and the assassination of Alexander II. He rose rapidly and with astonishing success. But his most important function was to articulate the aspirations of the New York East Side Jewish masses. In the words of Howe:

> Cahan was the kind of publicist who stands uneasily between intellectuals and masses, transmitting the sentiments of one to the other, yet soon making his position into a sort of fulcrum-point for a Bonapartist exercise of his will.[14]

In the life and activity of hundreds of men like Cahan, the Lower East Side created a distinct Jewish subculture which, years later and not until the Thirties, finally took a gigantic leap forward into the cultural and historic stream that is America.

The ghetto of the Jew is now a closed episode in the long history of these people. Dispersed and scattered in various parts of our great cities, but mainly removed to suburbia, the offspring of the Jewish immigrant holds but a rapidly fading memory, nostalgic and idyllic, of what life in the ghetto once was. Our present notion of the ghetto is, of course, built on our vision of the black ghetto: Harlem, Bedford-Stuyvesant, Chicago East Side. This is a far cry from the home of the newly arrived ethnic immigrant of the "new" immigration. Even in terms of health and living conditions, the old ghetto was preferable.

Politically, with the exception of the active and substantial minority of Jewish workers and intellectuals (professionals) who embraced the socialist and radical movement of their day while still retaining the kernel and flavor of their Jewishness, most Jews of the ghetto followed the traditional immigrant and American path. The Jewish wards were dominated by ward machines of the respective parties—generally the Democratic Party—votes were widely purchased as elsewhere, and the Jewish

14 Reprinted from Irving Howe, "Abe Cahan," *Commentary*, March 1970, p. 88.

voter tended to live and let live. The Jew was as patriotic as the next, serving in the army and in the various wars of the twentieth century.

To summarize, if the ghetto may properly be considered an organized cultural community, the New York City Lower East Side ghetto, the patriarch of them all, was the undisputed center of American Jewry and Jewish cultural life. The synagogue, dominated by the rabbinate and the Jewish elders, was the key institution of the culture. The ghetto was a physical fact, a geographic fact, and, perhaps most importantly, a state of mind. If we read the following chapter taken from Michael Gold's famous novel written in the social-realist style, we may obtain a more balanced picture of the ghetto—that is, how it appeared in the eyes of the children of these Jewish immigrants.

> I can never forget the East Side street where I lived as a boy.[15]
>
> It was a block from the notorious Bowery, a tenement canyon hung with fire-escapes, bed-clothing, and faces.
>
> Always these faces at the tenement windows. The street never failed them. It was an immense excitement. It never slept. It roared like a sea. It exploded like fireworks.
>
> People pushed and wrangled in the street. There were armies of howling pushcart peddlers. Women screamed, dogs barked and copulated. Babies cried.
>
> A parrot cursed. Ragged kids played under truck-horses. Fat housewives fought from stoop to stoop. A beggar sang.
>
> At the livery stable coach drivers lounged on a bench. They hee-hawed with laughter, they guzzled cans of beer.
>
> Pimps, gamblers and red-nosed bums; peanut politicians, pugilists in sweaters; tinhorn sports and tall longshoremen in overalls. An endless pageant of East Side life passed through the wicker doors of Jake Wolf's saloon.
>
> The saloon goat lay on the sidewalk, and dreamily consumed a *Police Gazette.*
>
> East Side mothers with heroic bosoms pushed their baby carriages, gossiping. Horse cars jingled by. A tinker hammered at brass. Junkbells clanged. Whirlwinds of dust and newspaper. The prostitutes laughed shrilly. A prophet passed, an old-clothes Jew with a white beard. Kids were dancing around the hurdy-gurdy. Two bums slugged each other.
>
> Excitement, dirt, fighting, chaos! The sound of my street lifted like the blast of a great carnival or catastrophe. The noise was always in my ears. Even in sleep I could hear it; I can hear it now.
>
> The East Side of New York was then the city's red light district, a vast 606 playground under the business management of Tammany Hall.
>
> The Jews had fled from the European pogroms; with prayer, thanksgiving and solemn faith from a new Egypt into a new Promised Land.
>
> They found awaiting them the sweatshops, the bawdy houses and Tammany Hall.

[15] Reprinted from Michael Gold, *Jews without Money* (New York: Liveright, 1930), pp. 13, 14, 15, 19, 20.

There were hundreds of prostitutes on my street. They occupied vacant stores, they crowded into flats and apartments in all the tenements. The pious Jews hated the traffic. But they were pauper strangers here; they could do nothing. They shrugged their shoulders, and murmured: "This is America." They tried to live.

They tried to shut their eyes. We children did not shut our eyes. We saw and knew.

On sunshiny days the whores sat on chairs along the sidewalks. They sprawled indolently, their legs taking up half the pavements. People stumbled over a gauntlet of whores' meaty legs.

The girls gossiped and chirped like a jungle of parrots. Some knitted shawls and stockings. Others hummed. Others chewed Russian sunflower seeds and monotonously spat out the shells.

The girls winked and jeered, made lascivious gestures at passing males. They pulled at coat-tails and cajoled men with fake honeyed words. They called their wares like pushcart peddlers. At five years I knew what it was they sold.

The girls were naked under flowery kimonos. Chunks of breast and belly occasionally flashed. Slippers hung from their feet; they were always ready for "business."

Earth's trees, grass, flowers could not grow on my street; but the rose of syphilis bloomed by night and by day. . . .

I will always remember that licking, not because it humiliated me, or taught me anything, but because the next day was my fifth birthday.

My father was young then. He loved good times. He took the day off from work and insisted that I be given a birthday party. He bought me a velvet suit with lace collar and cuffs, and patent leather shoes. In the morning he insisted that we all go to be photographed. He made my mother wear her black plush gown. He made her dress my sister in the Scotch plaid. Himself he arrayed in his black suit that made him look like a lawyer.

My mother groaned as we walked through the street. She hated new shoes, new clothes, all fuss or feathers. I was miserable, too. My gang saw me, and snickered at my velvet suit.

But my father was happy, and so was my sister, Esther. They chattered like two children.

It was solemn at the photographer's. My father sat stiffly in a dark carved throne. My mother stood upright beside him, with one hand on his shoulder, to show her wedding ring. My sister rested against my father's knee. I stood on the other side of the throne, holding a basket of artificial flowers.

The bald, eager little photographer disappeared behind a curtain. He snapped his fingers before us, and said, "Watch the birdie." I watched, my neck hurting me because of the clamp. Something clicked; the picture was taken. We went home, exhausted but triumphant. . . .

THE UKRAINIANS

Ukrainians have been known historically under a number of names, often used interchangeably or confused. At one time or another parts of the Greater Ukraine—called Ukrainia by the nationalists—have been overrun or subjugated by either the Russians, the Poles, the Austrians, or the Hungarians. Ukrainians today constitute parts of at least three countries: Soviet Russia, Poland, and Czechoslovakia; hence, in one form or another these people live under communist rule. The issue of national independence and Ukrainian sovereignty is therefore very much alive for the typical Ukrainian. Under the Russian Czar, these people were known as "Little Russians," indicative of their lowly status in the eyes of their Great Russian lords and masters. Historians have referred to subdivisions of the Ukrainians variously as "Carpatho-Russians" and even "Russians," much to the indignation of this proud people. Ethnically, whether living in that part of Russia known as the Ukraine (now the Soviet Ukrainian Republic) or in parts of Poland and Czechoslovakia, Ukrainians possess the same national language and the same general cultural background. It is this that has kept alive the spirit of Ukrainian nationalism, which foresees the day when all Ukrainians will be united in a nation of their own. It has also, however, encouraged sharp and bitter disagreements within the Ukrainian people between those who support Russia, including the present Soviet government, and those who advocate some form of independent Ukrainian nationalism.

Immigration began on a noticeable scale only in the 1870's, largely as a result of intensive political and religious persecution at the hands of the Russian Czar. The centers of resistance to both the Russian imperial authorities and the Russian Orthodox Church were the dioceses of the Ukrainian and Ruthenian Catholic Church. The church also regulated the migratory movement and, in fact, has always exercised a powerful influence over a deeply religious people. While there was never any major exodus of Ukrainians, it is estimated that by 1914 perhaps as many as 700,000 Ukrainians had entered the United States. Since ethnic differences between Russians, Ruthenians, and Ukrainians were not taken into account by the immigration authorities until 1896, this is at best a shaky estimate. Eastern Galicia, a part of Poland and, hence, a part of the Russian Empire, was the center from which most Ukrainians migrated.

Once settled in the New World, a tiny percentage of the Ukrainian immigration became wheat farmers in the West. But the bulk of these people helped to fulfill the seemingly inexhaustible need of the country for factory and industrial workers. The largest group of Ukrainians settled in southwestern Pennsylvania, in and around the city of Pittsburgh. They were employed in the soft coal mining areas of Pennsylvania and were often found in the iron foundries of the region. Others settled in Chicago, New York City, and the industrial centers of New Jersey. Some accumulated sufficient money to buy homesteads in the Dakotas, Montana, and western Canada. Still others went into small businesses (such as grocery stores) or, after obtaining the necessary education, became professional people. All, almost without exception, however, took their first job doing anything in order to pay off their debt (usually $100) for the initial trip to the New World. One notorious activity generally associated with Ukrainians was enlistment in strike-breaking activities and organizations, usually in connection with strikes initiated by the Irish in the western Pennsylvania coal fields. Other groups of Ukrainians moved into the coal mining districts of Ohio, West Virginia, Illinois, as well as the iron mines of Minnesota and Michigan. Wherever factory hands were needed in the urban and industrial centers, these powerful and long-enduring people could be found. Strongly imbued with the desire to hold onto their language and culture, they formed tightly knit groups and islands in the great sea of American life. Against heavy odds, they tried to distinguish themselves through their language and cultural associations from the Russians, with whom they were most frequently confused. It was largely a losing battle.

Wasyl Halich, author of *Ukrainians in the United States*, describes the process by which Ukrainians found a place for themselves within the American industrial order, and he relates the hardships endured by this particularly burdened ethnic group.

At Work in the Pennsylvania Mines[16]

A very large percentage of the newcomers settled in the mining communities, beginning with Pennsylvania. The first appearance of Ukrainians in the Pennsylvania anthracite-coal mines was in the seventies (1877) in the regions of Shenandoah, Shamokin, Mt. Carmel, Olyphant, and Scranton. They were induced to come to America by an agent of coal-mining companies whose workers were then on strike. The experience of the first Ukrainian group in America contains some of the basic elements of that of other pioneers on this continent. When they landed in New York, they did not understand a word of English; their colorful attire attracted much attention, and they were regarded as a curiosity. Being unable to get lodgings, they had to leave the city. They walked to Philadelphia, being forced to sleep outdoors because people were afraid to give shelter to such curious strangers. By the time they reached Harrisburg their energy was exhausted, but a kind-hearted American, seeing their condition, had pity on them and gave them food. Other people, however, fearful of such strangers, urged them out of town. One farmer gave them lodging, but the following night they had to sleep under a bridge. Finally they reached Shenandoah, Pennsylvania, where a Luthuanian immigrant, a business man, Carl Rice by name (in Lithuanian "Ruchus"), took care of them. Rice was a great friend of the Ukrainian immigrants to the end of his life.

This group of immigrants arrived in the mining communities during a labor strike. Not understanding the conditions, or probably because of necessity, they went to work as strike-breakers; consequently they brought upon themselves the hatred of old miners,

[16] Reprinted from Wasyl Halich, *Ukrainians in the United States* (Chicago: University of Chicago Press, 1937), pp. 28–29.

mostly Irishmen. There were frequent assaults on the strike-breakers which ended in riots. The influx of fresh immigrants tended to keep the wages low, and this prolonged the racial and labor antagonism between the Ukrainian and Irish groups. In connection with this racial animosity not infrequently the newcomer became a victim of "accidental" injury in the mine, or even death. Such were the prevailing conditions in 1884 . . . .

THE RUTHENIANS

Never a significant group in the history of American immigration, the Ruthenians—also known on occasion, particularly in the immigration records, as the Russniaks—had their biggest moment of migration in the year 1906 when approximately 16,000 left the northern part of what was then the Austro-Hungarian Empire and undertook the voyage to the New World.

A Slavic people, the Ruthenians had the misfortune of being oppressed by a succession of masters: first by Polish landlords under whom they were serfs when they occupied sections of eastern Poland; then by the Austro-Hungarian Empire; finally, by the Czarist Empire.

The word *Ruthenia* is the Latinized form of *Russia*. The term was originally applied to the Ukraine in the Middle Ages, when that area was ruled by the kings of Ruthenia. Later, under the Austro-Hungarian Empire, the term Ruthenians was used to designate the Ukrainian population of the western Ukraine, which included the Russian provinces of Galicia, Bukovina, and Carpathian Ukraine.

There is no ethnic or linguistic distinction between Ukrainians and Ruthenians. Culturally, however, there is a religious difference, since Ruthenians are or were affiliated with the Roman Catholic Church in distinction from the Ukrainians, who form part of the Greek Orthodox Church, which was fully restored in the seventeenth century in the Russian part of the Ukraine.

The Ruthenian immigration to America closely parallels that of the Ukrainian. Several hundred thousand came over in the years preceding World War I, entered industry along with similar Russian groups, and retained their identity for a considerable number of years through the formation of strong local clubs and language societies. Church was particularly important to these people and probably their strongest cultural bond. They settled in Pennsylvania, New York, and New Jersey, with a substantial distribution in our larger cities in the Twenties: Chicago, 45,000; Pittsburgh, 35,000; Cleveland, 30,000; Detroit, 30,000; Jersey City, 25,000; and New York City, 20,000. Playing no special or unusual role in the story of American immigration, they are by and large indistinguishable from their closely related ethnic and linguistic brethren, the Ukrainians.

Nevertheless, they had their full share of experiences as an ethnic group in America. This dimension of their lives is described in the following extracts taken from Jerome Davis, *Russians and Ruthenians in America*. Below, he records the impressions of the Ruthenians as a subculture within a culture, completely isolated from the American people.

First impressions.[17]—The majority of Russians and Ruthenians are almost as completely isolated from the American people as if they were in the heart of giant Russia. They have no points of contact with the sound elements of American life. The dream of the Russian as he leaves his native shore is that everything is beautiful in America. It is the land of liberty and equality but he begins to feel that perhaps he has been hoodwinked almost as soon as he reaches Ellis Island. The Russians claim that the coarse and brutal treatment they receive at the immigrant stations is far worse than that in the Russia of the Tsars. Certainly the wholesale tagging of the immigrant, the physical inspection, the turning back of the eyelids, rushed through with machine-like regularity resembles more the inspection of cattle than of thousands of human souls. Only this year Commissioner Wallis, head of the immigrant station at Ellis Island, has complained of the methods of his subordinates who seem to think that an immigrant's time is worth nothing at all. It is small wonder that their first taste of liberty does not appeal. Then as they push on to their destination at Gary, or Pittsburgh, or Chicago, there is no one who tries to help them. I remember meeting two Russians at the Grand Central Station in New York. They were wandering about trying to find out when their train would go. Their inquiries in broken English met no response from the busy ticket agent. They stood beside their bags and baggage, a little picture of Russia in New York. They would ask passers-by about the train but at no time did anyone stop more than to say, "We don't know." One richly dressed woman replied as she would to a dog, "Get away from me." The look on their faces when I helped them showed how deep their perplexity and apprehension had been.

Indeed, the treatment at Ellis Island and in the railroad trains frequently awakens other sentiments than love for the new home. The immigrant has to learn at once the dangers of exploitation which await him. If he goes into the railroad dining room he is usually hustled out. If he follows the advice of a seemingly kind friend as to where to eat he is often robbed of his money. Sometimes his baggage is stolen, and there have even been cases of the abduction of his daughter or wife before he has been on American soil twelve hours. At best, the first impressions of America are discouraging because the treatment of a vast throng of incoming strangers has not yet been put on a friendly enough basis. We still are doing largely only the things that will safeguard America from undesirables and not enough genuinely to help the foreigner.

He describes the hardship of bearing a Russian or Ruthenian name during the time of American animosity toward Russia.

[17] From Davis, *Russians and Ruthenians in America,* pp. 104–106.

Real Americanization.[18] Real Americanization is a spiritual thing. It means that the Russian or Ruthenian loves our country and is willing to sacrifice in its behalf. This love can be created only by his experiencing that which is worthy of loyalty and sacrifice. If you are traveling to England your opinion of that country is determined by your experience with the English. It rests with them more than it does with you. In the same, only in a more intensified way, because the Russian does not speak our language and knows little of our history or traditions, he must judge America on his own contacts with our people.

Furthermore, after the scare about Russian Bolsheviks had been widely flaunted by our press, the Russians began to be laid off right and left simply on account of their nationality. The inevitable result was that whereas these men had been good honest workers they became embittered and radical. This is expressed in a letter of an educated Russian from Worcester, Mass.: "Many thousands of Russians in this country while they work have hardly enough to live on, and now that the war is ended, they are discharged from factories, and told, 'you are a Bolshevik.' Many of them do not know what Bolshevism and what capitalism mean but they make real Bolsheviks out of them." Several large firms frankly told me that they refused employment to Russians. "We can get plenty of other nationalities," said one employer, "why take Bolsheviks?" Unfortunately from the standpoint of the Russian worker, it does not seem quite so fair. He comes to our country, works seven years in the steel plant, loses his best strength in the work and then is laid off because the Bolsheviks seize control in Russia. Can one wonder if some give up the struggle? On the bodies of two such Russians who were found dead on the railroad track, this explanation was found, "We prefer death to starvation. Have worked in the hell of a steel plant for seven years. Now they discharge us and we can't find a job."

KEY QUESTIONS

1. Explain the distinction between "old" and "new" immigration. Were there any connotations implicit in the use of such terms? Discuss.

2. Describe the mass of Russian immigration in terms of the following: when they came to the United States; why they came; where they located in the United States.

3. To what extent were the East European Jewish immigrants exploited in America upon their arrival at the turn of the twentieth century?

4. In Eastern Europe the Jew was compelled to live in the ghetto; in the United States the Jewish ghetto has been eliminated. Analyze the reasons for this development.

5. Compare the ethnic experiences of the Ukrainians and the Ruthenians in the United States.

[18] Ibid., p. 109.

7

The Mediterranean People

The increasing ethnic diversity characteristic of the "New Immigration" finds people originating in countries bordering the Mediterranean Sea well represented. Like that of people from Central and Eastern Europe the influx of the Mediterranean people in the 1880's and 1890's was new and disturbing, adding to the burdens of city officials and complicating urban reforms. The Mediterranean peoples to be covered in this chapter are the Italians, Greeks, Portuguese, and Syrians. Arriving in a strange country, with little or no knowledge of its language and customs, they were expected to find their own place in society largely without benefit of special services from either the federal or state governments.

Most of these foreigners fed into the country from the federal government's hopper at Ellis Island, with many of them intending to remain in New York City. When Americans thought about these people at all, they thought of them as "problems." As members of the new immigration, they became stereotypes for the "undesirable citizens." Yet they were vital to the development of the nation's burgeoning industries, supplying physical strength and bodily labor for digging ditches for the great waterways, for working the mines, and for manning the blast furnaces. Many of these foreign workers came through the padrone system, a method of immigrant recruitment first developed in southern Italy but used effectively among Greeks and Syrians as well. Under this system labor bosses rounded up young Italians and transported them to America in near-servile conditions for employment. The practice soon was outlawed and practically ceased to exist by the 1880's.

Many other agencies, such as steamship lines, railroad companies, and state-sponsored drives for emigrants, operated as influences in the migration; yet the underlying forces were the same that had brought over the first great wave of immigration in the period prior to 1815, that is, religious and political discontent and desire for economic opportunities.

One must not overlook the official temper of the nations from which these Mediterranean immigrants came. For the first two-thirds of the nineteenth century, their governments opposed emigration if they did not prohibit it. But after Italy achieved unification in the 1860's and as large parts of the ancient Ottoman Empire freed themselves from Moslem rule, official restraint eroded. The pressures of a vastly changing agrarian economy and the ending of feudalistic practices served as expulsive forces that compelled governments now to eye emigration as a solution to situations of chronic poverty and overpopulation. What is to be remembered as well is that not only were the lands of emigration changing but so was America herself. For the Italian, the Greek, the Portuguese, and the Syrian, this presented additional problems of adjustment.

THE ITALIANS

Italy is one of modern history's classic examples of an emigrating country. Compared to most of the other major countries of Western Europe— Great Britain, Ireland, Norway, and Germany—Italy entered the field of emigration at a relatively late date in history. What it lacked in terms of longevity, however, it made up for in numbers. By 1900, six million Italians had emigrated to various countries. This figure would be eclipsed by an even greater number in the twentieth century. While many of these people became return immigrants to their homeland, several million found new homes in new countries, with the largest number (over five million) entering the United States.

In the early period of Italian immigration most of the emigrants came from regions such as Venezia and Liguria, in Northern Italy. Later, during the accelerated period of immigration, the Southern portion of the peninsula (La Campagna and Sicily) provided the bulk. The very size of Italian immigration posed a threat to native Americans, and thus the Italians quickly became the stereotype of the undesirable element. Indeed, much of the force behind restrictive immigration laws, such as literacy tests and the quota system, was aimed at them. While some of these immigrants came from the artisan and factory-trained class, most were versed in agriculture as farmers, foresters, workmen, and shepherds, a type of work for which they would find few outlets in the United States.

The causes of their departure from their homeland were primarily economic. They inhabited one of the most densely populated nations in Europe; industrial development was retarded; and the overworked soil continually presented the country with health crises such as malaria. While Italians emigrated to escape from hunger, they also fled from the rural padroni to whose privileged position they owed ancient social deference. Thus, egalitarian principles intermingled with economic. It is also notable that numerous Italian public officials regarded emigration as a favorable solution to various Italian economic, social, and political problems.

The experience of the early immigrants was one of shock. They were confronted with a different and higher standard of living and with unfamiliar customs in lands vastly dissimilar to the provinces from which they came. Life in the alien lands was very trying at best. This caused one astute observer to remark:

> The Italian immigrant who does not become a delinquent or crazy— is a saint. No immigrant is normal; and America is a land of immigrants who do not speak the original tongue, nor follow its religion and its political habits and its social diversions, is in fact full of the abnormal. . . .[1]

Thus Italians found themselves marginal men in an unfriendly land, or if included in the new society, it was in the most elemental way, as in the underworld. But the majority of Italians had little to do with criminality, even if they did not oppose it strenuously. The majority worked long hours in humble occupations.

The Italian immigrant experienced tribulation at every step along the way. The emigrant ship in which he was borne was buffeted by rough seas, his courage was smothered by the crowds of immigrants, and he found no surcease of his difficulties upon reaching the American shore. He was now compelled to look for work, seek living quarters in towns and cities totally foreign to him, confront people with strange and even antithetical modes of dress, and communicate in an unfamiliar language, difficult at best to learn, especially for housewives. In order to cope with these handicaps, most Italians banded together in colonies which came to be known as "Little Italies," e.g., East Harlem, the Lower East Side of New York City, or the North End of Boston. Rarely did the immigrant leave the place of debarkation. This meant taking up residence in the industrial towns and cities along the eastern seaboard. It meant also that he would have little opportunity to practice his agricultural expertise, although he would have the opportunity to change his trade, and the comforting advantage of living next to his compatriots.

A smaller but significant number did, however, seek their fortunes in the regions west of the Mississippi River, and they seemed to experience important improvement in their living circumstances, despite encountering prejudice and adversity. It is to be remembered that in 1891 eleven Italians were hanged by a lynch mob in New Orleans and the same fate visited other Italians in the mining sections of Colorado.[2]

---

[1] Renzo De Felice, "L'emigrazione egli emigrante nell' ultima secolo," in *Terzo Programma*, ERI Edizione, N. 3, 1964, p. 176.

[2] For an excellent history of the Italians in the western part of the United States, see Andrew F. Rolle, *The Immigrant Upraised* (Norman: University of Oklahoma Press, 1966).

Not all Italians in the East remained in the "Little Italies." A minority energetically sought complete transformation of their lives rather than transplantation. They quickly learned the English language, intermarried with Anglo-Saxons, moved into non-Italian neighborhoods, scrupulously avoided contact with the old Italian compatriots, and changed their names and even their religion in their desire to be accepted. Most, however, had a conscious desire to transplant their old way of life to the New World. The first generation carried on their lives in the Italian language, shopped in Italian stores, read Italian newspapers, cooked Italian meals, went to Italian plays and movies, and continued Italian religious practices (this usually meant practices and devotions germane to a particular region of Italy). The second generation took greater strides into Americanization. They adopted American customs more readily at the expense of Italian culture and language. This often caused deep linguistic and cultural strains between first and second generation Italian-Americans. The second generation also produced individuals of some influence in American life: prominent political figures on state and local levels such as F. H. LaGuardia and Vito Marcantonio, union and industrial leaders such as Luigi Antonini of the ILGWU and the DiNapoli brothers in the construction industry, and various practitioners in the medical and legal professions.

The tenacity with which Italians held onto their culture was only one side of the picture, however. Thus, the Italo-American came to speak a language that was neither pure Italian nor pure English, but rather a combination. "Grosseria" became a new word for the grocery, "fruttistanne" for fruit stand, "ghella" for girl, and so forth. In a similar manner Italian culture has undergone great dissolution among Italian-Americans. A true fusion of Italian and American has not yet taken place. Somehow the Italian-Americans have not become fully assimilated but neither have they retained Italian culture. Language, the key to the maintenance of ties with the mother country, has not been extensively learned or cultivated by the newer generation of Italians in America. Nevertheless, ethnicity is still a force among many Italian-Americans. The majority of Italian-Americans still marry Italian-Americans; they continue to socialize (not exclusively) with Italian-Americans, and they take a certain pride in their ancient heritage in a kind of mystical way. At the very least they take serious umbrage at the popular notion that somehow Italians are more connected with or susceptible to criminal activities than other national groups by the mere fact of their Italian background. Thus, although greatly diluted, the persistence of ethnicity among Italians in America is an ongoing phenomenon.

One of the earliest and most complete historians of Italian emigration was Robert F. Foerster. His study runs the gamut of topics under which emigration can be studied. It also gives substance to the central theme of ethnicity that accompanied and developed among the Italians in America. In the first selection, Foerster relates the role of the Italians in industry. He demonstrates the way one ethnic group succeeds another —in this case the Italians replaced the Irish as longshoremen and railroad workers. This selection also includes evaluations of the Italians as workers (often unfavorably) and the impairment they suffered as a result of industrial accidents.

South Italians almost entirely, they first found employment on the New York waterfront about 1887.[3] Between 1890 and 1892 they increased, and by 1896 promised to threaten the supremacy of Irish and Irish-Americans. By 1912 they had become a close second to these older groups, and had forced them to speculate, or even confidently to predict, that within ten years the Italians would stand first. . . .

In its swiftness, this substitution of the Italian longshoremen for others is one of the most striking examples of racial displacement in American industry. It is by reason of their increasing numbers and not by superior qualities that they have come to the fore. In discharging Mediterranean fruit they may have a special fitness; but generally they have been ordinary coal shovellers and pier men, sometimes hold men, only rarely deck hands. They have had less strength than the Irish, if common opinion and some rough experiments may be accepted in testimony.

The Scandinavian-American Line, Hoboken, once worked a gang of Irish in one coal boat and a gang of Italians in another at the same time, and found by actual count that the Irish brought up two bucketfuls to the Italians' one. (Again.) A foreman . . . told of once having put Italians to work piling sugar. It had been the custom to pile it four and five bags high, but when they got it three bags high they had reached their limit. Another stated that he had seen Italians sink helpless under bags of sugar which the Irish handled easily. A third said there is a knack in the work which the Irish possess. He had seen two Irishmen grab a bag of sugar by its ears and swing it up, after Italians had tugged at it for some time without moving it.

It is worth noting that they have been inducted into the industry by contracting stevedores of their own people, who have usually withheld a part of their wages by way of commission. Because of this deduction and because their employment has commonly been less regular than that of the Irish, their earnings, in the period about 1912, were generally as little as $10 or $12 a week.

What is characteristic in the labor of Italian men in North America is nowhere so apparent as on the railways. Both relatively and absolutely, the South Italians, as construction and repair workmen, have there achieved a foremost position. The censuses are but blind aids to tracing these elusive armies. It is true that the cate-

[3] Reprinted by permission of the publishers from *The Italian Emigration of Our Times* by Robert F. Foerster (Cambridge, Mass.: Harvard University Press, 1919), pp. 356–58, 362, 389.

gory of general steam-railway employees gives to the Italians an altogether exceptional place, but it embraces only a part of them, while the others are mainly and indistinguishably collected in the group of general laborers. . . .

The Italians have succeeded as the predominant unskilled railway laborers of the country. Other people have played important parts—the Chinese, Germans, negroes, Slavs, and Hungarians, more recently the Mexicans and Japanese—but Irish and Italians, in successive epochs, have led all. Thirty odd years ago, when rag pickers and street musicians still seemed to many the very quintessence of Italian immigration, the pick-and-shovel laborers were silently being carried to the remoter places and set to work on the railways. A decade later, a contemporary non-statistical view held that "the Irish have ceased building railroads and doing the hard work of constructing public works. The Italians have taken their place." . . .

In an actual test made by this company to determine the efficiency of Italian laborers, they were shown to have performed in a given time only from 35 per cent to 50 per cent of the same work done by native laborers.

> From our experience it is generally agreed that (Southern) Italians run below Americans as to strength and efficiency. . . . It is the general opinion that the Northern Italian, together with the Austrian, is the best foreign laborer. The Southern Italian is a poor worker of low efficiency; and the Sicilian is a very poor, undesized laborer, incapable of heavy work.

What clearly emerges from this study is that the Italians are employed in great numbers partly because they are to be had, while other workmen are not, and partly because, in certain kinds of work especially, and with due organization and oversight, they produce good results. While demonstrating less power in accomplishment than some of their harder-fibered predecessors, they have been willing to fag in isolated places for many hours in the day. . . .

A constant source of bodily impairment or death is industrial accident. The occupational concentration of the Italians is precisely such as to subject them to risk; for few are in agriculture or the commercial callings, and many work in an environment of rocks, heavy machinery, sharp implements, and the elemental motive powers. Blasting, concrete mixing, coal gases, and the dangerous seams of coal mines dispose, typically, to many accidents. Ignorance of spoken English, inability to read, fatigue, that uncultivated intelligence which, after a mishap, is only too easily called carelessness, complicate the risk. . . . Now and then, as at Cherry, Illinois, and Dawson, New Mexico, a single accident may destroy a hundred or more Italians. No one can say how many industrial injuries or deaths take place each year in the length and breadth of the land. No one can say how many of those who escape injury in one year will not meet it in five or ten years, or twenty. Once it happened commonly that the worker was known to his employer only by number, so that identification was impossible, and friends were uninformed; and even today this occurs, or Pasquale suffers a sea change into Pat!

Foerster examines the dualistic aspect of Americanization.

What few Italians understand before they come to the United States—and I speak especially of those who will linger or stay permanently—is that a mysterious process of unmaking and remaking will take place in them.[4] In the older persons the inevitable resistance is greater than in the young. But all have come a long way, and their die is cast. Children of circumstance, they are under a spell of suggestion which makes them fertile ground for the seeds of assimilation—to good elements of our life or bad. America would "Americanize" them. But "Americanization" is a two-edged sword. Some the prodigious conflict will strengthen, others it will weaken. All that moral support that men derive from religious and social ties with the group they have grown up with is imperilled when they find themselves in the maelstrom of a strange land. The Italians are rural dwellers dropped into the unaccustomed brutal parts of great cities. The fascination of the new home may be unwholesome, but it is keen. For many the destiny is one of loneliness, disappointment, demoralization, sometimes transitional in its stay, but often enduring. The immigrant has pressed his steps into a "one-way street."

The Italian laborers are seen as competitors and threats to the native-born.

The non-immigrant laborers similarly have a point of view, which, like that of the employers, is echoed by many persons in the general population.[5] The Italian is a competitor, because of his numbers and his qualities deemed unwelcome. His saving grace is that he often enters trades in which his competition with Americans is not apparent or direct. He takes a low wage; even, according to a charge that is common and, I believe, sometimes well founded, a lower wage than others would require for equivalent work. Such is his tractability that strikes for increase of wages and all bargaining for better conditions are through his presence less likely to succeed, and so the general condition remains poor. That employers make capital out of racial rivalries, playing off "Wop" against "Hunkie," for example, and so preventing a united labor front, is well enough established. To American laborers the procedure has naturally been obnoxious, and they have perhaps been more willing to regard the Italian as blameworthy than as victimized. Equally they dislike the Italian's readiness to pay commissions for jobs and to accept a loss from a loose calculation of time served—for example, to take pay for 29½ hours when the work has lasted 30.

Italians have often been strike breakers. They helped to defeat the Pennsylvania coal strike of 1887–88. A few took employment during the longshoremen's strike of 1887, and their increasing numbers became the employers' means of preventing further trouble. The immediate cause of the introduction of Italians into the New York clothing industry is declared to have been the employers' desire to escape trade-union demands. With other workers they

[4] Ibid., p. 394.
[5] Ibid., pp. 402–404.

helped to break the Chicago meat packing strike of 1904. . . . During the war years, with the tremendous enhancement of the bargaining power of labor, Italians have frequently participated in strikes and at times, as in the case of the coal heavers of the New York piers in 1917, they were the first to quit work.

Yet it is still but a fraction of the Italians who are members of unions. Only one in ten of the South Italians was found by the Immigration Commission to be organized (among the less numerous and more skilled North Italians the rate was nearly four times as great). In many quarters their strike breaking history still condemns them and their competition is feared even when it is not detected. . . .

The reception Italians received in some parts of the United States was violent even to the point of death. The most notorious case of anti-Italian sentiment resulting in death was the lynching of eleven Sicilians in Louisiana in 1891. The role of emotion and outright ethnic prejudice was obvious as recorded in the account that follows.

In 1890 a series of Sicilian crimes, partly in the nature of vendettas, occurred.[6] They were due primarily to the interference in the local fruit trade of various capi mafiosi or Mafia chieftains, of the secret Black Hand (Mano Nera) society. Among these avaricious Sicilians were Antonio and Carlo Matranga, originally from Palermo, who allegedly levied tribute on every banana freighter that came into the harbor. Various Italian competitors who tried to muscle into this lucrative traffic were dumped into canals with their throats cut, or found virtually decapitated. Others became the victims of bombs, shotguns, and daggers.

Although a number of Mafia suspects were tried for these crimes, none were convicted. This led the public to believe that bribery had impeded the course of justice. Then came an even greater shock. On March 15, 1890, while investigating such criminal charges, New Orleans Chief of Police David Hennessy was murdered. This followed upon disclosures of complicity by two rival Sicilian dock-working gangs. Yet none of the witnesses could identify the assassins, although more than forty Italians were arrested the day Hennessy died. The New Orleans *Times-Picayune* reported that they "were as dumb as clams." Suddenly the timidity of the law enraged public opinion. In frontier vigilante fashion a New Orleans mob took justice into its own hands.

Edgar H. Farrar, a prominent white supremacist, headed a "Committee of Fifty" to "suppress the Mafia" and to hunt out Hennessy's assassins. Nine suspects were brought to trial. On March 12, 1891, six of these were acquitted, and a mistrial was declared for the other three. The *Times-Picayune* was indignant, inviting "all good citizens" to a mass meeting "to take steps to remedy the failure of justice in the Hennessy Case." Its readers were exhorted to "come prepared for action," and the newspaper published a list of prom-

6 From *The Immigrant Upraised: Italian Adventurers and Colonists in an Expanding America,* by Andrew F. Rolle, pp. 102, 103. Copyright 1968 by the University of Oklahoma Press.

inent Louisianans who endorsed its call to duty. In the opinion of
the *Times-Picayune* there was no doubt that the Sicilians cowering
in the city jail were linked to criminal elements. In this instance,
a lynching was virtually advertised beforehand in the New Orleans
press.

On March 15, 1891, one year after Police Chief Hennessy's
murder, a mob seized eleven of these unsuspecting Sicilians and
hanged them. Included were the nine who had been tried and two
others who had not. The *Times-Picayune* congratulated the mob,
moralizing that "desperate diseases require desperate measures."
The paper reported proudly that when the mob left the parish
prison eight culprits lay dead on its blood-stained floors and "behind
the crumbling walls of the gloomy old prison another lay dying on a
stretcher near where he had been shot."

Rev. Ladislao Dragoni, an Italian-speaking priest, offered his observations of life in Italian communities in the United States in a work
published in 1927. Reverend Dragoni recounts the strange experience
of how a small number of Italians became involved in a fiercely nativist
secret society whose objectives were inimical to their fellow Italians. He
reveals how some individuals with definite religious and ethnic ties can,
nevertheless, join in a movement to destroy their own ethnic group.

It was a few days since I was in a village in Pennsylvania, an
eminently workers' village, which lived on the work of the obviously
Italian coal miners, because for the most part the inhabitants were
Italians.[7] A little while after my arrival the usual hooded members
of the KKK had burned a cross. Among these arsonists—a new
style—there were also some Italians affiliated with this sect. Very
few in reality. A few units of them. Even in other cities, towns or
villages through which I travelled where this sect has members I
found a few Italians to swell this army—these few—who want to
increase the role of this exercise in marching and conquering for
the grand Invisible Imperial. This phenomenon of Italians is strange
—even the few. Even stranger is this association, still indefinite,
that recruits them and seemingly with such satisfaction.

I saw the publication entitled "Principles and Purposes of the
K.K.K." from which I will recall a passage which makes the proposition, "A large percentage of the foreign immigrants pouring into
this country, during the past few years, have been Roman Catholics,
and a big percentage of these immigrants are from the lower strata
of Italy. The policy of the Klan is to stop the stream of the undesirables and thus prevent the glutting of the American labor market."

I could also extract some other selection describing this type
of Italian character that takes part in this phenomenon, his moral,
social and civil psychology. . . . certainly not to eulogize him but to
condemn him pointing him out as an undesirable character to be
eliminated.

---

[7] Reprinted from Ladislao Dragoni, *Reflessi di Vita Americani e Contrariflessi* (*Reflections and Counter-Reflections on an American Life*) (New York: Catholic Polyglot Publishing House, 1927), pp. 58–60. Translation by Salvatore J. LaGumina.

Now isn't it strange that such an association of this type extends its arms to this undesirable Italian coming from the lowest strata in Italy? Even if it seems a curious phenomenon and strange, it is a fact that—even these few—even our countrymen live in the shadows of the temple of the hooded Klan. They have also become hooded themselves collaborating for the anti-Italian purpose of the sect. But even more strange is it to see Italians so definite . . . against their own who worked to exclude them in an absolute way from public life, ostracizing them who seek to be assimilated, affiliated with this sectarian society which is so hostile to us. Are these countrymen of ours Catholics? If so how can they became part of the Klan which is directly, desperately contrary to Catholicism? The classical motto of the Klan is "for Protestant Christianity first, last and all the time." Is not this order and word clear enough? Is it not a program of hatred towards Catholicism?

Those Italians who have become cavaliers in the K.K.K. are no longer Catholics, because they have renounced that fact. If in the event they have renounced their Catholic religion, I do not believe they have renounced their Italian heritage. How then can they become part of it? In either one case or the other the phenomenon is inexplicable. . . .

It is well to state the aim of the "National Vigilance Association" which pre-arranged to gain every state's approval of the Anti-Masking bill to make propaganda pressuring legislators who make laws to prohibit secret organizations from remaining secure under federal law in order to support the violence of the mob and the excess of fanaticism of the federal judges who offend the United States.

The Italians who more than others are threatened by the hooded ones ought to adhere in a body to the invitation of this Association in which our name and our faith are respected, to resist. They tell us especially that, because Italians are so Catholic, we have contributed to the development of American greatness, with the force of our arms, with the splendor of our faith, with purity of our Catholic morality, while men of the Klan, under the guise of triumphant America, compensate for our heroic sacrifice by fighting them, burning the glorious symbol, fleeing from our Catholicism and our Savoy banner.

Italians! Guard against your name to this strangling Society of some of our brothers on account of our faith and our country.

The religious pattern that emerged for many Italian families who migrated to the United States was often antagonistic to their ancient Catholic religion. For these people who had migrated from their small, peaceful villages, countryside, or mountaintop and who were accustomed to measure their daily routine by the sound of the church bell, the experience of being thrust into the hustle and bustle of a huge and alien metropolis proved to be disturbing and disorienting. A number of them either rebelled or developed habits in which their ties to the Catholic Church atrophied. The experience of Bella V. Dodd, a one-time prominent Communist and later famous convert to her original religion, is perhaps reflective of the pattern that emerged.

We had neighbors all about us—Scotch, Irish, and German families.[8] There were two Catholic churches not far from us. . . . We did not seem to belong to either church and Father and Mother soon ceased to receive the Sacraments and then stopped going to church. But Mother still sang songs of the saints and told us religious stories from the storehouse of her memories.

Though we still considered ours a Catholic family, we were no longer practicing Catholics. Mother urged us children to go to church but we soon followed our parents' example. I think my mother was self-conscious about her poor English and lack of fine clothes. Though the crucifix was still over our beds and Mother burned vigil lights before the statue of Our Lady, we children got the idea that such things were of the Italian past and we wanted to be Americans. Willingly, and yet not knowing what we did, we cut ourselves off from the culture of our own people and set out to find something new.

Almost from the outset of the tidal wave of immigration from Italy, a number of individuals became alarmed at the deplorable religious conditions of the transplanted Italians. At the forefront was Bishop John Scalabrini, whose concern for their material and spiritual welfare prompted him to establish first the St. Raphael Society and then the Missionary Society of St. Charles. Highly conscious of the ethnic sensitivities of the Italian people, the priests of the order made a deep impression among large segments of the Italian population in America. They exhorted their people to remain united in spirit with the land of their birth, while at the same time they fostered a respect for the culture of the new land. They opened national parishes and parochial schools and thereby provided a sense of security for their ethnic group as it began the long journey into the mainstream of American life. This background is described in the excerpt that follows.

The profound union between the missionary and the immigrants permitted the former to discover the secret for their regeneration and salvation, close as he was to their lives, to their very souls.[9] The establishment of national parishes was a great contribution to the moral, spiritual, and social adjustment of Italians in the United States.

The Scalabrinians, sent by their founder from Italy, were a link between the American bishops and the Catholic Italian immigrants. First and foremost, they organized as best they could large groups in the principal cities. They sought for the best way to keep these people loyal to their religion and to eliminate certain existing frictions among them. Experience and time prove the success of their efforts. They coaxed the immigrants to forget their differences, pull together, and raise a church of their own. The common efforts

[8] Reprinted from Bella V. Dodd, *School of Darkness* (New York: P. J. Kenedy & Sons, 1954), p. 15.

[9] Reprinted from Icilio Felici, *Father to the Immigrants: John Baptist Scalabrini* (New York: P. J. Kenedy & Sons, 1955), pp. 163–64. By permission of the Center for Migration Studies.

in building their own church turned out to be a spiritual and social bond. The immigrants of the Italian communities often found themselves united in their needs and in their different activities. The petty antagonism which might have existed, say, between Sicilians or Neapolitans, or between northern or southern Italians, became gradually a thing of the past.

A parish church awakened sympathy and cooperation among the people. Common sacrifices were to be met and shared and overcome by all for the fulfillment of a common task. The erection of their own church bound them to become acquainted with one another, engendered exchanges of opinions, made them brothers. A feeling of pride and achievement rendered them worthier sons and daughters of the country of their origin as well as of the country of their adoption.

Side by side with other nationalities, the Italians began to feel themselves more at home in the new environment. The sense of pride in their national origin and in their religious beliefs become a powerful factor in their moral and social development.

This solidarity also brought about generous response whenever aid was needed, whether in Italy or in the United States, no matter when or how misfortune raised its ugly head. With their missionaries as their leaders, the Italians who had been fortunate enough to better their condition answered generously any appeal for help for their less fortunate brethren. The concept that the Italians were a nation of beggars and filthy wretches, a concept which unfortunately they had acquired when they had first reached the New World, began to wane.

The Scalabrinians worked also in the field of education. The parochial schools that rose one by one in the shadow of the Church safeguarded the religious flame, cornerstone of a healthy, moral education, and also aided in the development of the new citizen.

The national parishes and their schools proved wrong the opinion of some in the matter of assimilation. Such parishes and schools, far from hampering, created and fostered the ideal atmosphere for the process of assimilation. They educated the immigrants and their children to adjust themselves to life in the United States and to become citizens of whom it could be proud.

Some Italians came over as contract laborers to work on public works, such as canals and roads, or on private works, such as lumber camps and brickyards. As they lived in makeshift labor camps, which often hosted different nationalities, it might be expected that substantial intermingling took place. However, this was not always the case, as Italian preference for ethnic similarity won out. The excerpt that follows is from a 1909 report of a Commission on Immigration in New York.

In these labor camps the various races mix together and in this crude form get their first contact with American institutions and ways of living.[10] The Italians, unlike other races, live or herd by

[10] Reprinted from Edith Abbott, *Immigration: Select Documents and Case Records* (Chicago: University of Chicago Press, 1924; reprint ed., New York: Arno Press, Inc., 1969), 485–86.

themselves in boarding houses under the management of the padrone. The padrone encourages the boarding house method of living
on account of the profits he realizes form the sale of food, and
because, through this system, he is continually in touch with his
countrymen and can control their movements and employment.
When work ceases with one employer, he can transfer them to
another and make a profit on the fee for each man. It is said that
the Italian laborer himself insists upon this system, because in this
way he can live more cheaply even if he must buy of the most unscrupulous padrone, and can have the food to which he is accustomed at home. Nearly every agency friendly to the Italian also
encourages him in this method of living. The Italian societies themselves, which aim to protect him from the misconduct of the padrone
and others, insist upon the establishment at labor camps of the
commissary or store, and of his own methods of cooking, they as
well as the padrone making it one of the conditions of employment.
This is disproved, however, by the fact that in emergency cases,
when a railroad finds it necessary to assemble a body of Italian and
other laborers quickly at some given point, the Italians not only use
the company's boarding cars, but accept without question the free
meals of soups and roasted and boiled meats prepared in the usual
American style.

The role of Italian-Americans in the labor movement has often been
assessed from a negative point of view stressing their reputation as strike-
breakers and their willingness to work for low wages. One of the industries in which they achieved a notable degree of prominence and success
was the garment industry, specifically the International Ladies Garment
Workers Union. Even in this instance, however, prejudice and discrimination were rendered the Italians by employers and employees of another ethnic group—in this case, Jewish. Italians received lower wages
than Jewish employees for the same work. The following extract points
up this ethnic factor in the labor movement.

It was, as we have indicated above, with the 1910 strike that the
Cloakmakers Union of New York acquired a true and genuine role
among people in the union movement.[11] Before 1910 the Cloakmakers Union had very little influence in the productive market
where the majority were elements of Jewish workers who, with the
favorable daily propaganda of the Jewish-language paper "Forward," had enlightened and educated them on the principles of the
struggle against capitalism. The Italian element, however, was
represented by such a scarce number that you could count them on
your fingers. Therefore, one could not talk about acquiring enlightened conscience of classes, and so Italian cloakmakers and
employees in cloak and suit making factories hastened enthusiasti-
cally and in large numbers to join the union which assumed the
aspect of a workers' organization worthy of its name, and then during the entire course of the strike the Italian workers revealed

[11] Reprinted from Raffaele Rende (ed.), *Twenty-Fifth Anniversary Italian Cloak, Suit
and Reefer Makers Union, Local 48, ILGWU, 1919–1941* (New York: 1941), pp.
78–81.

themselves animated by a militant spirit in which they had no prior
experience. Why? If the cause for their enthusiasm was not attributed to a class consciousness what was the true cause of the
enthusiastic support to the union struggle determined by the
Italian masses. The true cause, the only genuine cause, was made
in the rebellion which came against the system of exploitation that
had surpassed beyond every measure of endurance. . . .

In general, for to tell the whole story, management was constituted of Jewish capitalists who, either because of the influence of
the rabbi of the synagogue, or because they were annoyed by the
too-verbal insistence of their co-religionists, revealed themselves to
be less cutthroat with the latter than they were with the Italian
workers who, besides not being able to express themselves in
English, had a little disposition toward the niggardly characteristics
of Jewish cloakmakers. And the salaries that the Italians received
were very inferior to those that were realized by their fellow Jewish
cloakmakers, for the latter, if not inferior, at least were only equal in
technical capacity to the Italians. From the wage-earning viewpoint
the Italian element remained several steps below the Jewish cloakmakers. . . .

An important historian of Italian-American history is Giovanni
Schiavo, who has been laboring on this task for a few decades. In the
course of that time he has written some basic, if not classic, histories of
Italians in America, usually from a sympathetic viewpoint. The extract
that follows is from *The Italians in Missouri.* In this selection Schiavo
eulogizes the Italian immigrant and presents a valuable insight into the
well-integrated quality of the Italian ethnic community.

The immigration from Italy has differed from that from Anglo-Saxon
countries chiefly in two respects: First, the Italian had no affinity
with the language and customs of the new country; second, the
Italian came over with a hidden love for his native town and with a
powerful desire to make a moneyed return. . . .[12]

The district can yet be called a "Little Italy." Social life
centers around the Catholic Church of Our Lady Help of Christians,
on 10th and Wash. streets, the main business places being on 7th
Street, between Franklin and Carr. It is there that one finds the
Rome Drug store, the Viviano Macaroni establishment, the Selvaggi
and Coppolino steamship agencies, the wholesale house of Costa
and Sciales, Dr. Cataldi's office, the "pasticceria" and several gro-
ceries and butcher shops. One of the main events of the colony is
the celebration of the Congregation of Santa Fara, the patroness of
the town of Cinisi. There in the month of April the festival is held.
For the occasion solemn vespers are sung, a colorful parade takes
place and fireworks galore remind the immigrant of his days in the
"old country." But Santa Fara is not the only Saint that is venerated.
Almost everyone of the groups from the towns mentioned above has
its "patron" or "patroness" saint in whose honor large amounts of
money are lavished every year.

[12] Reprinted from Giovanni Schiavo, *The Italians in Missouri* (Chicago: Italian-American Publishing Co., 1929), pp. 13, 59–60.

The other Italian "Little Italy" of St. Louis is located in the Fairmount District, or "Dago Hill" as it has been kindly dubbed by our American friends.

The Fairmount district is of rather recent origin. In 1890 there were about ten shingle houses; today it contains over 1100 Italian families. That district was settled by the Italians on account of its proximity to their places of work, in the brickyards and clay pits nearby. It was originally settled by natives of Lombardy, almost exclusively men. In 1888, it is said, there were only three women in the whole district. No water connections, no gas, electricity, no comforts of any sort made the section almost uninhabitable. Yet, the Italians settled there, transforming it from a desert into one of the most picturesque and the most sanitary districts in the city. Today it is inhabited chiefly by natives of Lombardy and Sicily, a rather strange combination thirty years ago, if one realizes how dissimilar were the customs of the Lombards from those of the Sicilians. It is said that of the 10,000 or more people in the district about 5,000 are Sicilians, 4,000 Lombards, and 1,000 from other parts of Italy, chiefly Venetians. According to the registers of the Catholic Church of St. Ambrose, from 1925 to 1927 about 175 christenings a year took place in the district; in 1927 there were 40 weddings and 35 funerals.

At first the Lombards and the Sicilians could not get along. Today they understand each other much better. Their children, even against the will of their parents, marry into each other's families and harmony seems to be prevailing.

An interesting fact in the colony is the complete trust that the people of the community, regardless of their province of origin, have in the leading "banker" of the district, Mr. I. Riggio, a native of Sicily. With the exception of the priest, who is a native of Piedmont, the Lombards seem to have more faith in their Sicilian friend than in anybody else on the hill. A good omen, indeed, for the Italian people! The Fairmount Italian "colony" is a true community. It has its Church, its branch library, its clubs, its shops, its music store, its drug store, its lawyers, its physicians, its family theatre, its pool rooms, its factories, its business men's association, its boys' band, and its "speakeasies." It is said that over four hundred girls from the district work in the Liggett and Meyer tobacco plant, and over two hundred men in the nearby brickyards. It is in this district that are located the Ravarino and Freschi macaroni plant, one of the largest in the middle west, the Missouri Baking Company, undoubtedly one of the best in the city, the Sala Restaurant, the Blue Ridge Bottling Company, one of the largest in St. Louis, and the Volpi sausage manufacturing establishment, one of the few of its kind in Italian–American communities.

The center of all activities in the district is the Church of St. Ambrose. The priest indeed directs most of the activities of the Italians of this section, and it is only rarely that something is done without his advice. A religious event on Fairmount Heights assumes the importance of a national event. Parades, processions, fireworks, concerts, seem to hold the attention of the Italians more than a baseball game would for the average American.

The Fairmount district is considered the healthiest district in the whole city. As a matter of fact, according to figures and statements given out to the press by the St. Louis Community Council, that district, for quite some time has been leading all the 26 districts in which St. Louis is divided, in the "human welfare race."

THE GREEKS

In most of the important realms of thought—for example, the arts, government, and science—Western civilization has been inspired by the long and glorious history of ancient Greece. The apogee of Greek civilization, however, was followed by decline and subjugation until in 1827 Greece again gained its independence. Its experience with an autocratic monarchy proved to be a disappointment and led to important changes in the Greek government throughout the latter part of the nineteenth century. During that period Greece continued to grow with the accretion of various islands. By the end of the nineteenth century emigration to the United States also became an important feature of Greek society. Admiration for the United States was traceable to Greek gratefulness for American interest and sympathy as the Greeks struggled for independence early in the nineteenth century and to concern for the welfare of Greeks on the island of Crete in the later-nineteenth-century struggle between the Greeks and Turks of that island.

But there were other factors affecting Greek emigration to America. One of the influences was domestic Greek politics in the late nineteenth and early twentieth centuries. Since Greece's entry into the modern world was of relatively recent vintage and since its existence as an independent entity came later than the establishment of the nations of western and central Europe, traditional spiritual and economic influences persisted for years after its liberation. The force of Pan-Hellenism emboldened Greece to try to bring under one banner all the Greeks scattered over other parts of Asia Minor and the fading Ottoman Empire. The consequence was numerous conflicts between Greece and neighboring states like Turkey and Bulgaria. Caught in the vortex of these conflicts, many Greek inhabitants of these other countries came to America to escape oppression and persecution.

Unfavorable economic conditions constituted probably the greatest reason for Greek emigration to American shores. A mountainous nation with a primarily farming population, the Greek peninsula was in a backward state. For those aspiring to middle-class status, the home country offered limited possibilities for economic advancement, although a relative degree of prosperity had been reached by the early 1890's. However, before the turn of the century European markets for Greek currants collapsed. For many an enterprising Greek peasant, who despaired of a life of unrewarding toil on the farm which he often did not own, the solution was to migrate to the towns or to embark for the United States. Moreover, as in the case of other immigrants, many had been misled by letters from earlier immigrants from their homeland which exaggerated the ease with which one could achieve economic solvency and security. Even social customs like the dowry system played their role in promoting emigration to America. The custom of expecting substantial dowries from prospective brides often obligated faithful fathers and brothers to secure sizable amounts of money for daughters or sisters, and often this could best be realized by economic opportunities in the United States.

Add to these conditions the desire to avoid military service and the love of adventure that seemed to come naturally to the Greeks, and there emerges a picture of a lively emigration to the United States commencing in the 1890's. In all, over 500,000 Greeks came to live in this country, the peak of immigration coming between 1900 and 1920 when 351,720 transplanted their culture to the Western Hemisphere. (It is to be noted that overall totals are estimates rather than fixed, accurate figures.)

Many of the first emigrants were from the peasant class, mostly illiterate and poor, primarily young men, single or married. They were soon followed by cultivated and educated classes. Despite his background of the soil, the Greek immigrant found it preferable to live in the cities. In a new land, these people faced many hurdles, one of the foremost being the language barrier. Because of this obstacle many Greeks worked at lowly tasks in America, as street vendors or common laborers. Many Greek-Americans found their employment through the padrone system, which has been described by the historian Theodore Saloutos as "a modernized version of the indentured-servant system."

The common action of most Greeks on coming to America was to take up residence in a Greek colony. These were distinctive ethnic enclaves within the heart of some of the major American communities. Often this takeover of a geographic region by an ethnic group was accomplished by dispossession of another ethnic group, the new group's then starting its own ethnic organizations and changing the lifestyle from the previous ethnic orientation to the new one. The way this was accomplished by the Greeks is discussed in the selection below, wherein Fairchild describes the process by which the Greeks replaced the Italians in a section of Chicago early in the twentieth century.

The Greek Colony of Chicago[13]

Five years ago if a visitor to Chicago had alighted from a Blue Island Avenue street car at Polk Street, and had wandered around the neighborhood, along these two streets and South Halsted and Ewing Streets, he might almost have imagined that he was in Italy. The stores, the houses, the people, the sights and sounds all would have suggested a distinctly Italian character. Within the space of five years, an ethnic revolution has been worked in this district, until

[13] Reprinted from Henry Pratt Fairchild, *Greek Immigration* (New Haven: Yale University Press, 1911), pp. 122–23.

today it is just as distinctively Greek. Here, in the section of which Hull House is the social center, are gathered the greater part of the 15,000 Greeks who call Chicago their home.

Taking all things into consideration, Chicago is probably the oldest and most important Greek colony in the United States. Here, too, the Greeks have developed their characteristic industries to the fullest extent. Yet the Greek invasion of Chicago is comparatively a recent thing. In 1882 there were very few Greeks in the city, not enough to have a community of their own. But they united with the Slavs to form the "Graeco Slavic Brotherhood," and secured a Greek priest. . . .

As the Greeks became more numerous they began to do what they do in almost every city where they form considerable settlements—they invaded the Italian section and drove the Italians out of their homes and out of their businesses. The district which has been mentioned, around Blue Island Avenue and Polk and South Halsted Streets, is today more typically Greek than some sections of Athens. Practically all the stores bear signs in both Greek and English, coffee-houses flourish on every corner. . . .

Fairchild mentions a relatively high incidence of law-breaking among Greek immigrants and goes on to express open skepticism about successful Greek (and other) assimilation in the United States. Although a scholar, he placed more emphasis on immigrants' environmental handicaps, poverty, ignorance, and intense nationalism than on their capabilities. To that extent he exemplified the sense of superiority common to the typical Anglo-Saxon of his day:

The criminal record of the Greeks is less favorable.[14] While there are few major criminals among them, they are probably a greater tax on the police courts of the country, in proportion to their total number, than any other class of our population. But their record for the past decade gives us ground for hope that the years will bring an improvement in this direction. But it seems likely that the presence of this race in the country will add to, rather than diminish, the growing indifference to law as such, which is one of the most threatening signs of the times. This lack of reverence for law, and every form of authority, seems to be characteristic of the children of immigrants of every race. But the Greeks appear to have it when they come. What the character of their children will be in this respect we can only conjecture. . . .

The great question which, in the case of the Greeks, as well as of every other class of our alien population, is of vital importance and interest to the country, is, Will they make good citizens? The answer to this depends primarily upon one's individual opinion of what is a good American citizen. Some writers go so far as to intimate that there is no such thing as a distinctive American citizen. A large proportion of our population seems to look upon the ideal American citizen as the man who tends strictly to business, makes money, lets other people severely alone and expects them to do the

14 Ibid., pp. 239–40, 241–42.

same. If we adopt this point of view, we can have little hesitation in saying that the Greeks answer the requirements, for as we have seen, they are distinctly a money-making class in this country, and if some of the methods by which they do it will not bear investigation —that is nobody's business, according to the hypothesis.

But if we look at the matter more broadly, and think of the ideal American citizen as one who has the higher and better interests of himself, his neighbor and his country at heart, and who believes that he ought to contribute to the general betterment of his community during his lifetime, and give at least as much as he gets—from this point of view the answer to the question is much less certain. In this respect, the effect of the immigrant upon the country is the effect of the country upon the immigrant, viewed from a different angle. If the immigrant finds his change of residence an advantage, if he prospers morally and socially as well as financially, the chances are that he will give back to the country something in return for what he gets. But if the conditions in which he finds himself placed in his new home are such as to cause him to preserve, or even increase, any low ideals, vicious habits or degenerate propensities that he may have, he is, by so much, a hindrance to the country of his adoption.

As far as the Greeks are concerned, at least, it seems undeniable that the determination of the question, into which of these two categories the immigrant shall go, is largely a matter of distribution. It has been frequently remarked in the course of the preceding discussion, that the evil tendencies of Greek life in this country manifest themselves most fully when the immigrants are collected into compact, isolated, distinctively Greek colonies, and that when the Greek is separated from the group and thrown into relations with Americans of the better class, he develops and displays many admirable qualities. Our system and machinery for regulating the admission of aliens is very complete and well-organized. But we do practically nothing for them, after they are once inside the border. We talk with smug complacency of the marvelous assimilative power of America. We are, in fact, by no means sure that these great hordes of foreign nationalities are in any true sense assimilated, even after many years of residence in this country.

J. P. Xenides was a Greek-American clergyman who in 1922 wrote a short but sympathetic work entitled *The Greeks in America*. The result of numerous personal visits to Greek-American communities as well as of questionnaires, this offers some valuable observations into various aspects of Greek-American life at the height of the immigration. Xenides comments on the weak hold America had on some Greeks, while most accepted it as a second fatherland. He also discusses how Americanization will affect Greek family life.

Dr. S. I. Paul of Springfield, Mass., writes: "Go halfway with the Greeks and they will go halfway with you."[15] The Americanization of the Greeks, until recently, had been superficial, as they had come

[15] Reprinted from J. P. Xenides, *The Greeks in America* (New York: Doran, 1922), pp. 78–79, 91–92.

to the United States generally with the idea of making money and then returning to their native land. But this is no reason for despair, as the very names of Boston, New England, New York, etc., indicate that the early English in America were reluctant to separate themselves from their mother country. Since the war, due perhaps to the drafting of many Greeks in the service of the United States, there has been a marked change in their attitude toward this country, coming more and more to regard it as their own. Proof of this is demonstrated by the fact that many Greeks are now buying American realty.

The prosperous will stay.—Those who are accustomed to American ways and ideas with all the rush and hustle of life here, with ever-widening fields of enterprise and efficiency, cannot rest satisfied with the quieter and less active life in the Near East. Besides many own houses and other property. Some are engaged in real estate enterprises or other lines of business. Such will never return. One Greek now in real estate business in Wilmington, Del., owns property worth more than $1,000,000 and he is only one of a class of prosperous Greeks, some of whom started from the very bottom and have risen gradually to prosperity.

Working Greeks will return.—It is different with workers in mills and factories and those who cannot feel at home in America. I asked in 1918 scores of Greeks in Syracuse, N. Y., who were from Broosa and its villages in Asia Minor, if any planned to return home. "All of us," they replied. "Who would not go back to his home and his own? We are strangers in a strange land; we do not know the language of the country; neither can we learn it; we are working hard like slaves and then our earnings fly away from us, everything is so dear. At home we have our houses, fields, vineyards, and our relatives and friends are all there."

In general, however, Greeks are well satisfied with America. They love and adore it. They intend to stay here permanently. They call it "Their second fatherland." . . . .

Husband and wife.—Greeks are very much devoted to their families. Whatever freedom may be allowed to men during their pre-marital life, it is understood and expected that, after the marriage, a new chapter is to be opened and strictly clean records are to be entered in it. Women of course have always to be exemplary and pure in every way. Divorce is uncommon among the Greeks. Children are numerous and are regarded as blessings and gifts of God. However poor and ignorant parents may be they are anxious to educate their children in good schools.

There is not much data for comparing the first and the second generations, as to family life, but there are many indications that the new generation is getting Americanized and is learning both the good and bad aspects of American life.

Divorce.—A Greek young man was asked: "Would you marry a Greek or an American?" He replied "American." To the question, "Will you be able to agree together and be happy?" "If we do not, then we get divorced," was his emphatic reply. He would never have thought or said so in Greece or Turkey. There marriage is thought of as a matter of harmony and love to last till death.

Children are devoted to their parents and relatives. Young men gladly undergo many troubles and live a life of thrift and self-denial in order to save, and send money to their parents. They pay the old debts of their parents to keep up their good reputation or save paternal inheritance. They postpone or even forego marriage in order to get their sisters married. Unfortunately the evil custom of dowry continues in the old country. So fathers and brothers working here must save money in order to provide dowry for daughters and sisters. It is a good thing that the custom of dowry is getting broken in America, though not entirely abandoned.

Neighborhood life.—People from the same town or village in Greece are usually drawn together in America too. The newcomers find out first of all the whereabouts of their relatives and fellow-countrymen. In fact they may come directly to them, having already corresponded with them. Even those of different towns are very helpful to one another in finding work and if need be helping each other financially and otherwise. They room together; work together; frequent the same coffee-house, club and restaurant. Thus close attachments are formed.

Here people may live in the same neighborhood (even the same house), and not get acquainted with each other. Not so among the Greeks; they easily get acquainted and are friendly and neighborly to one another.

Xenides speculates on the meaning of assimilation.

Forces of Assimilation[16]

Americanization.—A great deal is being said and written regarding the Americanization or assimilation of the immigrants that seems strange. Some of the heated utterances sound like the nationalistic theories of the Pan-Germans or the Pan-Slavists. If the various races are to be forced to forget all their racial peculiarities and characteristic customs, usages, and language, and to adopt American ways instead, the result will be disappointing. Whenever a people is forced to accept, willingly or unwillingly, a certain course of action, the result has usually been the opposite of what was desired.

But if without being interfered with in their cherished customs, ideas, language and traditions, they are surrounded with a genial American atmosphere and are given suitable opportunities to learn American ways, ideas, language and institutions; in short, if they are gradually taught what is good in their new surroundings, while they retain what was good and useful in their former life, all the immigrants will be Americanized in due time.

Even the word "Americanization" sounds strange to many ears; it sounds like suppression, force. Let the immigrant have freedom to contribute his best to the welfare of America. As the various races have brought their national dishes, customs and usages, so let each contribute his peculiar talent and accomplishment in art, letters or business, though he may be deficient in the knowledge of the English language.

Americanization of the children.—Many a simple illiterate immigrant may turn out to be more loyal to America, than the so called cultivated theorists who can chatter, parrot-like, good English, but are unsound in morals and unprincipled in action. It is difficult and

[16] Ibid., pp. 112–13.

in some cases impossible to change the habits of the adult. It is different with the young and the children. They are open to impressions, and the future lies with them. They will all get Americanized through education. The public school is the melting pot where children of all races are being assimilated. Many Greek children who are being educated in American schools, answer their parents in English who speak to them in Greek.

The evening schools are of immense value. Both men and women are attending evening classes, in the public schools, Y.M.C.A. and the various Greek societies.

The most recent and most comprehensive English-language study of the Greeks in America is *The Greeks in The United States* by Theodore Saloutos. An historian, Saloutos traces the story of the Greeks in their adopted homeland, examining the impact that events in Greece had on immigrants in the United States and the reciprocal effects actions of these emigrants had on developments in the old country.

Below, Saloutos discusses the role of the coffeehouse (kaffeneion) in the Greek-American community.

No account of a Greek community would be complete without reference to one of the most widespread of all immigrant institutions, the kaffeneion, or coffeehouse.[17] For it was to the coffeehouse that the immigrant hurried after his arrival from Greece or from a neighboring community. It was in the coffeehouse that he sought out acquaintances, addresses, leads to jobs, and solace during the lonely hours. One could frequently hear him say: "I'll see you at the coffeehouse. . . . I went by the coffeehouse. . . . I heard it at the coffeehouse."

The coffeehouse appeared whenever a sufficient number of Greeks and an enterprising compatriot had settled in a particular neighborhood. Little capital was needed to start one. A store was rented; a few marble-top tables and wire-twisted chairs, several pounds of coffee, a few narghiles, and a dozen or so decks of playing cards were collected; and the coffeehouse became a reality. On the walls the proprietor was likely to hang lithographic portraits of his political favorites and those of his patrons; in communities in which Venizelos was the idol, pictures of the kings of Greece were not to be seen. There might also be posted battle scenes of some Greek victory over the Turks, a map of Greece, a military hero, a revolutionary leader, or some modern Greek Hercules. Coffeehouses bore names such as "Acropolis," "Parthenon," "Paradisos," "Venizelos," "Messinia," "Arcadia," "Synantisis," and "Lesche." In the rear of the house was the kitchen in which the proprietor brewed the coffee which he himself served to his patrons. Lokum, baklava, and other Near Eastern delicacies were in evidence, as were bottled soft drinks.

The coffeehouse was a community social center to which the men retired after working hours and on Saturdays and Sundays.

---

[17] Reprinted by permission of the publishers from *The Greeks in the United States* by Theodore Saloutos, Cambridge, Mass.: Harvard University Press, Copyright 1964 by the President and Fellows of Harvard College, pp. 78–79.

Here they sipped cups of thick, black Turkish coffee, lazily drew on narghiles, played cards, or engaged in animated political discussion. Here congregated gesticulating Greeks of all kinds: railroad workers, factory hands, shopkeepers, professional men, the unemployed, labor agitators, amateur philosophers, community gossips, cardsharks, and amused spectators.

The air of the average coffeehouse was choked with clouds of smoke rising from cigarettes, pipes, and cigars. Through the haze one could see the dim figures of card players or hear the stentorian voices of would-be statesmen discussing every subject under the sun. No topic was beyond them. European problems were resolved readily, and all were at their peak when the politics of Greece were discussed. . . .

Religious customs and Orthodox Church influence were strong in the early Greek communities.

The observance of religious holidays, at least in these early years, was another important social outlet.[18] Women often found their way to church on weekdays, as well as on Sundays, in observance of a saint's day or some special religious service. If a man also acquired the churchgoing habit, he soon discarded it; for attending church on weekdays meant the loss of a day's wages.

The nameday furnished still another occasion for celebration. In accordance with Old World customs, the nameday rather than the birthday was regularly observed. Friends and relatives visited the namesake to extend good wishes and share in the hospitality of the day. Music, dancing, and food were inevitable parts of these events. In the beginning the tendency was to celebrate them in a fashion reminiscent of the village from which the host came. With the passage of time, these celebrations were observed with declining regularity; only in the homes of the tradition-bound and the newer arrivals were they observed.

Christmas for the early immigrants was more of a religious holiday than a day of gift-giving and fun-making. Solemnity, the offering of greetings, and the singing of carols depicting the nativity predominated. Gift-giving was kept at a modest level. Unlike Christmas, New Year's Day, or St. Basil's Day, was the day for mirth. The zeal with which this was celebrated varied. In cities with large colonies and where tradition was strong, children carolers sometimes visited homes, coffeehouses, and stores singing "Agios Vasileos." They concluded their caroling by extending good wishes for the New Year and receiving small tokens from the listeners. Cutting the Vasilopita, or St. Basil's Cake, was also common. The eve of St. Basil's Day, and in some cases the entire holiday season, offered the men an excuse for swarming to the coffeehouses to test their luck at the gaming table.

Easter was far and away the most important holiday of the year. In Greece the pre-Lenten season was observed with much festivity and music, but in the United States this was rare, except perhaps in the earlier years. Palm Sunday, or Vaeion, was accom-

18 Ibid., pp. 83–84.

panied with the customary good wishes to friends and neighbors. During Holy Week, church services were held every night. At the Thursday evening services the priest read from the Twelve Gospels, and on Good Friday (Megale Paraskevi) the churches literally bulged with people. This was the one day of the year when the once-a-year churchgoers turned out en masse.

On the whole, Greek-Americans were highly nationalistic about their country of origin, but the World War I period proved to be a decisive one for Americanization.

> The First World War was the great transition period.[19] It gave many a feeling of belonging that the earlier years had not. Greece had been an ally of the United States; a feeling of kinship had blossomed; and American influences were being felt in Greece itself. Thousands fought with the American Expeditionary Forces. Still more contributed to the common war effort by investing their savings in government bonds and working in war industries. Many businessmen emerged financially stronger and securer as a result of the lush years. . . .
> The inroads that naturalization and Americanization were making on the immigrants ran counter to all that the frenzied nationalists had prophesied. For years they had boasted that their compatriots would not be absorbed by a foreign culture because they, more than any other nationality, adhered tenaciously to their language, customs, and traditions. The Greek-Americans, they claimed, possessed many of the admirable qualities of their ancient ancestors and the pioneers of America, but they differed in their determination that "the fire of the Mother Country should never be extinguished in their Hellenic souls." . . .
> This admonition was taken very seriously by some, ignored by many, and strongly opposed by others who found it impossible to reconcile such a philosophy with living in the United States. . . .

Despite the erosion of Greek nationalistic sentiment, some Greek-Americans organized a patriotic association, AHEPA (American Hellenic Educational Progressive Association), a semisecret, middle-class-oriented society dedicated to the promotion of Americanism among Greeks.

> What in effect was happening was that Greek-American businessmen, who felt the menacing hand of nativist opposition, were organizing for self-protection.[20] Instead of meeting kind with kind and resorting to violent action, marked by bigotry and hate, the Greek-Americans, the immigrants of yesterday, chose the method of peaceful assembly and democratic discussion. They decided upon organization, persuasion, and positive action. If their methods in the past had been inappropriate, they meant to right the situation. . . .
> From the outset AHEPA was middle-class in orientation. It appealed to those who were climbing the social and economic ladder

[19] Ibid., pp. 236–37.
[20] Ibid., pp. 249–50.

of success. It extended recognition to those who craved it but who found it difficult to obtain in "non-Greek" spheres. Its banquets, dances, and meetings furnished an outlet for many a harassed businessmen who preferred the company of compatriots facing identical problems. The element of secrecy and exclusiveness also had its charm, for men regardless of race or nationality like to believe themselves among the select. The times were relatively prosperous and the dues were no obstacle to the well-off businessman. AHEPA, after all, represented Americanism in a decade of conformity, when many Greek-Americans, reacting sharply against the politics of the Old World, were desirous of shaking off all traces of foreignism by joining the greater American community. In short, the social climate was favorable to the growth of the order. . . .

Greeks opened many small businesses in the United States, and many of them went into the restaurant field.

The trade usually associated with the Greeks is the restaurant business.[21] It represented a milestone in economic progress; for many it was a major step beyond working on the railroad or in the factory, pushing a cart or driving lunch wagon. Restaurant keeping marked the high point in the careers of many; to others it represented but another rung in the economic ladder, the opportunity to establish a chain of restaurants or to branch off into real estate, the theater business, summer resorts, and related enterprises. The restaurant business represented the first stable economic base on which many ambitious immigrants built their fortunes. The restaurant was important for other reasons as well. It brought the Greek businessman into closer contact with the general public, which in many instances found him to be a hard-driving and industrious person. Commercial, patriotic, and fraternal agencies solicited his services or sought contributions from him for a wide variety of causes. Many students also remember working in one of his restaurants as a means of meeting college expenses.

Second-generation Greek-Americans seemed to be less affected by ethnic ties than their parents.

The members of the second generation of Greeks in America did not find themselves in an easy position.[22] Born into families with strong paternal and national ties, and thrust into a society that had as one of its objectives the obliteration of those vestiges of foreignism that proud parents wished to perpetuate, they faced a bewildering and frustrating experience. This was especially true for those who reached maturity between the First and Second World Wars. . . .
For the most part, the members of the second generation wanted to be accepted by the society into which they were born, rather than become torchbearers in preserving the national identity of their parents. For a time it appeared as though an unbridgeable

[21] Ibid., p. 265.
[22] Ibid., pp. 310–12.

chasm separated the older generation from the younger, but the trend of events demonstrated that the chasm could be bridged. In appreciating the problems of second-generation Greek-Americans, as well as those of their parents, one must keep in mind the prevalence of strong family ties, the Greek language, the Greek school the child was expected to attend, and the role of and the reaction to the Greek Orthodox Church. All of these factors significantly shaped the attitude and behavior of the child born of immigrant parents.

Family ties in a Greek family, as we have seen, were quite close. Unquestioned authority was vested in the father who, in keeping with the ancestral tradition, made the laws and administered them. Decisions frequently were made without consulting his wife, who was expected to uphold and defend them. The major concern of the closely regulated family was to preserve the language, faith, and traditions. And deviation from this norm could create a crisis. . . .

Besides being raised in strict obedience, the children had specific chores to perform. Every girl was expected to become an expert in housekeeping; she had to help with the housework, the family wash, the shopping, and the cooking. The boys also had duties outlined for them. There were physical labors to be performed around the house, parents to accompany to the store whenever they needed interpreters or assistance, and errands to run. Moreover, there were the studies in Greek. From the public school the children went home, then to the late afternoon and early evening school, and home again for supper and studies. Leisure time in most families was at a minimum.

The early years in the lives of children born of immigrant parents were hardly joyous ones, for they were exposed to the realities of life at a tender age. They heard parents and their friends tell of their hardships in Greece and the early years in the United States, the unemployment, discrimination, and difficulties with the language. They were told in clear and often blunt language that their principal purpose in life was not to have fun, but to work, take advantage of the opportunities denied their parents, assume responsibilities, make a success of themselves, see their sisters happily married, and provide for their parents in old age. All children did not abide by this regimen, but it was the kind of rhetoric to which almost all were exposed.

The first contacts of the children usually were with peers of identical background, as were the associations of their parents and friends. This is understandable, for they spoke a common language, understood each other's problems, and could be counted upon for sympathy and advice. Some parents made a point of seeing to it that their children associated with children of Greek backgrounds. This was part of the family and cultural discipline, as well as a matter of convenience. In fact, some children felt uncomfortable and insecure in the company of people of non-Greek backgrounds.

This cultural isolation, self-imposed in numerous instances, broke down as the children advanced in the elementary and high-school grades. This is when they began to draw comparisons, complain about having to attend the Greek school and the Greek church, and wonder about the observance of customs and traditions that were so different from those of their classmates. This was a natural reaction for children who were thrown into contact with those reared in other faiths, and who saw other children playing after school instead of performing household chores and attending a second school.

THE PORTUGUESE

Portuguese influence in the United States, although moderate, has been of long duration. Portuguese explorers charted the California coast in the sixteenth century, and small numbers of colonists settled in the eighteenth century. This latter migration was largely from Portugal's Azores Islands, and these early immigrants worked primarily in the American fishing industry. There are records of some Portuguese migrating to California during the gold rush of 1849. However, it was not until the last years of the nineteenth century that a significant number of Portuguese entered this country, with even greater numbers coming in during the first three decades of the twentieth century. By 1920 Portuguese stock in the United States was estimated to be 126,000, of whom two-thirds resided in several New England cities. The bulk of the remainder settled in California and Hawaii. The 1940 census gives a figure of 176,407. Together with descendants from earlier generations, the Portuguese stock probably numbers a few hundred thousand, although accurate figures are not available.

The social and cultural background of these people forecast divergencies between them and the majority of older inhabitants in the United States. In addition, Portuguese-Americans themselves did not possess homogeneity, as they were composed of several distinct groups. Those from mainland Portugal included Portuguese of Moorish or Negro admixture, while the Flemish element was featured in the Azores. Steeped in backgrounds of agriculture and fishing, a significant number of Portuguese-Americans carried on their pursuits in the New World as hard-working farmers in California or in the fishing communities of New England. However, for perhaps most of them the mills in Massachusetts and Rhode Island were the economic support. As for other immigrants, life for these people in a new country was hard. In addition, Portuguese-Americans were burdened by other problems—they had an excessive infant mortality rate compared to other nationalities, and they took less advantage of education than most of the other national groups.

Attachment to ethnic Old World patterns continues in many Portuguese-American homes. In the areas of language, religion, education, marriage, the family, and social relations, they remain strongly ethnically oriented.

Donald R. Taft's *Two Portuguese Communities in New England*, first published in 1923, is the pioneer work about Portuguese-Americans in the English language. Taft concentrated on two communities with a high percentage of Portuguese, Fall River and Portsmouth, one urban, the other rural. He was able to examine the social contacts they had as one of many immigrant elements in Fall River and such contacts as they had with primarily native-born non-Portuguese in Portsmouth. Taft's description of the Portuguese immigrants' first contact with Americans is revealing for its exposure of economic hardship and social isolation.

Contacts with Americans[23]

When the peasant from St. Michael's arrives either in Portsmouth or in Fall River, he finds himself in America but not of America. The innumerable differences between himself and the native-born American isolate him; and this isolation is also promoted by peculiar conditions of the environment in which he finds himself.

In Portsmouth the Portuguese immigrant is fortunate if he begins as a farm laborer for one of the more progressive American farmers or for a fellow-countryman who knows the farming and marketing methods of the community. The Portuguese bring with them patient industry and some knowledge of cultivation, but there is much to learn under new conditions.

Work as a laborer is only an apprenticeship, however, for every true Portuguese is ambitious to farm for himself, and his next step is to rent a farm from a native family where the man has either died or moved to the city. Then the Portuguese immigrant sends for his wife, if she has not already come, and a life of real isolation begins. This isolation is especially pronounced if he has chosen a farm off from the main highway as is frequently the case. Even then he has some contacts, of course, when he takes his vegetables to market, purchases seed or supplies, or goes to the town hall to procure a license for the inevitable dog. But these contacts are for the new-comer very transitory and he has no share in such active community life as there is. For his wife the isolation is well-nigh complete for she toils all day in the fields, bends over the wash-tub in the yard, or minds or neglects the rapidly accumulating brood of children. About every year she gets a very few days vacation from these occupations to bear another child. Her life is altogether at home and she seldom talks with a native woman and never on the same social plane. As for the children, they run wild until the school age is reached when the mother is only too glad to get them out from under foot until they are strong enough to work in the fields, when their attendance becomes less regular. If a visitor drives up to such a secluded farm house these younger children may be seen peeking out from behind the curtains or from around corners. On the visitor's nearer approach they scurry away like rabbits, to return, perhaps, when the conversation with the mother reassures them. In school, of course, they do learn American ways and see some American children, but there is some evidence that they tend to form separate play groups. In one school, as we shall see, there are but two non-Portuguese children; but this is unusual and to some "Ports" school opens a new world. In general, however, life for the new-

---

[23] Reprinted from Donald R. Taft, *Two Portuguese Communities in New England* (reprint ed., New York: Arno Press, Inc., 1969), pp. 205–207.

comer in Portsmouth is one of isolation. His illiteracy, foreign ways, and inability to speak English would create this isolation even if he were welcomed by the old stock. As compared with some other foreign communities Portsmouth evidences remarkably little open hostility to the Portuguese, but they certainly are not "of" the community which, though fast going to seed, is nevertheless Yankee, Protestant, relatively clean and just a little self-satisfied.

The isolation we have just described applies to new-comers. After considerable time has elapsed and the Portuguese have become semi-"Americanized" the isolation decreases. Not a few Portuguese farmers are respected, some even admired, by the older native stock. One resident of long standing delights in telling of kindly neighborly acts by the Portuguese nearby. On the occasion of illness one of them did all the farm chores for a considerable period and refused to accept payment for his work. The fact, also, that there is but one Catholic church in the town brings the few non-Portuguese Catholics into contact with the Azoreans and contacts reach even the women. . . .

Taft cautioned against sweeping generalities about these people because of the economic and social differentiation inherent in the different communities and because of their heterogeneous background. Nevertheless, he did see much similarity in their attachment to their own ethnic culture, and he arrived at some conclusions about them, not always flattering.

There seems no doubt that for the great majority of Portuguese, immigration to New England has meant an improved status.[24] Granting that they are poverty-stricken here, that they live far below our standards of comfort and decency, that women often work outside the home and that children leave school as soon as the law allows, that homes are unattractive and wages low; nevertheless their lot is far better than in the homeland, except perhaps in its picturesqueness. America gives the Portuguese a small wage but a higher one, a poor house but a better one, a meager sixth grade education but more than they know enough to want, and it is universal and compulsory.

What does the coming of the Portuguese mean to Fall River and Portsmouth? Immediately it means industrious labor on the farms, and perhaps less industrious labor in the mills. But it also means all the evils of an ignorant population. The presence of these people undoubtedly handicaps the public schools, complicates the work of public health organizations, increases the births where they should be fewest, and the death rates at all ages but especially of little children. It also makes possible economic and political exploitation whether by unscrupulous natives or by their own leaders. Indeed the presence of the Portuguese goes far to account for the poor record of our two communities in official statistics and for the not altogether enviable reputation which they may have among sociologists. If Fall River could dispense with the Portuguese tomorrow she would probably benefit.

[24] Ibid., pp. 348–349.

But the Portuguese are a permanent element in our two communities. Moreover if they should leave, a substitute labor supply would have to be found. Whether the securing of this labor supply would compel the payment of higher wages than are now offered in the mills the writer does not know. There are, of course, plenty of cotton-mill communities without Portuguese. Portsmouth would probably miss the Portuguese more than Fall River, for there are few enough men to-day willing to struggle with New England farmland at its best. As a people willing to work abandoned farms and able to make a living from them the Portuguese seem to be a real asset. If they could be induced to leave the city for the farms in large numbers, and if greater efforts could be made to aid them—to promote their assimilation and educational progress—they would constitute productive and useful rural citizens. There seems to be evidence that they have proven their worth on Cape Cod. But the movement from city to farm is not marked. They are to-day a permanent and a backward element in our city (Fall River) population.

To test the persistency of cultural patterns in the face of acculturative processes, Hans Howard Leder undertook an in-depth study of a Portuguese-American enclave in Bayside, California. As a result of extensive field work, Leder became an active participant in the life of that ethnically heterogeneous community. The typical resident of the area was aware of ethnically identifiable groups, such as Italian-Americans or Mexicans, usually living in a given section. Although this residential pattern, presenting a picture of a hermetically sealed people living and working totally within a single neighborhood, did not apply to the area's Portuguese-Americans, they nevertheless presented ample examples of ethnic persistence. In the extracts that follow, we see descriptions and evaluations of these people in regard to working practices, for which they were held in high regard; aspects of social life, such as the great emphasis on the compradrazoo (godparent system); and the existence of ethnic voluntary organization that satisfied their associative needs.

> In the offices of the city's planning commission, where I had gone to obtain general information on the demography of Bayside, the Anglos with whom I discussed this subject definitely felt that, despite their lack of advanced education and their following of "lower status" occupations, the Portuguese-Americans were "defininitely middle class," had "high standards" (i.e., morally and ethically), and, in general, were among "the best people in Bayside."[25] Representative of the conversations I am referring to are these excerpts from a talk I had with the planning commission's senior statistician:
>
> > We have some younger men of Portuguese descent on the staff here. None in my own department, so I can't tell you anything

[25] Reprinted from Hans Howard Leder, "Cultural Persistence in a Portuguese-American Community" (Ph.D. diss., Stanford University, 1968), pp. 56–57, 75–76, 79, 87–88.

there that you might want to know. They are not attracted to work of this kind, under these conditions; furthermore, there are not many who are qualified educationally to step in even at a trainee level. . . . There were any number of Portuguese youngsters in my class at High School, but I don't recall that any of them went on to college. They were quiet, polite, did their work. No scholars, but no dunces either. . . . Of course you know a lot more about this than I do, but I would say that most of them, after High School—that is, the group I am familiar with—joined some sort of family enterprise, or followed in their fathers' footsteps. Agriculture is their big vocation. I say "vocation" because that is what it is with them. With the Mexicans—and you could even say with the Italians —a job in agriculture is just that, a job, to work at because nothing else is available. . . . The Portuguese have done their share of stoop labor in California, but with them it was a means to an end. Now you'll see their children out there picking, but on their own land. . . . They have a dignity about their work, whatever it happens to be.

I discussed this one evening with a group of people who had gathered in the Sameiro home to view my slides of Portugal, and there was general agreement with the host's view that

No matter what we might think, when it comes right down to it, where something is really needed—money, advice, I don't care what—the Portuguese will think first of his *compadre*. Or, if it's a young man, of his *padrinho*. Even where there is a rich father, say, or uncle. One big reason is because—to speak for myself and Mr. Freitas, here—because we know that the spirit is the same for both of us.

That "spirit," as I learned through later discussions, is one of pure friendship, unalloyed by the inequalities and involuntary obligations that are inherent in actual kin relationships. Among such relationships, the one that most closely resembles that of *compadre* is the essentially equalitarian, non-compulsive bond that exists between cousins of the same sex and of approximately the same age— and which helps to explain why cousins are so often counted as "friends" and selected as *compadres*. . . .

As Frank Azevedo, a cabinet maker who earns $7,000 annually, explained it to me when he and his family were responding to the questionnaire:

I told you, I have my insurance with the I.D.E.S. (i.e., the *Irmandade do Divino Espirito Santo*—the various *sociedades* are usually referred to in the Community by their initials). That's because I've always been a member, since when I was a very young man, still under twenty. Maybe it's not the best insurance—we think it's pretty good but who knows, I don't doubt there's better, you know? But I was a member, like my father, so it was natural, when I got married. But that's not anything to do, really, with why I'm in the I.D.E.S. Heck, half the members around my age have got this government insurance, from when they were in the service. You hear a lot of talk, especially from the older people, about how the Portuguese like the "old ways" as they call them. To hear it, you would think—like a lot of Americans *do* think—we were just against the times. Let me tell you, this has always been a misunderstanding; we like what is *good*, is all, new or old.

Measured against such ethnic organizations as the German-American Turnverein, the voluntary associations of the Portuguese-Americans have consistently entered more widely into the lives of their members. Despite their specific ethnic orientation, the number and importance of the affiliations they provided was great enough to enable the bulk of the Community to satisfy, within the Luso-Californian context, the great majority of their associative needs. Whereas individuals from other immigrant groups who wished to rise socially or occupationally had to enter into "the social cliques, organizations, institutional activities, and civic life of the receiving society" (had, in other words, to undergo extensive structural assimilation), individual Portuguese-Americans who had such desires could fulfill them without having to pass out of the group of their origin. . . .

Contrary to Oscar Handlin's prognostication that newcomers to the democratic experience would quickly be won over to active participation, the Portuguese-Americans evinced little interest in politics.

I do not know what political experiences the Portuguese-Americans have had in California in the past half-century (even the Portuguese-American newspapers I have consulted have had virtually nothing to report on the subject, and none of my informants had anything to say about it) but I do know that there is in the Community today a widespread mistrust of politics and politicians.[26] For example, here is how Jose Carvalho, the grocer in my sample, saw Bayside's last mayoralty election:

On both sides, the same old bunch. What you would expect, considering the kind of man that goes into politics. And if a man is honest to begin with, how long can he stay that way and keep in with that crowd? Souza, a nice-looking young Portuguese feller, was running for something here just a while back. There was some talk around about how the Portuguese should vote for him. Well, for one thing, the Portuguese in this town never would get behind one of their own anyway, never have. For another, you find yourself wondering just what he's doing up there, you know what I mean?

One of the few studies about Portuguese-Americans in the West was written by Gerald A. Estep, "Portuguese Assimilation in Hawaii and California." American encouragement of Portuguese to move to the West, especially to Hawaii, was in part fear of the Oriental "Yellow Peril." In his study Estep estimates that some 200,000 Portuguese-Americans re-

[26] Ibid., p. 105.

sided in California in 1941 and that Hawaii housed over 27,000. About half of this ethnic group in California carried on agricultural pursuits, while a smaller percentage concentrated on farming in Hawaii. Some of Estep's conclusions are contained in the extract that follows. He discusses, among other things, the impact of education and differences in degree of retention of ethnic identity between Portuguese-Americans in Hawaii and in California.

Portuguese coming to California—whether from their native lands: the Azores, Madeira Islands, and Portugal; or by way of Hawaii or Massachusetts—were mostly farmers and artisans, striving to improve their socio-economic lot.[27] Their homelands were poverty-torn, overpopulated, and controlled by the aristocracy. Working conditions in Hawaii were not always the best. Then, too, the pioneer spirit brought many a Portuguese immigrant westward to seek gold, or simply land and a home on the frontier. . . .

While the Portuguese in Hawaii have worked their way urbanward as fast as possible to escape the stigma attached to lowly plantation labor and to better their economic conditions, approximately 50 per cent of those in California are in rural areas, and the migration appears to be outward from centers of population. In consequence, the types of labor of the two groups are different, as well as is the degree of contact with other groups. In Hawaii the tendency is away from agriculture and chiefly into occupational pursuits designated in census records as "Manufacturing and Mechanical" and "Transportation and Communication." In California, on the other hand, specialization has been in dairying, fishing, and to a lesser extent in agricultural fields. In 1920 the Portuguese ranked third highest in ownership of land and fourth highest in value of farms in California. In addition, they are said to control 75 per cent of the cattle of the state.

The Portuguese are known as an honest, proud, thrifty people. They are hard workers, conscientious, home lovers, and home owners. They came, not to make their "pile" and then return to the old country, but to settle, to raise their families in America. Both in Hawaii and in California the Portuguese have attained middle-class economic status. They are proud of their achievement as well as of the fact that they have seldom needed welfare aid in times of depression.

The largest urban Portuguese population in California is in Oakland, where the group numbers more than 12,000 and represents 9.1 per cent of the foreign white stock, as compared with 3.1 per cent for the state as a whole. In Hawaii they represent approximately 12 per cent of the Island population.

In order to induce a stable Portuguese population into Hawaii, plantation interests guaranteed transportation for both laborers and their families. As a result, the sex ratio of the Portuguese in Hawaii today is 101.1 males to 100 females, while that for California, where there was no paid sponsorship of the group, is 154.7 to 100. From this situation one might expect to find the rate of outmarriage higher

[27] Reprinted from Gerald A. Estep, "Portuguese Assimilation in Hawaii and California," *Sociology and Social Research* 26, University of Southern California (September 1941):61–69.

in California than in Hawaii. Such, however, is not the case. While in Hawaii 36.2 per cent of Portuguese males and 51.4 per cent of females marry outside their own group, in California an estimated 10 per cent marry outside.

Those marrying into other groups in California marry almost entirely with Catholics, while in the Islands, despite the fact that 98 per cent of the Portuguese profess Catholic religion, outmarriage is based on other grounds. Portuguese there have married into more than a dozen different racial groups and have shown considerable religious toleration in so doing.

There is a wide cultural differentiation between the Portuguese in the Island setting and those in California today. Four decades of separation have shown the influence that environment can have in remolding a people. Although there have been changes in the cultural patterns of the Portuguese in California, it is in Hawaii, where the Portuguese people have gone through the processes of competition, conflict, and accommodation, and assimilation and have broken down social distance, that the distinction from old-world family pattern [is most evident.] The man is distinctly the head of the family. The wife may drive the family car to the market, but she remains far more the housewife than is the American woman.

Compulsory education is tending to break down family influence over children.

Religious and fraternal festivals play a far greater part in the lives of California Portuguese than is the case with their brothers in Hawaii. In California there are at least four active Portuguese fraternal organizations, with two or more women's auxiliaries. Some of their meetings are conducted in Portuguese and others in English. In Hawaii, on the other hand, the two such organizations still in existence have lost much of their membership in recent years.

In Hawaii the Portuguese have but a single small newspaper today. Its circulation is confined, for the most part, to first-generation Portuguese. In California there are five newspapers printed in the Portuguese language. In Hawaii few second- and third-generation Portuguese can speak or read the language, whereas in California approximately 50 per cent of Portuguese children are bi-lingual. In both areas, contrasted with the 70 per cent illiteracy of their immigrant forebears, Portuguese youths are highly literate today. At least two radio stations in California, one in Oakland and the other in Long Beach, broadcast programs in Portuguese each week. Hawaii has no such radio programs.

Seldom do Portuguese of Hawaii take trips back to the mother country. In California the proportion of those returning has been one out of four.

Why have the Portuguese in California not assimilated as thoroughly as have those in Hawaii? The answer is to be had through an analysis of the political forces and geographic setting of each group. While Portuguese are Caucasians of southern European origin, the controlling element in the Hawaiian Islands is of north European extraction and considers itself superior. Then enters the fact that the Portuguese came to the Islands in relatively large numbers and formed a rather high percentage of the European laboring class in the Islands at the time. Their cultural patterns—language, names, gestures, religion, and other institutions—differed from those of the controlling group under whom they worked. Add to this the fact that the Portuguese had but little worldly goods and accepted work in the lowest brackets, and the picture is complete.

As they were looked down upon, the Portuguese quite naturally were subjected to many prejudicial practices. For instance, in order to insure plenty of social distance between themselves and the Portuguese, the controlling group held themselves apart from these lowly laborers through a special census classification, calling themselves the "Other Caucasians." Many other such practices were instituted to keep Portuguese out of "haole," or Anglo-Saxon, society, such as refusing admittance to them in certain haole organizations.

Being a sensitive people, the Portuguese rebelled against their position as "under dogs." Through years of hard labor they have elevated themselves into the better-paying jobs; they have moved cityward, working as carpenters, cabinet makers, machinists, and in any other kinds of work they could find. They sought positions away from the cane fields in order to give expression to their ability and receive recognition. Gradually, they neared middle-class economic status. But they found themselves now face to face with members of the controlling group, who, fearful lest the Portuguese gain too much power, instituted the practice of minimizing their ability and of calling attention derogatorily to the group's lowly beginning in the Islands.

To dispose of this matter of stereotyping, the Portuguese disbanded as a nationality group, settled apart from one another and, preferably, in haole-occupied areas. They associated with others than their own group, modifying old-world customs and taking on new ones, marrying outside the group and especially into the haole group, giving up old-world institutions and language, even changing their names in some instances. Anything and everything was justified in order to obliterate the haole stereotype of a "Portagee." Every action was a positive one. Such negative acts as segregation and isolation were impossible in so small and thickly populated a community. Therefore, accommodation and assimilation had to come the hard way. The Portuguese in Hawaii after forty years of struggle have finally gained a fair degree of assimilation and of status.

The picture in California is somewhat different. Since the Portuguese came to the United States of their own accord to gain new freedom and to improve their economic-social status, they were not paid much attention by the controlling group on the mainland. Then, too, their percentage to the total population of the state was, and is, so small that their competition with other groups has been insignificant. Add to this the fact that in California the group has tended to move outward from densely populated urban areas where competition with established businesses would inevitably bring on conflict, and the reason for lack of notice of the Portuguese by other groups is fairly evident.

THE SYRIANS

Although an ancient people who traced their heritage to the Phoenician and Canaanite tribes of the Ancient World, Syrians of modern history found themselves under the yoke of Turkish rule through the first half of the nineteenth century. During their struggle to be rid of Turkish domination, the Syrians, a minority, were driven from their homes by persecution which reached extraordinary proportions in the 1860's. Hundreds of thousands of Syrians fled the Ottoman Empire, with a considerable number discovering America in the late 1870's. The desire to avoid military duty in the Ottoman forces was one reason for this move. Other factors operative in the Syrians' removal to America were the stories of fabulous wealth awaiting them as told by earlier emigrants and the promotion efforts of money lenders and steamship agencies. Finally, there was the influence of American missionaries stationed in Syria as well as of tourists to the Holy Land. The result was the migration of many Syrians and the growth of small ethnic colonies in principal United States cities.

By the early 1890's, Syrian migration to America reached large proportions, so much so that hardly a village in all Syria was not represented in the United States. When Syria was annexed to Lebanon in the twentieth century, a significant number of Christian Syrian-Lebanese migrated to America. In the absence of reliable figures, the Christian Syrian-Lebanese population is estimated to be 200,000, a small figure but, nevertheless, one of the more significant groups of immigrants from that area of the world.

From the beginning of their entry into their new homeland, Syrians were interested in promoting an ethnically oriented social and cultural life. This was evidenced by the creation of The Syrian Society of the City of New York in 1893. In the excerpt that follows, Dr. Ameen F. Haddad, the "Father" of the Society, educated at Beirut College and New York University, describes the tremendous handicaps confronting his fellow Syrians, yet remains confident that their determination will guarantee their success, despite the inhospitality they are encountering.

> On reaching America, they find to their disappointment no chances for employment and are thus forced to become peddlers.[28] You would probably ask me, how do they get their goods, if they are poor? There are quite a few Syrians among them who are quite well-to-do, who have stores and keep such articles as are needed. They deal with wholesale business houses and retail to peddlers, and many are supplied by on credit. I might state right here, and do it with great pleasure, that the dealings of the Syrians with American business houses have always been honest, and their credit with them is good.
>
> Washington Street near Rector Street is their headquarters in this city, where over a thousand reside and from whence they scatter all over North and South America. Strangers in a strange land, ignorant of the English language, customs and manners, laws and

[28] Reprinted from Ameen F. Haddad, *First Annual Report with Constitution and By-Laws of The Syrian Society of the City of New York* (May 1893), pp. 7–8.

everything American, who will become citizens without conception of American institutions or love of their adopted country. They roam from one point to another seeking to earn their living, not knowing what to do, having no one to advise them. They endure great hardships and privations, and even persecutions at the hands of other foreigners around them, learning their customs and adopting their manners. Notwithstanding all this, they came with their families, no matter who or what stands in their way. Their hope of bettering their condition stimulates them to overcome all difficulties which confront them. No more peaceable people have ever landed on these shores than the Syrians, and yet the Christians have singled them out of all other immigrants by ignoring them and doing nothing for their encouragement until within a year.

The next extract was written by Philip K. Hitti, a highly regarded scholar and historian. He lived among the Syrians in the United States for many years and became thoroughly acquainted with and sympathetic to the plight of Syrian immigrants. In later life he returned to live in Syria. The extract that follows depict the habits and customs of Syrians, their reputation among Americans, their relations with other groups and with the old country, and their problems with Americanization.

Beyond a certain number of stabbing and shooting affrays, cases of smuggling and fraudulent bankruptcy, the only serious accusations brought against Syrians in the United States is that their standards of business probity and veracity are not up to the American mark.[29] There may be an element of truth in that. It should be borne in mind, however, that the Oriental manner of speech which the Syrian uses is meant to convey impressions rather than accurate scientific information. The fine niceties of distinction between various shades of thought, in which the Anglo-Saxon indulges, are not deemed necessary. The Syrian is fond of exaggeration and figures of speech, but does not expect his hearer to take him literally. He has a poet's license, and uses it, though he may not have the poetry. His language has behind it the same psychology as lies behind the various advertisements or the statements of the different presidential campaign managers which we read in our papers. The hotel in which I am writing these lines has its walls placarded with this legend "THE CLEANEST, MOST REASONABLE IN PRICE, AND MOST SANITARY IN ALL CHICAGO." If this is to be taken seriously, I must not believe the proprietor. But I know exactly what he means. He means to say the hotel is good enough for me, and I believe it.

Considering the business tradition which the Syrian brings with him from a country where a "one-price" system is not known and bargaining is the rule, and where political oppression often makes truth unpopular and unsafe, special credit should be given to the Syrians for maintaining the standards of integrity and truth which they do maintain. A new type of Syrian business man with

[29] Reprinted from Philip K. Hitti, *The Syrians in America* (New York: Doran, 1924), pp. 87–89, 99–100.

all the traditions of American business is rapidly forging to the front. As early as 1906 *The New York Evening Post* had this to say, "Those among them who have risen to a higher degree of wealth than the majority of their countrymen possess the complete confidence of the business men with whom they deal."

Relation to the old country.—The relation of the Syrian immigrants, not so much to the old country, as to their folks in the old country, has been kept alive and cordial. Their sympathy with them during the years of famine and war, as expressed in terms of relief, furnishes the best evidence therefor.

Relation with other racial groups.—Aside from a few business partnerships and marriages between Syrians and Greeks or Armenians, the Syrians have no special relationship with any other racial group. They prefer to intermarry among themselves, and those of them who are not fortunate enough to find brides here have to go to Syria for them.

Racial prepossessions and aspirations.—It is not safe to generalize regarding the racial prepossessions of a heterogeneous people. In the case of the Syrians, however, certain characteristics are especially pronounced. They are as a rule adventurous, though easily discouraged, adaptable, industrious, but not persevering, frugal, and individualistic. . . .

Relation to American people.—The Syrians did not make their debut into the social consciousness of the American people until 1905 when their exaggerated "factional war" was waged in their Manhattan colony. It was a poor introduction and the undue publicity given it left an enduring and unfavorable impression.

One would expect at least a Sunday school acquaintance with this people of the Holy Land, yet this is not always the case.

In 1909 we find the United States District Court in St. Louis holding that Syrians could not be naturalized because they come within the category of aliens other than white. The case was carried to the Circuit Court of Appeals and the decision of the lower court was reversed. The same question was later raised in the Southern District of New York, and the decision of the lower court that they could be naturalized was affirmed by the Circuit Court of Appeals of that district.

Even at present the colossal ignorance and prejudice, on the part of some, is amazing and constitutes the chief obstacle in the way of better understanding. In an amusing printed bill, circulated in the spring of 1920 in Birmingham, Alabama, we read:

FOR CORONER
VOTE FOR
J. D. GOSS
"THE WHITE MAN'S CANDIDATE"

They have disqualified the negro, an American citizen, from voting in the white primary. The Greek and Syrian should also be disqualified. I DON'T WANT THEIR VOTE. If I can't be elected by the white men, I don't want the office.

Aside from these few unhappy points of contact the relationship between Syrians and Americans has been on the whole cordial. . . .

Political relations.—Syrians cut no figure in the political life of this nation. Very few of them interest themselves in politics or aspire to office. Nothing else could be expected from a people coming from a country where "We the People" does not exist. The case of one who in 1910 ran as Republican nominee to represent the Fifth Senatorial District in New York, and was defeated, stands as a conspicuous exception.

Americanization.—With the decline of belief in naturalization and assimilation as infallible processes, there came into favor within the last few years the so-called process of Americanization. Numberless organizations sprang up like mushrooms, large sums of money were raised and numerous "drives" were instituted to convert the alien. The trouble with an Americanization "drive" is that it does not Americanize. Americanization is a spiritual process, and like all spiritual processes, it is subject to the laws of growth. It is invisible and subtle, if it is to be real and enduring. It involves the problem of environment pitted against heredity. The knowledge of English is a step towards Americanization, but it is not Americanization itself. Donning American clothes and eating American food does not constitute Americanization. America, being more than a geographic entity, is a set of ideas, institutions and ideals; and Americanization means divesting one's self of a certain deep rooted patrimony of ideas, sentiments, traditions and interests, and an acceptance of, and participation in, a certain new spiritual inheritance. Such a thing cannot be accomplished completely in one generation. Even the second generation among immigrants cannot be fully assimilated.

Americanization is not solely a "foreign" problem. It is essentially an American problem. The fact that the foreigner is within our gates indicates his belief in our ability to teach him. The question is not so much whether the foreigner is responsive and open minded, as it is to whether the American is virile and broad enough to adopt him into his spiritual heritage. In the words of a writer in The Atlantic Monthly, "The greatest obstacles to the speedy Americanization of 'foreigners' are the ridicule of, contempt for, and prejudice against them on the part of native Americans." The case of the lady in Philadelphia whose sister was a missionary in the Orient and who refused to rent her room to an Oriental student, and the case of a church which sold its downtown building because of the increasing number of foreign neighbors and sent the money to the foreign field are interesting illustrations of an inconsistency in the working of the human mind.

Agencies.—There are practically no American agencies specializing on the Syrians. In only a few cities—New York, Detroit, St. Louis, Cleveland, Lawrence, Fall River and Boston—are they found in sufficient numbers to attract the attention of any agency; and even in these cities they are too widely scattered to be dealt with as a racial group. In Minneapolis, the University of Minnesota sends its students in Americanization classes to teach English to Syrians.

Among the Syrian agencies the work of the Syrian-American Club, with headquarters in Brooklyn, has been notable along the line of naturalization. Its last report shows that during the year 1919 the Club filled out 485 applications for first, and 112 for second, papers. An investigation made by the Club shows that only one half of those Syrians in Brooklyn eligible for citizenship are actual citizens.

Use of languages.—The old generation of Syrians still hold the Arabic in almost sacred regard, and, true enough, their souls cannot be thrilled other than through its instrumentality. They throng to hear a speaker in this rich and musical mother tongue, but see no reason why they should tolerate anyone lecturing to them in another language. The reverse is true of the native born generation. In answer to a question as to whether she spoke Arabic, a three-year-old girl crossing Chouteau Avenue in St. Louis, replied, "No, ma'am, I speak American." But her elder sister companion confided to me that at home her sister did speak Syrian.

Use of racial sentiment.—If the absence of a strong sense of national pride facilitates the working of the process of assimilation, then the Syrians are among the easiest to assimilate. In many cases they do not like to be classified as Syrians. A five-year-old boy in Brooklyn protested against being called Syrian on the ground that he was a "Yankee." Their names often undergo strong metamorphoses in a vain attempt to Anglicize them. Thus "Milad" becomes "Christmas," "Sham'ūn" Shannon, "Hurayz" Harris, and "Ashshi" Cook. This is especially true where the original patronymics are hard for Americans to handle, and stands in marked contrast with the case of an American-born Frenchman, named Robert, who insisted on my calling him Ro-ber (the French pronunciation for Robert).

"Did you not receive any aid from American sources?" asked I of the Maronite priest in Detroit who was showing me his newly built church and priding himself on its being one of the finest Syrian church buildings in the country. No sooner had his negative reply been made than my eyes caught "Edward A. Maynard," on the altar, and, asking for an explanation, the priest replied, "O, well, that is Wadi' Mu'auwad."

A more recent investigator of Syrian-Lebanese mores observed that the power of the concept of the evil-eye was lessening. Belief in the evil eye contained many of the characteristics typical of a backward people. The Christian Syrian-Lebanese were ready to attribute a victim's affliction to the phenomenon, and the appropriate exorcism was rather elaborate. Once a strongly held belief, it has weakened considerably as a result of Americanization.

The strong Mediterranean belief in the power of the evil eye was imported intact with the cultural baggage of the Christian Syrian-Lebanese immigrants who joined the tide of new immigrants to America in the late nineteenth and early twentieth century.[30] But despite the significant place the eye once held in the beliefs of these tradition-bound people, its practice in America is greatly diminished. This was evident from conversations with first-generation immigrants whom I had the opportunity to interview in the summer

[30] Reprinted from Alixa Naff, "Belief in the Evil Eye Among the Christian Syrian-Lebanese in America," *Journal of American Folklore* (January 1965):46–47.

of 1962. Of 87 informants only 21, all women whose average age was about 65, responded to questions about the evil eye, frequently with embarrassment. And of those who did proffer any information, credence ranged from strong conviction to complete disavowal, while the majority were skeptical. An early immigrant, expressing the skeptical view, frankly admitted that she had once strongly feared the evil eye, ". . . but then," she added, "I got to thinking and it didn't make sense to me so I stopped believing in it." This development can be partly attributed to their remarkable integration into American life which was accomplished within the lifetime of the first generation.

The Christian Syrian-Lebanese who came to America had been predominantly small land-owning peasants and minor craftsmen from the villages of Syria and Lebanon. Many of the immigrants interviewed emigrated from an area which before World War I was a part of Syria and was annexed to Lebanon only after their departure to America. Until Lebanese independence in 1941 they had always referred to themselves as Syrians and some among them still retain that identification. No reliable figures on the number of Christian Syrian-Lebanese in the United States are available, but a rough estimate is 200,000.

The majority of the immigrants began life in America as notions and dry goods peddlers operating from several scattered communities all over the country. Peddling as a way of life was generally temporary but its contribution to their integration was substantial. While it both demanded intercourse with the American community and tended to keep their own communities relatively loose and fluid, it was also a means for these highly individualistic people, unfamiliar with the English language and the American customs, to accumulate capital, establish a business of their own, and move up the ladder of economic success. In addition to being scattered, mobile, and success-oriented, they suffered no particular group discrimination. Their integration process on the whole was favorable enough to minimize anxieties which in turn not only devitalized superstitions but gradually weakened the transmission of folk beliefs to subsequent generations. Where the belief in the evil eye does persist, it is in relatively isolated small-town communities or in rural areas. Here, the children of early immigrants and those who came with their parents at a young age seem to fear the evil eye more than the older women of the first generation.

KEY QUESTIONS

1. Analyze and compare America's views of Italians and Greeks as workers (favorable or unfavorable impressions) and their impact on the labor movement.

2. In what important respects did Italian and Greek colonies in America manifest similarities and differences?

3. Compare and contrast the experiences of the Italians, Greeks, Portuguese, and Syrians in America by commenting on the durability of

their traditions and how these served to keep them aloof from American influences.

4. Compare and contrast the causes for emigration to America on the part of Greeks and Portuguese.

5. Could it be said that the sense of inferiority strengthened when immigrant children entered the American public school atmosphere? Answer this by reference to the Italian experience and by comparing it with the Portuguese experience.

6. If the Greek experience in America is taken as an example, what was encompassed by the term "Americanization"?

8

Native American Indians and Immigrants from the Western Hemisphere: CANADIANS AND MEXICANS

The history of the United States of America over the centuries leaves little doubt as to the role various ethnic peoples have played in contributing to the population growth and mix. There is little question as to the relationship of the New World to the Old, so that although there is a distinctiveness about Americans, on the whole the European ancestry is the preponderant one. It is a simple fact that, numerically speaking, most Americans descended from European forbears. Having said that, however, it is important to remember that significant influxes of people came to this country from other continents, many of which have already been discussed in this text. In this chapter and the next, the focus will be on the ethnic impact on and experiences in the United States of people from the Western Hemisphere.

Emigration from the Western Hemisphere was discernible in the pre–Civil War period with approximately a quarter of a million inhabitants from British America settling in the United States during that time. Canadian emigration accelerated in tempo in the generation following the Civil War. Altogether, nearly four million people have moved from Canada to the United States, a figure exceeded only by a few European countries.

Immigration to the United States from the rest of the Western Hemisphere, although a more recent movement than the Canadian, is nevertheless sizable. The best estimates are that of a total of 7,307,862 emigrants from the Western Hemisphere, including 3,336,004 people from Latin America, have emigrated to the United States. Not hampered by quota restrictions and only recently limited to an overall yearly maximum figure, Latin-Americans have come to be an important ethnic minority.

According to the data of the Census Bureau, March 1971, there were approximately 9 million persons of Spanish origin in the United States. Of this number over 5 million persons were of Mexican origin;

1,450,000 persons were of Puerto Rican origin; 626,000 persons were of Cuban origin; 501,000 persons were of Central and South American origin; and 1,356,000 persons were of other Spanish-American origin. Three-fifths of the population of Spanish origin lived in the five Southwestern states of Arizona, California, Colorado, New Mexico, and Texas. Additionally, foreign-born persons of Spanish origin made up the largest group of foreign-born people in the United States.[1]

CANADIANS

The 3,941,858 people who migrated from Canada to the United States between 1820 and 1969 make the Canadians the largest group of immigrants among all people from the Western Hemisphere. Of course, the raw figures must be considered advisedly, since among other things they do not take into account the number of return immigrants, which in the case of French Canadians was considerable. Nevertheless, Canadian migration to the United States still constitutes a major phenomenon. In view of the large number of people involved, it is surprising that research concerning this group is not more extensive.

Part of the reason for the limited research may have been caused by the peculiarities of relationship between the United States and her northern neighbor. The absence of artificial physical barriers renders it unsurprising that there has been considerable interchange between the populations of the two countries. One idea of how extensive the movement from Canada to the United States was can be gleaned from a 1930 statistic showing that over 9 percent of the foreign-born in the country at the time were Canadian immigrants. The few hundred thousand Americans to migrate to Canada did not offset the influx from Canada southward, an exodus so massive that at one point it represented 20 percent of the entire Canadian population, thereby promoting fear of depopulation.

Although the movement to the United States was discernible from the beginning of the country's history, it picked up momentum in the 1850–1900 period and continued well into the twentieth century. However, the bulk of the Canadian immigrant population in the twentieth century easily assimilated with the native population of the United States because most twentieth-century Canadian immigrants were of English stock. By contrast, the experiences of the French-Canadians have been markedly different. Although the majority of immigrants were French-speaking, over a million were English-Canadians.

The social and linguistic backgrounds of the English- and French-Canadians necessarily resulted in differing assimilation patterns. French-

[1] U.S., Bureau of the Census, "Selected Characteristics of Persons and Families of Mexican, Puerto Rican, and Other Spanish Origin: March 1971," *Current Population Reports*, Series P-20, No. 224, p. 3. [See Appendix.]

Canadians, because of the homogeneity of language and religion, formed a compact minority. Their religion and language served to maintain ethnic identity. While these factors bound French-Canadians one to another, they also constituted barriers restricting intercourse with non-French-Canadians. The heterogeneity and less definite ethnic characteristics of English-Canadians posed few assimilative problems and probably explain the paucity of material about their ethnic experience in the United States.

After emigrating, the majority of newcomers from Canada settled in the northeastern states and along the Atlantic Coast, where most flocked to urban centers. A smaller number moved into the Pacific Coast region. The main cause of their migration was economic. Canada's limited financial and economic development, as contrasted with the hope or expectation of receiving good wages in the factories and industries in the United States, told the story for most.

The significance of the Canadian migration to the United States is further demonstrated in the following figures estimating the percentage of Canadian stock in various American states in 1930; Maine, 25.3 percent; New Hampshire, 29.5 percent; Vermont, 20.6 percent; Massachusetts, 17.1 percent; Rhode Island, 16.1 percent; and Michigan, 10.3 percent. In some instances they were the predominant ethnic group in cities such as in Worcester, Fall River, and Providence.

Employed upon arrival almost completely in the factory system, a considerable number also entered the commercial and professional life of their adopted country. Although not generally the recipients of prejudicial abuse, French-Canadians felt a need to preserve their ethnic characteristics. Their ethnic concerns found them erecting hospitals, schools, churches, benevolent and literary institutions, and newspapers with an indelible French stamp.

Canadian emigration to the United States became a source of major concern for some Canadian journalists and officials. Indeed, in the case of two French-Canadians, the movement to the United States was a serious threat to French-Canadian culture. In 1875 one of them, Ferdinand Gagnon, was designated an agent of repatriation for the Quebec government to promote reimmigration from New England. An account of his activities makes it possible to glimpse the core of French-Canadian society in the United States in its first phases. The excerpt that follows is from Donald Chaput, "Some Repatriement Dilemmas." Notice that although Gagnon began his drive convinced that residence in America would bring evil to his ethnic compatriots, he changed his harsh attitude toward the end of his career as he saw his repatriation efforts fail. Indeed, he finally became an American citizen, claiming he could take that step and remain at heart a Canadian.

On his appointment as *agent de repatriement* Gagnon immediately sought the assistance of the most powerful *Canadien* group in New

England—the clergy.[2] The parish priests who had only recently arrived to look after the expatriates generally held the view that residence in the United States was only temporary. Thus they were easily convinced by Gagnon that the time had arrived for repatriation: work was slow; salaries were low; working conditions in the factories were far from ideal.

One proof of Gagnon's sincerity came in the fall of 1875, when he persuaded his parents to return to *la patrie*. Gagnon continued to spread his repatriation message throughout the New England states. He did more than merely explain Quebec's plan for colonizing the eastern townships; he dangled every possible lure in front of his audiences. In his speeches to patriotic and fraternal organizations he spoke glowingly of the contributions of Champlain, of Perrot, of Talon, and often concluded with a poem or remark on the majestic scenery along the St. Lawrence. When speaking before labour groups he began by contrasting the grime, sweat, and long hours of New England's factories with the pure, healthy air of Quebec's forests and fields, and then pointed to the colonization plan as the solution: "Retournez donc au pays; retournex donc vers notre cher et bien-aimé Canada; allez y fonder, au milieu des forêts, de puissantes familles canadiennes et catholiques."

Gagnon decried the materialistic values of American life, values which *Canadiens* should not share. The American search for the dollar, the American natural law of assimilating minority cultures ("flotsam of foreign nationalities"), were evils that *Canadiens* should avoid. Patriotism, respect for the church, love of family— these great *Canadien* characteristics could best be preserved by returning to *la patrie* and living among one's *concitoyens:* "Serions-nous donc déjà prêts à tout oublier, respect humain, gloire, souvenirs, épreuves, troubles, difficultés, pour nous jeter dans les bras des autres peuples?" Gagnon also used effective legal arguments to encourage a return to Canada. He detailed all the ramifications of becoming a naturalized American citizen. Though he was fair in pointing out some advantages, he emphasized that if one became an American citizen, and then wanted to repatriate, his path would not be easy. Certain professional activities and other protections accorded British subjects could only be enjoyed after a three-year period in Canada.

Where he could not go, Gagnon's message was carried in his newspapers, and in the many communications he had with other editors and the clergy. Even at this period, though he had lived in the United States for only seven years, he was regarded as the "father of French American journalism. The Gagnon message was strong and consistent: some, he admitted, were probably right in deciding to remain in the United States, but the majority of *Canadiens* must, for patriotic, cultural, social, religious, and economic reasons, return to Canada.

Gagnon, however, was not to be a prophet. Although at times he showed great perception in understanding American economy and politics, it took him much longer to realize that though the *Canadiens* in New England valued their French heritage and Cath-

---

[2] Reprinted from Donald Chaput, "Some Repatriement Dilemmas," the *Canadian Historical Review*, vol. 49, no. 4 (December 1968):403–408; by permission of the author and of the publisher, University of Toronto Press.

olic religion, they also valued American wages and potential social mobility. In the late 1870s, Gagnon's position gradually shifted. He still glorified *Canadien* culture, but he no longer spoke or wrote about the dismal aspects of American life. In earlier years he had preached against the evils and corrupt values of American culture. By the end of the decade he made a distinction between cruel factory owners and the rest of American society.

By 1881 it was obvious that the campaign for repatriation was a failure, not through any fault of Gagnon's or any lack of appreciation for *Canadien* culture but rather because the *Canadiens* were adjusting admirably to the Yankee environment. In 1881 the state of Massachusetts published a report prepared by Colonel Carroll Wright, which denounced *Canadien* immigration and blamed the *Canadiens* for many of New England's economic and social problems. Gagnon replied to this accusation in a speech entitled "Plaidoyer patriotique," given in Boston on 25 October 1881. He answered the charges point by point, emphasizing the great progress the *Canadiens* had made in the previous ten years: thirty churches, many schools, and a sound record of home ownership. He criticized Wright for maintaining that the *Canadiens* took no interest in public affairs, failed to become American citizens, and had no interest in voting. Gagnon showed that, in a survey of thirty-one communities, almost 13,000 of the 66,000 students were *Canadiens* and claimed that 4,000 had been naturalized. Admitting that the *Canadiens* in New England had not made their presence known by any series of great deeds, Gagnon stressed that they deserved respect because of their behaviour as good, loyal, obedient citizens.

This cataloguing of the *Canadiens'* progress over the years was no listing of facts by a repatriation agent. The dream of resettlement in eastern Quebec had vanished, not only for most *Canadiens,* but also for Gagnon. On 19 October 1882, Gagnon himself became a naturalized American citizen. In a speech at Cohoes, New York, Gagnon explained why he no longer believed in repatriation and why he had become an American citizen. It *is* possible, he now claimed, to be a good citizen of the United States and remain at heart a *Canadien.* To prove this he cited cases of well-known, Canadian-born men who became successful American businessmen and politicians, yet still took pride in their French heritage. "L'allégéance à un pouvoir ne change pas l'origine du sujet ou du citoyen; elle ne change que sa condition politique." The solution, he maintained, was to be completely loyal to the government of the United States, but at the same time to conserve the *Canadien* language, religion, and culture. Apparently forgetting his earlier examples of the great American tendency toward assimilation of other cultures, he felt that a continuing French culture was possible in New England. . . .

Telesphore St. Pierre, the other journalist, while not officially connected with the repatriation movement, did exert his energies among his ethnic compatriots in the midwest in his concern that French culture not be swallowed up by Yankee culture. After a number of years, however, he concluded that although French culture was largely kept intact, it was merely a matter of time before it died out and assimilation into the predominant culture followed.

Telesphore St-Pierre was never officially connected with the re-patriation movement, but his activities in the midwest helped to shape the thinking of the *Canadien* expatriates.[3] He was born in Lavaltrie, 10 July 1869; his father, Jean-Baptiste, was a farmer. While still in his teens, St-Pierre moved to the Windsor-Detroit region and began work as a printer. He was self-educated and had developed a lifelong interest in the story of French exploration and settlement in the Great Lakes area. Belisle mentions that St-Pierre spent every spare moment in the Detroit libraries and became an authority on New France. He joined *Le Progrès* of Windsor in 1885 and staunchly defended the Riel rebellion; in 1888 he founded *L'Ouest Français*, at Bay City, Michigan. Late in 1889 he moved to Lake Linden, Michigan, a community on the south shore of Lake Superior, where he founded *L'Union Franco-Américaine;* under St-Pierre's direction, this became the best French journal in the mid-west.

But St-Pierre only stayed with *L'Union* for about a year, and then he moved on to found or edit several other French newspapers in Michigan. He felt from his first days in Michigan that the drama of French settlement deserved a chronicler. During his years there he kept copious notes from his readings, hoping eventually to write such a work. So dedicated to that task did he become that he temporarily retired from journalism to complete it. The work, *Histoire des Canadians du Michigan et du comté d'Essex, Ontario,* was published in Montreal in 1895. The newspapers, magazine articles, and books by St-Pierre prior to 1900 show his belief that all other ends should be subordinate to encouraging knowledge and love for *la patrie....*

Though large numbers of French immigrants had settled in Michigan, as in New England, after the American Civil War, French influence in Michigan had a long history. Sault Ste Marie had been founded by the Jesuits Dablon and Marquette in 1668, Michili-mackinac (Fort de Buade, at St Ignace) in the 1670s, Fort St Joseph (Niles) in 1693, and Detroit in 1701. Even after the successive British and American regimes, the majority of Michigan residents were French. By the 1840s, however, heavy immigration from the eastern states led to a rapid decline in French influence; by the time of the Civil War, Frenchmen were centred around Detroit, St Ignace, and Sault Ste Marie. Michigan's great copper and iron discoveries of the 1840s led to rapid industrial expansion during the Civil War years. These mining developments, in addition to the large lumbering operations of the 1870s and 1880s resulted in a critical labour shortage, which was met in part by thousands of emigrants from Quebec. The same impulses which drove the *Canadiens* into New England also pushed them into Michigan; only the lure was different.

St-Pierre saw in this movement of Frenchmen to Michigan a chance to revitalize French culture. He felt it his duty to assure that the newly arrived *Canadiens* would not be swallowed by the Yankee culture. At the same time, he hoped that Frenchmen in the older communities would look upon these immigrants as a means to reopen contact with Quebec. French history, culture, and language became the dominant themes of St-Pierre's newspaper articles. Sketches of

[3] Ibid., pp. 410–11.

personalities such as Jacques Cartier and Samuel de Champlain appeared in every issue of *L'Union.* St-Pierre felt that the newcomer must retain his pride in his origins; he deplored the practice of anglicizing names, which he claimed was "unworthy of honest people." But St-Pierre knew that a French press alone could never preserve French culture. He realized that strong support would be found among the resident *Canadien* clergy who would look after the spiritual, cultural, and economic well-being of their flocks. He also believed that strong fraternal societies would aid cultural survival. . . .

If, then, emigration were an unwise choice, what of the tens of thousands who had already come to Michigan? Here, St-Pierre's fierce nationalism was dominated by his realism. Many *Canadiens* had put in years of hard labour in Michigan. Repatriation would mean selling their property at a loss, and leaving friends and relatives. Repatriation would also handicap the work of the already shaky parish and fraternal organizations. And, indeed, what would a repatriate find in Quebec? He had no land, little money, and did not wish to begin the struggle anew. What happened, according to St-Pierre, was that many of those who were repatriated returned to the United States after a short stay in Quebec, and he cited a repatriation movement in Lake Linden in 1894. Widely acclaimed at the time, the major effects of this affair, however, were the disruption of the French community and hardship for many families.

Though he regretfully rejected repatriation as a solution, and though he was aware of the tendency towards assimilation in the United States, St-Pierre felt that French culture could be retained to some degree by encouraging nationalism—through the church, schools, and press. Yet, his normally keen perception seems here to have been blurred. He wrote: "Loin de favoriser l'anglicisation des peuples catholiques qui vivent aux États-Unis, c'est notre humble opinion que l'église devrait les encourager à conserver leur langue et leurs traditions, tout imprégnées qu'elles sont de l'ésprit catholique." He gave tribute to a dying cause, however, for already he had noted the americanization of the churches and the schools in French communities in which English had become the language of instruction. . . .

St-Pierre, like Gagnon, believed to the end that it was possible to keep the French language and traditions alive, even in the midst of Anglo-Saxon influences. Both men gave consideration to repatriation of their countrymen; Gagnon even acted as an agent for the Quebec government. At the peak of their careers, however, both men rejected repatriation, urging rather that the *Canadiens* in the United States and western Canada do everything possible to retain heritage, while remaining loyal to their new political sovereigns.

Cultural and ethnic trait retention was strongest among the first and second generation French-Canadians, with evidence of its power lasting well into the 1930's. It was manifest in their language, their religion, and their "Frenchness." The ethnic experience was so deeply engrained that it attempted to affect the course of religious development. Thus at one point early in the twentieth century, French-Canadians in

Maine, although sharing the same religion with other Catholics in the state, undertook a vigorous campaign to have the Diocese of Maine take cognizance of their ethnic heritage. This was the reasoning behind their insistence on the appointment of French-Canadians to membership in the hierarchy in the Diocese of Maine. The excerpt that follows is from Kenneth B. Woodbury, Jr., "An Incident Between The French Canadians and the Irish in the Diocese of Maine in 1906."

One of the most pressing of the many problems created by the great influx of immigrants to the United States at the turn of the century was the assimilation of the new arrivals into American culture.[4] Every facet of American life witnessed the tensions of creating a unified, vibrant culture out of a diverse and pluralistic society. Emigrants from French Canada were as much a part of these tensions as those from the Old World. The French Canadians, who vehemently resisted any loss of their national identity, struggled fiercely to preserve their own culture and language even within their Church. Consequently, this conflict in the Catholic Church may be viewed as essentially materialistic, rather than religious, in origin. The struggle between the French Canadians and the assimilators, the Irish, was dramatized by the attempts of each group to control the administration of the Church. This conflict became intensified in the diocese of Maine in 1906 when a vacancy occurred in the episcopal throne. The question at issue was how and with whom the position should be filled.

Of the sixty-three parishes of the Portland diocese comprising the entire state, thirty-three or slightly more than half were French Canadian in September, 1901. Of the remainder, four were French, one Dutch, one Belgian, and twenty-four were Irish. In 1903 the French Canadians claimed from eighty to one hundred thousand parishioners as compared with estimates from twenty-six to forty thousand Irish Catholics in the diocese.

During the period 1900–1910 in the Portland diocese ten parishes were established. Three of these were created for the French Canadians, and one of the three was strictly a national as distinct from a territorial parish. A territorial parish serves all the Catholics of a district regardless of nationality. A national parish ministers only to one nationality, and a Catholic may elect to attend either the church in his area or the church of his nationality if there is one nearby. The establishment of national parishes was a bone of contention between the French Canadians and the Irish. A national parish was meant to be created sparingly since canon law recognized it as a "transitory institution, destined to care for the spiritual needs of immigrants who do not understand the local language. Its purpose obviously is not to perpetuate foreign elements at the cost of national unity." Furthermore, the establishment of a national parish required an apostolic indulgence even if the parish language was one of the official languages of the country. This requirement

---

[4] Reprinted from Kenneth B. Woodbury, Jr., "An Incident Between the French Canadians and the Irish in the Diocese of Maine in 1906," *The New England Quarterly* 15 (June 1967):260–69.

was even extended to those national parishes assigned a specific territory.

Priests assigned to the national parishes were able to speak the language of the parish, and it was the diocesan policy to appoint bilingual priests to serve the territorial parishes where there was a majority of French Canadians. The assignment was made according to the language needed, the priest's seniority, and the "adaption of the talents of various priests to needs of the individual parishes."

The Reverend Louis S. Walsh, D.D., was consecrated Bishop of Portland on October 18, 1906, and during his episcopacy he created fourteen French Canadian parishes with the assignment of French Canadian priests. There is no record of any pastor other than one of French Canadian descent being assigned to a French Canadian parish.

Another issue between the French Canadians and the Irish was the composition of the Diocesan Council or Board of Consultors, and the role it should play in the administration of the Church. During the first decade of the present century the Council was composed of nearly an equal number of each nationality— French Canadian and Irish. For instance, of the six Diocesan Consultors in 1900 three were French Canadian and each of the three was an extern priest incardinated into the Portland diocese. The membership of the Council was appointed by the bishop for a five-year term and the Consultors were supposed to come from the immediate vicinity of the Chancery Office so that they could meet quickly at the call of the bishop. It seems that the Irish bishops of this decade made unusual efforts to appoint French Canadians to the Council since those chosen came from considerable distances. The Council of 1905 included French Canadian priests from Old Town, Waterville, and Biddeford. The Council of 1910 had French Canadian priests from Old Town, Lewiston, and Eagle Lake in Aroostook County. The bishop was under no obligation to see that any nationality was represented on the Council in any specified proportion. . . .

As the strength of the French Canadian community in Maine grew, its awareness of its national identity increased. At the turn of the century, the French Canadians were the most numerous foreign nationality in Maine, bound together by their national societies, Church, culture, national newspapers, and above all, their language. The national societies held frequent conventions in an effort to hold the French Canadian community together, calling upon the French Canadians to preserve their language and culture. These conventions and the national language newspapers were effective instruments in giving the French Canadian community a sense of its cultural identity.

In December, 1905, *Le Messager* reprinted an article entitled "Un Amoreux de la Canadienne" from *l'Opinion Publique* of Lynn, Massachusetts, urging that the French Canadian fraternity must be established outside of the guardianship of the foreigner. The French Canadians were advised to band together and to avoid mixing with the other national groups. In another article of the same date, *Le Messager* lamented that the struggle to maintain the French Canadian language had been lost in the Northwest of the United States. It asserted, however, that this surrender was not a result of the strength of the enemies of the French Canadians, but rather of the timidity of the French Canadians themselves. *Le Messager* considered the preservation of the language to be the cornerstone of the French Canadian culture. Asserting that the French Canadian "race" was the most intelligent in North America, the author declared that the best way to preserve this superiority was to remain loyal to the French Canadian language: "That the English remain loyal to their language is just, but I don't see why we should abandon our language for theirs, since ours is superior."

Any attack on the French Canadian language was interpreted as an attempt to subvert the French Canadian "race." Thus *Le Messager* reported that in Jewitt City, Connecticut, the Irish secured a Polish vicar for the Church even though the French Canadians numbered twelve hundred as compared with four hundred Poles and with five or six hundred Irish. In Putnam, Connecticut, an Irishman was elected to the office of mayor although the Irish numbered only six hundred and the French Canadians totaled twenty-five hundred.

The Diocesan Synod of Chicago had decreed that all children must learn the catechism in English. Would this decree be extended to the Portland diocese, asked *Le Messager*. This was one of the worries of the ardent French Canadian nationals who feared being "Saxonized."

In January, 1906, when Monsignor William H. O'Connell, Bishop of Portland, was promoted to the post of coadjutor to the Archbishop of Boston, *Le Messager* quickly seized the opportunity to demand a French Canadian successor to O'Connell. The editor demanded that French Canadians had a right to have a bishop who knew the diocese, its population, its needs, and especially its language. Since the French Canadians were the most numerous group of Catholics in the diocese, he insisted that their interests be taken into consideration. *Le Messager* even went so far as to suggest the names of suitable candidates for the episcopacy. . . .

Early in February, the French Canadian community was startled to read in *Le Messager* that a Portland newspaper had announced that Patrick B. Supple, a close friend of Bishop O'Connell had been named to succeed Monsignor O'Connell as bishop. *Le Messager* was indignant that another Irishman had been named. It asked how much Supple had paid for the post, and reported a rumor that the Holy See had scorned the majority of the Catholics in Maine. *Le Messager* again took the position that the majority must be taken into consideration and that the Pope should heed their wishes.

In mid-March a convention of French Canadians met in Lewiston. It not only went on record in favor of a French Canadian bishop, but also passed four resolutions: (1) demanding that rights and privileges of the French Canadian community must be preserved; (2) declaring that the French language is the only safeguard of the Catholic faith among the French Canadians; (3) decreeing that bilingual parish schools be maintained and strengthened; and (4) insisting that French Canadian parishes have their own priest and missionaries. These resolutions added support to the crusade of *Le Messager* for a French Canadian bishop. . . .

Four Irishmen and three French Canadians comprised the Council. Walsh was the first elected, Hurley second, and Mc-

Donough third: all were Irishmen. Later in the month *Le Messager* printed the results of the Council balloting. . . .

The French Canadians did not vote as a bloc and all supported the election of Walsh. The other Irish members voted for Hurley. Thus an Irish priest was nominated as the first preference of the Council by the French Canadians. *Le Messager* printed numerous articles condemning the election of Walsh, overlooking the crucial role that the French Canadian priests had played. *Le Messager* wanted a majority of French Canadians on the Council in order that the election of a French Canadian would be assured and justice done. . .

Meanwhile trouble between the French Canadians and the Irish broke out in Connecticut and in Fall River, Massachusetts. *Le Messager* asserted that "Irish priests are everywhere the same, they persecute their faithful French Canadians." The newspaper concluded that the French clergy (the Dominicans) were attempting to "chase the French Canadian priests from our parishes in the United States." Editorials appeared throughout July attacking the Dominicans.

On August 13, *Le Messager* reported that the Associated Press had learned that Pope Pius X had approved the nomination of Louis S. Walsh as Bishop of Portland. Walsh even admitted that he had been confirmed as the new bishop. *Le Messager* then advised its readers to submit to the confirmation of Walsh, but warned that "we will not cease to protest the injustice. With the present organization of the diocesan administration, the French Canadians will never get justice." It further contended that the election of Walsh was not a defeat, "only a retreat—the struggle begins." *Le Messager* thought that help must come from Rome, but if it did not come, the French Canadians must continue to protest.

Bessie Bloom Wessel, in a study entitled *An Ethnic Survey of Woonsocket, Rhode Island* (originally published in 1931), made an important effort to collect scientific data on ethnic change in one geographic region of the United States in the early 1920's. When she examined Woonsocket, Rhode Island, she found that individuals of French-Canadian descent represented two-thirds of the community's population. The majority (three-fourths) of the population attended French-Canadian parochial schools, intermarriage outside the ethnic group was the lowest of almost all the groups in the city, and they retained language usage to a high degree, although they became bilingual as their residence in the United States lengthened. In sum, French-Canadians in this community demonstrated a remarkable tenacity to their cultural values, while not remaining indifferent to the lifestyles of their new environment. The selection that follows discusses bilingualism and bicultural traits.

Bilingualism and Biculturalism[5]

It is in its bilingualism and in its biculturalism that the French-Canadian group is peculiarly distinctive and assertive. The data on

[5] Reprinted from Bessie Bloom Wessel, *An Ethnic Survey of Woonsocket, Rhode Island* (reprint ed., New York: Arno Press, Inc., 1970), pp. 242–46.

language usage as obtained from the case histories of children cor-
robate the impressions obtained in home visits by Mlle Bossavy, and
confirm the theories asserted by leaders in brochures on the subject
and in conversation.

French Canadians even when native born and English speaking assert, with pride, their French-Canadian descent. About 90 per
cent of all individuals who are native born can speak both languages; about half claim bilingualism in the home. They assert,
most emphatically, that their tenacity for French culture is not inconsistent with loyalty to America or with full acquaintance with
American institutions and the English language. They are French
speaking even in the third generation. But they are English speaking, too, and become so in the very first generation. Our previous
analysis of language usage indicated that with the exception of the
Jews no other group in Woonsocket learns English more readily or
uses it more extensively. But they differ from the Jews in one regard: Given time, the Jews drop their ancestral language; the
French retain it as the familial and ancestral tongue. With the
French the attachment to the French language and to French-Canadian ancestry was noted among families when even grandparents
were native born. In other families one or more of the grandparents
were brought here as babies, or the first member of the family came
to the United States sixty, seventy, or even eighty years ago, or "too
far back to remember," and yet "these families frankly and even
proudly claim their French-Canadian ancestry, and still use the
French language."

Mlle Bossavy offers three possible causes in explanation of this
tenacity for the French language even among Old Americans. She
calls attention to the extensive intramarriage between French Canadians of different generations. Numerous marriages occur between
two French-Canadian persons, one of whom is native born and the
other foreign born. This was noted in our own investigations, but
she finds evidence of the same procedure among grandparents and
even among great grandparents. Second, frequent migration back
and forth to Canada keeps the contacts and the language alive. Third,
internal migration in the United States from one community to another where there are centers of French-Canadian life serves to perpetuate ancestral traditions.

"The West, whether American or Canadian, seems to have a
fatal influence on the mother-language. But one does not need to
move across the continent. It makes a difference in what New England town one happens to settle. The district of Woonsocket a
family lives in may make a difference. One may cease to use French
for a few years and adopt it again because one's neighbor uses that
and no other." This explanation was offered by some of the mothers
and was obviously indicative of the situation in numerous homes.

The French Canadians in Rhode Island are essentially a bilingual people. That this is characteristic of the group in other situations has been attested by many writers dealing with the same
problem, particularly in Canada.

"It is an outstanding fact," writes Helen C. Munroe in a recent
article "that the educated French Canadian speaks almost flawless
English in addition to speaking a French that can be understood
anywhere in a French-speaking country."

French Canadians who came under our observation expect

their children to be bilingual as a matter of course. Native-born children know English and are being taught French and French tradition.

This biculturalism is not limited to use of French as a language. There is an ardor for all things French. Nor is this devotion necessarily French Canadian. The Canadian flag is rarely exhibited, but the French flag is seen alongside the flag of the United States. To the French the former is the symbol of his culture; the latter, of his country. Loyalty to Canada as a homeland is seldom heard expressed, but loyalty to French culture and American citizenship is urged in every page of their literature. This is a conscious policy indorsed and fostered by those who represent leadership in the group. Its manifestation in Woonsocket is obviously typical of the situation in other communities.

The dependence upon language is closely related to the religious problem. Indeed, the devotion to one gathers strength from the other. To them the French Canadian church and the parochial schools are the custodians of culture values. It is here that the dominance of the Irish, and particularly the "Irish theory of Americanization"—which assumes that the use of English as the primary language is an essential characteristic in an Americanization program— evokes resentment.

The French Canadian conceives Americanization as a process which brings into harmonious relation two diverse cultures. It is a plea for diversity in American community life. In this they are not alone among foreign nationalities in this country. But they are probably unique in having promulgated, some thirty years ago, a theory of Americanization which anticipated various theories of Americanization now current, one in particular which is in practice among numerous groups in this country. . . .

Franco-Americans

In Woonsocket no other group, excepting possibly the British, can claim to represent old settlers in greater degree or can claim larger contribution to stock. In their group life here the French Canadians are true to the policies articulated in conventions, in their press, and by their leaders.

The French Canadians insist and our data would corroborate the assertion that their adherence to the French language is not inconsistent with the use of English. The indications are that we have here a people that long remains not only bilingual but bicultural. In general, this "biculturation" is uniquely American. They themselves like to describe it as Franco-American, not French Canadian, and this point is made an issue in the educational programs which they foster. "We want an American-trained French clergy," said one Rhode Island priest, "a clergy that is 'American minded.'" Looking toward the clergy for leadership, the need is expressed for leaders trained in the United States, steeped in Catholic French tradition, and cognizant of the problems arising from migration and settlement in a still new homeland. No other nationality can claim to have enunciated a theory of Americanization more clearly or to have organized its group life more consciously toward a given end than have the French Canadians. It is manifestly a theory of adjust-

ment of Americanization, and one of frank "resistance" to certain
Anglo-Saxon (and Irish) traits in American life. It is with them "a
way of life" to be defended against certain encroachments which
they fear, and to be harmonized with a political theory which they
support.

One of the most recent and most interesting examples of ethnic retention was an announcement that a group of French-Canadians in Louisiana are currently attempting to implement French language courses
in that state's public school system. Since French culture was imbedded
in Louisiana over two centuries ago, it is revealing that this belated attempt to preserve French language and culture in Louisiana has received
sanction from the state legislature.

A committee of the Lafayette Parish School Board is looking into
the possibility of implementing compulsory French language courses
at the elementary level in the parish public school system.[6]
    The committee was appointed by board president George
Dupuis to study ways and means of funding French programs, the
kinds of programs that could be implemented, and the priority
French could take over other subjects already on the curriculum.
    The committee was created at the request of James Domen-
geaux, chairman of the Council for the Development of French in
Louisiana (CODOFIL). He warned that the French language in
this state would "die forever" unless parish school boards take the
leadership in initiating French language programs at the elementary
level.
    Domengeaux reminded board members of the 1968 legislative
act which urges school boards throughout Louisiana to implement
French programs in their elementary schools "as expeditiously as
possible" but not later than the beginning of the 1972–73 school
year.
    Domengeaux told the board he would see to it that hundreds
of teachers from France would be sent to Louisiana to teach French
in the state's public schools. The French government in cooperation
with CODOFIL would send the teachers, he said.
    Lafayette Parish has done "very little" toward implementing
French education programs in its schools, Domengeaux said, and he
suggested that the school board take steps toward starting the programs.
    Board members applauded Domengeaux after his remarks,
and they passed a resolution commending him for his leadership in
the movement to preserve and expand the French language and
culture in Louisiana.

MEXICAN-AMERICANS

Spanish-speaking people make up the largest minority in the southwest part of the United States, and of this minority Mexican-Americans

[6] *Times Picayune* (New Orleans), 10 April 1971.

comprise the largest segment. As a result of the Mexican War, the Mexicans in this region automatically became part of the United States. In the last half of the nineteenth century there was a constant flow of people between Mexico and the United States, with little regard to the border line. The numbers were not many, and there was little interest shown by either government.

Mexican migration has taken place mainly in the twentieth century because of rising regional industries: railroad construction, mining, and agriculture. Economic advancement was the major attraction drawing the Mexicans to the United States. In *North From Mexico* (originally published in 1948), Carey McWilliams estimated that about 10 percent of Mexico's adult population entered the United States from 1900 to 1930. Although the Quota Act did not apply to Mexicans, the depression caused a drop in their immigration in the 1930's. It has been difficult to maintain accurate records because of the number of Mexicans who have entered illegally and the number who have returned to their homeland. These latter were called "wetbacks" (mojados) because they swam the Rio Grande and entered the United States illegally.

Legal and illegal entries into the United States increased sharply during World War II because of the increase of employment opportunities. For example, both governments agreed to allow agricultural workers (braceros) to enter the United States on a temporary basis, a program ended in 1964. The Mexican-born population in the United States in 1945 was estimated at 2.5 million, with this number increasing as the wetbacks and braceros continued to arrive. The braceros were not immigrants.

As indicated, Mexicans have been concentrated geographically and economically, becoming isolated in insular communities and jobs in this country. The wetbacks have remained around the border area, and large numbers of agricultural workers have been migratory, serving as a fundamental force in the agricultural development in the southwest. Discriminated against because of their lower socio-economic background, the color of their skin, and their lack of skills, they were further exploited by the Anglos. Thus, the Mexicans experienced serious ethnic setbacks in their attempts to integrate and adapt to the North American culture.

With the rise of the civil rights movement and a growing sensitivity concerning the treatment of ethnic minorities, attention has begun to focus on the Mexican-Americans. Their problems and achievements were suddenly "discovered." Only recently do we find a growing literature on the Mexican-Americans that may be able to dispell false images of this large minority.

The Mexicans who have emigrated to the United States have come mainly from the working class with few skills and little education. The lure of economic improvement motivated their movement to the north. Dr. Manuel Gamio, who studied Mexican immigration under a grant from the Social Science Research Council in 1926–1927, concluded that Mexican-Americans have very little chance of vertical social mobility.

Let us now analyze the vertical social mobility of the immigrant, or the conditions of his rise from lower social strata to higher.[7] From the time of their arrival in the United States the great majority of Mexican immigrants are automatically and inevitably incorporated into the lowest American social strata. In these strata they will remain until conditions in Mexico make possible and desirable their repatriation. The color of their skin, more or less dark, the small pay which they find themselves obliged to accept, their traditions of slavery and servitude which weighed upon them in the colonial period and even during the nineteenth century, the fact that in their own country they occupied the lower social strata—all these and many other factors bring it about that their social situation is in various respects similar to that of the colored race, though it should be recognized nevertheless that the race prejudice which exists toward the Mexican has never been so pronounced or exaggerated as that felt toward the Negro.

Previously we made the statement that the improvement which the Mexican immigrant in the United States experiences with regard to physical condition, food, clothing, and shelter, industrial and agricultural knowledge, is undeniable. In other words, his culture can rise to the level of the culture of the white Americans with whom he associates at the lower social strata of society. However, speaking generally, he cannot continue his vertical mobility. He is condemned to remain in the lower social strata in which he was incorporated from the time of his arrival in the country. This social situation does not only affect the non-nationalized immigrants, but also those who are nationalized, and even children who are, through birth, American citizens. This explains in part why the immigrant very rarely becomes naturalized, since he finds in this no social advantage, while it attracts the unfavorable criticism of those Mexicans who have kept their nationality. Let us examine what in actual fact are the chief means toward social improvement in the United States and what opportunities they offer to the nationalized immigrant and his children. Such persons cannot rise by means of intermarriage, or successive marriages with whites each time of a higher social stratum, since race prejudice prevents this. Political activity, and especially the filling of public offices won by this activity, are strictly forbidden to them. This is proved by the fact that although there are parts of America in which the Mexicans form a large majority of the population, very few public officers are of Mexican origins. The very few cases of Mexicans who are filling unimportant public offices are no more than a confirmation of the rule. In the army and the navy there have been no Mexican generals or admirals, and the number of Mexican officers has been very few. The churches have been more liberal since they accept Mexicans as ministers and priests, but these are generally destined for Mexican parishes which the white Americans probably would not be willing to take. The schools offer them a primary education, but they rarely enter high school or college and almost never the universities. The very few number of individuals who succeed in entering professions such as those of law or medicine find themselves forced to carry on their professions almost exclusively among the residents of Mexican origins. To bring out more clearly the state of horizontal social immobility of these social elements, one needs only to compare this situation with that presented by the immigrants from Europe and their children. These latter can ascend to the highest social strata of the nation.

In conclusion we should state that we are referring in these pages to Mexicans, principally mestizos or Indians, who are classified as unskilled labor and who have always constituted the great body of the immigration.

Like the Negro, the Mexican-American is a visible minority. Discrimination persisted until the end of World War II, with segregation of Mexican-Americans in the public schools, job discrimination, and segregated housing patterns continuing to deny them the equal protection of the laws. The visibility of and prejudice against the Mexican-American was accentuated by the "zoot suit," a popular garb developed during the early 1940's.

The zoot suit originated in the northeast and was worn extensively by Negroes in Harlem, while in California Mexicans favored this type of suit. A zoot suit consisted of a very long suit jacket, padded shoulders, wide lapels, pegged trousers at the cuffs, and draped trousers at the knees. From June 3 to June 7, 1943, riots broke out in Los Angeles against zoot suiters. Servicemen, accompanied by civilians, attacked mostly Mexicans, but also Filipinos and Negroes. "Zoot suiter" became synonymous with Mexican as the press whipped up anti-Mexican emotions.

On Thursday evening, June 3, 1943, the Alpine Club—made up of youngsters of Mexican descent—held a meeting in a police substation in Los Angeles.[8] Usually these meetings were held in a nearby public school but, since the school was closed, the boys had accepted the invitation of a police captain to meet in the substation. The principal business of the meeting, conducted in the presence of the police captain, consisted in a discussion of how gang-strife could best be avoided in the neighborhood. After the meeting had adjourned, the boys were taken in squad cars to the street corner nearest the neighborhood in which most of them lived. The squad cars were scarcely out of sight, when the boys were assaulted, not by a rival "gang" or "club," but by hoodlum elements in the neighborhood. Of one thing, the boys were sure: their assailants were not of Mexican descent.

Earlier in the same evening a group of eleven sailors, on leave from their station in Los Angeles, were walking along the 1700 block on North Main Street in the center of one of the city's worst slum areas. The surrounding neighborhood is predominantly Mexican. On one side of the street the dirty brick front of a large brewery hides from view a collection of ramshackle Mexican homes. The

[8] From *North from Mexico* by Carey McWilliams, published by Greenwood Press, 1968, pp. 244–51, by special permission of the author.

other side of street consists of a series of small bars, boarded-up store fronts, and small shops. The area is well off the beaten paths and few servicemen found their way this far north on Main Street. As they were walking along the street, so they later stated, the sailors were set upon by a gang of Mexican boys. One of the sailors was badly hurt; the others suffered minor cuts and bruises. According to their story, the sailors were outnumbered about three to one.

When the attack was reported to the nearest substation, the police adopted a curious attitude. Instead of attempting to find and arrest the assailants, fourteen policemen remained at the station after their regular duty was over for the night. Then, under the command of a detective lieutenant, the "Vengeance Squad," as they called themselves, set out "to clean up" the gang that had attacked the sailors. But—miracle of miracles—when they arrived on the scene of the attack, they could find no one to arrest—not a single Mexican —on their favorite charge of "suspicion of assault." In itself this curious inability to find anyone to arrest—so strikingly at variance with what usually happened on raids of this sort—raises an inference that a larger strategy was involved. For the raid accomplished nothing except to get the names of the raiding officers in the newspapers and to whip up the anger of the community against the Mexican population which may, perhaps, have been the reason for the raid.

Thus began the so-called "Zoot Suit Race Riots" which were to last, in one form or another, for a week in Los Angeles.

1. The Taxicab Brigade

Taking the police raid as an official cue,—a signal for action,— about two hundred sailors decided to take the law into their own hands on the following night. Coming down into the center of Los Angeles from the Naval Armory in Chavez Ravine (near the "Chinatown" area), they hired a fleet of twenty taxicabs. Once assembled, the "task force" proceeded to cruise straight through the center of town en route to the east side of Los Angeles where the bulk of the Mexicans reside. Soon the sailors in the lead-car sighted a Mexican boy in a zoot suit walking along the street. The "task force" immediately stopped and, in a few moments, the boy was lying on the pavement, badly beaten and bleeding. The sailors then piled back into the cabs and the caravan resumed its way until the next zoot-suiter was sighted, whereupon the same procedure was repeated. In these attacks, of course, the odds were pretty uneven: two hundred sailors to one Mexican boy. Four times this same treatment was meted out and four "gangsters,"—two seventeen-year-old youngsters, one nineteen, and one twenty-three,—were left lying on the pavements for the ambulance to pick up.

It is indeed curious that in a city like Los Angeles, which boasts that it has more police cars equipped with two-way radios than any other city in the world (Los Angeles *Times*, September 2, 1947), the police were apparently unable to intercept a caravan of twenty taxicabs, loaded with two hundred uniformed, yelling, bawdy sailors, as it cruised through the downtown and east-side sections of the city. At one point the police did happen to cross the trail of the caravan and the officers were apparently somewhat embarrassed over the meeting. For only nine of the sailors were taken into custody and the rest were permitted to continue on their merry way. No charges, however, were ever preferred against the nine.

2. Operation "Dixie"

The stage was now set for the really serious rioting of June seventh and eighth. Having featured the preliminary rioting as an offensive launched by sailors, soldiers, and marines, the press now shipped public opinion into a frenzy by dire warnings that Mexican zoot-suiters planned mass retaliation. To insure a riot, the precise street corners were marked at which retaliatory action was expected and the time of the anticipated action was carefully specified. In effect these stories announced a riot and invited public participation. "Zooters Planning to Attack More Servicemen," headlined the *Daily News;* "Would jab broken bottlenecks in the faces of their victims. . . . Beating sailors' brains out with hammers also on the program." Concerned for the safety of the Army, the Navy, and the Marine Corps, the *Herald-Express* warned that "Zooters . . . would mass 500 strong."

By way of explaining the action of the police throughout the subsequent rioting, it should be pointed out that, in June, 1943, the police were on a bad spot. A man by the name of Beebe, arrested on a drunk charge, had been kicked to death in the Central Jail by police officers. Through the excellent work of an alert police commissioner, the case had finally been broken and, at the time of the riots, a police officer by the name of Compton Dixon was on trial in the courts. While charges of police brutality had been bandied about for years, this was the first time that a seemingly airtight case had been prepared. Shortly after the riots, a Hollywood police captain told a motion picture director that the police had touched off the riots "in order to give Dixie (Dixon) a break." By staging a fake demonstration of the alleged necessity for harsh police methods, it was hoped that the jury would acquit Dixon. As a matter of fact, the jury did disagree and on July 2, 1943, the charges against Dixon were dismissed.

On Monday evening, June seventh, thousands of Angelenos, in response to twelve hours' advance notice in the press, turned out for a mass lynching. Marching through the streets of downtown Los Angeles, a mob of several thousand soldiers, sailors, and civilians, proceeded to beat up every zoot-suiter they could find. Pushing its way into the important motion picture theaters, the mob ordered the management to turn on the house lights and then ranged up and down the aisles dragging Mexicans out of their seats. Street cars were halted while Mexicans, and some Filipinos and Negroes, were jerked out of their seats, pushed into the streets, and beaten with sadistic frenzy. If the victims wore zoot-suits, they were stripped of their clothing and left naked or half-naked on the streets, bleeding and bruised. Proceeding down Main Street from First to Twelfth, the mob stopped on the edge of the Negro district. Learning that the Negroes planned a warm reception for them, the mobsters turned back and marched through the Mexican east side spreading panic and terror.

Here is one of numerous eye-witness accounts written by Al Waxman, editor of *The Eastside Journal:*

At Twelfth and Central I came upon a scene that will long live in my memory. Police were swinging clubs and service-men were fighting with civilians. Wholesale arrests were being made by the officers.

Four boys came out of a pool hall. They were wearing the zoot-suits that have become the symbols of a fighting flag. Police ordered them into arrest cars. One refused. He asked: "Why am I being arrested?" The police officer answered with three swift blows of the night-stick across the boy's head and he went down. As he sprawled, he was kicked in the face. Police had difficulty loading his body into the vehicle be-cause he was one-legged and wore a wooden limb. Maybe the officer didn't know he was attacking a cripple.

At the next corner a Mexican mother cried out, "Don't take my boy, he did nothing. He's only fifteen years old. Don't take him." She was struck across the jaw with a night-stick and almost dropped the two and a half year old baby that was clinging in her arms. . . .

Rushing back to the east side to make sure that things were quiet here, I came upon a band of servicemen making a systematic tour of East First Street. They had just come out of a cocktail bar where four men were nursing bruises. Three autos loaded with Los Angeles policemen were on the scene but the soldiers were not molested. Farther down the street the men stopped a streetcar, forcing the motorman to open the door and proceeded to inspect the clothing of the male passen-gers. "We're looking for zoot-suits to burn," they shouted. Again the police did not interfere. . . . Half a block away . . . I pleaded with the men of the local police substation to put a stop to these activities. "It is a matter for the military police," they said.

Throughout the night the Mexican communities were in the wildest possible turmoil. Scores of Mexican mothers were trying to lo-cate their youngsters and several hundred Mexicans milled around each of the police substations and the Central Jail trying to get word of missing members of their families. Boys came into the police stations saying: "Charge me with vagrancy or anything, but don't send me out there!" pointing to the streets where other boys, as young as twelve and thirteen years of age, were being beaten and stripped of their clothes. From affidavits which I helped prepare at the time, I should say that not more than half of the victims were actually wearing zoot-suits. A Negro defense worker, wearing a defense-plant identification badge on his workclothes, was taken from a street car and one of his eyes was gouged out with a knife. Huge half-page photographs, showing Mexican boys stripped of their clothes, cowering on the pavements, often bleeding profusely, sur-rounded by jeering mobs of men and women, appeared in all the Los Angeles newspapers. As Al Waxman most truthfully reported, blood had been "spilled on the streets of the city."

At midnight on June seventh, the military authorities decided that the local police were completely unable or unwilling to handle the situation, despite the fact that a thousand reserve officers had been called up. The entire downtown area of Los Angeles was then declared "out of bounds" for military personnel. This order immediately slowed down the pace of the rioting. The moment the Military Police and Shore Patrol went into action, the rioting quieted down. On June eighth the city began issuing statements. The district attorney, Fred N. Howser, annouced that the "situation is getting entirely out of hand," while Mayor Fletcher Bowron thought that "sooner or later it will blow over." The chief of police, taking a count of the Mexicans in jail, cheerfully proclaimed that "the situation has now cleared up." All agreed, however, that it was quite "a situation."

Unfortunately "the situation" had not cleared up; nor did it blow over. It began to spread to the suburbs where the rioting continued for two more days. When it finally stopped, the Eagle Rock *Advertiser* mournfully editorialized: "It is too bad the servicemen were called off before they were able to complete the job. . . . Most of the citizens of the city have been delighted with what has been going on." County Supervisor Roger Jessup told the newsmen: "All that is needed to end lawlessness is more of the same action as is being exercised by the servicemen!" While the district attorney of Ventura, an outlying county, jumped on the bandwagon with a statement to the effect that "zoot-suits are an open indication of subversive character." This was also the opinion of the Los Angeles City Council which adopted a resolution making the wearing of zoot-suits a misdemeanor! On June eleventh, hundreds of handbills were distributed to students and posted on bulletin boards in a high school attended by many Negroes and Mexicans which read: "Big Sale. Second-Hand Zoot Suits. Slightly Damaged. Apply at Nearest U.S. Naval Station. While they last we have your Size."

Another distinctive development involving Mexicans was the "wetback" movement, occurring on a large scale in the 1940's. The "wetback" was an illegal entrant to this country from Mexico; the term derives from the individual who swam northward across the Rio Grande. It has been estimated that in 1949 there were 400,000 wetbacks in the United States. The situation had become so bad that the United States Immigration and Naturalization Service in 1954 began "Operation Wetback" in an attempt to deport illegal Mexican entrants. Within five years 3.8 million Mexicans were deported, many to return, and to be deported again. It is evident the condition of the wetback was dreadfully primitive because he was unskilled, illiterate, and without legal status. The following selection presents the ethnic experience of the wetback, who must be considered one of the most peripheral minorities in the United States.

The most extensive effort to apprehend illegal entrants was known as Operation Wetback.[9] By the early 1950s it had become evident that large numbers of Mexicans were continuing to cross the border illegally, despite the existence of the *bracero* program. Growers strenuously resisted proposals to make it a crime to employ "illegals,"

[9] Reprinted with permission of Macmillan Publishing Co., Inc. from *The Mexican-American People* by Leo Grebler, Joan W. Moore, and Ralph C. Guzman. Copyright © 1970 by The Free Press, a division of Macmillan Publishing Co., Inc., pp. 521–23.

and normal control measures did not seem to work. Widespread alarm about the "wetback invasion" led to official recommendations to Congress that the United States Army be called upon to "stem the tide." In fact, Operation Wetback was conducted by a retired general, and was organized with military precision by an expanded and better-equipped Border Patrol. The roundup effort—raids and interrogations—got under way in June 1954. A special mobile force concentrated first on California and then on Texas, and extended to points as far from the border as Spokane, Chicago, Kansas City, and St. Louis.

Expulsions under this program reached vast proportions. The number of apprehensions rose from 875,000 in fiscal year 1953 to 1,035,282 the next year. As Operation Wetback was phased out, it fell to 256,290 in 1955 and 90,122 in 1956. In mid-1955, the Immigration and Naturalization Service reported that "for the first time in more than ten years, illegal crossing over the Mexican border was brought under control." In the first half of the 1950s as many as 3.8 million expulsions of Mexican aliens were recorded. (These include multiple counts of men who had entered and been expelled more than once.)

The sweep included persons of long residence in this country as well as those of only a few weeks' tenure. United States-born children were known to have been expelled with their parents. Many American-born adults were stopped and asked for proof of citizenship in cities far removed from the border—and some, reacting with anger as well as amazed incredulity, came into conflict with the officers. Because of its large scale and allegations of rough treatment, Operation Wetback became one of the most traumatic recent experiences of the Mexican Americans in their contacts with government authority. No Mexican-American community in the Southwest remained untouched.

But it should be noted that growers and other employers resented the stepped-up activities of the Border Patrol almost as much as the Mexican Americans. In a heavily satirical article. Bill Helmer, a native of one of the Texas border cities, comments on the "passing of the Valley's happy wetbacks" and shows the importance of the wetbacks in the economy—and ideology—of the lower Rio Grande Valley.

> Before the big Border Patrol crackdown in the early 1950's wetbacks were as contraband and commonplace as liquor in Mississippi. They picked the cotton and citrus, harvested the vegetable crops, dug the irrigation ditches, cut the weeds, cleaned up the messes, trimmed the palms, and kept the Valley's lawns pretty. They didn't cost much, either. A dollar or two a day kept them in beans and tortillas; if you paid them more than that they would just go out and spend it foolishly. Anyhow, it was more than they could make in Mexico, God knows, and they were happy.

Wetbacks were often found and deported, but the "deportation" was usually just a drop across the Rio Grande, and

> the Valley people thought it quite amusing the way a wetback could get back "home" so quickly after being deported. Some

could make it back the same day they were taken across. This pleased anyone who employed wetbacks; it meant the system was working smoothly and dependably, and that his wetbacks liked him, which was important to the community conscience. It justified the breaking of the law and paying of low wages. It was also a good joke on the unpopular Border Patrol.

The journalist's report of the Anglo's view of the Border Patrol illustrates the complexity of the "contact" between Mexican and Border Patrol. It underscores the point that the Anglo employer—usually an exploiter of wetback labor—was also deeply involved. It further emphasizes the important point that the Border Patrol *was not subject to local controls*:

> Nobody liked the Border Patrol, and the Border Patrol didn't like nobody either. . . . I remember they were a surly bunch who always kept to themselves, wouldn't tell tales, and wouldn't wave back at kids on bicycles the way other cops would. . . . The Patrol was frequently accused of mistreating wetbacks and of using Gestapo tactics, but the accusations didn't even have lurid stories to go with them, and I suspect they were largely false. In some ways, the Patrol even helped wetbacks. One day, to everyone's surprise, they instituted a policy of making employers pay off arrested wetbacks . . . before deporting them. This was intended to discourage unscrupulous employers from hiring a flock of wetbacks and then instigating a deportation raid to avoid paying them, which was said to happen from time to time.
>   . . . The tougher the Border Patrol got, the more people liked wetbacks. . . . Immigration officials, conceding it was pointless to deport wetbacks across the river if they would only swim right back again, hit upon an idea that outraged the entire Valley. . . . Wetbacks would be . . . transported by planes to the interior of Mexico so they couldn't get back so easily. Such a scheme not only jeopardized the Valley's economy and (therefore) the nation's welfare, but was *inhumane*. . . . The newspapers and the public closed ranks in righteous opposition to the green-clad devils who were sweeping down on the helpless wetbacks.

Although the transportation of Mexicans deep into Mexico was not new in the 1950s, it was not until September 1956 that Mexicans were airlifted to points from which the Mexican Government could return them to their home towns. By the end of 1956, 81,078 persons had been airlifted to Guanajuato, and 107,939 moved by train to Chihuahua. This procedure greatly reduced the number of repeaters.

Helmer's ironic report on the wetbacks concludes with these words on the aftermath:

> By the time I left the Valley in 1954 . . . the wetback was nearing extinction. A few survived on isolated farms and ranches as permanent help, but the migratory wetbacks, depended on to pick the seasonal crops, were too conspicuous to escape the Patrol's suddenly efficient efforts. The new Bracero

program kept Valley crops from "rotting in the fields," but Braceros weren't as loyal and trustworthy and hardworking as the good old wetbacks, and also they cost more. They kept the cotton farmers in business just long enough to equip themselves with cotton-picking machines.

Despite the increasing mechanization of Southwestern agriculture, the economic significance of the wetback is indicated in Helmer's conclusion that the 1966 melon strike in the Rio Grande Valley would have been inconceivable during the era of wetback labor. Organizers in that strike actually welcomed Border Patrolmen searching for wetbacks (who were working as strikebreakers). The union itself launched a boat to patrol the Rio Grande for wetbacks, just as in an earlier agricultural strike unions had mounted their own guards to close the California border. Organized or organizing labor has generally been in alliance with the Border Patrol, whereas grower's associations are reported to have lobbied in Washinton to keep the agency's budget as small as possible. That organizing labor is often Mexican American means that their feelings about the Border Patrol's activities are deeply ambivalent: On the one hand, wetbacks jeopardize union efforts, but on the other hand many have wetback relatives and friends. The same deep and probably unresolvable ambivalence is evident in many Mexican Americans' discussions of restricting even legal immigration from Mexico.

The United States Civil Rights Commission held a series of hearings in San Antonio, Texas, in early December 1968 in order to collect data regarding the rights of Mexican-Americans in the Southwest. The hearings resulted in a voluminous record of nearly 1,300 pages. The following extract contains the testimony of Dr. Jack Forbes, a research program director with the Far West Laboratory for Educational Research and Development in Berkeley, California. Dr. Forbes points out sharp distinctions between the Mexican-American population and the European immigrants. Interestingly enough, he indicates the effect of conquest on a people's behavior, specifically the Mexican-American. Dr. Forbes also shows the negative impact that the Anglo-American schools have had on the culture of the Mexican-Americans in the Southwest.

Well, I would say that it's not a valid analogy to compare the Mexican American population with particularly European immigrant groups in the United States for a number of reasons.[10] It will probably take me a couple of minutes to respond to this question, but I will try to get through various points.

First of all, the Mexican American population is in great part a native population in the Southwest. It is not an immigrant population. Now this nativity in the Southwest stems not only from the pre–1848 period, that is, the so-called Spanish colonial and Mexican

[10] Reprinted from U.S., Commission on Civil Rights, *Extract from Hearing Before the United States Commission on Civil Rights,* 9–14 December 1968 (Washington, D.C.: Government Printing Office, 1969), pp. 25–31.

periods, but it also stems from the fact that many people who today identify as Mexican Americans or in some areas as Hispanos, are actually of local Indian descent. That is particularly in California, a great deal of California Indian descent and New Mexico a great deal of Pueblo Indian and Plains Indian descent and quite a bit of Pima-Papago descent in Arizona and so on, so that not only do we have people who are native in the sense of coming in from what is now Mexico before 1848, prior to the Anglo, but also in the sense that these people are descended from the aboriginal groups of the area.

Now a second point is that the Mexican American population today, as always, represents a northward extension of Mexico, and this is very, very different from European immigrant populations because with the European population you have a geographical, a special, as well perhaps a cultural ideological separation from the homeland.

But in the case of the Mexican American population you have direct continuity with the homeland, and the area in question is an extension of Mexico, that is the Southwest.

Now this means that the Mexican American people are perhaps one [that] would best classify as a border minority in a European sense. That is, that they compare with Hungarians in Roumania, with Arabs in Israel, with Greeks in Turkey, and groups of that nature—very, very long term minorities that overlap national boundaries. Now again this is not an immigrant situation, it is quite distinct.

We must remember in this connection that Mexico has been one of the world's great vital centers for cultural creativity, and this creativity has been flowing into the area of the present United States now for at least ten and perhaps twenty thousand years continuously.

At the same time, of course, in more recent times the Northern part of the United States has become a very creative area and its influences flow into the Southwest also. So this is an area where two great cultural streams as well as two great peoples meet and interact.

Now another point which needs to be made also is that the Mexican American population, although it is biologically heterogeneous in some degrees, is predominantly of native American origin, that is, of what the white man calls Indian origin. And this means that many Mexican Americans, the majority undoubtedly, exhibit physical characteristics which are different from that of European populations, and although this has been kind of an ignored subject in literature for many, many years, I am convinced from going through documents and Anglo–American newspapers and so on, studies of Mexican labor in the 1920's, and various other kinds of documentation, that the Anglo–American population is a racial minority in the United States, and this racial difference has played a key role. Now, again, this is distinct from European immigrant groups.

Now another very significant difference which is, I suspect, one of the most crucial of all for understanding present day situations is that when we talk about minority populations we have to break them down into several kinds of categories.

You have already identified one in the immigrant group, but another kind of category of minority we need to concern ourselves with here . . . is the culturally different, the racially different minority which is also a conquered population.

Now, unfortunately, the concept of conquest has very, very often been ignored, but here I can't emphasize it too much, because we're beginning to learn that the process of conquest—particularly a harsh and intensive long enduring situation of conquest—has tremendous effect upon people's behavior.

For example, a conquered population tends to exhibit certain characteristics such as apathy, apparent indifference, passivity, a lack of motivation in relation to the goals of the dominant society. Such things as alcoholism, alienation, negative self-image, inferiority complex, personalistic factionalism with the conquered population because this is a powerless group and people's bitterness and so on must be taken out within the group on each other. These things are turned inward instead of being reflected outward against a group which has in a real sense been the oppressor in relation to this population. So this process of conquest is a very significant one indeed. . . .

And if we are to do this, we would see that the U.S. conquest of the Southwest is a real case of aggression and imperialism, that it involved not only the military phase of immediate conquest, but the subsequent establishment of a colonial society—a rather complex colonial society because there was not one single colonial office to administer Mexican American people and also to enable the dominant population to acquire almost complete control of the soil and the other forms of wealth, of the social institutions, cultural institutions, and so on.

Now this conquest and colonial period can be further understood if we think about a community such as the city of Los Angeles in California which has long had a large Mexican American population but in which no major institution of any kind is controlled even proportionally to numbers by the Spanish-speaking population.

The schools, for example, are completely controlled by Anglo–Americans, the city government, the police department, the fire department, the public library, the department of water and power, I mean, you name it, going down the public institutions that presumably serve this population, all are now and actually have been controlled essentially by Anglo-Americans.

Now at the same time, of course, the economic sector, the private sector, is largely controlled by Anglo-Americans. So that we can say that in Los Angeles as in many, many comparable communities the Mexican American population exists as a powerless population that functionally in many significant respects, although things are perhaps gradually changing, but in a very significant aspect is a colonialized population that exists in a colonial relationship to the dominant group, even though I know that we really don't like sometimes to use those terms, but I think that if we are going to understand the situation that exists in the Southwest we have to do that. . . .

You see in terms of the Southwest, which is a very distinct region of the United States, the Anglo–American is quite obviously the newcomer, and as a newcomer he had the option available to him of assimilating into the native cultures which already existed in this area.

Now, we all realize, I suspect, that the Anglo–American like most nationalities around the world is not anxious as a group . . . to give up its identity. It is not anxious to change its way of life. I mean one really finds very few people around the world who simply, all of a sudden, decide to abandon their identity and culture, especially when the group is the conqueror, especially when the group already has visions of superiority complex and messianic ideas of his role in the world and so on. But the essential point is that one cannot expect the Mexican American as a distinct people with a distinct identity and a cultural heritage to be proud of, a very beautiful and extremely useful language and so on, to do what the Anglo–American obviously would not do. . . .

We did have in the old days, around the 1850's through the 1870's in many areas some schools that were controlled by local Mexican American people and that were bilingual and bicultural schools. They did exist—primarily because in certain areas such as southern California the Anglo had not yet moved in and taken over.

However, since that time the schools that haxe existed in the Southwest have not been neutral, culturally speaking. Those schools have been controlled by the Anglo–American population and the curricula throughout has been Anglo in character. It doesn't take but a moment visiting a typical school to find that the history is Anglo white history, that the sewing is Anglo sewing, that the cooking is Anglo cooking, that the literature is Anglo literature, and that the music is Anglo music and so on right down the line.

Now occasionally in recent years one can find a few little changes taking place, but these are still I think more at the level of token changes bringing in a little bit of exoticism rather than significant changes. The character of the school is that of the dominant population politically and economically.

Now the school cannot be understood and changing, it cannot be understood unless we remember that the school is simply one of those institutions which the dominant population uses as a device for perpetuating a colonial relationship and as a device for transforming the heritage of the Mexican American child. In fact one can really not deal accurately with the school apart from other institutions because if the school is going to be run as an Anglo institution this is because the dominant population wants to run all institutions as Anglo ones—all that can be run in that way. And so it is perhaps unlikely to expect the school to be changed apart from wider changes that take place in the total relationship of these two groups.

Now another aspect of this that must be mentioned is that this kind of school quite obviously has not been good for Mexican American children. The same kind of school has not been good for American Indian children; it's not been good for other non–Anglo children. It tends to lead to a great deal of alienation, a great deal of hostility. It tends to lead also to a great deal of confusion where the child comes out of that school really not knowing what language he should speak other than English, being in doubt as to whether he should completely accept what Anglo people have been telling him and forget his Mexican identity, or whether he should listen to what his parents and perhaps other people have said and be proud of his Mexican identity. There is a state of great vacillation on the part of many people. And when this kind of thing happens, children drop out of school.

We know from research that . . . the degree of alienation and low achievement rates correlate very highly. We know from the Coleman study that the feeling of powerlessness felt on the part of pupils—and of course, therefore, on the part of their parents—to be two of the key factors relating to the problem of minority education.

Now, before I go any farther with that, I should mention one thing else, too, and that is when we think of education which I think is what you are really interested in here, we have to think of more than just the formal school. We have to remember that there are many other kinds of educational agencies that affect young people and these would include stereotypical motion pictures, stereotypical television, and so on which contain anti-Mexican items. It would contain things like the San Antonio greeter magazine which I picked up in a hotel lobby and which had the statement about the history of San Antonio that said nothing about the Mexican heritage of this region, talking only about the glorious Spanish colonial era and things of this nature. It includes all of these kinds of influences, including the parents and the family and the status of the total community. This is all a part of the educational process.

Alfredo Cuellar classifies four periods of political development in the United States for the Mexican-Americans. The first phase, from the 1840's to about 1920, he considered "apolitical" because the Mexican-Americans were submerged and suppressed. The second phase, from the 1920's to the 1940's, was a time of accommodation and adaptation for them to the Anglo culture and the beginnings of a Mexican middle class in the Southwest. The third period saw Mexican-American aggressiveness and involvement in the political system. The last period emerged in the 1960's and may become the most dramatic and influential in the Mexican-American ethnic experience. The Chicano movement, as it is called, is the most radical, questions the present American and Mexican-American leadership and institutions, and seeks to reap the fruits of ethnic pride and identification. In the following account Alfredo Cuellar details the development and significance of the Chicano movement.

The Chicano Movement[11]

Throughout this chapter we have suggested that Mexican American political activity has often been related to social structural factors. Because much of this political activity was possible only after certain structural changes in Mexican American life, there were seldom any real alternatives beyond simple reaction to Anglo

[11] Reprinted from Joan W. Moore with Alfredo Cuellar, *Mexican Americans,* © 1970, pp. 148–154. Reprinted by permission of Prentice-Hall, Inc., Englewood Cliffs, New Jersey.

pressure. The importance of the Chicano movement as an alternative to pressures from the majority society can hardly be overemphasized. It is a distinctively novel development in the Mexican American community. The Chicano movement developed in southern California no earlier than 1966, and it is already a sharp new force in the political expression of Mexican Americans throughout the southwest.

The Chicano ideology includes a broad definition of political activity. Ironically, such thinking was possible only for a new generation of urbanized and "Anglicized" (that is, assimilated) young Mexican Americans, who were much less burdened by social and class restrictions than their elders were and whose education had exposed them to new ideas.

The exact beginnings of the movement are obscure. There is some evidence that the Chicano movement grew out of a group of conferences held at Loyola University in Los Angeles in the summer of 1966. As originally conceived by its Catholic sponsors, the conferences were to create a fairly innocuous youth organization for the middle-class Mexican students attending various colleges throughout California. Very quickly the movement grew beyond the intent or control of its sponsors (Loyola has never been very noted for its interest in Mexican American education) and it drew in yet others, not students and not middle class, who were attracted by the ideology of the chicanismo. Thus it cannot be understood as a movement limited to the young, to students, or even to urban areas. It must also be understood as including the followers of Reies Tijerina in northern New Mexico and Cesar Chavez' embattled union of striking farm workers in central California. In 1969 Rodolfo (Corky) Gonzales was the principal leader and inspiration of the Chicano movement in Denver although his interests were mainly in urban civic action. Moreover, "Corky" has organized regional youth conferences and his influence spreads far beyond the local area. No one leader has yet emerged in southern California or in Texas.

As this wide range of activity shows, the Chicano movement is extremely heterogenous, and its elements have different aims and purposes. In this way the movement cuts across social class, regional, and generational lines. Its aims range from traditional forms of social protest to increasingly more radical goals that appear as a sign of an emerging nationalism. It is a social movement, in that it can be described as "pluralistic behavior functioning as an organized mass effort directed toward a change of established folkways or institutions." The dynamic force of the movement is its ideology—chicanismo.

The new ideology is advanced as a challenge to the dominant Anglo beliefs concerning Mexicans as well as to the beliefs of Mexican Americans themselves. Although we have emphasized that students are by no means the only element of the Chicano movement, we will reconstruct chicanismo primarily as it has been developed among students. Actually, this is only one of several ideological strands but it is the most consistently developed, thus the best illustration of the change from protest to nationalism and a synthesis of the ideology of chicanismo.

The first student form of the Chicano movement coincided with the development of new student organizations in California universities and colleges in 1966 and 1967. Some of these groups were the United Mexican American Students (UMAS), the Mexican American Student Association (MASA), Mexican American Student Confederation (MASC), and Movimiento Estudiantil Chicano de Aztlan (MECHA). More recently the Mexican American Youth Organization (MAYO) has appeared, with particular strength in Texas (MAYO is also the name adopted by the new organization of Chicanos in California prisons.) These student groups were at first concerned with a rather narrow range of problems in the field of education, particularly those concerned with increasing the number of Mexican American students in college. To the extent that these student groups were active in the Mexican American community, they were involved with various forms of protest against specific and long-standing grievances, such as police brutality and inferior educational facilities, although other forms of community activity also involved political campaigns.

Chicano student groups thus have never repudiated ordinary forms of political activity, although for them such forms as voting constitute only one political alternative. Actually, given the wide range of problems facing the Mexican American community, Chicanos view conventional forms of political activity as perhaps the least effective. Instead, they favor forms of confrontation as the most effective means to gain access for the traditionally excluded Chicano, even though it has, on occasion, led to violence. In general, this conception of politics contrasts sharply with the ideas of more conservative Mexican American leaders, most of whom adhere to very limited and "safe" politics with an emphasis on voting and "working within the system" to gain political leverage. This is not to say that Chicanos reject working for social change within the system; as a matter of fact, much recent activity has focussed on bringing about change in the universities and colleges as well as in the public school system. Nevertheless, whereas the moderates seek to bring major change in American society through nonviolent means, the more militant speak of the need for "revolutionary activity," though they often leave the details and direction of this revolution unspecified. While they admire the life style and aspirations of revolutionary leaders like Che Guevara, they have thus far made no systematic theoretical connection between the Chicano movement and the general literature on revolution. The theoretical underpinnings of the Chicano movement thus often lack a strong direction.

And yet, the advent of the Chicano movement does represent a revolutionary phenomenon among Mexican Americans. As we shall see, most of the change from traditional forms lies in (or is reflected in) the ideology of chicanismo. Basically eclectic, chicanismo draws inspiration from outside the United States and outside the Mexican American experience. The Cuban Revolution, for example, exerts some influence, as do the career and ideals of Che Guevara. For instance, the Brown Berets (a Chicano youth group) affect the life style of this revolutionary. Black Power also offers something of a model. Most recently, Chicanos have resurrected the Mexican revolutionary tradition.

Basically, however, chicanismo focuses on the life experience of the Mexican in the United States. It challenges the belief system of the majority society at the same time that it attempts to reconstruct a new image for Mexican Americans themselves. Chicanos assume that along with American Indians and black Americans, Mexicans live in the United States as a conquered people. This idea allows chicanismo to explain the evolution of the Chicano as essentially conflictful. In each conflictual relationship with Anglos, the Mexicans lost out and were thus forced to live in the poverty and degradation attendant upon those with the status of a conquered people. This is no better illustrated than by the Mexicans' loss of communal and private property. As a result, they had no choice but to work the land for a patron (usually an Anglo, but sometimes a Mexican, who exploited his own people). When the Mexican was thrown off the land, he was forced to become an unattached wage-earner, often a migrant farm worker; or he might migrate to a city, where the exploitation continued. In any event, chicanismo emphasizes that the Mexican was transformed into a rootless economic commodity, forced either to depend on migrant farm work or to sell his labor in the urban centers, where his fate depended upon the vicissitudes of the economy. Ironically, indispensable as Mexican labor was for the economic development of the Southwest, the Mexican got little recognition for his contribution and even less benefit from it.

Chicanos therefore see the economic expansion of the Southwest as essentially a dehumanizing process. They also point out that during periods of economic depression in the United States, when the Mexican became "superfluous" and "expensive," Anglo society had no qualms about attempting to eliminate Mexicans from the United States, as in the repatriations of the 1930s. The repatriations are viewed as a conscious attempt to eliminate the Chicano from American society.

The thrust of chicanismo is not only economic, but also cultural. In many ways, the exploitation and suppression of his culture is what most angers the Chicano, who views the attempt to deracinate Mexican culture in the Southwest as the reason why Mexican Americans are disoriented about their culture and often attempt to deny it. The Chicano points out that the Anglo often views Mexicans with a great degree of ambivalence. Anglos oftentimes take over aspects of "Spanish" (which is really Mexican) culture and at the same time deny it to the Mexican himself. In this fashion Mexicans were denied the development of a more autonomous cultural life, especially as it touches upon Spanish language use, the arts, and so on. (This was done in spite of the agreements made in the signing of the Treaty of Guadalupe Hidalgo. Early drafts of the treaty contained Mexican government efforts to make formal recognition of language rights for Mexicans who chose to remain in the United States after the Mexican War. These provisions were not approved by the U.S. Senate.)

Worse yet, the ideology goes on, the cultural suppression continues to the present day, reinforced by Anglo institutions, particularly the schools. The extreme position (although by no means infrequent) is represented by the fact that Mexican American students in the public schools are corporally punished for using Spanish, their native language. Under these circumstances, it is understandable that the Mexican American student remains ignorant and often ashamed of his past. When the Mexican is mentioned in textbooks, it is in a romanticized and stereotypically Anglicized version of "Spanish culture" that may be congenial to Anglos but is remote and irrelevant to the Mexican American. The Chicano considers this type of whitewashed "Spanish" culture particularly galling because he feels that while Anglos may selectively choose certain motifs from Mexican culture, the person behind the culture, the Mexican himself, is given neither recognition nor respect.

Chicanismo also focuses on race, and in some ways this emphasis constitutes one of the most controversial aspects of chicanismo. It is argued that Anglo racism denies the Mexican his ethnicity by making him ashamed of his "Mexican-ness." Mexican ancestry, instead of being a source of pride, becomes a symbol of shame and inferiority. As a consequence, Mexicans spend their lives apologizing or denying their ancestry, to the point that many dislike and resent being called "Mexican," preferring "Spanish American," "Latin," "Latin American," and similar euphemisms. For these reasons, the term "Chicano" is now insisted upon by activists as a symbol of the new assertiveness.

Advocates of chicanismo therefore hope to reconstruct the Mexican Americans' concept of themselves by appeals to pride of a common history, culture and "race." Chicanismo attempts to redefine the Mexicans' identity on the basis not of class, generation, or area of residence but on a unique and shared experience in the United States. This means that appeals for political action, economic progress, and reorientation of cultural identity are cast in terms of the common history, culture, and ethnic background of *la raza*.

Chicano ideologues insist that social advance based on material achievement is, in the final analysis, less important than social advance based on *la raza*; they reject what they call the myth of American individualism; if Mexicans are to confront the problems of their group realistically they must begin to act along collective lines. Hence, the stirrings of a new spirit of what chicanismo terms "cultural nationalism" among the Mexican Americans of the Southwest.

Chicanismo has led not only to increased participation in community activities, but also to a heightened and often intense interest in cultural life. Chicano poets, playwrights, journalists, and writers of all varieties have suddenly appeared. There are Chicano theater groups in several large cities (often known as the *teatro urbano*) and one nationally known and well-travelled group from Delano, California (*El teatro campesino*), which tells the story not only of the striking California farmworkers but of Chicanos in general. Newspapers and magazines also reflect this desire to disseminate the idea of chicanismo. Throughout the Southwest numerous Chicano "underground" newspapers and magazines publishing literary materials have emerged. There is even a Chicano Press Association, a regional association representing Chicano publications from Texas to California. Furthermore, because of the strong base in colleges and universities, a serious and generally successful drive to develop "ethnic studies" programs has appeared, especially in California. As part of the drive to spread the idea of chicanismo in education, Chicanos place an emphasis on Mexican contributions to American society, thus giving Chicano college students a new conception of their past and present.

Chicano student groups share an orientation similar to that of black students, and on occasion they cooperate and support each other on similar demands. (There is more mutual support between black and brown students than between their counterparts at the community level.) The alliance between black and brown students, however, has not been close, harmonious, or continuous. Chicano student organizations have not yet been significantly involved with Anglo radical student groups, although these groups sometimes claim their support or claim that they are working for the benefit of Chicanos.

THE INDIANS

Having discussed the neglected and heroic past of the American Indian in the period up to the Civil War, we must consider briefly the road traversed by this ethnic group since that time. While a full account of this people's history is not going to be attempted, some highlights of this history will be mentioned so as to illumine aspects of white man–Indian relations. In point of fact, the record of this relationship is a dismal story acknowledged by virtually all quarters. Thus President Rutherford B. Hayes said in 1877:

> The Indians were the original occupants of the land we now possess.[12] They have been driven from place to place. The purchase money paid to them, in some cases for what they called their own, has still left them poor. In many instances, when they had settled upon lands assigned to them by compact and begun to support themselves by their own labor, they were rudely jostled off and thrust into the wilderness again. Many, if not most, of our Indian wars have had their origin in broken promises and acts of injustices on our part.

Much of the problem centered around the Indian's desire above all to continue his own way of life, and the white man's denial of that wish. Indians were pressured to "settle down" and engage in agricultural pursuits like the rest of American citizens. This pressure was accompanied by invasion of hunting grounds, wanton destruction of buffalo, and disregard for Indian rights. American legislative policy attempted to persuade Indians to abandon tribal identification in preference to individual land ownership or live on government rations on a reservation. The Dawes Severalty Act of 1887 provided for the dissolution of Indian tribes as legal entities and the division of their tribal lands among individual members. Rights of disposal were withheld for twenty-five years. For the most part, the latter policy was a failure as the lot of the Indian continued to deteriorate. By an act of Congress in 1924 all Indians born in the United States were admitted to full citizenship. In 1934 the Indian Reorganiza-

12 From *Messages and Papers of the Presidents*, Vol. X, edited by James B. Richardson (New York: The Bureau of National Literature, Inc., 1897), p. 4427.

tion Act ended land allotments in severalty and provided for reinvestment to tribal ownership of surplus lands hitherto open to all.

In recent years it has become apparent that the national Indian scene is undergoing an extraordinary stirring. This stirring is undergirded by the phenomenon of population growth which shows the Indian population on the reservations increasing from 269,388 in 1901 to 523,591 in 1960 to 791,839 in 1970. It is estimated that these figures include only half of the Indian population in the United States, namely those on reservations. Moreover, Indian ethnic consciousness gathers momentum as individual Indians rejoin their tribes and speak increasingly about Indian tribal sovereignty. Thus the contemporary scene once again seems to confirm the tenacity of ethnicity within a social order.

Indian leaders throughout the second half of the nineteenth century were consistent in their assertions that the white man exploited them and left them with little hope. Typical is the lament of a Comanche chief in the selection that follows.

> My people have never first drawn a bow or fired a gun against the whites.[13] There has been trouble on the line between us, and my young men have danced the war dance. But it was not begun by us. It was you who sent out the first soldier and we who sent out the second. Two years ago I came upon this road, following the buffalo, that my wives and children might have their cheeks plump and their bodies warm. But the soldiers fired on us, and since that time there has been a noise like that of a thunderstorm, and we have not known which way to go. So it was upon the Canadian. Nor have we been made to cry once alone. The blue-dressed soldiers and the Utes came from out of the night when it was dark and still, and for campfires they lit our lodges. Instead of hunting game they killed my braves, and the warriors of the tribe cut short their hair for the dead. So it was in Texas. They made sorrow come in our camps, and we went out like buffalo bulls when their cows are attacked. When we found them we killed them, and their scalps hang in our lodges. The Comanches are not weak and blind, like the pups of a dog when seven sleeps old. They are strong and farsighted, like grown horses. We took their road and we went on it. The white women cried and our women laughed. . . .
>
> You said that you wanted to put us upon a reservation, to build us houses and make us medicine lodges. I do not want them. . . .
>
> The white man has the country which we loved, and we only wish to wander on the prairie until we die.

One of the most famous Indians was the Apache Geronimo. Proud, bellicose and durable, he spent the last twenty years of his life as a prisoner of the United States in the late 1800's, during which time he wrote a re-

---

[13] From *Bury My Heart at Wounded Knee* by Dee Brown, pp. 241–42. Copyright © 1970 by Dee Brown. Reprinted by permission of Holt, Rinehart and Winston, Inc. and the Harold Matson Company.

markable autobiography in which he "told it like it was." In his story he reveals some of the problems encompassed by the victor-to-vanquished relationship between white man and Indian.

These problems were encountered despite the trust the Indians had in the white man, particularly in the person of General Miles who was to administer a mutually-agreed-to treaty backed by the President of the United States. Impressed by General Miles' exhortation that by entering into a treaty with each other they would be acknowledging a fraternal relationship, the emissary of the United States government also promised that the material needs of the Indians would be met, i.e., horses, cattle, houses, farm implements, water and grass land. With some misgivings Geronimo agreed to sign the treaty. In later years he came to believe that he never violated this treaty, although General Miles failed to live up to its provisions.

In the following extract, Geronimo confesses his feelings near the close of his life as he reviewed the ethnic difficulties encountered and the prospects for the future.

I am thankful that the President of the United States has given me permission to tell my story.[14] I hope that he and those in authority under him will read my story and judge whether my people have been rightly treated.

There is a great question between the Apaches and the Government. For twenty years we have been held prisoners of war under a treaty which was made with General Miles, on the part of the United States Government, and myself as the representative of the Apaches. That treaty has not at all times been properly observed by the Government, although at the present time it is being more nearly fulfilled on their part than heretofore. In the treaty with General Miles we agreed to go to a place outside of Arizona and learn to live as the white people do. I think that my people are now capable of living in accordance with the laws of the United States, and we would, of course, like to have the liberty to return to that land which is ours by divine right. We are reduced in numbers, and having learned how to cultivate the soil would not require so much ground as was formerly necessary. We do not ask all of the land which the Almighty gave us in the beginning, but that we may have sufficient lands there to cultivate. What we do not need we are glad for the white men to cultivate.

We are now held on Comanche and Kiowa lands, which are not suited to our needs—these lands and this climate are suited to the Indians who originally inhabited this country, of course, but our people are decreasing in numbers here, and will continue to decrease unless they are allowed to return to their native land. Such a result is inevitable.

There is no climate or soil which, to my mind, is equal to that of Arizona. We could have plenty of good cultivating land, plenty

[14] From the book *Geronimo: His Own Story*. Ed. by S. M. Barrett Newly with an Intro. and Notes by Frederick W. Turner III. Intro. and Notes Copyright © 1970 by Frederick W. Turner III. Published by E. P. Dutton & Co., Inc. and used with their permission. Pp. 172–73.

of grass, plenty of timber and plenty of minerals in that land which the Almighty created for the Apaches. It is my land, my home, my fathers' land, to which I now ask to be allowed to return. I want to spend my last days there, and be buried among those mountains. If this could be I might die in peace, feeling that my people, placed in their native homes, would increase in numbers, rather than diminish as at present, and that our name would not become extinct.

I know that if my people were placed in that mountainous region lying around the headwaters of the Gila River they would live in peace and act according to the will of the President. They would be prosperous and happy in tilling the soil and learning the civilization of the white men, whom they now respect. Could I but see this accomplished, I think I could forget all the wrongs that I have ever received, and die a contented and happy old man. But we can do nothing in this matter ourselves—we must wait until those in authority choose to act. If this cannot be done during my lifetime—if I must die in bondage—I hope that the remnant of the Apache tribe may, when I am gone, be granted the one privilege which they request—to return to Arizona.

The American Indian has been accorded a second-rate position in the rapid development of this country. As the "superior" civilization of the white man conquered that of the Indian, it was expected that the Indian would be acculturated by the white man's ways; and to some extent he is, adopting many aspects of the American system—technology, materialism —and becoming more involved in the educational, economic, and political systems. But the Indian, seeking to maintain his ethnic identity and pride, has resisted complete assimilation through the retention of much of his socio-cultural traditions. Cultural pluralism, then, will continue in the future. A recent development that is distinctly Indian and that attempts to make meaningful his own aboriginal cultures is the Pan-Indian movement. The following selection examines Pan-Indianism and concludes that it will develop into a political force to "speak more effectively for a more highly organized American-Indian minority. . . ."

> Since a kind of ultimate lid or ceiling has been placed upon full acculturation and assimilation in the United States, it is now pertinent to raise the question as to what is happening to Indian groups who become reasonably well educated by our standards and move a great distance from their aboriginal ways of life without becoming fully integrated in the larger United States society.[15] One way of looking at the problem is that we shall continue with a type of cultural pluralism for some generations to come. But in a vast number of cases, the process has moved too far for Indian groups to continue to find much meaning in their own particular aboriginal cultures, and what appears to be emerging is an interesting type of "Pan-Indianism."
>
> This Pan-Indianism is assuming a form in which increasing

[15] Reprinted from "The Acculturation of American Indians" by Evon Z. Vogt in volume no. 311 of *The Annals* of The American Academy of Political and Social Science. Pp. 145–46. © 1957 by The American Academy of Political and Social Science.

numbers of American Indians are participating in customs and institutions that are describable only as Indian. These customs and institutions are being synthesized from elements derived from diverse Indian cultures and to some extent from white American culture. There exists also in many regions, and especially in Oklahoma, a loosely knit, informally organized grouping of Indians who have joined forces to participate in these Pan-Indian activities.

Historically, the beginnings of this type of Pan-Indianism are found in many of the nativistic movements which followed in the wake of conquest, the spread of the Ghost Dances being a classic type of example. The later emergence of the Peyote Cult, which involved not only the exchange of customs and ideas among Indian tribes and the incorporation of Christian concepts, but also intertribal participation in the same ceremonies, carried the process much further and continues to be one of the focal points in Pan-Indianism.

Conspicuous more recent developments are the various pow-wows and intertribal ceremonial gatherings. Some are organized by the Indians themselves, especially in Oklahoma and the Middle West; others, like the annual Gallup Inter-Tribal Indian Ceremonial, are managed by white businessmen to promote local business interests. But in both types, there is enthusiastic intertribal participation on the part of the Indians and a strong encouragement of Pan-Indianism.

Although the cultural elements found in this emerging Pan-Indian movement are derived from diverse Indian sources, it is highly significant that a high proportion of these elements are drawn from Plains culture: the war bonnet, the Plains-type war dance, and so forth. These elements have become symbols of Indianism to the Indians themselves to a degree that bears little relationship to the aboriginal facts. And it is probable that their importance as symbols derives in part from the fact that these elements are central features of the prevailing white-American stereotype of the American Indian.

Vine Deloria is one of the most effective American Indian writers of today. In the account that follows, he describes vividly the way of life on the reservation. In America, yet not part of the mainstream of American culture, life on the reservation as he describes it provides a provocative comment on contemporary Indian-white relationships from the viewpoint of an Indian in the twentieth century. Whether he describes life during the depression or the disruption caused by World War II, it is always with an eye for the ethnic experience involved.

In those days the reservation was isolated and unsettled.[16] Dirt roads held the few mail routes together. One could easily get lost in the wild back country as roads turned into cowpaths without so much as a backward glance. Remote settlements such as Buzzard Basin and Cuny Table were nearly inaccessible. In the spring every

[16] Reprinted from Vine Deloria, "This Country Was a Lot Better Off When the Indians Were Running It," in *A Nation of Nations*, ed. Theodore L. Gross (New York: The Free Press, 1971), pp. 522–27; originally published in *The New York Times Magazine*, 8 March 1970. © 1970 by The New York Times Company. Reprinted by permission.

bridge on the reservation would be washed out with the first rain and would remain out until late summer. But few people cared. Most of the reservation people, traveling by team and wagon, merely forded the creeks and continued their journey, almost contemptuous of the need for roads and bridges.

The most memorable event of my early childhood was visiting Wounded Knee where 200 Sioux, including women and children, were slaughtered in 1890 by troopers of the Seventh Cavalry in what is believed to have been a delayed act of vengeance for Custer's defeat. The people were simply lined up and shot down much as was allegedly done, according to newspaper reports, at Songmy. The wounded were left to die in a three-day Dakota blizzard, and when the soldiers returned to the scene after the storm some were still alive and were saved. The massacre was vividly etched in the minds of many of the older reservation people, but it was difficult to find anyone who wanted to talk about it.

Many times, over the years, my father would point out survivors of the massacre, and people on the reservation always went out of their way to help them. For a long time there was a bill in Congress to pay indemnities to the survivors, but the War Department always insisted that it had been a "battle" to stamp out the Ghost Dance religion among the Sioux. This does not, however, explain bayoneted Indian women and children found miles from the scene of the incident.

Strangely enough, the Depression was good for Indian reservations, particularly for the people at Pine Ridge. Since their lands had been leased to non-Indians by the Bureau of Indian Affairs, they had only a small rent check and the contempt of those who leased their lands to show for their ownership. But the Federal programs devised to solve the national economic crisis were also made available to Indian people, and there was work available for the first time in the history of the reservations.

The Civilian Conservation Corps set up a camp on the reservation and many Indians were hired under the program. In the canyons north of Allen, S. D., a beautiful buffalo pasture was built by the C.C.C., and the whole area was transformed into a recreation wonderland. Indians would come from miles around to see the buffalo and leave with a strange look in their eyes. Many times I stood silently watching while old men talked to the buffalo about the old days. They would conclude by singing a song before respectfully departing, their eyes filled with tears and their minds occupied with the memories of other times and places. It was difficult to determine who was the captive—the buffalo fenced in or the Indian fenced out.

While the rest of America suffered from the temporary deprivation of its luxuries, Indian people had a period of prosperity, as it were. Paychecks were regular. Small cattle herds were started, cars were purchased, new clothes and necessities became available. To a people who had struggled along on $50 cash income per year, the C.C.C. was the greatest program ever to come along. The Sioux had climbed from absolute deprivation to mere poverty, and this was the best time the reservation ever had.

World War II ended this temporary prosperity. The C.C.C. camps were closed; reservation programs were cut to the bone and social services became virtually nonexistent; "Victory gardens" were suddenly the style, and people began to be aware that a great war was being waged overseas.

The war dispersed the reservation people as nothing ever had. Every day, it seemed, we would be bidding farewell to families as they headed west to work in the defense plants on the Coast.

A great number of Sioux people went west and many of the Sioux on Alcatraz today are their children and relatives. There may now be as many Sioux in California as there are on the reservations in South Dakota because of the great wartime migration.

Those who stayed on the reservation had the war brought directly to their doorstep when they were notified that their sons had to go across the seas and fight. Busloads of Sioux boys left the reservation for parts unknown. In many cases even the trip to nearby Martin was a new experience for them, let alone training in Texas, California or Colorado. There were always going-away ceremonies conducted by the older people who admonished the boys to uphold the old tribal traditions and not to fear death. It was not death they feared but living with an unknown people in a distant place.

I was always disappointed with the Government's way of handling Indian servicemen. Indians were simply lost in the shuffle of 3 million men in uniform. Many boys came home on furlough and feared to return. They were not cowards in any sense of the word but the loneliness and boredom of stateside duty was crushing their spirits. They spent months without seeing another Indian. If the Government had recruited all-Indian outfits it would have easily solved this problem and also had the best fighting units in the world at its disposal. I often wonder what an all-Sioux or Apache company, painted and singing its songs, would have done to the morale of elite German panzer units.

After the war Indian veterans straggled back to the reservations and tried to pick up their lives. It was very difficult for them to resume a life of poverty after having seen the affluent outside world. Some spent a few days with the old folks and then left again for the big cities. Over the years they have emerged as leaders of the urban Indian movement. Many of their children are the nationalists of today who are adamant about keeping the reservations they have visited only on vacations. Other veterans stayed on the reservations and entered tribal politics.

The reservations radically changed after the war. During the Depression there were about five telephones in Martin. If there was a call for you, the man at the hardware store had to come down to your house and get you to answer it. A couple of years after the war a complete dial system was installed that extended to most of the smaller communities on the reservation. Families that had been hundreds of miles from any form of communication were now only minutes away from a telephone.

Roads were built connecting the major communities of the Pine Ridge country. No longer did it take hours to go from one place to another. With these kinds of roads everyone had to have a car. The team and wagon vanished, except for those families who lived at various "camps" in inaccessible canyons pretty much as their ancestors had. (Today, even they have adopted the automobile for traveling long distances in search of work.)

I left the reservation in 1951 when my family moved to Iowa. I went back only once for an extended stay, in the summer of 1955, while on a furlough, and after that I visited only occasionally during summer vacations. In the meantime, I attended college, served a hitch in the Marines, and went to the seminary. After I graduated from the seminary, I took a job with the United Scholarship Service, a private organization devoted to the college and secondary-school education of American Indian and Mexican students. I had spent my last two years of high school in an Eastern preparatory school and so was probably the only Indian my age who knew what an independent Eastern school was like. As the program developed, we soon had some 30 students placed in Eastern schools.

I insisted that all the students who entered the program be able to qualify for scholarships as students and not simply as Indians. I was pretty sure we could beat the white man at his own educational game, which seemed to me the only way to gain his respect. I was soon to find that this was a dangerous attitude to have. The very people who were supporting the program—non-Indians in the national church establishments—accused me of trying to form a colonialist "elite" by insisting that only kids with strong test scores and academic patterns be sent east to school. They wanted to continue the ancient pattern of soft-hearted paternalism toward Indians. I didn't feel we should cry our way into the schools; that sympathy would destroy the students we were trying to help.

In 1964, while attending the annual convention of the National Congress of American Indians, I was elected its executive director. I learned more about life in the N.C.A.I. in three years than I had in the previous 30. Every conceivable problem that could occur in an Indian society was suddenly thrust at me from 315 different directions. I discovered that I was one of the people who were supposed to solve the problems. The only trouble was that Indian people locally and on the national level were being played off one against the other by clever whites who had either ego or income at stake. While there were many feasible solutions, few could be tried without whites with vested interests working night and day to destroy the unity we were seeking on a national basis.

In the mid-nineteen-sixties, the whole generation that had grown up after World War II and had left the reservations during the fifties to get an education was returning to Indian life as "educated Indians." But we soon knew better. Tribal societies had existed for centuries without going outside themselves for education and information. Yet many of us thought that we would be able to improve the traditional tribal methods. We were wrong.

For three years we ran around the conference circuit attending numerous meetings called to "solve" the Indian problems. We listened to and spoke with anthropologists, historians, sociologists, psychologists, economists, educators and missionaries. We worked with many Government agencies and with every conceivable doctrine, idea and program ever created. At the end of this happy round of consultations the reservation people were still plodding along on their own time schedule, doing the things they considered important. They continued to solve their problems their way in spite of the advice given them by "Indian experts."

By 1967 there was a radical change in thinking on the part of many of us. Conferences were proving unproductive. Where non-Indians had been pushed out to make room for Indian people, they had wormed their way back into power and again controlled the major programs serving Indians. The poverty programs, reservation and university technical assistance groups were dominated by whites who had pushed Indian administrators aside.

Reservation people, meanwhile, were making steady progress in spite of the numerous setbacks suffered by the national Indian community. So, in large part, younger Indian leaders who had been playing the national conference field began working at the local level to build community movements from the ground up. By consolidating local organizations into power groups they felt that they would be in a better position to influence national thinking.

Robert Hunter, director of the Nevada Interracial Council, had already begun to build a strong state organization of tribes and communities. In South Dakota, Gerald One Feather, Frank La-Pointe and Ray Briggs formed the American Indian Leadership Conference, which quickly welded the educated young Sioux in that state into a strong regional organization active in nearly every phase of Sioux life. Gerald is now running for the prestigious post of chairman of the Oglala Sioux, the largest Sioux tribe, numbering some 15,000 members. Ernie Stevens, an Oneida from Wisconsin, and Lee Cook, a Chippewa from Minnesota, developed a strong program for economic and community development in Arizona. Just recently Ernie has moved into the post of director of the California Intertribal Council, a statewide organization representing some 130,000 California Indians in cities and on the scattered reservations of that state.

By the fall of 1967, it was apparent that the national Indian scene was collapsing in favor of strong regional organizations, although the major national organizations such as the National Congress of American Indians and the National Indian Youth Council continued to grow. There was yet another factor emerging on the Indian scene: the old-timers of the Depression days had educated a group of younger Indians in the old ways and these people were now becoming a major force in Indian life.

KEY QUESTIONS

1. In regard to Canadian migration to the United States, compare the ethnic patterns of the English-Canadians and the French-Canadians.

2. Define wetback, bracero, "zoot suiter." What significance do these terms hold in United States-Mexican relations? Explain.

3. Describe the origins, meaning, and future of the Chicano movement.

4. In the numerous selections dealing with the Indians in this chapter, what are the recurring themes that you detect?

5. In spite of the persistent exploitation of the Indians, their population has rapidly increased. How do you account for this growth?

9

Immigrants from the Western Hemisphere: PUERTO RICANS, CUBANS, VIRGIN ISLANDERS, AND HAITIANS

The Puerto Ricans, Cubans, Virgin Islanders, and Haitians were chosen for inclusion in this chapter dealing with immigrants from the Western Hemisphere because of their proximity to and historical relationships with the United States. Many of their ethnic experiences and problems have derived from the fact that they are dark-skinned people. Additionally, their Latin origins, with their distinct customs, dress, and language, have contributed to their difficulties in the process of cultural assimilation in the United States.

The Puerto Ricans, the most numerous of the four groups, have made the greatest impact on the mainland. They have attempted to aid themselves and to preserve their ethnicity by retaining their language and customs and by joining numerous Puerto Rican clubs and associations. The Puerto Ricans are not so much immigrants as they are migrants, since they are already American citizens.

The selections covering the Puerto Rican ethnic experiences in this chapter include a dramatic account of a young Puerto Rican growing up in East Harlem and a New York City suburb; a realistic picture of the education of Puerto Ricans in Spanish Harlem; the influence that Catholicism and Protestantism have had on the Puerto Ricans; and finally a critical evaluation of the Americanization process on the island of Puerto Rico itself.

The considerable Cuban exodus to the United States since 1959 has been the direct result of the recent Castro revolution. Increased disenchantment with the new regime has accelerated the movement. The United States has benefitted because this immigration has been qualitative as well as quantitative and the Cuban immigrants proved to be easily assimilated in the alien society. The skills and the education they possessed allowed them to contribute to their own and the nation's well-being. The extract in this section focuses upon the successful adaptation in the 1960's of the Cuban immigrants in Miami.

The Virgin Islanders, though not so numerous, also share American citizenship with the Puerto Ricans. Though they seek more readily to assimilate, they simultaneously wish to maintain their ethnic identification through Virgin Island associations. This paradox strikes at the very essence of the phenomenon of ethnicity as the selection in this chapter shows.

The last ethnic group covered in this chapter are the Haitians. Although Haiti was discovered in 1492 by Columbus, it became a French colony in 1677 and gained its freedom in 1804. The French have played a more prominent role than the Spanish in the development of Haitian institutions. Nevertheless, the Haitians who migrated to the United States came here for social, political, and economic reasons similar to those of the other groups. The concluding article in this chapter presents an account of the Haitians' experiences in New York City.

PUERTO RICANS

Puerto Rico holds an unusual place among American possessions. Discovered by Columbus in 1493, it became a strategic stronghold for the Spanish as they used the island to protect their position in the Caribbean. Unsurprisingly, Spanish culture made an indelible impression on the island during the next few centuries. Although Indians first inhabited the island, in the course of time they became virtually extinct.

As a result of the Spanish-American War in 1898, the United States secured Puerto Rico. However, this country did not devote much of its energies to the island's development until 1941 when Rexford Tugwell became its governor. Under his leadership efforts were made to improve public education, sanitation, and social services—activities which had been sadly neglected in the prior period, during which the island was known as a "poor house." Slowly, the economic face of Puerto Rico began to change from that of a poverty-stricken land to that of a fairly healthy self-governing entity. This transformation has been attributed to several factors. First was the overwhelming support for Luis Muñoz Marin, Puerto Rico's first elected governor, whose innovative leadership proved invaluable. Second, credit is given to Operation Bootstrap, which concentrated on economic development through such steps as the attraction of new industries, breaking up large acreage holdings, and slum clearance. The result has been that per capita income has risen perceptibly, although still far below that of the United States. A third factor is the political status of the island: Its free commonwealth association with the United States was confirmed in its first constitution in 1952. This seems to have majority endorsement, although a vocal minority has demanded complete independence.

The Puerto Ricans, therefore, hold a unique place in the study of American ethnic groups. Very soon after the United States acquired the island, free access to the United States was available to its inhabitants. Together with the extension of American citizenship in 1917, this prompted 70,000 Puerto Ricans to live on the mainland prior to the beginning of World War II. It was not until after World War II that really great numbers migrated. After 1946, with the improvement of transportation, especially the airplane, hundreds of thousands relocated so that in 1971 the population figure of individuals of Puerto Rican origin is placed at 1,450,000. In the process, considerable numbers returned home, many to return again. Because of its location and its cosmopolitanism, New York City became the primary residence for most of the Puerto Ricans, especially in such areas as East Harlem, South Bronx, and other sections of Brooklyn and Queens. Nearly 70 percent of the Puerto Rican population in the United States lives in the New York City Metropolitan Statistical Area. They came for economic and social improvement. They took the unskilled jobs, and, though partially Americanized, they experienced many difficulties because of their color, religion, and lower socioeconomic background. They were also prey to exploitation. Yet the Puerto Ricans with their rich heritage have made a major impact on such places as New York City and have begun to emulate the role of the Jews and Italians who came before them.

A searing, savage view of life is recounted in Piri Thomas' *Down These Mean Streets*. The autobiographical account is a vivid description of a black Puerto Rican's teenage years in East Harlem during the 1940's. What is depicted is not only Thomas' painful search for himself as a man, but also his need to discover the dimensions of his ethnic being. His ethnic experience is complicated by the fact of his Puerto Rican background in an American setting and his color. As such, Thomas' autobiography is important because of the insights it offers about the position that color creates for a Puerto Rican.

In the excerpt that follows, Thomas gives an authentic, earthy glimpse of what it is like for a Puerto Rican living on an "Italian block." The simple point, as he put it, is that "sometimes you don't fit in," despite the Latin background.

Alien Turf[1]

Sometimes you don't fit in. Like if you're a Puerto Rican on an Italian block. After my new baby brother, Ricardo, died of some kind of germs, Poppa moved us from 111th Street to Italian turf on 114th Street between Second and Third Avenue. I guess Poppa wanted to get Momma away from the hard memories of the old pad.

I sure missed 111th Street, where everybody acted, walked, and talked like me. But on 114th Street everything went all right

[1] Reprinted from Piri Thomas, *Down These Mean Streets* (New York: Random House, Inc., 1967), pp. 33–35.

for a while. There were a few dirty looks from the spaghetti-an'-
sauce cats, but no big sweat. Till that one day I was on my way
home from school and almost reached my stoop when someone
called: "Hey, you dirty fuckin' spic."

The words hit my ears and almost made me curse Poppa at
the same time. I turned around real slow and found my face pushing
in the finger of an Italian kid about my age. He had five or six of his
friends with him.

"Hey, you," he said, "What nationality are ya?"

I looked at him and wondered which nationality to pick. And
one of his friends said, "Ah, Rocky, he's black enuff to be a nigger.
Ain't that what you is, kid?"

My voice was almost shy in its anger. "I'm Puerto Rican," I
said. "I was born here." I wanted to shout it, but it came out like
a whisper.

"Right here inna street?" Rocky sneered. "Ya mean right here
inna middle of da street?"

They all laughed.

I hated them. I shook my head slowly from sided to side.
"Uh-uh," I said softly. "I was born inna hospital—inna bed."

"Umm, paisan—born inna bed," Rocky said.

I didn't like Rocky Italiano's voice, "Inna hospital," I whis-
pered, and all the time my eyes were trying to cut down the long
distance from this trouble to my stoop. But it was no good; I was
hemmed in by Rocky's friends. I couldn't help thinking about kids
getting wasted for moving into a block belonging to other people.

"What hospital, paisan?" Bad Rocky pushed.

"Harlem Hospital," I answered, wishing like all hell that it
was 5 o'clock instead of just 3 o'clock 'cause Poppa came home at
5. I looked around for some friendly faces belonging to grown-up
people, but the elders were all busy yakking away in Italian. I
couldn't help thinking how much like Spanish it sounded. Shit, that
should make us something like relatives.

"Harlem Hospital?" said a voice. "I knew he was a nigger."

"Yeah," said another voice from an expert on color. "That's
the hospital where all them black bastards get born at."

I dug three Italian elders looking at us from across the street,
and I felt saved. But that went out the window when they just
smiled and went on talking. I couldn't decide whether they had
smiled because this new whatever-he-was was gonna get his ass
kicked or because they were pleased that their kids were welcoming
a new kid to their country. An older man nodded his head at Rocky,
who smiled back. I wondered if that was a signal for my funeral
to begin.

"Ain't that right, kid?" Rocky pressed. "Ain't that where all
black people get born?"

I dug some of Rocky's boys grinding and pushing and punching
closed fists against open hands. I figured they were looking to shake
me up, so I straightened up my humble voice and made like proud.
"There's all kinds of people born there. Colored people, Puerto
Ricans like me, an'—even spaghetti-benders like you."

"That's a dirty fuckin' lie"—*bash*, I felt Rocky's fist smack
into my mouth—"you dirty fuckin' spic."

I got dizzy and then more dizzy when fists started to fly from everywhere and only toward me. I swung back, *splat, bish*—my fist hit some face and I wished I hadn't, 'cause then I started getting kicked.

I heard people yelling in Italian and English and I wondered if maybe it was 'cause I hadn't fought fair in having hit that one guy. But it wasn't. The voices were trying to help me.

"Whas'sa matta, you no-good kids, leeva da kid alone," a man said. I looked through a swelling eye and dug some Italians pushing their kids off me with slaps. One even kicked a kid in the ass. I could have loved them if I didn't hate them so fuckin' much.

"You all right, kiddo?" asked the man.

"Where you live, boy?" said another one.

"Is the bambino hurt?" asked a woman.

I didn't look at any of them. I felt dizzy. I didn't want to open my mouth to talk, 'cause I was fighting to keep from puking up. I just hoped my face was cool-looking. I walked away from that group of strangers. I reached my stoop and started to climb the steps.

"Hey, spic," came a shout from across the street. I started to turn to the voice and changed my mind. "Spic" wasn't my name. I knew that voice, though. It was Rocky's. "We'll see ya again, spic," he said. . . .

In the next excerpt Thomas reflects on his feelings, ethnic feelings, when he, a Puerto Rican, moved to the suburbs.

In 1944 we moved to Long Island.[2] Poppa was making good money at the airplane factory, and he had saved enough bread for a down payment on a small house.

As we got our belongings ready for the moving van, I stood by watching all the hustling with a mean feeling. My hands weren't with it; my fingers played with the top of a chalkboard box full of dishes. My face tried hard not to show resentment at Poppa's decision to leave my streets forever. I felt that I belonged in Harlem; it was my kind of kick. I didn't want to move out to Long Island. My friend Crutch had told me there were a lot of paddies out there, and they didn't dig Negroes or Puerto Ricans.

"Piri," Momma said.

"Yeah, Moms." I looked up at Momma. She seemed tired and beat. Still thinking about Paulie all the time and how she took him to the hospital just to get some simple-assed tonsils out. And Paulie died. I remember she used to keep repeating how Paulie kept crying, "Don't leave me, Mommie," and her saying, "Don't worry, nene, it's just for a day." Paulie—I pushed his name out of my mind.

"Dios mio, help a little, hijo," Momma said.

"Moms, why do we gotta move outta Harlem? We don't know any other place better'n this."

"Caramba! What ideas," Momma said. "What for you talk like that? Your Poppa and I saved enough money. We want you kids to have good opportunities. It is a better life in the country. No like Puerto Rico, but it have trees and grass and nice schools."

"Yeah, Moms. Have they got Puerto Ricans out there?"

[2] Ibid., pp. 86–87.

"Si, I'm sure. Senora Rodriguez an' her family, an' Otella—
remember her? She lived upstairs."

"I mean a lotta Latinos, Moms. Like here in the Barrio. And
how about morenos?"

"Muchacho, they got all kind." Momma laughed. "Fat and
skinny, big and little. And—"

"Okay, Momma," I said. "You win. Give me a kiss."

To some observers residence in an ethnic enclave such as Spanish
Harlem offers little of real value to the Puerto Ricans. Although the role
and value of ethnic neighborhoods have historically been significant, they
contained their share of problems. In order to gain insight into some of
these problems, Dan Wakefield, a graduate of Columbia College, lived in
Spanish Harlem in the 1950's. His record of this experience reveals much
about the educational problems of this Puerto Rican community. He
found that the high expectations of the Puerto Ricans as they left their
native land to make a better life in the United States were followed by
disenchantment as the result of bitter experiences in their newly adopted
land. In the following extract, the Assistant Principal of P.S. 168 in Spanish Harlem explains to Reverend George Todd of an East Harlem Protestant parish the unique difficulties encountered in educating the Puerto
Rican children.

"The most trouble in discipline seems to be among the kids themselves, mainly between the Puerto Ricans and the Negroes.[3] You
might expect it would be between the whites and the Puerto Ricans,
or whites and Negroes, but that doesn't seem to be the main problem in our school. The principal found that it was better to have
separation in classes—Puerto Ricans in one section, the rest in
another—for these social as well as educational reasons. A fight
between a Puerto Rican and another boy was liable to carry on from
the playground to the classroom. But if the Puerto Ricans are kept
in separate classes, they come into class and the fight's all over.

"Also, our principal found it was better from the standpoint of
learning to read and write that the kids be separated. If the children
don't know English, you teach them reading and writing in a different way than you would teach children who speak English
already." . . .

"That's the way it was worked out here, according to experience," he said, "But it's not being done like that right now. You see,
there was a policy recently instituted of extra state appropriations
for schools with classes having fifty per cent or more Spanish-
speaking enrollment. Actually it was for classes with fifty per cent or
more 'foreign language' enrollment, but Spanish is of course what
they mean. Now, the more classes you have with fifty per cent or
more Puerto Ricans, the more appropriation money you get, so
we've had to switch our classes all around and make a lot of changes
to work it out to the best advantage. We now have close to sixty per

[3] Reprinted from Dan Wakefield, *Island in the City* (Boston: Houghton Mifflin, 1959),
pp. 151–57.

cent Puerto Rican students out of our whole enrollment of about fifteen hundred students—five years ago we only had twenty per cent Puerto Ricans—and we had twenty-six out of sixty-one classes with fifty per cent or more Spanish-speaking children. In these classes, the children have to be taught all together, and we don't think that's the best system, but we feel the best thing is to get more money to be able to do more things for the schools, and that's the best way to help children. Maybe later on they'll change this about the appropriations.

"Right now we have one teacher who can speak Spanish— she's a Negro herself and she likes the Puerto Rican kids, so of course we give them to her in classes—but the principal doesn't want her speaking Spanish to them in class. None of our teachers speak Spanish in class. Our principal thinks the best way is to have nothing but English spoken and read in the school—after all, they come to school to learn English. We have two other Spanish-speaking teachers who are substitutes, but they don't usually work with the classes. Their main job is to work with the parents when the parents can't speak English and the children are in some sort of difficulty or there are things wrong at home."

The Reverend Todd wondered what the teachers did at first with the children who couldn't speak English and couldn't understand what was happening in class.

"In that case, they just have to wait till they pick it up—and in the meantime, if there is something urgent to tell the child, the teacher gets one of the other children to translate. There are always children in the class who can speak both Spanish and English." . . .

The assistant principal, smiling, led the visiting minister out through the back of the hall while the chorus chanted a concluding affirmation of the dignity of man. The assistant principal explained, as he led Reverend Todd down the long, empty corridor, that the class they were about to visit was an "opportunity" class, consisting of "holdovers," children with emotional problems and Puerto Ricans. The holdovers, he continued, were children who had trouble with reading tests or I.Q. tests or both; the Puerto Ricans, unless they knew English well before coming to school, of course had trouble with reading.

Reverend Todd wondered if I.Q. tests were given to Puerto Rican children, and if so, how their language problem was taken into account in scoring their intelligence.

"For a while," the assistant principal explained, "they tried giving I.Q. tests in Spanish to the Puerto Rican kids, but that wasn't fair either, because most of them knew a little English and it was all mixed up in their mind. They were actually illiterate in two languages. Now, we just let the individual teachers judge the I.Q. of these children until they're far enough along to take the tests in English. You can usually judge. You can't get it right on the nose, of course, but you can pretty well judge what group they ought to be with." . . .

"You can see," he said, "there are many problems. And many aren't obvious, either. One of the biggest is turnover. Many of the parents are constantly moving. If they move four blocks away they are likely to be in another school district—the neighborhood is that heavily populated. Also there are the housing projects, and when the

old houses are torn down it means a whole movement of hundreds
of families. Some move out of the neighborhood altogether, and
then when the new projects go up there's a whole set of new students moving in. And in September there's always a big influx from
Puerto Rico. The sugar cane season is over and a lot of them have
the money to come and be here when school opens in the fall.
There's always a lot who are only here for a little while and go
back to Puerto Rico again. And, of course, those who come up from
Puerto Rico and are already in school have done different work in
their school down there."

Although most Puerto Ricans are nominally Catholic, the Church
has not made as great an impact on the Puerto Rican community in New
York City as it has on other ethnic groups. This can be ascribed to their
experience in the homeland, the lack of Spanish-speaking priests, and the
nature and size of the Catholic parish. On a smaller level, but in a more
intense manner, Protestant denominations have made considerable headway in attempting to serve the religious and social needs of the New York
Puerto Rican population, as indicated in the following selection.

We have already referred to the weakness of Catholicism in
Puerto Rico.[4] Roman Catholicism is not a national church, as it is in
Ireland and Poland. It sets the general frame of life by baptizing
(most), marrying (less), and burying, and its calendar sets the
holidays and festivals, but its impact on the people, in guiding their
lives and molding their ideas, and in serving as a vessel for their
social life, is relatively small. It is, as elsewhere in Latin America, a
church for the women. In New York the Catholic Church is engaged
in an energetic program to increase the number of Spanish-speaking
priests, and to widen the circle of activity among the Puerto Ricans.
Since the Puerto Ricans have spread so widely through the city, the
Church has for the most part carried on its Puerto Rican work in
established parishes. The Puerto Ricans have not created, as others
did, national parishes of their own. Thus the capacities of the
Church are weak in just those areas in which the needs of the
migrants are great—in creating a surrounding, supporting community
to replace the extended families, broken by city life, and to supply a
social setting for those who feel lost and lonely in the great city.
This is a task that smaller churches, with an active lay leadership,
and a ministering group that is closer to and of the people, can
do better.

Most of the Puerto Ricans in the city are Catholic, but their
participation in Catholic life is small. It is interesting for example
that there are but 15,000 Puerto Rican children in parochial schools
in the New York Archdiocese, against almost ten times as many in
the public schools, a much smaller percentage than for any other
Catholic group in the city. There are only 250 Spanish-speaking
priests in the Archdiocese of New York for the Puerto Rican popul-

[4] Reprinted from *Beyond the Melting Pot* by Nathan Glazer and Daniel P. Moynihan
by permission of The MIT Press, Cambridge, MA. Pp. 103–107.

ation, and most of these—as many in Puerto Rico itself—have learned Spanish to minister to the group. In 1961, in 42 Catholic parishes in New York City with Spanish-speaking priests, there was only one Puerto Rican. And the proportion of the Spanish-speaking priests to the Catholic Puerto Rican population was still one-third or one-fourth what it was for other New York Catholics.

As the problems of the first generation are overcome, as families become stabler, incomes higher, and the attachment to American middle-class culture stronger, Catholicism will probably also become stronger among the Puerto Ricans. But it does not seem likely that it will play as important a role among them as it plays in the European Catholic ethnic groups. For there is already well established a strong rival to Catholicism among the Puerto Ricans, and if we were to reckon religious strength not by mild affiliation but by real commitment, it would be likely that there are not many less committed Protestants among the Puerto Ricans than there are committed Catholics.

Protestantism's history on the island dates from the American occupation, when some major denominations divided up the island and began work there. A 1947–1948 study of the island showed that about 82 per cent called themselves Catholic, that 6 per cent of the population belonged to the major Protestant denominations, 2 per cent to Protestant sects, and 2 or 3 per cent were Spiritualists. The Mills-Senior-Goldsen 1948 study of New York Puerto Ricans showed about 83 per cent Catholic and slightly higher proportions of Protestants in the major denominations—9 per cent—and in the sects—5 per cent. But the fervor of the Protestants seems greater than that of the Catholics; and the fervor of the members of the Pentecostalist and similar sects of the hundreds of the storefront churches that dot the Puerto Rican neighborhoods is even greater.

There are about 70 Spanish-language Protestant churches of major denominations in the city, and close to another 50 that have both English and Spanish services. Another 70 have some Spanish members. All told, there are about 14,000 Spanish-speaking members of major Protestant denominations in the city, about 10,000 in their own all-Spanish churches. Attendance in the Spanish churches is high, evangelical zeal puts most Anglo-Saxon Protestantism to shame, and the willingness to spend money to support the church is also great.

This is now largely an indigenous movement, staffed by Puerto Rican ministers. The Protestant church leaders of the city have been anxious to have the English language churches also reach out to the surrounding Puerto Rican population. But for regular, denominational Protestantism, this is not an easy task. The strength of Protestantism is that it forms a community, and its weakness is that in forming a community it finds it difficult to reach out from its original ethnic or class base to attract other groups. The most catholic of the Protestant groups, the Protestant Episcopal Church, has been most successful in developing integrated churches of mixed native Protestant and Puerto Rican members, just as it is also this church that is most successful in developing churches that integrate white and colored members. Father James Gusweller's West Side Church of St. Matthew and St. Timothy is the best-known example of such an integrated church.

But the most vigorous and intense religious movements among the Puerto Ricans are the Pentecostal and independent Pentecostal-type churches. The 1960 study of the Protestant Council of New York located 240 such churches—there are certainly more than this. Their membership was conservatively estimated at about 25,000. These tiny churches generally run services every day of the week. They demand of their members that they give up smoking and alcohol and fornication. They are completely supported by their memberships, and often a church of 100 members will support a full-time minister. The Pentecostal movement, which began in America, has for reasons that are not clear been successful in pentrating a number of Catholic areas, for example, Italy and Chile. Two Catholic sociologists who have studied the Pentecostal churches in New York suggest that they derive their strength from Catholicism's weakness. Many migrants feel lost in the city; many search for a community within the Church, and the integrated Catholic parish, whose base is another ethnic group and whose priests are not Spanish, cannot give this. The preachers and ministers of the Pente-costal Church in New York are almost all Puerto Ricans. Though it was initially spread to the island by English-speaking evangelists, working through translators, the requirements for preaching and ministering make it possible for devout members to rise rapidly to such positions. "In the Catholic Church," one member told the in-vestigators, "no one knew me." Here, if a stranger comes in, he is warmly greeted; if a member falls sick, he is visited; the tight con-gregation is one of the most important expressions of a community that is found among Puerto Ricans in New York.

Protestantism is an interesting if minority phenomenon among the Puerto Ricans; and there exists here a real field for competition between Catholicism and Protestantism in the city. It is impossible now to predict how things will come out. There are some potential areas for conflict. For example: Will Protestant social welfare agen-cies try to serve Puerto Ricans? Up to now this has been left to city agencies and to Catholic agencies. A third to a half of the clients of the family and child-serving agencies of Catholic Charities are now Puerto Ricans; since the Protestants have to take some responsibility for the Negroes, it is understandable that they have dragged their feet somewhat in staking out a claim to lost souls among the Puerto Ricans too. But according to the press releases of Billy Graham's three-day crusade to the Spanish-speaking of New York in 1960, 500,000 of New York's Spanish-American population are considered unchurched—which means that the religious organization of New York Protestantism considers most of the field available for sowing. If Protestant agencies should also make this claim, some serious headaches will arise for the public agencies (such as the New York City Youth Board) which distribute cases to private agencies and help support them.

In any discussion of Puerto Rican culture, a seminal question is the one that asks about Americanization of the Caribbean island. For nearly three-quarters of a century, American influence has continued to pene-trate the island, and the question remains whether it will result in drab uniformity of culture or in the persistency of cultural diversity. Gordon

K. Lewis, in *Puerto Rico, Freedom and Power in the Caribbean,* discusses
the problem and concludes that the process of Americanization of Puerto
Rican society goes on relentlessly and that this becomes more significant
as it proceeds largely in the absence of contact with other Latin cultures.
If this continues, he concludes, the Puerto Ricans will lose their virtues,
and intellectualism becomes sterile.

The American record in Puerto Rico since 1900—whatever the
future may hold—does not warrant any more optimistic conclusions
about the Puerto Rican place in the national picture.[5] The Puerto
Rican child, from the beginning, has been taught American rather
than Puerto Rican history. His attributes have been built up in a
colonial atmosphere, where the mass media have portrayed to the
populace a culture that is not their own and to which they have been
taught to attribute everything that is worthwhile in their experience.
The very linguistic symbols of merit and authority become those of
the dominant power; thus the Puerto Rican student still manages,
only too frequently, to address his teacher as "Mister," rather than
maestro or professor, as if the teacher were an American. Nor is
this applicable to the past only for, as Rene Marques has pointed
out, the ancestral sense of helplessness in the individual Puerto Rican
is still psychologically worked upon through modern methods of
education that are only somewhat more subtle than those used previously. Since the burden of taking on the inconvenient aspects of
communications between the ruled and the rulers has always been
the compulsory lot, in colonial situations, of the ruled, Puerto Ricans
have been compelled to learn English rather than Americans Spanish. The depreciation of the local culture has encouraged a corresponding self-depreciation in individuals. For some it has taken the
form of a blind submission to the American style, expressing an
urgent drive, frequently only half understood by its victims, for
identification and incorporation with the elite of the governing
power; and the guilt feelings thereby engendered have frequently
been covered up by the device of identifying Puerto Rico with
"Western civilization" rather than with the United States, so that
terms like this and others—"the crisis of the West," "Western culture," the free world," and so on—play a therapeutic role in the
psychology of that type of Puerto Rican. For others again the response to a situation so basically intolerable to sensitive spirits and
so powerfully buttressed by all the institutions of the society, private
and public, political and economic, has been a retreat into feelings
of bitterness, inferiority, chauvinism; and the life of a spirit like
Pedro Albizu Campos is a tragic monument to those elements in
Puerto Rican politics.

Even when the individual American in the picture has been
genuinely liberal, the liberalism has only too often blandly assumed
the natural superiority of American values (just as, in the case of the
British Caribbean, even the sympathy of British Fabian Socialists
with local aspirations has been grounded on the assumption that
West Indian nationalism ought to perpetuate English modes and

[5] Reprinted from Gordon K. Lewis, *Puerto Rico, Freedom and Power in the Caribbean*
(New York: Harper and Row, 1963), pp. 244–46, 258–60.

manners). The matter of race is an apt illustration. Americans liberal on everything else have drawn the line (with some individual exceptions) at accepting the Latin principle of race mixing. It has been a widespread, and quite unscientific, belief among them that the mixing engenders a decline in mental and physical capacities, and Dean Fleagle felt compelled to issue a stern warning about its "degenerating effect" on family life in his book of 1917. Nor is this a thing of the past only, for Alfred Kazin's crass reference to "Step'n Fetchit sloth" in Puerto Ricans suggests that there may sometimes lurk a latent anti-Negro prejudice underneath the gleaming armor even of the New York Jewish liberal. The Peace Corps is supposed to have been one of the more imaginative ideas of Kennedy liberalism, but the liberalism did not prevent the organizers of the Peace Corps training camp in Puerto Rico from countenancing the insulting suggestion that individual Puerto Rican independentistas should be asked to play the role of anti-American critics, like nothing so much as sparring partners, to the young members of the Corps. More generally, much of the liberal American literature on the islanders tends to exhibit an air of generous paternalism, but paternalism nonetheless. It is full of the sort of remark—that young Puerto Ricans who have come to American universities "have shown themselves to be fully equal to Orientals and other students from other lands," or that the underlying traits of the average Puerto Rican, "even though they may not be such as to build empires or produce Shakespeares, are qualities of which his peers in the world community stand in great need"—which infuriates thinking Puerto Ricans even more than a posture of rank hostility. At best the attitude tolerates Puerto Ricans; it sees them, in the indignant phrase of one of the victims, as just "damn nice stupid people."

There is not much more truth in the second assumption that Puerto Rico can be viewed as an overseas crucible of Hispanic culture. The Spanish legacy, as already noted, did not transplant to the island any of the outstanding features of Spanish life—a ceremonial urban culture, a complex bureaucracy (except in the military government), a sophisticated agricultural economy. Nor did it introduce any of its imposing civil and ecclesiastical hierarchies, as it did in its Mexican and Peruvian viceroyalties: the missions of the religious orders, the great peninsular universities, the tradition of splendid architecture, both civil and religious. There was nothing like the strong institutional fabric of the continental colonial societies to form a foundation for later emancipation from peninsular suzerainty. The psychological consequences of all this have been momentous, not least of all the continuing dependency of the Puerto Rican spirit upon external deliverance and the comparable failure to look inwards for national salvation. So, if there are unique Puerto Rican characteristics, it is profoundly misleading to expect them to be Caribbean echoes of the original Hispanic. Indeed the expectation is grossly unfair, for it presupposes a sort of tribal ancestor worship of merely snobbish utility. The American critic who compares the twentieth-century Puerto Rican with the sixteenth conquistadores, to the disadvantage of the former, rarely pauses to reflect upon the conclusions that might be derived from comparing his own type with the independent American farmer we read of in the pages of Crevecoeur. The modern Puerto Rican must be judged by what he is, not by what his ancestors were: the warning applies to both the Puerto Rican and American cultivators of the myth of Puerto Rico as a bridgehead between two world cultures. Consequently the attempt to explain the island culture and institutions as a crossing between two growths of pre-established national entities, the one Spanish, the other American, unavoidably results in shallow analysis. The metaphor has too easily seduced even critical observers, so that the cultural reality—that Puerto Rico exists as a local Creole culture in its own right, not merely as a tropical mirror of metropolitan Europeans or American societies—is too readily lost sight of. For what has really taken place in the last sixty years is not the growth of an ideal common life shared on equal terms by both Puerto Ricans and Americans—the ideal was typically expressed in a book like Juan Bautista Soto's volume of 1928, *Puerto Rico ante el Derecho de Gentes*—but the relentless imposition of American standards upon a dependent society helpless to resist the process. . . .

For the truth of the matter is that as the Americanization of the society proceeds apace its isolation from other cultural influences becomes more and more pronounced. Apart from the odd trip, the insular artists and intellectuals are starved of any fruitful contact with the Latin American world. The fact that the general output of the Institute of Puerto Rican Culture is weak in the field of painting, so powerfully resurgent elsewhere in the Caribbean in Mexico and Haiti, and strong in those fields that are not Pan-Caribbean in character—mural decoration, wood sculpture, lithography, and poster art—suggests a regrettable separation from what is going on elsewhere. Everything, increasingly, is seen through the American perspective. The strident tones in which so many Puerto Ricans congratulate themselves upon enjoying political "stability"—which really means the protection afforded by the virtual protectorate of the United States military power—shows how deeply they have removed themselves from a sympathetic identification with the Latin-American peoples. The humiliation, frequently self-imposed, of that situation is no better exhibited than in the spectacle of the Puerto Rican statehood fan pleading with the American people to take on an assimilation policy which would mean the erosion of all the social and cultural characteristics which distinguish his people from those of the United States. In such a context, people come to despise their own virtues. So, there are private hospitals in San Juan where all signs are in English despite the fact that the staff are overwhelmingly Spanish-speaking. The man in the street will convert himself into a pathetic comedy as he tries to parade the little store of mangled English phrases he has somewhere picked up. The comic strips in the newspapers are all of them American, with Spanish titles, even although some of them, "Blondie," for example, or "Bringing up Father," portray the type of abject American husband so far removed from the Puerto Rican male's image of himself.

CUBANS

Cubans had little influence on the ethnic mix of American society until the 1960's. In fact, there is a direct relation between the success of Fidel Castro's revolution, beginning in 1959, and the increase of Cuban immi gration to the United States. Cuba, long a possession of Spain, received her nominal independence in 1898. During the major portion of the intervening years, the United States exercised significant control on the island through the Platt Amendment and economic investments. The Good Neighbor Policy of the 1930's attempted to promote a new era of friendship and equality with Cuba. Though World War II alerted the United States to the strategic value of the entire Caribbean area, the United States funneled most of her energies and resources to Europe and Asia after the war. The Alliance for Progress and other programs are the recent responses to the needs of Latin-American neighbors.

In the immigration statistics recorded by the U. S. Bureau of the Census, Cuba is included with the West Indies from 1820 to 1950. During this period a total of 496,696 migrated here from the West Indies.

When it became clear that the Cuban revolution under Fidel Castro would go much further than many had assumed, the exodus from Cuba escalated to immense proportions. It accelerated after the Bay of Pigs invasion in 1961 and the missile crisis in 1962. As a result, the Cubans are the most recent foreign minority to enter the United States. When Castro announced in September 1965 that he would permit Cubans to leave the country, it is believed that the waiting list ranged from 50,000 to 700,000.

It soon became obvious that the original intention of many Cubans to return to the homeland had to evaporate overnight and the Cubans had to adjust to making the United States their permanent residence, since little chance remained of overthrowing the Castro regime. Thus, since 1959 over 400,000 Cubans have emigrated here. The remarkable thing about the Cuban immigrants is their rapid adaptability to American society and life. In fact, because they are so well educated and skilled, they have been referred to as the "golden exile." In many ways the United States has gained from their knowledge and expertise.

The Cuban immigration in the 1960's made a great impact on the city of Miami. At first, relations between the Cubans and Miamians were strained, but eventually adjustments were made to the benefit of each group. Both private and public aid hastened the transitional period of adjustment. The Cuban success actually resulted from their own private initiative and their advanced backgrounds. The following selection concentrates on the Cuban ethnic experience in Miami.

A Plus for Miami[6]

Virtually all the Cubans who come directly to the U.S., rather than by way of some other country, come first to Miami for processing. There they are screened by immigration and naturalization authorities who, among other things, investigate the possibility that Cuban

[6] Reprinted from Tom Alexander, "Those Amazing Cuban Emigrés, *Fortune Magazine,* vol. 74 (October, 1966), pp. 144–49. By permission of the editors.

Government agents are included among the arrivals. Once cleared, however, the immigrants are technically free to do what they please. What would please most of them would be to settle in Miami, where the climate is agreeable and where previous immigrants have virtually created a little bit of old Havana. Something over a quarter of the 300,000 refugees are now living in Miami.

For some time this concentration was viewed as a social problem that might get out of control. Ripples of dread have passed through Miami as each of the successive waves of refugees hit town. In the early 1960's there was, indeed, a plausible case for being worried about the immigrants. Miami's was a depressed economy. Nearly 100,000 Cubans had recently been dumped into the metropolitan area, raising its total population by over 10 percent. Over two-thirds of the refugees were then on public assistance. The area's total unemployment rate hung around the 10 percent mark, and loud, anguished cries came from the Negro community and some labor unions because Cubans were going to work for half the prevailing wages. Miami schools had trouble accommodating the 18,000 refugee children, most of whom spoke only Spanish. Furthermore, preoccupied with overthrowing Castro and returning to their homeland, many of the refugees were devoting a lot of their energies and spare capital to roiling agitation and sometimes even to harassing raids on the Cuban mainland.

Most of the refugees have long since given up any ideas about freeing Cuba by their own efforts and are now devoting their talents to getting along in their adopted home. Miami unemployment is down to about 4 percent. Cubans on welfare have declined from nearly 70,000 to about 12,000, with most of these being elderly, juvenile, sick, or otherwise unemployable.

Though some ill-feeling still persists in Miami, by and large the city has come to count its new Cuban community as its own good fortune. "There is no doubt in my mind that the Cubans boosted Miami immeasurably," says William Pallot, president of Miami's fast-growing Inter National Bank. Pallot believes, and others agree with him, that thousands of Miami's houses, apartments, and stores would be vacant had the Cubans not come. There is even something of a real-estate boom in Miami—one of the few cities in the U.S. where housing markets are strong—and an estimated 30 percent of the new FHA commitments there are to Cubans. Enterprising Cubans have been credited with bringing a new commercial vigor to much of the downtown area, especially the former commercial center of Flagler Street, which had been rapidly running down. Many of the former Havana cigar manufacturers and their employees have set up nearly a dozen companies in Miami, helping the city to displace Tampa as the hand-rolled-cigar capital of the U.S. At least one cigarette company, Dorsal & Mendes, is thriving; there are also sizable and prosperous Cuban-owned garment companies, shoe manufacturers, import houses, shopping centers, restaurants, and night clubs. To the northwest of Miami, Cuban entrepreneurs have set up sugar plantations and mills.

Though Miami still has by far the largest Cuban community, several other cities—notably New York, Chicago, and Los Angeles —have each received thousands of refugees. Large colonies of Cubans are now to be found in the northern New Jersey area that encompasses Newark, Elizabeth, Union City, and West New York: the total in the area is estimated to be over 30,000. In part the recent immigrants have congregated there because the area already had a Cuban community dating back as far as 1850. Some estimate that Union City itself has 20,000 Cubans in a total population of 40,000—the highest proportion of any city in the U.S. Just as in Miami, Cubans are credited with having done much to spruce up some of the city's run-down areas, notably the neighborhood around Bergenline Avenue and Forty-eighth Street.

"Send Us a Thousand More"

Most Cubans would almost certainly still be in Miami but for some pressures exerted on them by the Cuban Refugee Center, which has charge of financing and coordinating most of the government and voluntary agencies' aid to refugees. Registration with the center is voluntary, but anyone who fails to register forgoes a wide range of benefits: temporary financial assistance (up to $100 a month per family), medical care, food, hospitalization, and education loans for Cuban college students, plus a variety of adult-education programs that include English and vocational courses, teacher training, and refresher courses for physicians. At the same time, it is made clear to the refugees that those who register must agree to resettlement as soon as suitable jobs are found for them.

Most of the resettlement work is handled through the center's contracts with four voluntary agencies: the National Catholic Welfare Conference, the Church World Service (a Protestant agency), United HIAS (Hebrew Immigrant Aid Society), and the nonsectarian International Rescue Committee. The refugee is free to choose any one of these agencies and it then helps him find a job outside Miami. Within twenty-four to forty-eight hours of their arrival in the city, most Cubans are on their way to somewhere else. John Thomas, who directs the program from Washington, is convinced that the worst thing that can happen to refugees is to be detained for long periods while they are being "processed." Says Thomas: "Only two weeks in a refugee camp is enough to destroy a person."

Wherever Cubans have settled, they have elicited remarkably consistent praise for their energy, ability, and exemplary conduct. Many of the firms that have employed a few send back to Miami for more. And one company in Texas, which had taken on a lot of Cuban construction workers, later sent a wire to the refugee center, "Send us a thousand more."

Like Miami, most other cities have found that some widespread fears and prejudices about the Cubans are groundless. In Miami, where Cubans make up between 10 percent and 15 percent of the population, they account for only 2.9 percent of the arrests, with most of these being for traffic violations—Cubans seem not to be very good drivers, for some reason. In most communities where Cubans have settled, welfare officials have noted with astonishment their powerful urge to stay off relief rolls whenever jobs are available—and, with even more astonishment, have noted the effort that some Cubans make to pay back any welfare money they may have received. Of New York's 30,000-odd Cubans, only about 500 are on relief. Robert Frutkoff, a management expert with the New York

State Employment Service, testified in Senate hearings on refugee problems this past spring that Cubans are "a highly motivated group. We found, for example, that they would prefer to take any type of job than apply for welfare."

A Kind of Limbo

Despite the over-all success of the Cuban immigration, however, it seems clear that from 80 to 90 percent of Cuban refugees are "underemployed"—i.e., working at jobs that are beneath their real qualifications. One reason for this is their difficulty with the English language. Another reason is the peculiar legal status of the refugees. Because most entered after the U.S. had severed diplomatic relations with Cuba, the usual visa requirements have been waived; this leaves the refugees in a "parolee" status, a kind of limbo that does not permit them even to apply for citizenship without first going to another country and then re-entering under a permanent-resident visa—an expensive and uncertain business. Citizenship or declaration of intent, however, is a precondition for licensing in virtually all the professions in most states. It is also a precondition for civil-service qualification, for jobs requiring bonding or travel abroad, and for many others—such as selling real estate—that require licensing. . . .

Of all the professional men, the Cuban lawyers have the hardest time obtaining employment that uses their talents, since they were trained in the Napoleonic Code rather than the common law practice in the U.S. To help the lawyers, the refugee program has sponsored a special series of training programs aimed at turning lawyers into Spanish teachers, and by now several hundred of them are teaching in U.S. schools and colleges.

There is also a special problem about nearly 2,000 Cuban physicians, in some ways the most valuable single human resource of all to be received from Cuba. The problem is that most states require doctors to be citizens and to serve as interns before they can be licensed for private practice. To get around these barriers, most of the refugee doctors are placed in clinics and hospitals, where they can practice so long as they do so under the direction of an American citizen. Recently, a team of six Cuban physicians went to South Vietnam to aid war refugees—and thereby to get in their licks against Communism.

VIRGIN ISLANDERS

Another area of the West Indies is the Virgin Islands, an unincorporated territory of the United States. The Virgin Islands were acquired in 1917 from Denmark for $25,000,000, and the Virgin Islanders have been United States citizens since 1927. There are about 30,000 Virgin Islanders who have migrated to this country; this figure represents about half of the population at home. Along with the Puerto Ricans and the Haitians, most of them have migrated since the 1940's. Living mainly in New York City, the Virgin Islanders have successfully made the transition to the new culture. They tend to adapt very readily and are less apt to cling to traditions; however, they maintain their ties with the homeland.

The ethnic experience of the Virgin Islanders in this country has been similar to that of the Haitians and less troubled than that of the Puerto Ricans. Perhaps it is because of the difference in numbers. Nevertheless, the Virgin Islanders seek to retain their ethnic identity, as the following account shows. They gather at a place in Harlem to get the latest news of the homeland. Even though they are proud of their heritage, they lead middle-class lives, hold professional and civil-service jobs, and like to be referred to simply as Americans. The most serious problem they have faced here has been that of color. Coming from a society where skin color is no barrier, the Virgin Islanders have experienced racial prejudice.

The problems of most Virginlanders—as Virgin Islanders on the mainland call themselves—are, despite Mrs. Moorehead's lament, less severe than those of most Puerto Ricans.[7] Come and see. Up a flight of stairs on West 145th Street in Harlem, one of the sections of New York City into which Negro citizens are segregated, is the the office of VIPAC, the Virgin Islands Public Affairs Council. VIPAC is news headquarters for Virginlanders hungry to hear what's happening back home. A meeting is scheduled tonight. It's a summer night, hot enough to suit the Virginlanders. The open windows let in a musty breeze, together with the occasional shriek of a siren on a patrolling police car. The meeting room is clean, but the window sills have been blackened by sunken-in city grime from summers of open windows.

The walls are plastered with posters and photographs. The posters show the broad beaches, the purple reefs, the blue-green waters, and flowering trees of home. The photographs, most of them taken by VIPAC members, have been snapped at picnics, steel band dances, baptism and birthday parties. Some are beginning to haze with age.

The members idle in and help themselves to the Virgin Islands rum standing on a table. One man supplies a box of crackers and another some cheese. They talk of home.

"Salmon go home, and they are only fish," says one.

"Mon, what's the matter with us, we can swim as good as they?" kids another.

"Yeah and the salmon die when they get there," comments a third. There is a short laugh.

"I was just back," announces a young man, "visiting my aunt." The others question him eagerly. Did he eat fish and fungi? Mangos? Catch any lobster? How about that new road to John's Folly? Does it go all the way? Can you really make it in twenty minutes?

"Uh-huh, I did all that. I had a good vacation. Got tan." He lifts the short sleeve of his sport shirt to show the line between the shades of brown on his skin.

"And the bands are real hot. It's a real good place to visit." He does a few calypso dance steps. The others clap. "Say, why don't we get a record player here?" he asks. "And have a social next week? I brought some records back with me."

At the corner of the street where he lives, there's a record shop. After work, he stops in there often, or sometimes stands outside, listening. To him, the throb of a record on air sizzling with the aroma of hamburgers frying at the next-door stand are the sound and smell of home. He was born in New York, went to school and college in New York, now has a full-time job in a post office branch in New York where he has worked every summer since he was sixteen. He expects to be drafted but when his service is over, he hopes to become a computer-programmer. He's taking courses, nights.

He had a great two weeks in the islands, and he's glad his aunt lives there. With relatives, you visit free. But the vacation is over. He comes to VIPAC meetings sometimes with his father, but he can't quite understand the pining of the members.

A recruiter from the Virgin Islands Department of Labor arrives at the meeting and the formal session starts. The recruiter describes government job openings back home and invites questions.

"How much an hour would I get in your tax or audit division?" asks an accountant. He shakes his head at the answer. "I get almost twice that. And even supposing I could afford such a cut, considering the advantages of living there, what if things didn't work out and I had to come back and look for another job here, how could I explain to a next employer why I'd been working for so little?"

"What about Jerry?" asks another.

"What about him?" the recruiter parries.

"I hear he lost a promotion because he shot his mouth off about the government. That true?"

"Well, you don't go round making loud talk about your boss, do you?" the recruiter challenges.

"If I did, he couldn't do nothing about it," the man answers. "He can't come easy by a foreman good as me." He lapses into emphatic island dialect. "I born free, mon, and I stayin' free. I feels good wit'out lickin' anybody's hand."

The recruiter isn't making any headway. The islands offer fun and fresh air—the continent offers greater freedom of opportunity. The Virginlanders have made their choice. They have their Virgin Islands Clubs, like VIPAC, dozens of them. They hold Virgin Islands dances and card games and talk of home. But their daily lives in their jobs and homes are middle-class mainland American. They don't even like to be called West Indians. They call themselves Virginlanders but they prefer others to speak of them simply as Americans.

In New York City, where three quarters have settled, more of them live in outlying boroughs than in the central borough of Manhattan, and their apartments are roomy. In the country, some own neat homes. Their jobs are mostly white collar, many are in civil service and the professions. Few plan to give up what they have achieved unless and until they retire. The returning fraction the labor analyst mentioned are mostly elderly people still capable of work but no longer requiring substantial salaries. They have the pensions Albert Abel and Asta Moorehead's husband are still after.

There is one ragged exception to this pattern of absorption in the American mainstream. Color. As for all people of color in the States, it is harder for Virginlanders to find the homes they can afford, harder to rise to the professional levels for which they're trained, harder to get that training. This struggle was even more difficult for those who came before the civil rights decisions and laws of the 1950's and '60's. The born islander grew up in a society which is innately prejudice-free and so is he. It is a tremendous shock to him to be classified by the color of his skin.

"I don't understand how people can be so rude," says Mrs. Moorehead. After nine years of northern living, she continues to be shocked, daily. Yet even this affront doesn't shake the Virginlanders' choice, and they do manage it "wit'out lickin' anybody's hand" as the man said. The islander brings his dignity with him and all the meanness of human nature cannot tarnish it.

HAITIANS

During the twentieth century large numbers of immigrants have arrived from the West Indies. Through the period of the Great Depression it has been estimated that over 300,000 entered the United States from Haiti, Cuba, the British West Indies, and the French West Indies. They brought with them varied backgrounds and settled in cities along the eastern seaboard, such as New York and Boston. Many were professional people, some entered the garment industry, and most took lower paying jobs. They kept to themselves because of American racial patterns and the friction between themselves and American Negroes.

The British West Indians, the largest of this group, were permitted to use the unfilled British immigrant quota up until 1952, when the McCarran-Walter Act provided a maximum quota of 100 per unit: 100 for Trinidad, 100 for Jamaica, etc. The new Immigration Act of 1965 established more generous provisions: effective July 1, 1968, a ceiling of 120,000 was set for immigrants from the Western Hemisphere countries on a first-come, first-served basis with no limit on the number from any one country.

A small but prominent ethnic group that has developed its own communities in New York in the past decade is that of the Haitians. Most are escapees from the late dictator Francois Duvalier's iron rule in Haiti, and most are Catholic, French-speaking, and proud of their ethnic heritage. They appear to have made a smooth transition in their adopted land, as the following selection states.

They are perhaps New York's most invisible minority.[8] Perhaps 200,000 of them now live in the metropolitan area, but one rarely

[8] Reprinted from Michael Pousner, "Haitians: the Invisible Minority," *New York Daily News*, 11 January 1971. Courtesy of the New York News.

reads about them or sees their problems echoed on television news. Maybe it's because they have no crime problem, no welfare problem, nothing.

In that they are French-speaking and Catholic, they are in some ways different from other New Yorkers. In that they are black, however, they fit right into the New York scene.

They are the Haitians, a proud, strong people who have streamed to the New York area during the past decade to escape political persecution at home under the regime of Francois (Papa Doc) Duvalier, dictator and self-proclaimed president of Haiti for life. Under Duvalier, the lush but impoverished Caribbean country has become a police state, where "law" is administered by the dreaded secret police, the "Tonton Macoute."

Changes in the United States immigration quota system in 1968 and the decision by Duvalier to let malcontents emigrate have given an average of 30,000 Haitians a year the opportunity to come here.

Doctors, lawyers, accountants, artisans, the cream of the crop of a country with the highest rate of illiteracy in the western world (90%), they left Haiti on the first available flights. Most were not allowed to sell their possessions, which subsequently were confiscated. Many immigrated without knowing a word of English.

So, thousands of them live with friends or in cheap hotels, tenements and a small number of brownstones in a slice of the upper West Side of Manhattan stretching from West 72nd St. north to around 110th St. and from Columbus Ave. to Broadway.

Thousands of others live in shabby quarters in Brooklyn's crime-ridden Brownsville or nearby Crown Heights. The small but growing number of Haitian-Americans who have made it in New York live in one- and two-family houses in Crown Heights or in Cambria Heights, South Jamaica, or Corona in Queens.

Haitians with professional qualifications have no guarantee of a position here—in part because of the language gap, in part because of licensing requirements. Then, too, Haitian institutions—no doubt out of spite, refugees feel—rarely cooperate by forwarding evidence of degrees and honors.

So, physicians and lawyers from Haiti find themselves competing for factory or restaurant jobs here.

And they do so without, oddly enough, complaining. "They haven't caught on yet to the idea that the groups who scream the loudest get the most help," one Haitian community organizer comments.

Another reason is that to most of the immigrants, anything is better than Haiti. "Of course," said Jacob-Jean Gilles, an accountant in Haiti, as he waited at the Brooklyn Haitian center for jobs in a factory to materialize, "I would rather be an accountant here, too. But at least I'm free here."

Many Haitians seem chary of organizing or keeping other than a low profile because, in their minds, the tentacles of Papa Doc's rule-by-fear stretch here. They are afraid any political activity on their part will somehow reflect badly on relatives remaining in Haiti.

But perhaps an even more important reason why Haitians maintain their independent, quiet life here is their nature—the Haitians are a very proud people. They are reserved, civil and courteous, and, above all, proud. This is a refrain they consistently turned to when asked why they do not complain.

They are proud of their tradition of independence and self-sufficiency and boast of Haiti's becoming the first independent black republic in the Western Hemisphere in 1804. In addition, Haitians take great pride in their close-knit families and indigenous culture, both of which they strive to maintain here.

"Generation gap," "drug culture" and "new life style" are terms foreign to Haitian communities.

There also is a tradition of a strong emphasis on education. Other disadvantaged people marvel at the Haitian fathers who almost literally break their backs to send their children to college. They are convinced hard work will bring success and scorn welfare as soul-destroying.

Community leaders report they literally have to sell many Haitians on social security, medicare, and other general benefits to which they are entitled, but refuse to take because they don't want to depend on others for help.

In the sense that they tend to perpetuate their problems by not seeking such help, the Haitian pride can be self-defeating.

Several groups, however, are striving to remedy the situation. In Brooklyn, lines of quiet Haitians seeking assistance form early in the morning at the Centre Communautaire Haiten, at 163 Remsen Ave. in Crown Heights. The small staff here, funded by Catholic Charities, provides such services as locating jobs for unemployed Haitians, advising on health matters, and providing a forum for community activities.

In musty rooms above the Riviera Theater at 2575 Broadway, the Manhattan Haitian Neighborhood Service Center, which is funded by the city, provides similar services, and, in addition, offers legal counsel to French-speaking citizens.

Both agencies have classes where rudimentary English is taught, but complain of lack of funds to tackle the language problem effectively.

The community centers do their best to find Haitians employment in these hard economic times and enjoy surprising success.

"Making our initial contact is by far the hardest part," said Lyderic Bonaventure, director of the Haitian Center in Brooklyn. "Once we send our men somewhere, the employers always want them back. The men make a reputation for good, hard work."

Restaurant chains like Horn and Hardart and Schraffts seeking busboys, waiters and waitresses, and factories in Brooklyn and Long Island, have been wont to employ Haitians. The United States Extrusion Corp., a Long Island firm, has been so enthusiastic, according to Bonaventure, that the factory sends a van twice daily to the Haitian Center to pick up workers.

The long-range goal of Haitian leaders is that the problems of the Haitian immigrants be considered equal to those of the Cuban refugees. Because the Cuban immigrants were officially classified as "political refugees," complete well-funded, multi-service centers were set up to handle their problems. Haitians, however, are not classified as "political refugees," possibly because our government continues to maintain limited, if not cordial, relations with the Duvalier regime.

Despite the lack of service centers and the continued Haitian migration, some community leaders are guardedly optimistic. "The police department is teaching French to officers who patrol in Haitian neighborhoods and more and more city hospitals are putting signs up in French," comments community worker Anne Jaeger-huber. Likewise several schools with large populations of Haitian children now have special classes in English for French-speaking youths.

Perhaps the scene at a Haitian-American social club, "La Canne a Sucre" (Sugar Cane) in Corona, Queens, is an indication of how the Haitian-American identity will be shaped as more and more Haitians begin to overcome the language problem and enjoy success here.

At the club, a six-piece tropical band was playing a typically gentle Haitian melody as Haitian-Americans danced a brisk merengue. A singer imported from Haiti was belting out a slow ballad in French, under a canopy of nets.

Meanwhile, others at the club, clad not in Haitian tropical dress, but in elegant American suits, were sampling a delicious Haitian cuisine which featured a scrumptious Creole-styled lamb and "poisso rose," red snapper, "pala," fried bananas on rice, and "cremasse," a drink made with coconut milk and rum.

They were conversing in broken English about, of all things, American politics, as their wives, their hair done in Afros (a distinctly non-Haitian trait), chatted about new styles.

A young man, about 25, his arms around his cute, pregnant wife, was questioned as he left the club: "If there were no Duvalier, would you like to return to Haiti?"

The man, who like most Haitians refused to allow his name to be used, pondered a moment and then spoke softly, "I'll always miss Haiti. It's a beautiful country and I still have relatives there."

"But I'm an American now—although it took me several years to start feeling like one."

KEY QUESTIONS

1. "The Puerto Ricans are not so much immigrants as they are migrants." Explain the meaning of this statement. Has this made a difference in their treatment and status on the mainland?

2. Piri Thomas, a Puerto Rican American, describes his experiences in Harlem and his questions about moving to a Long Island suburb. Relate them. What is their significance?

3. What has been the influence of Catholicism and Protestantism on the Puerto Rican in the United States?

4. Explain why the Cubans who have immigrated to the United States since 1959 have been called the "golden exile."

5. Is there any evidence that the Virgin Islanders and the Haitians want to become assimilated into American society? What role has their color played in New York City?

10

The Black Man's Experience

To say that World War II had a major impact upon all peoples, especially Afro-Americans, is to voice the obvious. What may not be as obvious is the nature and extent of the war's consequences upon the Afro-American. Although Afro-Americans were an integral part, though not an integrated part, of the United States' effort to defeat the racist Nazi regime of Hitler, Afro-Americans found themselves the victims of extensive racism within the United States itself. The Afro-American soldier returned to a land that quite clearly stated, in terms of its practices and laws, that he was a second-class citizen. In fact, the United States was one of the most internally racist countries in the world. The Afro-American found legalized segregation and discrimination the rule rather than the exception.

Coexisting with institutionalized racism was a panoply of myths upon which American racism was rationalized. The Afro-American was thought to be innately intellectually inferior, slovenly, amoral, and hypersexual. Moreover, the images of Afro-Americans presented by the mass media served to reinforce white supremacy and black inferiority. On movie screens one saw the ignorant black being the butt of insensate "humor" and the white American the master of the universe.

World War II's impact upon the Afro-American was dramatic. It became clear to him not only that he had to tear down the laws and practices of a racist society but that he had to redefine himself as well, for the myths built by white society had had major deleterious effects upon many Afro-Americans. American racism was so effective that some Afro-Americans did, indeed, believe they were inferior. Others enacted "Uncle Tom" roles that whites assigned them. Many lived in fear of death. Starvation and malnutrition were rampant, and inferior education was the rule. Insidious exploitation of Afro-American employees was widespread. Too frequently, Afro-American families were torn apart by the psychological and socioeconomic conditions under which they were forced to survive.

These were the conditions faced by Afro-Americans after World War II. Their responses to these conditions have been variegated, for the United States itself has been a constantly shifting society. After World War II, it was the United States which dramatically became the leader of the Western world. Rapid industrialization produced profound effects upon all institutions and all peoples living in this country. For the Afro-American, it meant vast migration from rural to urban areas, a fact that by itself brought about vast changes in the life style of Africans living in the United States. The one constant he experienced wherever he moved was segregation and discrimination.

The shift of power to the federal government signalled important strategic considerations for Afro-Americans. The increased power of the Supreme Court as a force for social change was significant, as was the effect of an increased mass media. The widespread impact of instant news via television in part made this one nation. Its use by civil rights demonstrators was extensive. The increasing necessity of education in a technological society was to make it a major battleground. The political independence gained by many African nations served as an impetus to the civil rights movement. The fact that many African leaders had studied at American colleges, many of them Afro-American colleges, and lived in Afro-American communities was also highly significant. The entire revolution against exploitation in the "Third World" was not lost upon Afro-Americans. America's wars in Asia continue to have tremendous impact upon Afro-Americans.

From 1945 to the present one sees not only strategic shifts in the Afro-Americans' struggle to attain full equality but also a constantly shifting and changing America and world. From 1945 to 1956, the major emphasis of Afro-Americans, led by the National Association for the Advancement of Colored People (N.A.A.C.P.), was the repeal of laws which enforced and legitimatized their caste status. From 1956 to 1966, the major emphasis was on a largely nonviolent confrontation with racist institutions in order to change their practices. The most charismatic leader of this period was Dr. Martin Luther King, president of the Southern Christian Leadership Conference (S.C.L.C.). The next period, 1966 to the present, witnessed a shift from the legal to the economic and the political. "Black Power" became its rallying cry. At present political leadership is reflected by such individuals as Congresswoman Shirley Chisholm, Atlanta mayor Maynard Jackson, Los Angeles mayor Tom Bradley, Newark mayor Kenneth Gibson, and Georgia legislator Julian Bond.

To categorize periods of history is blatantly a device of convenience. Each of the above strategies coexisted before World War II, and they still coexist presently. What is significant is that each strategy received greater support and had greater impact during the period mentioned.

Moreover, it should also be obvious that each phase was also requisite for each succeeding phase. If segregation laws had not been outlawed, Dr. King probably could not have had the degree of influence he had. And Black Power might have been lost in the winds of history if it were not for the foundation laid by the N.A.A.C.P. and S.C.L.C.

Will there be a next phase? What will it be? One thing is clear: The future of the Afro-American movement will depend to a large degree upon the United States' reaction to its cry for freedom, equality, power, and peace.

This will obviously not be a one-way street in which the white American community does give out rights to Afro-Americans. The Afro-American's impact upon the United States will most certainly lead to changes in both her foreign and domestic policies. Most Afro-Americans at one time seemed only to want a piece of the pie, but today the apple pie itself is being questioned. The changes and events that have occurred since World War II have been so rapid and of such import that selecting articles for this chapter was a challenge. Indeed, an entire volume would be needed to deal with them. Since the issues of this period—sit-ins, Freedom Rides, ghetto rebellions (or riots), Panther trials, March on Washington, community control, assassinations, civil rights legislation, welfare, war in Vietnam, etc.—could not be dealt with in depth, what has been done is to select writings that have analyzed the living and psychological conditions under which Afro-Americans exist, to include writings that have vividly portrayed the Afro-American condition, and finally to include writings by men who have been judged to be leaders and whose views have had major impact.

The Afro-American struggle in the United States to achieve black ethnic identification and to secure full equality is a continuing and incomplete struggle. Hopefully, the following selections do capture the fervor, import, and dynamics of this time.

A. Philip Randolph, the leading black labor leader, includes in this first extract an appeal for ethnic equality. The appeal, made in the early 1940's at the height of World War II, called particular attention to the roles played by economics and politics in the strictures placed on blacks. Randolph's invectives have a current ring.

> This statement is being presented at an hour when the lamps of civilization are burning low.[1] If the Axis powers win, the lamps may go out, and if they do, they may not be relighted in a thousand years. The lamps of enlightenment have gone out before. They may go out again. Thus, the Nazism of Hitler, the Militarism of Hirohito, and the Fascism of Mussolini and now Badoglio must be destroyed.
> The cause of the United Nations must prevail.

[1] Reprinted from A. Philip Randolph, "March on Washington Movement Presents Program for the Negro," in *What the Negro Wants*, ed. Rayford W. Logan (Chapel Hill: University of North Carolina Press, 1944), pp. 133–47.

But the colored peoples know from a tragic experience that it is not enough for the arms of the United Nations to win.

Aims of the Negro

The oppressed darker races want something more.

They want much more.

They want the cause of true democracy to march forward.

They want the Brotherhood of man to triumph.

They want a durable and just peace.

They want security and plenty with freedom.

They want to put an end to the vile and sinister doctrine of the Master Race.

They want ethnic equality.

They want economic, political and social equality.

They want to abolish the racism and colonialism of the Anglo-American empire systems.

"Will this ever come?" ask the Negro bootblack, jitterbug, and Ph.D.

Darker Races Must Fight for Freedom

It will not come if the Axis powers win.

It may not come if the United Nations win.

Albeit, it will not come automatically.

It will come only if the downtrodden peoples fight for it.

The darker races can get no solace from the proclamations of Prime Minister Churchill or President Roosevelt. With inept Machiavellian diplomacy the Atlantic Charter states its concern only for the European countries under the Nazi yoke. And, Mr. Churchill observes in the unvarnished language of the "brass hat" imperialists, that he has not become the first minister of the King to preside over the liquidation of the British Empire. He also adds in a note of somber and sullen militant imperialism, that they will hold their own.

Thus the Negro, labor and liberals might well demand to know:

Are we fighting this global war to restore Singapore, Malaya, and Burma to Great Britain?

Will the peace reestablish the ill-fated Italian Empire, and give back to notorious Belgium the African Congo? Are the "natives" of Africa to continue to live in slavery of the mandated colonialism of white powers?

Free Africa

The March On Washington Movement proclaims the slogan of a free Africa. It joins the cry of a "Fight for a Free India and China." It hails the struggle for the freedom of the common man everywhere—the common man, whether black, white, brown, yellow, red, Protestant, Catholic, Jewish, native or foreign, worker, storekeeper, artist, teacher, minister.

Not A War for Freedom

But be not deceived. This is not a war for freedom.

It is not a war for democracy.

It is not a war to usher in the Century of the Common Man.
It is not a Peoples' Revolution.

It is a war to maintain the old imperialistic systems. It is a
war to continue "white supremacy," the theory of Herrenvolk, and
the subjugation, domination, and exploitation of the peoples of color.
It is war between the imperialism of Fascism and Nazism and the
imperialism of monopoly capitalistic democracy.

Under neither are the colored peoples free.

But this war need not be a world movement of reaction. The
people can make it a Peoples' Revolution—a Revolution whose
dynamism against Axis tyranny will be greater and more powerful
because it will possess the fighting faith and crusading confidence of
the masses of all colors and races. The people can cause this war to
usher in the Century of the Common Man. This is the meaning of
the call of Gandhi for an independent and free India. It is the reason
for the stirrings of the "natives" of Africa, the war by the Chinese
against the dominion of Nippon, the rebellion of the blacks in the
Caribbean Islands against a bare subsistence wage, and the fight of
the Negro people of the United States for equality.

What the Negro Wants

Now the basic phase of the Negro problem is economic.
Why?

The origin of the Negro problem was economic, for it had its
seat in the slave trade.

The reason for subjecting Negroes to slavery was economic.
It had residence in cheap labor.

The reason for the abolition of slavery was economic.

It rests upon the rise of capitalist industrialism and the growing uneconomic character of slave labor in the production of cotton,
rice, sugar and tobacco.

Verily, the biggest problem confronting Negroes today is economic, that is, getting work and wages to buy food, clothing and
shelter.

Thus the March On Washington Movement sets forth as the
cardinal and primary cornerstone of its program: economic action.

ECONOMIC
Labor Union

The major and paramount form of economic action by the Negro people must necessarily be the building of trade and industrial
unions and the employment of the technique of collective bargaining. This is so because well-nigh 99 and 9/10 per cent of the Negro
people are workers of hand and brain who earn their living in the
sweat of their brow by selling their labor in the market for wages.
Hence, the biggest business of the Negro consists in his selling at
the highest price, that which he has the most of, namely his ability
to work. But this business of the Negro worker selling his labor is
not as simple as it sounds. For immediately he enters the market
for jobs, he is met with a color bar in some of the trade unions, or
prejudice on the part of some employers. Not only is he the last
hired and first fired, but he meets this vicious cycle when applying
for work or a union card. The employer rejects him because he does

not have a union card and the union rejects him because he hasn't got a job.

Thus, the progress of the Negro in the modern industrial system will depend in a large measure upon cleansing the labor unions and personnel manager systems of the sins of race prejudice. This is one fight Negro and white workers must wage which they cannot afford to lose since trade unions are the main bulwark of democracy. But this bulwark cannot stand if part of the workers possess economic citizenship and another part is economically disfranchised because of color and race.

The March On Washington Movement sets its face resolutely toward the complete integration of the Negro workers into the organized labor movement. If an industry in which Negroes work is controlled by the A. F. of L. or C.I.O., they are urged to organize and become part of these federated labor bodies.

Cooperatives

But, labor through trade unions may win decent wages at the point of production and lose them at the point of consumption, when, as consumers, the workers go back into the market to buy back, with their wages, the goods they produced with their labor. Consumers' cooperatives are agencies through which the workers can conserve and increase their purchasing power by eliminating the middle man, and buying from themselves on the Rochdale principle and they offer the Negro as well as white workers an important economic force for their liberation. The importance of the workers directing attention to the price of goods they buy is shown by the struggle now being waged to force OPA to roll back prices.

Employment for Negroes

No greater wrong has been committed against the Negro than the denial to him of the right to work. This question of the right to work is tied up with the right to live. But Negroes are not only denied the right to work on certain jobs but they are sentenced in some industries to a sort of blind alley position. For instance, the Negro may be employed as a Pullman porter but not as a Pullman conductor, although he demonstrates his ability to perform this service by running-in-charge, at a slight differential in pay.

A Negro may be employed as a waiter on the dining cars but not as a steward, although here, too, he demonstrates his ability to perform the services of a steward, in which event he receives a slight differential in pay. The Negro may operate as a brakeman or flagman but, because of custom, practice and tradition resulting from racial discrimination, he is not promotable to the job of train conductor, although all train conductors were former brakemen or flagmen. It is a matter of common knowledge that Negro train porters teach hundreds of white brakemen how to operate as train conductors. And Negro waiters break in white stewards, and Negro Pullman porters instruct white Pullman conductors how to make out their diagrams.

The March On Washington Movement rejects this economic discrimination and segregation of the Negro worker and calls for the abolition of the racial blind alley job.

POLITICAL

But economics is only one arm with which the Negro people
may fight for their liberation. The struggle of all oppressed peoples
shows that economic action requires the supplementation of political
action. To this end, the March On Washington Movement suggests
as a major strategy for the effective employment of the political
power of the Negro, the building of a national non-partisan Negro
political bloc, with branches in the various local communities in the
country. This does not require that Negroes come out of the
Republican, Democratic, Socialist or Communist parties. But it does
require that, when a crucial question of universal concern and importance to the Negro arises, Negroes will express their united
political strength regardless of party politics. When this is done, it
will strengthen the position of Negro leaders in the Republican and
Democratic parties and make the white boss politicians more disposed to give serious consideration to all questions affecting the
interest of the Negro. It will prove that Negroes are not so died-in-
the-wool Republicans or Democrats that they will not ignore political labels when a crisis comes, for the benefit and advancement of
the Negro. It goes without saying that any form of political action
which favorably serves the interest of the Negro people also favorably serves the interest of our country. It is a matter of common
knowledge that Negroes as Democrats do not amount to much.
They can get but little done for Negroes. Similarly, Negroes as Republicans are not very strong and their voice is seldom heeded. Negroes as Socialists or Communists are helpless, but when Negro
Republicans and Democrats step forward in a united front expressed
in a powerful non-partisan political block, they will be heard and
heeded by political boss or mayor, governor, president, Senate or
House Committees. The value of a non-partisan political Negro
block consists in the fact that it represents power. It is well-nigh the
law of the life of the politician that he respects nothing but votes.
Politicians are seldom, if ever, moved by questions of principles,
ideals, or human justice. Politicians are hungry for power and jobs.
This is true of white and black politicians. They fear votes and the
righteous wrath of the people. They will only do the right thing for
the people when they are made to do so by pressure, public opinion
and votes.

Therefore, upwards of 15 millions of Negroes need not forever
play the role of political mendicants. They have power if they will
mobilize by registering in mass for non-partisan political action.
Such a political block should be financed by Negroes entirely. It
is still true that the power over man's subsistence is the power of his
will, and he who pays the fiddler calls the tune. Therefore, such a
non-partisan political block should not accept any money from
Republican, Democratic, Socialist or Communist party. It should be
entirely free. It cannot be free if it is subsidized by any politicians.

How Political Block May Function

This piece of political machinery, during campaigns, could send
speakers into districts to oppose the enemies of the Negro and
support their friends on a basis of their record in office and public
life. Literature on the issues and candidates could be prepared and

distributed widely throughout the country, expressing the position
of the Negro on them.

Whole page advertisements setting forth the position and demands of the Negro people should be carried in strategic papers,
dailies and weeklies, during a campaign to let the world know that
Negroes are not asleep or weak.

If such a powerful non-partisan political bloc is honestly,
courageously and intelligently directed, it could transform the political status of the Negro people in our American community, put a
Negro on the United States Supreme Court, Negroes on Federal
courts, a Negro in the Cabinet, Negroes on policy making commissions, get Negroes their rightful share of jobs in government
agencies, elect them to municipal and state legislatures as well as to
the Senate and the House of Congress, abolish anti-Negro legislation,
reverse anti-Negro court decisions, eliminate racial bias in adminis-
trative agencies, and secure for Negroes the respect enjoyed by
other citizens. It could effectively in passing anti-poll tax legislation,
put a federal anti-lynching law on the statute books and enable the
Negroes to have their voice heard above the ranting and raving of
the Bilbos and Rankins.

The uniqueness of the black's ethnic experience is acknowledged
by numerous observers of society. To most Americans, one black was
indistinguishable from another, leading to the "they-all-look-alike" syn-
drome. There was an incongruous irony about the situation. The nation's
most visible ethnic group left its people as invisible men. It is this aspect
of Afro-American life that is explored in the excerpt that follows from
Ralph Ellison's *The Invisible Man.*

I am an invisible man.[2] No, I am not a spook like those who haunted
Edgar Allan Poe; nor am I one of your Hollywood-movie ectoplasms.
I am a man of substance, of flesh and bone, fiber and liquids—and
I might even be said to possess a mind. I am invisible, understand,
simply because people refuse to see me. Like the bodiless heads you
see sometimes in circus sideshows, it is as though I have been
surrounded by mirrors of hard, distorting glass. When they approach me they see only my surroundings, themselves, or figments of
their imagination—indeed, everything and anything except me.

Nor is my invisibility exactly a matter of a bio-chemical accident to my epidermis. That invisibility to which I refer occurs
because of a peculiar disposition of the eyes of those with whom I
come in contact. A matter of the construction of their inner eyes,
those eyes with which they look through their physical eyes upon
reality. I am not complaining, nor am I protesting either. It is sometimes advantageous to be unseen, although it is most often rather
wearing on the nerves. Then too, you're constantly being bumped
against by those of poor vision. Or again, you often doubt if you
really exist. You wonder whether you aren't simply a phantom in

[2] Reprinted from Ralph Ellison, *The Invisible Man* (New York: New American Library, 1952), pp. 2–3. Copyright © 1947, 1948, and 1952 by Ralph Ellison. By permission of Random House, Inc.

other people's minds. Say, a figure in a nightmare which the sleeper tries with all his strength to destroy. It's when you feel like this that, out of resentment, you begin to bump people back. And, let me confess, you feel that way most of the time. You ache with the need to convince yourself that you do exist in the real world, that you're a part of all the sound and anguish, and you strike out with your fists, you curse and you swear, to make them recognize you, and, alas, it's seldom successful.

To Louis Lomax, the Supreme Court's "separate but equal" doctrine of 1954 had little direct bearing in uplifting the black American. Discrimination, humiliation, segregation, and even brutality continued to be experienced by the blacks. Lomax presents statistical evidence to show the social and economic impact that discriminatory practices had on the blacks six years after the Brown decision.

As of May 17, 1954, "separate but equal" was the law of the land; however, "separate but unequal" was, and still is, the practice and reality.[3]

The American Negro of the fifties lived in a state of constant humiliation. His dignity as an individual was not admitted, in the North or the South, and his worth was so demeaned that even other nonwhite peoples of the world had little respect for him. School desegregation, disfranchisement, segregation of public facilities and overt police brutality aside, the true condition of the Negro is best reflected by his relative position as a wage earner and professional man in American society.

Professional Pollyannas, particularly among white liberals, point with pride to the fact that the American Negro has more income today than he has ever had before. That is not the issue; everybody has more income today than he ever had before, and consumer goods cost more today than they ever have before. The crucial issue is that the income of the American Negro family showed no progress in relation to the income of the white family during the decade of the fifties. As a matter of fact, the relative average income of the Negro family declined during the last two years of the fifties. As of 1960, the median income of the Negro family was only three-fifths that of the white family; and there were almost three times as many whites as there were Negroes in business and professions. The statistics are almost exactly reversed on the other end of the economic scale: there are three times as many Negroes as there are whites in such menial occupations as common labor and housework. . . .

This economic straitjacket has everything to do with the breakdown of family life and general morality in the Negro community; it is the basic explanation for the inordinate Negro crime rate; it is the fundamental cause of our high welfare rolls and abundant relief chiseling; this is why we live in slums, and this is precisely why we have to gang up—brothers, sisters, cousins, aunts, every family we

[3] From pp. 67–71 in *The Negro Revolt* (hard cover) by Louis E. Lomax (beginning with the words "As of May 17, 1954 . . ." to ". . . assistance was non-white."). Copyright © 1962 by Louis E. Lomax. By permission of Harper & Row, Publishers, Inc.

can gather—to buy homes outside the Negro ghetto; and as a result of ganging up we bring social and economic deterioration to the once all-white communities.

Let us take a swift, but comprehensive, look at the relative social and economic status of the American Negro as of January 1, 1960:

* The Negro population had a net increase of 25 percent during the decade of the fifties; the white population's increase was only 18 percent.
* For the first time in history the end of the fifties found more than half of America's Negroes living outside the Deep South. The greatest numerical increase was in the Far West, where the Negro population doubled in the decade of the fifties.
* Seventy-two percent of the Negro population now lives in urban areas; only 70 percent of the white population is now urban. (This should be contrasted with the 1950 census, which showed that 63 percent of the white population were urban dwellers.)
* As of 1960, one out of six nonwhite dwelling units was dilapidated, compared with one out of thirty-two white dwellings: 29 percent of the nonwhite dwellings were deteriorating, compared with 12 percent for white dwellings; nonwhites are less likely to own their homes and when they do the chances are one out of three that the home is substandard: two-fifths of the nonwhite dwellings lacked some or all plumbing, compared with only one-tenth of the white-occupied units.
* These are national figures. The problem in the South is particularly serious: One out of four nonwhite dwellings (rentals) are dilapidated as compared with one out of ten for white dwelling units. Not only is nonwhite housing of an inferior quality; the non-white dweller must pay more for his housing.
* To compound the difficulty, nonwhite families (4.4 members) are, on the whole, larger than white families (3.6 members).
* Whereas public housing has improved the quality of housing available to low-income Negroes, it has not noticeably increased the quantity of good housing available to Negroes. This seeming contradiction arises from the fact that public housing usually displaces slum units and the former slum dwellers cannot afford to occupy the new units. The lowest-income Negroes have slums and will travel, and that's precisely what they do: Chicago affords a classic case where Negro slum dwellers are moved out by public housing or urban renewal and transplant, sometimes en masse, into another section of town, carrying all of the "slum" elements with them. In a matter of months their new homes are slums also. Even so, Negroes, only 10 percent of the national population, occupy 47 percent of the public housing.
* These economic and housing factors are reflected in the Negro family characteristics: One out of three nonwhite women above fourteen years of age who have married was, as of 1960, separated or divorced from her husband; the corresponding ratio for white women is one out of five. The higher mortality rate among Negro males leads to a higher ratio of nonwhite widows. This creates another financial burden. The Negro crime rate—which takes the Negro man, principally, from the social scene—adds even more of a burden.

* Broken homes lead to broken morality. One out of five non-white births is illegitimate, as compared with one out of every fifty white births. Moreover, nonwhite unwed mothers find the doors to many adoption agencies closed to them. Little wonder, then, that over two-fifths of the unwed mothers receiving public aid are nonwhite.

* The economic disadvantage suffered by the Negro family spills over into such areas as old-age assistance and aid to the blind. As of 1960, the number of Negroes receiving old-age assistance was three times that of white persons and one out of every three blind persons receiving federal assistance was nonwhite.

Perhaps the most poignant ethnic experience for the black man is that described by Dr. Martin Luther King, Jr., in his "Letter from Birmingham Jail" of 1963. Placed in jail for protesting Birmingham's white racist practices, Dr. King was criticized by the white religious establishment for being a troublemaker. Dr. King responded in a spirit of love and understanding, presenting his reasons for an appeal for justice, nonviolence, his goals and, most important, a dramatic description of what it is like to be a black man in America.

My Dear Fellow Clergymen:[4]

While confined here in the Birmingham City jail, I came across your recent statement calling my present activities "unwise and untimely." Seldom do I pause to answer criticism of my work and ideas. If I sought to answer all the criticisms that cross my desk, my secretaries would have little time for anything other than such correspondence in the course of the day, and I would have no time for constructive work. But since I feel that you are men of genuine good will and that your criticisms are sincerely set forth, I want to try to answer your statement in what I hope will be patient and reasonable terms. . . .

But more basically, I am in Birmingham because injustice is here. Just as the prophets of the eighth century B.C. left their villages and carried their "thus saith the Lord" far beyond the boundaries of their home towns, and just as the Apostle Paul left his village of Tarsus and carried the gospel of Jesus Christ to the far corners of the Greco-Roman world, so am I compelled to carry the gospel of freedom beyond my own home town. Like Paul, I must constantly respond to the Macedonian call for aid.

Moreover, I am cognizant of the interrelatedness of all communities and states. I cannot sit idly by in Atlanta and not be concerned about what happens in Birmingham. Injustice anywhere is a threat to justice everywhere. We are caught in an inescapable network of mutuality, tied in a single garment of destiny. Whatever affects one directly, affects all indirectly. Never again can we afford to live with the narrow, provincial "outside agitator" idea. Anyone who lives inside the United States can never be considered an outsider anywhere within its bounds.

You deplore the demonstrations taking place in Birmingham. But your statement, I am sorry to say, fails to express a similar concern for the conditions that brought about the demonstrations. I am sure that none of you would want to rest content with the superficial kind of social analysis that deals merely with effects and does not grapple with underlying causes. It is unfortunate that demonstrations are taking place in Birmingham, but it is even more unfortunate that the city's white power structure left the Negro community with no alternative.

In any nonviolent campaign there are four basic steps: collection of the facts to determine whether injustices exist; negotiation; self-purification; and direct action. We have gone through all these steps in Birmingham. There can be no gainsaying the fact that racial injustice engulfs this community. Birmingham is probably the most thoroughly segregated city in the United States. Its ugly record of brutality is widely known. Negroes have experienced grossly unjust treatment in the courts. There have been more unsolved bombings of Negro homes and churches in Birmingham than in any other city in the nation. These are the hard brutal facts of the case. On the basis of these conditions, Negro leaders sought to negotiate with the city fathers. But the latter consistently refused to engage in good-faith negotiations. . . .

You may well ask: "Why direct action? Why sit-ins, marches and so forth? Isn't negotiation a better path?" You are quite right in calling for negotiation. Indeed, this is the very purpose of direct action. Nonviolent direct action seeks to create such a crisis and foster such a tension that a community which has constantly refused to negotiate is forced to confront the issue. It seeks so to dramatize the issue that it can no longer be ignored. My citing the creation of tension as part of the work of the nonviolent-resister may sound rather shocking. But I must confess that I am not afraid of the word "tension." I have earnestly opposed violent tension, but there is a type of constructive, nonviolent tension which is necessary for growth. Just as Socrates felt that it was necessary to create a tension in the mind so that individuals could rise from the bondage of myths and half-truths to the unfettered realm of creative analysis and objective appraisal, so must we see the need for nonviolent gadflies to create the kind of tension in society that will help men rise from the dark depths of prejudice and racism to the majestic heights of understanding and brotherhood.

The purpose of our direct-action program is to create a situation so crisis-packed that it will inevitably open the door to negotiation. I therefore concur with you in your call for negotiation. Too long has our beloved Southland been bogged down in a tragic effort to live in monologue rather than dialogue.

One of the basic points in your statement is that the action that I and my associates have taken in Birmingham is untimely. Some have asked: "Why didn't you give the new city administration time to act?" The only answer that I can give to this query is that the new Birmingham administration must be prodded about as much as the outgoing one, before it will act. We are sadly mistaken if we feel that the election of Albert Boutwell as mayor will bring the millennium to Birmingham. While Mr. Boutwell is a much more gentle person than Mr. Connor, they are both segregationists, dedicated to maintenance of the status quo. I have hope that Mr. Boutwell will be reasonable enough to see the futility of massive resistance to desegregation. But he will not see this without pressure from devotees of civil rights. My friends, I must say to you that we have not made a single gain in civil rights without determined legal and nonviolent pressure. Lamentably, it is an historical fact that privileged groups seldom give up their privileges voluntarily. Individuals may see the moral light and voluntarily give up their unjust posture; but as Reinhold Niebuhr has reminded us, groups tend to be more immoral than individuals.

We know through painful experience that freedom is never voluntarily given by the oppressor; it must be demanded by the oppressed. Frankly, I have yet to engage in a direct-action campaign that was "well timed" in the view of those who have not suffered unduly from the disease of segregation. For years I have heard the word "Wait!" It rings in the ear of every Negro with piercing familiarity. This "Wait" has almost always meant "Never." We must come to see, with one of our distinguished jurists, that "justice too long delayed is justice denied."

We have waited for more than 340 years for our constitutional and God-given rights. The nations of Asia and Africa are moving with jetlike speed toward gaining political independence, but we still creep at horse-and-buggy pace toward gaining a cup of coffee at a lunch counter. Perhaps it is easy for those who have never felt the stinging darts of segregation to say, "Wait." But when you have seen vicious mobs lynch your mothers and fathers at will and drown your sisters and brothers at whim; when you have seen hate-filled policemen curse, kick and even kill your black brothers and sisters; when you see the vast majority of your twenty million Negro brothers smothering in an airtight cage of poverty in the midst of an affluent society; when you suddenly find your tongue twisted and your speech stammering as you seek to explain to your six-year-old daughter why she can't go to the public amusement park that has just been advertised on television, and see tears welling up in her eyes when she is told that Funtown is closed to colored children, and see ominous clouds of inferiority beginning to form in her little mental sky, and see her beginning to distort her personality by developing an unconscious bitterness toward white people; when you have to concoct an answer for a five-year-old son who is asking: "Daddy, why do white people treat colored people so mean?"; when you take a cross-country drive and find it necessary to sleep night after night in the uncomfortable corners of your automobile because no motel will accept you; when you are humiliated day in and day out by nagging signs reading "white" and "colored"; when your first name becomes "nigger," your middle name becomes "boy" (however old you are) and your last name becomes "John," and your wife and mother are never given the respected title "Mrs."; when you are harried by day and haunted by night by the fact that you are a Negro, living constantly at tiptoe stance, never quite knowing what to expect next, and are plagued with inner fears and outer resentments; when you are forever fighting a degenerating sense of "nobodiness"—then you will understand why we find it difficult to wait. There comes a time when the cup of endurance runs over, and men are no longer willing to be plunged into the abyss of despair. I hope, sirs, you can understand our legitimate and unavoidable impatience.

You express a great deal of anxiety over our willingness to break laws. This is certainly a legitimate concern. Since we so diligently urge people to obey the Supreme Court's decision of 1954 outlawing segregation in the public schools, at first glance it may seem rather paradoxical for us consciously to break laws. One may well ask: "How can you advocate breaking some laws and obeying others?" The answer lies in the fact that there are two types of laws: just and unjust. I would be the first to advocate obeying just laws. One has not only a legal but a moral responsibility to obey just laws. Conversely, one has a moral responsibility to disobey unjust laws. I would agree with St. Augustine that "an unjust law is no law at all."

Now, what is the difference between the two? How does one determine whether a law is just or unjust? A just law is a man-made code that squares with the moral law or the law of God. An unjust law is a code that is out of harmony with the moral law. To put it in the terms of St. Thomas Aquinas: An unjust law is a human law that is not rooted in eternal law and natural law. Any law that uplifts human personality is just. Any law that degrades human personality is unjust. All segregation statutes are unjust because segregation distorts the soul and damages the personality. It gives the segregator a false sense of superiority and the segregated a false sense of inferiority. Segregation, to use the terminology of the Jewish philosopher, Martin Buber, substitutes an "I-it" relationship for an "I-thou" relationship and ends up relegating persons to the status of things. Hence segregation is not only politically, economically and sociologically unsound, it is morally wrong and sinful. Paul Tillich has said that sin is separtion. Is not segregation an existential expression of man's tragic separation, his awful estrangement, his terrible sinfulness? Thus it is that I can urge men to obey the 1954 decision of the Supreme Court, for it is morally right; and I can urge them to disobey segregation ordinances, for they are morally wrong. . . .

I hope you are able to see the distinction I am trying to point out. In no sense do I advocate evading or defying the law, as would the rabid segregationist. That would lead to anarchy. One who breaks an unjust law must do so openly, lovingly, and with a willingness to accept the penalty. I submit that an individual who breaks a law that conscience tells him is unjust, and who willingly accepts the penalty of imprisonment in order to arouse the conscience of the community over its injustice, is in reality expressing the highest respect for law.

Of course, there is nothing new about this kind of civil disobedience. It was evidenced sublimely in the refusal of Shadrach, Meshach and Abednego to obey the laws of Nebuchadnezzar, on the ground that a higher moral law was at stake. It was practiced superbly by the early Christians, who were willing to face hungry lions and the excruciating pain of chopping blocks rather than submit to certain unjust laws of the Roman Empire. To a degree, academic freedom is a reality today because Socrates practiced civil disobedience.

We should never forget that everything Adolf Hitler did in Germany was "legal" and everything the Hungarian freedom fighters did in Hungary was "illegal." It was "illegal" to aid and comfort a Jew in Hitler's Germany. Even so, I am sure that, had I lived in Germany at the time, I would have aided and comforted my Jewish brothers. If today I lived in a Communist country where certain principles dear to the Christian faith are suppressed, I would openly advocate disobeying that country's antireligious laws.

I must make two honest confessions to you, my Christian and Jewish brothers. First, I must confess that over the past few years I have been gravely disappointed with the white moderate. I have almost reached the regrettable conclusion that the Negro's great stumbling block in his stride toward freedom is not the White Citizen's Council or the Ku Klux Klanner, but the white moderate who is more devoted to "order" than to justice; who prefers a negative peace which is the absence of tension to a positive peace which is the presence of justice; who constantly says: "I agree with you in the goal you seek, but I cannot agree with your methods of direct action"; who paternalistically believes he can set the timetable for another man's freedom; who lives by a mythical concept of time and who constantly advises the Negro to wait for a "more convenient season." Shallow understanding from people of good will is more frustrating than absolute misunderstanding from people of ill will. Lukewarm acceptance is much more bewildering than outright rejection.

I had hoped that the white moderate world would understand that law and order exist for the purpose of establishing justice and that when they fail in this purpose they become the dangerously structured dams that block the flow of social progress. I had hoped that the white moderate would understand that the present tension in the South is a necessary phase of the transition from an obnoxious negative peace, in which the Negro passively accepted his unjust plight, to a substantive and positive peace, in which all men will respect the dignity and worth of human personality. Actually, we who engage in nonviolent direct action are not the creators of tension. We merely bring to the surface the hidden tension that is already alive. We bring it out in the open, where it can be seen and dealt with. Like a boil that can never be cured so long as it is covered up but must be opened with all its ugliness to the natural medicines of air and light, injustice must be exposed, with all the tension its exposure creates, to the light of human conscience and the air of national opinion before it can be cured.

In your statement you assert that our actions, even though peaceful, must be condemned because they precipitate violence. But is this a logical assertion? Isn't this like condemning a robbed man because his possession of money precipitated the evil act of robbery? Isn't this like condemning Socrates because his unswerving commitment to truth and his philosophical inquiries precipated the act by the misguided populace in which they made him drink hemlock? Isn't this like condemning Jesus because his unique God-consciousness and never-ceasing devotion to God's will precipitated the evil act of crucifixion? We must come to see that, as the federal courts have consistently affirmed, it is wrong to urge an individual to cease his efforts to gain his basic constitutional rights because the quest may precipitate violence. Society must protect the robbed and punish the robber.

I had also hoped that the white moderate would reject the myth concerning time in relation to the struggle for freedom. I have received a letter from a white brother in Texas. He writes: "All Christians know that the colored people will receive equal rights eventually, but it is possible that you are in too great a religious hurry. It has taken Christianity almost two thousand years to accomplish what it has. The teachings of Christ take time to come to earth." Such an attitude stems from a tragic misconception of time, from the strangely irrational notion that there is something in the very flow of time that will inevitably cure all ills. Actually, time itself is neutral; it can be used either destructively or constructively. More and more I feel that the people of ill will have used time much more effectively than have the people of good will. We will have to repent in this generation not merely for the hateful words and actions of the bad people but for the appalling silence of the good people. Human progress never rolls in on wheels of inevitability; it comes through the tireless efforts of men willing to be co-workers with God, and without this hard work, time itself becames an ally of the forces of social stagnation. We must use time creatively, in the knowledge that the time is always ripe to do right. Now is the time to make real the promise of democracy and transform our pending national elegy into a creative psalm of brotherhood. Now is the time to lift our national policy from the quicksand of racial injustice to the solid rock of human dignity.

You speak of our activity in Birmingham as extreme. At first I was rather disappointed that fellow clergymen would see my non-violent efforts as those of an extremist. I began thinking about the fact that I stand in the middle of two opposing forces in the Negro community. One is a force of complacency, made up in part of Negroes who, as a result of long years of oppression, are so drained of self-respect and a sense of "somebodiness" that they have adjusted to segregation; and in part of a few middle-class Negroes who, because of a degree of academic and economic security and because in some ways they profit by segregation, have become insensitive to the problems of the masses. The other force is one of bitterness and hatred, and it comes perilously close to advocating violence. It is expressed in the various black nationalist groups that are springing up across the nation, the largest and best-known being Elijah Muhammad's Muslim movement. Nourished by the Negro's frustration over the continued existence of racial discrimination, this movement is made up of people who have lost faith in America, who have absolutely repudiated Christianity, and who have concluded that the white man is an incorrigible "devil."

I have tried to stand between these two forces, saying that we need emulate neither the "do-nothingism" of the complacent nor the hatred and despair of the black nationalist. For there is the more excellent way of love and nonviolent protest. I am grateful to God that, through the influence of the Negro church, the way of nonviolence became an integral part of our struggle.

If this philosophy had not emerged, by now many streets of the South would, I am convinced, be flowing with blood. And I am further convinced that if our white brothers dismiss as "rabble-rousers" and "outside agitators" those of us who employ nonviolent direct action, and if they refuse to support our nonviolent efforts, millions of Negroes will, out of frustration and despair, seek solace and security in black-nationalist ideologies—a development that would inevitably lead to a frightening racial nightmare.

Oppressed people cannot remain oppressed forever. The yearning for freedom eventually manifests itself, and that is what has happened to the American Negro. Something within has reminded him of his birthright of freedom, and something without has reminded him that it can be gained. Consciously or unconsciously, he has been caught up by the Zeitgeist, and with his black brothers of Africa and his brown and yellow brothers of Asia, South America and the Carribbean, the United States Negro is moving with a sense of great urgency toward the promised land of racial justice. If one recognizes this vital urge that has engulfed the Negro community, one should readily understand why public demonstrations are taking place. The Negro has many pent-up resentments and latent frustrations, and he must release them. So let him march; let him make prayer pilgrimages to the city hall; let him go on freedom rides—and try to understand why he must do so. If his repressed emotions are not released in nonviolent ways, they will seek expression through violence; this is not a threat but a fact of history. So I have not said to my people: "Get rid of your discontent." Rather, I have tried to say that this normal and healthy discontent can be channeled into the creative outlet of nonviolent direct action. And now this approach is being termed extremist.

Yours for the cause of Peace and Brotherhood,
Martin Luther King, Jr.

The next selection includes excerpts from a variety of anonymous individuals who express the bitterness of their lot as black people.

If a man qualifies, it should be first come, first serve, You understand what I mean?[5] Regardless of whether we're black or white, we all have families! It should be first come, first serve. But that's not how they do you! If you're black, you're automatically turned down on a lot of jobs. They'll take your application, but no sooner than you walk out of the office, or wherever it is, they take the application and put it in the wastebasket, and tell you they'll let you know in a couple of weeks.

—Man, age about 24

No one with a mop can expect respect from a banker, or an attorney, or men who create jobs, and all you have is a mop. Are you crazy? Whoever heard of integration between a mop and a banker?

—Man, age about 38

[5] From pp. 1–4, 6, 7 in *Dark Ghetto* by Kenneth B. Clark. Copyright © 1965 by Kenneth B. Clark. By permission of Harper & Row, Publishers, Inc.

The way the Man has us, he has us wanting to kill one another. Dog eat dog, amongst us! He has us, like we're so hungry up here, he has us up so tight! Like his rent is due, my rent is due. It's Friday. The Man wants sixty-five dollars. If you are three days over, or don't have the money; like that, he wants to give you a dispossess! Take you to court! The courts won't go along with you, they say get the money and pay the Man, but they don't say how to get it. Now, if you use illegal means to obey his ruling to try to get it—which he's not going to let you do—if you use illegal means to pay your bills according to his ruling—he will put you in jail.

—Man, age 31

If you could get onto the ninth floor of the Tombs, you would see for yourself. They are lying there like dogs, vomiting and what not, over one another. It is awful. It smells like a pigpen up there. If you look, you'll see nothing but Spanish. And the black man. You'll seldom see a white man. When you do, he is from a very poor group. They are 20 years old, looking like they were 40.

—Drug addict, male, age about 37

I want to go to the veins.
You want to do what?
I want to go to the veins.
You want to go to the veins; you mean you want to get high?
Yeah.
Why do you want to get high, man?
To make me think.
You can't think without getting high?
No.
Discrimination is even in the school I attend right now. I know my teacher is very prejudiced because I have certain questions that have to be answered for my knowledge, but he will never answer. He would always call on a little white boy to give the answer. I told him one night, to his face, that if he didn't want to answer my questions just tell me and I would leave. There are always other teachers. He didn't say anything. He just looked at me and figured I was going to—so he said, "Well, maybe next time." There is no next time—this is the time and I'm not taking second best from any white man.

—Boy, age 17

The conditions here are the way they are because of white domination of this community, and when that changes, as is being attempted here, by these [Black] Nationalists, or by any other nationalist groups, or by the Muslims; when they can unite and change these conditions, change the white domination for Black domination, the conditions will change.

—Man, age 28

Why in the hell—now this is more or less a colored neighbor-hood—why do we have so many white cops? As if we got to have somebody white standing over us. Not that I am prejudiced or any-thing, but I can't understand why we have to have so many white cops! Now if I go to a white neighborhood, I'm not going to see a lot of colored cops in no white neighborhood, standing guard over the white people. I'm not going to see that; and I know it, and I get sick and tired of seeing so many white cops, standing around.

—Woman, age 38

I don't see why we've got to always look up to the white man's life. That's what we've been exposed to, you know. Be like the white man. I think we have to have criteria of our own. They had "Amos and Andy" on radio, they were done by white men. You hear the fellows saying, "Oh, I'm going to get me a white broad." We should form our own criteria. We should try and have some more people like Martin Luther King, like James Baldwin. We can send some draftsmen to school, some engineers; people can come back and build a city for Negroes to live in, or you know, not just for Negroes but for Negroes and anyone else who wants to live there. Why do we always have to get up—come up to the white man's level? We struggle like the devil to get up there, and we hardly ever do it. Why can't we form our own level?

—Girl, age 15

The main thing is to know just where he comes from, knowing about his race. The main thing. He will then disregard every time he turns on the television that he sees a white face. That won't mean anything to him; it will be just another program because he will know that the conditions of the way of this world are based on only the white man's psychology, that makes these things. It won't be because this man is better fitted than he is on the television; it is because he dominates, he capitalizes, he corrupts.

—Man, age 35

First stop wearing the white man's clothes. Dress in your ancestral clothes. Learn your history and your heritage. This is part of my culture and I'm proud. Wear your clothes! Put on your abdaba, your dashiki and your fella. You can do it.

—Woman, age about 45

One of the most controversial advocates of Black Power in recent years has been Stokely Carmichael. An exponent of the need for black people to know and to identify with their heritage, he sees this as akin to the route traveled by each new ethnic group as it sought social and political integration into American society. Carmichael, in "Toward Black Liberation," does not apologize for the strident cry for power, but insists that it is something that must be granted.

One of the most pointed illustrations of the need for Black Power, as a positive and redemptive force in a society degenerating into a form of totalitarianism, is to be made by examining the history of distortion that the concept has received in national media of publicity.[6] In this "debate," as in everything else that affects our lives, Negroes are dependent on, and at the discretion of, forces and institutions within the white society which have little interest in repre-

[6] Reprinted from Stokely Carmichael, "Toward Black Liberation," *The Massachusetts Review* 7, © 1966 by The Massachusetts Review, Inc. Pp. 639–51.

senting us honestly. Our experience with the national press has been that where they have managed to escape a meretricious special interest in "Git Whitey" sensationalism and race-mongering, individual reporters and commentators have been conditioned by the enveloping racism of the society to the point where they are incapable even of objective observation and reporting of racial incidents, much less the analysis of ideas. But this limitation of vision and perceptions is an inevitable consequence of the dictatorship of definition, interpretation and consciousness, along with the censorship of history that the society has inflicted upon the Negro—and itself.

Our concern for black power addresses itself directly to this problem, the necessity to reclaim our history and our identity from the cultural terrorism and depredation of self-justifying white guilt.

To do this we shall have to struggle for the right to create our own terms through which to define ourselves and our relationship to the society, and to have these terms recognized. This is the first necessity of a free people, and the first right that any oppressor must suspend. The white fathers of American racism knew this—instinctively it seems—as is indicated by the continuous record of the distortion and omission in their dealings with the red and black men. In the same way that southern apologists for the "Jim Crow" society have so obscured, muddied and misrepresented the record of the Reconstruction period, until it is almost impossible to tell what really happened, their contemporary counterparts are busy doing the same thing with the recent history of the civil rights movement.

In 1964, for example, the National Democratic Party, led by L. B. Johnson and Hubert H. Humphrey, cynically undermined the efforts of Mississippi's black population to achieve some degree of political representation. Yet, whenever the events of that convention are recalled by the press, one sees only that version fabricated by the press agents of the Democratic Party. A year later, the House of Representatives, in an even more vulgar display of political racism, made a mockery of the political rights of Mississippi's Negroes when it failed to unseat the Mississippi Delegation to the House which had been elected through a process which methodically and systematically excluded over 450,000 voting age Negroes, almost one-half of the total electorate of the state. Whenever this event is mentioned in print it is in terms that leave one with the rather curious impression that somehow the oppressed Negro people of Mississippi are at fault for confronting the Congress with a situation in which they had no alternative but to endorse Mississippi's racist political practices.

I mention these two examples because, having been directly involved in them, I can see very clearly the discrepancies between what happened, and the versions that are finding their way into general acceptance as a kind of popular mythology. Thus the victimization of the Negro takes place in two phases: first it occurs in fact and deed, then—and this is equally sinister—in the official recording of those facts.

The "Black Power" program and concept that is being articulated by SNCC, CORE, and a host of community organizations in the ghettoes of the North and South has not escaped that process.

The white press has been busy articulating their own analyses, their own interpretations, and criticisms of their own creations. For example, while the press had given wide and sensational dissemination to attacks made by figures in the civil rights movement—foremost among which are Roy Wilkins of the NAACP and Whitney Young of the Urban League—and to the hysterical ranting about black racism made by the political chameleon that now serves as Vice-President, it has generally failed to give accounts of the reasonable and productive dialogue which is taking place in the Negro community, and in certain important areas in the white religious and intellectual community. A national committee of influential Negro churchmen affiliated with the National Council of Churches, despite their obvious respectability and responsibility, had to resort to a paid advertisement to articulate their position, while anyone shouting the hysterical yappings of "Black Racism" got ample space. Thus the American people have gotten at best a superficial and misleading account of the very terms and tenor of this debate. I wish to quote briefly from the statement by the national committee of churchmen which I suspect that the majority of Americans will not have seen. This statement appeared in *The New York Times* of July 31, 1966.

> We an informal group of Negro Churchmen in America are deeply disturbed about the crisis brought upon our country by historic distortions of important human realities in the controversy about "black power."[7] What we see shining through the variety of rhetoric is not anything new but the same old problem of power and race which has faced our beloved country since 1619.
>
> . . . The conscience of black men is corrupted because, having no power to implement the demands of conscience, the concern for justice in the absence of justice becomes a chaotic self-surrender. Powerlessness breeds a race of beggars. We are faced now with a situation where powerless conscience meets conscience-less power, threatening the very foundations of our Nation.
>
> . . . We deplore the overt violence of riots, but we feel it is more important to focus on the real sources of these eruptions. These sources may be abetted inside the Ghetto, but their basic cause lies in the silent and covert violence which white middleclass America inflicts upon the victims of the inner city.
>
> . . . In short; the failure of American leaders to use American power to create equal opportunity in life as well as law, this is the real problem and not the anguished cry for black power.
>
> . . . Without the capacity to participate with power, i.e., to have some organized political and economic strength to really influence people with whom one interacts—integration is not meaningful.
>
> . . . America has asked its Negro citizens to fight for opportunity as individuals, whereas at certain points in our history what we have needed most has been opportunity for the whole group, not just for selected and approved Negroes.

[7] © 1966 by The New York Times Company. Reprinted by permission.

. . . We must not apologize for the existence of this form of group power, for we have been oppressed as a group and not as individuals. We will not find our way out of that oppression until both we and America accept the need for Negro Americans, as well as for Jews, Italians, Poles, and white Anglo-Saxon Protestants, among others to have and to wield group power.

Traditionally, for each new ethnic group, the route to social and political integration into America's pluralistic society has been through the organization of their own institutions with which to represent their communal needs within the larger society. This is simply stating what the advocates of Black Power are saying. The strident outcry, particularly from the liberal community, that has been evoked by this proposal can only be understood by examining the historic relationship between Negro and white power in this country.

Negroes are defined by two forces, their blackness and their powerlessness. There have been traditionally two communities in America: the white community, which controlled and defined the forms that all institutions within the society would take; and the Negro community, which has been excluded from participation in the power decisions that shaped the society, and has traditionally been dependent upon, and subservient to, the white community.

This has not been accidental. The history of every institution of this society indicates that a major concern in the ordering and structuring of the society has been the maintaining of the Negro community in its condition of dependence and oppression. This has not been on the level of individual acts of discrimination between individual whites against individual Negroes, but as total acts by the white community against the Negro community. This fact cannot be too strongly emphasized—that racist assumptions of white superiority have been so deeply ingrained in the structure of the society that it infuses its entire functioning, and is so much a part of the national subconscious that it is taken for granted and is frequently not even recognized.

Let me give an example of the difference between individual racism and institutionalized racism, and the society's response to both. When unidentified white terrorists bomb a Negro church and kill five children, that is an act of individual racism, widely deplored by most segments of the society. But when in that same city, Birmingham, Alabama, not five but five hundred Negro babies die each year because of a lack of proper food, shelter and medical facilities, and thousands more are destroyed and maimed physically, emotionally and intellectually because of conditions of poverty and deprivation in the ghetto, that is a function of institutionalized racism. But the society either pretends it doesn't know of this situation, or is incapable of doing anything meaningful about it. And this resistance to doing anything meaningful about conditions in that ghetto comes from the fact that the ghetto is itself a product of a combination of forces and special interests in the white community, and the groups that have access to the resources and power to change that situation benefit, politically and economically, from the existence of that ghetto.

It is more than a figure of speech to say that the Negro community in America is the victim of white imperialism and colonial exploitation. This is, in practical economic and political terms, true. There are nearly twenty-three million black people comprising 11.2 per cent of this nation. They, for the most part, live in well-defined areas of the country—in the shantytowns and rural black-belt areas of the South, and increasingly in the slums of Northern and Western industrial cities. If one goes into any Negro community, whether it be in Jackson, Mississippi, Cambridge, Maryland, or Harlem, New York, one will find the same combination of political, economic and social forces is at work. The people in the Negro community do not control the resources of that community; its political decisions, its law enforcement, its housing standards, and even the physical ownership of the land, houses and stores lie outside that community.

It is white power that makes the laws, and it is violent white power in the form of armed white cops that enforces those laws with guns and nightsticks. The vast majority of Negroes in this country live in these captive communities and must endure these conditions of oppression because, and only because, they are black and powerless. I do not suppose that at any point the men who control the power and resources of this country ever sat down and designed these black enclaves, and formally articulated the terms of their colonial and dependent status, as was done, for example, by the apartheid government of South Africa. Yet, one cannot distinguish between one ghetto and another. As one moves from city to city, it is as though some malignant racist planning-unit had done precisely this—designed each one from the same master blueprint. And indeed, if the ghetto had been formally and deliberately planned instead of growing spontaneously and inevitably from the fascist function of the various institutions that combine to make the society, it would be somehow less frightening. The situation would be less frightening because, if these ghettoes were the result of design and conspiracy, one could understand their similarity as being artificial and consciously imposed, rather than the result of identical patterns of white racism which repeat themselves in cities as far apart as Boston and Birmingham. Without bothering to list the historic factors which contribute to this pattern—economic exploitation, political impotence, discrimination in employment and education—one can see that to correct this pattern will require far-reaching changes in the basic power-relationships and the ingrained social patterns within the society. The question is, of course, what kinds of changes are necessary, and how is it possible to bring them about?

In recent years, the answer to these questions which has been given by most articulate groups of Negroes and their white allies— the "liberals" of all stripes—has been in terms of something called "integration." According to the advocates of integration, social justice will be accomplished by "integrating the Negro into the mainstream institutions of the society from which he has been traditionally excluded." It is very significant that each time I have heard this formulation it has been in terms of "the Negro," the individual Negro, rather than in terms of the community.

This concept of integration had to be based on the assumption that there was nothing of value in the Negro community and that little of value could be created among Negroes, so the thing to do was to siphon off the "acceptable" Negroes into the surrounding middle-class white community. Thus the goal of the movement for integration was simply to loosen up the restrictions barring the entry of Negroes into the white community. Goals around which the struggle took place, such as public accommodation, open housing, job opportunity on the executive level (which is easier to deal with than the problem of semi-skilled and blue-collar jobs which involve more far-reaching economic adjustments), are quite simply middle-class goals, articulated by a tiny group of Negroes who had middle-class aspirations. It is true that the student demonstrations in the South during the early Sixties, out of which SNCC came, had a similar orientation. But while it is hardly a concern of a black sharecropper, dishwasher, or welfare recipient whether a certain fifteen-dollar-a-day motel offers accommodations to Negroes, the overt symbols of white superiority and the imposed limitations on the Negro community had to be destroyed. Now, black people must look beyond these goals, to the issue of collective power.

The violent, enigmatic and brilliant figure of Malcolm X occupies a special niche in the recent history of Afro-America. A self-educated man, he experienced a religious conversion to the Black Muslim faith which was later followed by a break with that group, although he remained a Muslim. In the extract below he exhorts his fellow blacks to take on a unified nationalist approach to their problems. He emphasizes the concept that blacks were Africans in America, not Americans, and that in that respect their experience was basically different from that of other ethnic groups.

Mr. Moderator, Brother Lomax, brothers and sisters, friends and enemies:[8]

I just can't believe everyone in here is a friend and I don't want to leave anybody out. The question tonight, as I understand it, is "The Negro Revolt, and Where Do We Go From Here?" or "What Next?" In my little humble way of understanding it, it points toward either the ballot or the bullet.

Before we try and explain what is meant by the ballot or the bullet, I would like to clarify something concerning myself. I'm still a Muslim, my religion is still Islam. That's my personal belief. Just as Adam Clayton Powell is a Christian minister who heads the Abyssinian Baptist Church in New York, but at the same time takes part in the political struggles to try and bring about rights to the black people in this country; and Dr. Martin Luther King is a Christian minister down in Atlanta, Georgia, who heads another organization fighting for the civil rights of black people in this country, and Rev. Galamison, I guess you've heard of him, is another Christian minister in New York who has been deeply involved in the school boycotts to eliminate segregated education; well, I myself am a minister, not a Christian minister, but a Muslim minister; and I believe in action on all fronts by whatever means necessary.

Although I'm still a Muslim, I'm not here tonight to discuss my religion. I'm not here to try and change your religion. I'm not here to argue or discuss anything that we differ about, because it's time for us to submerge our differences and realize that it is best for us to first see that we have the same problem, a common problem— a problem that will make you catch hell whether you're a Baptist, or a Methodist, or a Muslim, or a nationalist. Whether you're educated or illiterate, whether you live on the boulevard or in the alley, you're going to catch hell just like I am. We're all in the same boat and we all are going to catch the same hell from the same man. He just happens to be a white man. All of us have suffered here, in this country, political oppression at the hands of the white man, economic exploitation at the hands of the white man, and social degradation at the hands of the white man.

Now in speaking like this, it doesn't mean that we're anti-white, but it does mean we're anti-exploitation, we're anti-degradation, we're anti-oppression. And if the white man doesn't want us to be anti-him, let him stop oppressing and exploiting and degrading us. Whether we are Christians or Muslims or nationalists or agnostics or atheists, we must first learn to forget our differences. If we have differences, let us differ in the closet; when we come out in front, let us not have anything to argue about until we get finished arguing with the man. If the late President Kennedy could get together with Khrushchev and exchange some wheat, we certainly have more in common with each other than Kennedy and Khrushchev had with each other.

If we don't do something real soon, I think you'll have to agree that we're going to be forced either to use the ballot or the bullet. It's one or the other in 1964. It isn't that time is running out—time has run out! 1964 threatens to be the most explosive year America has ever witnessed. The most explosive year. Why? It's also a political year. It's the year when all of the white politicians will be back in the so-called Negro community jiving you and me for some votes. The year when all of the white political crooks will be right back in your and my community with their false promises, building up our hopes for a letdown, with their trickery and their treachery, with their false promises which they don't intend to keep. As they nourish these dissatisfactions, it can only lead to one thing, an explosion; and now we have the type of black man on the scene in America today—I'm sorry, Brother Lomax—who just doesn't intend to turn the other cheek any longer.

Don't let anybody tell you anything about the odds are against you. If they draft you, they send you to Korea and make you face 800 million Chinese. If you can be brave over there, you can be brave right here. These odds aren't as great as those odds. And if you fight here, you will at least know what you're fighting for.

I'm not a politician, not even a student of politics; in fact, I'm not a student of much of anything. I'm not a Democrat, I'm not a Republican, and I don't even consider myself an American. If you and I were Americans, there'd be no problem. Those Hunkies that just got off the boat, they're already Americans; Polacks are already

Americans; the Italian refugees are already Americans. Everything that came out of Europe, every blue-eyed thing, is already an American. And as long as you and I have been over here, we aren't Americans yet.

Well, I am one who doesn't believe in deluding myself. I'm not going to sit at your table and watch you eat, with nothing on my plate, and call myself a diner. Sitting at the table doesn't make you a diner, unless you eat some of what's on that plate. Being here in America doesn't make you an American. Why, if birth made you American, you wouldn't need any legislation, you wouldn't need any amendments to the Constitution, you wouldn't be faced with civil-rights filibustering in Washington, D.C., right now. They don't have to pass civil-rights legislation to make a Polack an American.

No, I'm not an American. I'm one of the 22 million black people who are the victims of Americanism. One of the 22 million black people who are the victims of democracy, nothing but disguised hypocrisy. So, I'm not standing here speaking to you as an American, or a patriot, or a flag-saluter, or a flag-waver—no, not I. I'm speaking as a victim of this American system. And I see America through the eyes of the victim. I don't see any American dream; I see an American nightmare.

These 22 million victims are waking up. Their eyes are coming open. They're beginning to see what they used to only look at. They're becoming politically mature. They are realizing that there are new political trends from coast to coast. As they see these new political trends, it's possible for them to see that every time there's an election the races are so close that they have to have a recount. They had to recount in Massachusetts to see who was going to be governor, it was so close. It was the same way in Rhode Island, in Minnesota, and in many other parts of the country. And the same with Kennedy and Nixon when they ran for president. It was so close they had to count all over again. Well, what does this mean? It means that when white people are evenly divided, and black people have a bloc of votes of their own, it is left up to them to determine who's going to sit in the White House and who's going to be in the dog house.

Much of recent literature about the black people's experience unsurprisingly revolves around the themes of racial discrimination and exploitation, and the consequent irreparable damage to their family life. While there is no gainsaying that this is a truism for many Afro-Americans, it is still, nevertheless, true that family life was a warm and rewarding experience for many other blacks. Commenting on the paucity of material on this aspect is the following article by Mary E. Mebane, "Daddy Wasn't a Numbers Runner."

ORANGEBURG, S.C.[9]—Daddy wasn't a numbers runner, Mama wasn't a loose woman, my two brothers were neither pickpockets nor pimps, and I have never seen heroin in my life.

[9] Reprinted from Mary E. Mebane, "Daddy Wasn't a Numbers Runner," *The New York Times,* 18 February 1971. © 1971 by the New York Times Company. Reprinted by permission.

When I read reviews of current fiction by and about black Americans, I wonder if I should turn in my membership card, or better still I wonder how I'll ever be able to become a member of the black community.

I mean where are my family, friends, schoolmates, teachers, the deacons, missionary sisters, usher board members, and choir that made up the world that I inhabited in rural Durham County, North Carolina, in the mid-twentieth century? Were they phantoms, fantasies, dreams that somebody dreamed?

Daddy, a tall bone in a dark Sunday suit, shiny with age, was a deacon in the Baptist church. Though he was a drinking man in his youth, by the time we children came along, he had quit and in the evening, after he quit plowing, he loved to pore over mathematics books.

Daddy loved to make things, and I can remember standing around him, a question mark on matchstick legs, while he made a pulpit for his church. He didn't want it simple and went to some trouble to put little decorative touches on it.

Daddy, a city boy, was a strikingly unsuccessful tobacco and cotton farmer, but we always had a big vegetable garden. He sometimes peddled vegetables through white neighborhoods in Durham and he took us children on the wagon with him—the greatest adventure in the world. Five miles on a wagon. You who haven't had it, eat your heart out.

Mama canned a lot. My job was to go to the fields and get corn and squash that were too hard, too ripe tomatoes, too large cucumbers, bring them to the house and cook them in a huge, iron pot for the hogs.

We had hogs, a mule, and a cow. Daddy would sometimes come in very mad when the cow had kicked over the bucket. My job was to churn the milk to make the butter. I stood forever and pounded the plunger up and down, but then the butter formed and Mama shaped it into a cake.

Mama wasn't a loose woman. She worked in a tobacco factory, leaving while I was still in bed and coming home late. She wore a blue uniform with matching blue cap and a white apron. Powder-like brown dust filled every wrinkle in her clothing.

But we met her in town on Fridays and went with her into a place with shiny pretty bottles and beautiful cans called a store. When I was in a play, she took me to Belk's basement and bought me cloth for a dress. Sunday she fried chicken early in the morning and in the afternoon she sat and talked with her friends. In the summer they sat on the lawn and fanned lazily with church fans. In the winter they sat in the gloomy front room near the fireplace.

Daddy made locust beer, Mama made blackberry wine and peach brandy, and every Christmas we had a black walnut cake made from the walnuts of a neighbor's tree. We children gathered scuppernongs, plums and the sweet persimmon.

On a bitter cold day, hogs would be killed and all of us would scrape the hair. Daddy had two nails on which he hung a rabbit to be skinned and a barrel in which he kept the possum for days before it was cooked.

My brothers never played hooky. What was there to do? Look at the trees? All they had waiting for them was a long row, a sweating mule, and a half gallon fruit jar of water at the end. No, they went to school, because that's where the other children were. The boys went down to the privies in the woods and discussed whatever it is that boys discuss and the girls sat on the rocks in a grove with lime-treated trees and rehearsed their feminine roles.

The principal sometimes gave bad boys a whipping with a strap and the girls sometimes got a lick in the hand with a ruler. To this day, no one seems to harbor any grudges against any teacher who punished them. Everybody was glad that it was the teacher, rather than their parents.

My classmates and I went to school, learned how to read, ate our biscuit sandwiches, the envied ones brought "light" bread and cold sweet potato lunches, popped the whip, and sang in "chapel" every day. We went to Sunday School on Sunday, staying once a month for preaching.

I never could bear to read Faulkner and other writers like him because I hated the image that he portrayed of blacks. But I could intellectualize him by saying that he didn't know any better. But how to explain . . . how to explain the images currently jumping out of the pages of fiction by blacks? Is this all there is? Where are we residents of Durham County? Rural, black farmers and factory workers, domestic workers, common laborers all. Don't our lives have meaning? Are we not worthy of being celebrated in song and story? Or should we turn to drugs and crime before we can exist in the pages of literature?

In recent years every medium of mass communication has thrown open its facilities to black people, and blacks have taken advantage of it. Much of what emanates from this seems to be from radical leaders with large followings and radical leaders who are speaking virtually only for themselves. Even though some conservative and middle-of-the-road blacks find little difficulty in being heard, there seems to be some question as to whether they receive "equal time" in recent collections of writings by contemporary black leaders.

Roy Wilkins is one of the most durable leaders of the oldest black civil rights organization, the N.A.A.C.P. He has called the nation's attention to its responsibilities to the country's black people, but he has also taken issue with a number of "black power" radicals. Thus he argues forcibly against a black separatist policy and comes out in favor of an integrationist approach, although he clearly disclaims any interest in assimilation.

Given the position of the Negro American population as a numerical minority of one-tenth and an economic, political and social minority of far less than one-tenth, the only tactical road for the black minority is integration into the general population.[10]

The word "integration" as used here is not employed as a synonym for "assimilation." The policy of integration does not mean,

[10] Reprinted by permission of *Ebony* Magazine from Roy Wilkins, "Integration," *Ebony*, August 1970. Copyright 1970 by Johnson Publishing Company, Inc.

as so many opponents seem to contend, a melting into other peoples, the loss of color, identity and the racial heritage that 350 years of life as Americans have built into the Negro population.

It is intended, generally, to accord with the definition in most dictionaries: "The making up of a whole by adding together or combining the separate parts or elements; a making whole or entire." Nothing in this or other definitions suggests assimilation. As a component, the race would be equal under the Constitution and the laws, with such equality woven into every fabric of American life. Thus far, equality has not been achieved and therein lies the disillusionment of the properly impatient young Negro Americans and of older ones as well. In their frustration they have sought other ways of winning self-esteem, dignity and accelerated—almost instant— progress as individuals and as a group.

Which way out for black Americans? Separatism—a complete severing of all ties to white people in the United States and to their often glaring hypocrisy on race? A separate state outside the U.S.? One within our borders? A withdrawal for a time, a re-grouping of forces, an inventory, a shoring up of spiritual and physical resources, a sort of partial and temporary self-segregation? Or integration— long, slow, difficult, beset by all the booby-traps of an imperfect democratic society as well as by stubborn racial prejudices expressed in a thousand ways?

Despite the clamor of a minority of the minority, despite penetration of its spokesmen and ideological followers into key spots in electronic communications, the daily press, the magazine and book-publishing industry, the arts and high school and college faculties, the overwhelming majority of the Negro American population, ranging as high as 95 per cent and as low only as 78 per cent, chose integration. The age groups include at least half of those "under 30" and in some sections of the country the percentage of these runs above 70.

Thus, while ways out are still being debated, the choice of the day is integration. This is so in the face of the almost daily examples of crass racial proscriptions—by individuals, by corporations and institutions and by government.

The anti-integrationists have forgotten that the siren song of separatism has fallen flat several times before in the history of American black-white relations. The first serious effort is now believed to have been made about 1714, less than 100 years after the 1619 landing of the first black slaves at Jamestown.

About 100 years elapsed before the advent of the best financed effort, the American Colonization Society, founded in 1816. In 50 years the society spent $2½ million and managed to send only 12,000 free Negroes to Africa (about half went because they had been freed from slavery on condition that they leave). Roughly, one and a half per cent of the free Negroes voluntarily emigrated at a period when the Negro future here was dark, indeed. An anti-colonization (anti-separatist) convention of free Negroes in 1831 declared:

"We do not believe that things will always continue the same. This is our home and this is our country."

The next great stirring of black nationalism was to occur in another hundred years with the advent of Marcus Garvey and his Universal Negro Improvement Association. Through Garvey's native intelligence, plus his showmanship (plumed, gold braided uniforms, titles and other unabashed apings of the British ruling clique), he recruited a large following. Garvey, of course, had an advantage which present-day separatists also enjoy: he was advocating something that many millions of white Americans wish in their secret (and not so secret) hearts could occur. Garvey, hopefully, was going to remove millions of blacks from their midst and with them all the headaches and moral ironies that stem from their presence.

But Garvey, like the black separatists and some of the black militants today, exemplified the racism that today's militants see behind every bush and in front of every comma. The Garvey creed was simply reverse racism. White was inferior and black superior. In his African church, God was black, as was the Virgin Mary, but Satan was white. The Garvey "black Christ" concept has been taken over, lock, stock and barrel, by some of today's Negro clergymen-entrepreneurs. Garveyism was rejected by Negro Americans.

In the 1930s the Communist Party brought brief life to the black separatist movement with its "self-determination for the black belt," but the party reversed this campaign with a change in the party line a few years later to that of the Popular Front. Still later the party was to switch policies literally overnight when Hitler attacked the Soviet Union. Negro Americans were told to forget "self-determination for the black belt" and to cease complaining about all aspects of Jim Crow.

The separatists today are lifting loud voices, but they are but a tiny minority in the black population. They have found, to no one's surprise, that they are not welcomed to Africa by black Africans. Dr. Robert E. Browne, an intellectual spokesman for separatists, puts it most delicately in this soft-sell language: ". . . we were no longer quite at ease there—we are left with only one place to make our home and that is the land to which we were brought in chains." The view is here underscored (not advanced, since perceptive Negro Americans steadfastly advanced the course more than 150 years ago) that integration into American life remains today the best way out of our situation.

The long struggle toward basic integration began when the illusion of the Reconstruction Era became apparent. It ended—theoretically—in 1954 with the Supreme Court's decision in *Brown v. Board of Education of Topeka, Kansas*. For the Brown decision ended an era in which the Negro population had been neither fish nor fowl. Despite the 14th Amendment, the Negro was only as much of a citizen of the United States as each individual state or court permitted. The *Brown* pronouncement, at long last, raised the umbrella of the U.S. Constitution over the black citizen. Although it dealt specifically with the cases of five segregated school systems, it had the effect of forbidding states and subdivisions thereof to differentiate between citizens on the basis of skin color.

Until *Brown*, Negro citizenship rights had no recognized, across-the-board protection in the Constitution. Since the Plessy case of 1896, the Negro American had set himself to the monumental task of winning the integration fight in the courts, in legislation and in the court of public opinion. The history of this struggle against an adamant system and against a public opinion that had been conditioned against black aspirations is an incredibly inspiring document. For sheer drama, for tenacity, for getting up off the floor to fight again, for undisputed testimony to the determination of a race, the period from the Civil War to the present day has no equal for heroism. Only the struggle of the slaves from 1619 to 1863 approaches it.

Negro American young people who yearn so much for heroes that they have gone to China, the French Caribbean islands, Cuba and Africa in search of images have overlooked the black American heroes and heroines who brought them to the places they now occupy. The rooms and tiny offices and literature of the young militants and revolutionaries boast the posters and the books of latter-day soldiers in the civil rights wars. Among those ignored are Harriet Tubman, a conductor on the Underground Railroad—a device that brought slaves from the Deep South to freedom in Canada. Have today's black militants ever walked a mile, to say nothing of 1,000 miles, dodging sheriffs with guns and dogs? Can a weak-hearted people walk from the Carolinas to Ontario?

Is it any less of an accomplishment to knock out, say, the White Primary laws, and enfranchise, overnight, 750,000 Negro Americans, than to shoot it out with a deputy sheriff?

Were the elections of Mayors Kenneth Gibson of Newark, Howard Lee of Chapel Hill, N. C., Richard Hatcher of Gary, Ind., Charles Evers of Fayette, Miss., and Carl Stokes of Cleveland, the result of confrontation? Were not voter registration, close study of the strategies of politics, adaptation to the realities in an urban situation all integral parts of the victories?

The nominations to the Supreme Court of Clement F. Haynsworth, Jr., of G. Harrold Carswell and, in 1930, of the late John J. Parker, were all defeated through organizations backed up with a voting public, through familiarity with the workings of the federal government and through meticulous and painstaking day-to-day lobbying with senators and with the voters back home.

Is it better to aid black contractors to bid on projects and help them to hire more black artisans than to promise them relief some day in a separate Soul state? The idea of challenging suburban zoning restrictions so that Negroes may follow the factory jobs in low income housing makes sense in the realities of the day.

All this and more can be acknowledged, even praised, and then dismissed as too little, too late and too slow. Yet such an appraisal and dismissal in effect chooses revolution as the way out. Revolution with its trappings of barricades, violent struggle with the minions of the Establishment and summary executions feeds the ego. But does a revolution bring real change or does it just switch ruling cliques?

For black Americans this is an important issue. They seek dignity and opportunity and an end to racial and religious discrimination. If their efforts which now seem to them rewarding should be tossed aside as insignificant, they will continue their struggle in whatever regime is set up. Integrationists believe that a joining together in full partnership with other Americans who seek change is the way to a new life.

Even the deception and hostility, the use of politics in public school desegregation have not induced them to alter their course. And they find themselves, in this topsy-turvy race relations era, fighting a two-front war. Out in front are the opponents, mostly white, who have defied the *Brown* decision in every conceivable manner since 1954 and those, mostly outside the South, who have given *Brown* lip service only. And for the first time in all civil rights history, there are black proponents of segregated schools in small but extremely vocal groups.

While there have been divisions in the black ranks on nearly all questions, the opposition to segregation has been muted. The Negro businessmen, protected by segregation, and some of the Negro teachers have soft-pedaled their obvious stakes in a segregated system. Even the new black caucuses in predominantly white denominations are seeking to keep their segregation-inspired black-jacking of funds within the church. Never shouters, all these factions are being smothered by the actions and pronouncements of black students on campuses across the nation.

The highly vocal minority of students startled the black majority and delighted the whites by openly demanding racial segregation. It also abruptly rejected any but the most minimal contacts with white people. It demanded black studies departments, more black faculty members and a change in college admissions policies and practices so that more Negro students could be enrolled.

They capped off these demands by insisting on all-black dormitories or sections of dormitories. To their demands for black studies, they added that all such courses must be headed by a black director and taught only by black teachers. They also demanded all-black centers on campuses. Some groups demanded that they approve all courses in black studies and all black faculty members, including, of course, all directors of black studies departments and campus black centers.

The reaction of universities and colleges has been mixed. None has denied the plea for more Negro history, enrollment and faculty. They are scrambling to get qualified black faculty members and have caused protests by predominantly Negro colleges for their raiding of these less-endowed institutions. Most colleges are not dodging the fact that they have been deficient, even though the posturing and the rhetoric of black student groups have often bordered on the absurd.

When a total black enrollment of 250 out of a student body of 41,000 can muster only 70 of their own at a rally, the claim of the militants that they represent the black students and their "demand" that certain steps be taken on a "non-negotiable" basis are patently without much substance. Their free-wheeling operation has given rise to rumors that they have intimidated the bulk of black students with threats of bodily harm.

The rest of the black students and the general black public are not likely to buy a return to 1920. The Negro citizens over 30 years of age know all about the cruelties and acute disabilities under racial segregation. They don't need the examples of Rhodesia and South Africa and their abhorrent racial policies. They have their green memories (and some lingering present-day examples) of what segregation means in schools, housing, employment, the administration of justice, public recreation, travel, public accommodation in theaters, restaurants, hotels and in voting and politics.

Their answer may not be a swift and unqualified "No," but it is definitely in the negative. They do not have before them now the utter hopelessness of the decades after 1896, when the U. S. Supreme Court fastened the iniquitous "separate-but-equal" albatross about their necks and threw them to the states' rights wolves. Moreover, the young black militants, who either declare openly for separatism or whose beliefs, when spelled out, lead inevitably to separatism, know little, apparently, about planning for 22 million people scattered into 50 states. This requires something more than a slogan or a press conference.

These 22 million are multiplying and are longer-lived. They are better educated and some are superbly so. They are acquiring skills in employment, in government and in the general business of living. With this steadily improving equipment, they are facing, eagerly and unafraid, the manifold problems of the rough world outside the enervating cocoon of racial segregation.

For arousing the black community from a dead-end apathy and for the infusion of pride and dignity, the militants rate the deep gratitude of Negro Americans. They have wit, ingenuity, talent, energy, skill and innovative abilities to spare. For the great leap forward of Negro Americans here in America, as an integral functioning part of the whole, Negro militants need all these abilities and skills. Their own people need these skills in order to build on a past of which no people need be ashamed. In the process they cannot help but engineer the changes in America that will redeem the nation's basic promise, made nearly 200 years ago, of individual liberty for all men, with achievement limited only by ability.

"We are left with only one place to make our home," wrote Dr. Browne. That is the place of Denmark Vesey, Frederick Douglass, John Brown and the millions who said, with the free men of 1831: "This is our home and this is our country."

Afro-Americans have generally adopted the culture of the white man's society, although some aspects of African civilization survive. Nevertheless, blacks have been compelled to maintain separate institutions within the black community. There is very little direct social contact between the blacks and the nonblacks. In the following selection, Alphonso Pinkney analyzes the question of black assimilation in American society.

The extent to which black Americans are assimilated into the larger society is the subject of considerable debate.[11] They were among the earliest arrivals to North America, but they were quickly stripped of their native African cultures. Their tribal organization, religion, family life, and language were systematically destroyed. It thus became necessary for them to adopt the patterns of life of the white Europeans with whom they were forced to live. The adoption of Western culture became a difficult task, for they were permitted to assimilate into the society only to the extent that their services could be utilized by their white rulers. In general, they were forced to live a dual existence: their lives had to be structured in terms of

[11] Reprinted from Alphonso Pinkney, *Black Americans*, © 1969, pp. 162–167. Reprinted by permission of Prentice-Hall, Inc., Englewood Cliffs, New Jersey.

the demands made on them by the larger society and in terms of the necessity to survive in a generally hostile environment. When formal slavery ended more than a century ago, it was replaced by a caste system which prevented substantial alteration of the dual environment within which black people lived. A rigid system of segregation and discrimination replaced the institution of slavery, and this system continues to preclude assimilation into the larger society.

Being in the society but not a part of it has fostered a conflict among black Americans. Some strive to identify with white middle-class values, and others reject all aspects of white culture. The former attitude sometimes leads to negative identification (self-hatred), while the latter frequently manifests itself in black nationalism. The majority of Negroes would no doubt welcome the chance to become assimilated into the larger society. To the extent that there are forces among Negroes resisting such an eventuality, these forces are a result of widespread rejection by white Americans. . . .

Cultural Assimilation

To what extent have black Americans adopted the cultural patterns of the larger society in which they find themselves? The systematic stripping of the slaves of their African cultures has been detailed previously. Debate persists, however, on the extent and nature of the survival of African cultures among black people in the United States. In the more than three and one-half centuries that black people have inhabited what is now the United States, they have adopted the culture of the larger society to the extent that it is difficult to detect any significant vestiges of their original cultures. In North America small numbers of slaves were scattered over a large area on numerous plantations and farms. Even when a sizable number of slaves were held by the same owner, they were likely to have been from a variety of cultures in Africa. Under such circumstances the retention of aspects of their original cultures was difficult. In addition, it was forbidden for them to speak their native languages, and their family patterns were systematically destroyed. Although it is still possible to detect survivals in religious life, Christianity made significant inroads among the slaves, and their religious practices developed along the lines of those of white Christians. Indeed, ". . . the religion of the slaves was, in essence, strikingly similar to that of the poor, illiterate white men of the antebellum South." In other aspects of culture as well, few survivals of African civilization remain.

There have been frequent attempts by some individual Negroes and organizations to re-emphasize aspects of traditional African cultures, but among the majority of Negroes these attempts have been unsuccessful. Historically the most successful of these movements was the Universal Negro Improvement Association, led by Marcus Garvey. The most recent is the Nation of Islam (popularly known as the Black Muslims), led by Elijah Muhammad. In urban areas throughout the United States Black Nationalist groups continue to search for aspects of their past that were destroyed by the institution of slavery.

According to Milton M. Gordon, the extent to which black people have adopted the cultural patterns of the host society varies by class. He sees the middle- and upper-class Negroes as being totally acculturated, while ". . . lower-class Negro life . . . is still at a considerable distance from the American cultural norm." A vast majority of black Americans are poor (lower class), and in some respects their cultural patterns deviate from those of the larger society. To a large extent, however, these differences are a function of class rather than race. Gordon's analysis posits "middle-class white Protestant Americans as constituting the 'core society.'" Clearly many lower-class Negroes deviate from the norms of this group, as do lower-class white Protestant Americans. In the sense that lower-class Negroes adhere to lower-class American culture patterns, they may be said to be acculturated. Poor Negroes in the rural South are not significantly different from their poor white counterparts in, for example, food habits or religious practices. They eat the less expensive foods and tend to be more emotional in their religious practices, but the same phenomena are true of poor rural white Southerners. Negroes in non-Southern urban areas may differ in these regards from poor whites in the same areas, but the differences are a function of their Southern, not their African, heritage.

Middle- and upper-class Negroes are hardly distinguishable from white Americans of comparable social class level in cultural patterns. There is even some evidence that they frequently over-conform to middle-class standards of behavior in religious observances, in dress, in sexual behavior, and in child-rearing practices. In virtually all aspects of life, then, Negroes have adopted the cultural patterns of the host society. When differences occur, they are more likely to be functions of their being victims of oppression than of their systematic retention of elements of the cultures which they left in Africa. Such differences are of American, not African, origin. The acculturation process is virtually complete for black Americans. Culturally, they are clearly products of life in the United States.

Structural Assimilation

Black Americans usually maintain their own separate institutions within the black community. Historically this situation has not been a result of voluntary isolation; rather, a caste system of segregation and discrimination against them has tended to preclude their large-scale entrance into cliques, social clubs, and other social organizations and activities along with white Americans on a primary-group level. However, with increasing racial pride among black people today, voluntary racial separation is not uncommon. In the "rank order of discriminations" against Negroes by white Southerners, as enumerated by Gunnar Myrdal, activities specifically concerned with personal relations, such as dancing, bathing, eating, and drinking together with Negroes, followed closely after intermarriage and interracial sexual relations as forbidden behavior. Such practices are more characteristic of the South than elsewhere, but, in general, they characterize the relations between black and white persons throughout the United States. The caste system, which separates Negroes and whites, dictates that members of these two social categories should not associate in any relationships which imply social equality. This ban generally extends to marriage, dancing, eating together, and social visiting.

The traditional pattern of relations between black and white Americans has been slightly altered in recent years, but, in general, the pattern of almost total isolation of the black community from the white community persists. As black people continue to settle in the central cities of the largest urban areas, the isolation is becoming more pronounced. Studies of black-white relations in the South show the pervasiveness of rigid segregation along racial lines insofar as the major social groups and institutions are concerned. The tradition in the South is deeply rooted in the mores, and social change in this regard is slow. Indeed, it is unlikely that any significant change will occur in the near future.

Outside the South the isolation of the black community is only slightly less pronounced than in the South. Most white Americans live their lives with only the slightest awareness of the lives of their black fellow citizens, except during periods of racial unrest. A vast majority of the Negroes who live outside the South live in urban areas, but those who live in small towns live isolated lives compared to their urban counterparts. Two studies illustrate the dearth of interracial association between blacks and whites in smaller Northern cities. In Elmira, New York, it is reported that the Negro community is so isolated that its inhabitants think of themselves not as citizens of Elmira but as citizens of the black community. Such references as "all over town" or "the prettiest girl in town" do not refer to Elmira but to the specific section in which the Negroes are concentrated. Given such conditions as these, it is clear that Negroes have not entered into social groups and activities with their white co-residents. Social contacts between the two groups are minimal.

In a small Connecticut town it is reported that, "while Negro-white neighborhood relations are friendly, they are characterized for the most part by lack of contact between the two races." The Negroes maintained their own church, and in public social activities sponsored by other churches, discrimination against Negroes was evident. There were few adult interracial social contacts. Only two of the many formal organizations, the Chamber of Commerce and the town band, had black members. On the adolescent level a similar pattern was discerned. Social contact between black and white persons was, in this case, limited to athletic and recreational activities. The school system was found to be the only institution in which black and white citizens participated with some degree of equality.

In large cities outside the South there is little social contact between blacks and whites. Black social life tends to be centered around their own social, civic, and religious organizations. Recently, however, middle- and upper-class Negroes have often participated freely with whites in social groups. Nevertheless, the vast majority of Negroes continue to have only superficial social contact with white persons. The maintenance of rigid residential segregation is a strong deterrent against the structural assimilation of Negroes into the life of the larger society.

Structural assimilation may be subdivided into primary and secondary assimilation. Those social institutions which are rooted in the black community (e.g., schools) are primary, and those either partially (e.g., schools) or totally (e.g., economic activities) located in the white community are secondary to the black community. When this dichotomy is made, it is clear that assimilation has progressed at a much more rapid pace in secondary institutions than in those which are primary. Inasmuch as primary institutions tend to be in the private sector of American life, and those which are secondary tend to be public, it appears that the interest of black people has been more in secondary assimilation than in primary assimilation.

KEY QUESTIONS

1. To what extent is the black man's ethnic experience similar or dissimilar to the experiences of the European immigrants?

2. Ralph Ellison's book, *The Invisible Man,* is one of the most significant in the understanding of race relations in the United States. Why did he use this title for his book?

3. Trace the impact that each of the following three men had on the recent rise of Afro-American rights: Martin Luther King, Jr., Stokely Carmichael, and Malcolm X. What has been the place of each in the development of the civil rights movement?

4. What does "Black Power" mean? Does it mean the same thing to the white man as it does for the black man?

5. Is there any evidence today that the black man has retained elements of African culture?

11

Immigration Policy and Ethnicity

The story of American immigration is unique and one of the most fascinating of all the sagas of this country's past. It is the story of one of modern history's greatest mass movements of population. The familiar epic is found in traditional texts in American history and society as they narrate the odyssey of one group of sojourners after another who came to this land, some of their own free will, others in bondage, some to escape religious, economic, or political persecution, and others to seek happiness. And yet there is a paradox in this picture of the United States as a country welcoming all, rich and poor, mighty and weak, black and white, Jew and gentile.

It is a picture best epitomized by the poem written by the Jewish immigrant, Emma Lazarus, and inscribed on the base of the Statue of Liberty, part of which reads: "Give me your tired, your poor, your huddled masses yearning to breathe free, The wretched refuse of your teeming shore. Send these, the homeless, tempest-tossed to me, I lift up my lamp beside the golden door." Thus, on the one hand, immigration truly has been America's *raison d'être*. It has been the most persistent and pervasive influence in her development. On the other hand, the history of immigration, both before and after the Civil War, has been marked by racism and discrimination. This has produced a picture that could very well have changed Lazarus' description to read "Give me your energetic and solvent, your educated and healthy, The cream of the crop of your teeming shore. Exclude the undesirable, the illiterate, the poor, the uneducated, the sick to whom is closed the golden door."

It is this divergence between romanticism and reality that pervades the succession of laws that established United States immigration policy, which will now be explored.

When President Lyndon B. Johnson signed the immigration bill of 1965, he stated, it "corrects a cruel and enduring wrong in the conduct of the American nation. . . . Yet the fact is that for over four decades the immigration policy of the United States has been twisted and distorted by the harsh injustice of the National Origins Quota System." This chapter will examine the ethnic concern of the generation that brought about the policies that were applicable in these decades alluded to by President Johnson. Particular attention will be placed on the quota system of the 1920's, the demand for total restriction, the more progressive legislation of 1965, and the reaction to these policies.

United States restrictive policies were fashioned out of a matrix of ethnocentrism, which encompasses the powerful human desire for acquiescence to one's own ways and the simultaneous fear that the indigenous population will be overwhelmed by hordes of inferior alien peoples. The need for uniformity was not in and of itself a new phenomenon. From the beginnings there were indications of its strength as a basic social force. This strength would exact a heavy price from the newcomers of the "New Immigration" period. Since a painless and a rapid transition from one culture to another is not common, the more the immigrant group differed from the old stock, the more it excited the wrath of the dominant group, and the more the dominant group demanded the annihilation of all that was peculiarly ethnic among the newcomers. This was what was referred to as the "Americanization" process, and because it did not seem to be progressing swiftly enough, the old immigrant stock sought refuge in restrictive immigration policies against the spectre of ethnic mongrelization.

The first general immigration law was passed in 1882. It established a head tax on immigrants, excluded convicts, lunatics, idiots, and others liable to become public charges. That same year also saw ethnic discrimination, as Chinese were excluded from lawful immigration to the United States. Likewise, the "Gentlemen's Agreement" of 1907 had the same effect on Japanese immigrants. Efforts to establish qualitative ethnic distinctions among European immigrants was attempted by means of literacy test legislation. The issue was, as Prescott F. Hall, a Boston Brahmin and guiding spirit of the Immigration Restriction League, put it, whether this country wanted "to be peopled by British, German, and Scandinavian stock, historically free, energetic, progressive, or by Slav, Latin and Asiatic races, historically down-trodden, atavistic and stagnant." Negative value judgments were at the core of the drive for restrictive legislation. Proponents of the literacy test were not immediately successful, as presidential vetoes stymied the drive during the years of and between the administrations of Cleveland and Wilson. Nevertheless, in 1917, Congress overrode Wilson's veto, and the literacy test became law.

The first selection in this chapter is an appeal for immigration restriction through literacy tests by Senator Henry Cabot Lodge. Lodge was joined by pressure groups from organized labor, racists, and superpatriots, who feared a radical ethnic impact on American society. In part, official substantiation for this prejudice came from the report of the Dillingham Commission in 1911, an extract of which is the second article in this chapter. This is followed by extracts from Oscar Handlin's criticism of the Dillingham Commission philosophy. The fourth extract is from a United States senator's defense of "New Immigration" and rebuke of the ethnocentrism of Americans. Other selections cover the negative impact that immigration policies and American attitudes had on various ethnic groups during the Depression, the relationship of immigration and national origins, and the changes brought by the 1965 immigration act.

One of the most vigorous voices urging immigration restrictions was that of Senator Henry Cabot Lodge, Sr., of Massachusetts. In the extract that follows, he suggests that because increasing immigration is deteriorating in quality and producing many serious domestic problems, illiterate immigrants should be barred. In 1917, after more than two decades of debate on the issue, the literacy test provision was enacted into law, although it did not significantly reduce immigration.

As it is thus apparent that immigration is increasing in quantity, the next point is to determine its quality.[1]

In the consular reports on "Emigration and Immigration," published by the State Department in 1887, when Mr. Bayard was Secretary, a table is given which classifies the immigration into the United States from 1873 to 1886, inclusive, as follows:

Professional	31,803
Skilled	587,349
Miscellaneous	2,052,294
Occupation not stated	128,782
Without occupation	2,506,188

Taking the table as it stands, and throwing out those immigrants "with occupations not stated," it appears that of all the vast immigration during those fourteen years 48.1 per cent, or nearly one-half, are persons avowedly without occupation or training, or, in other words, unskilled labor of the lowest kind, while professional and skilled labor amounts to only 11.49 per cent of the whole. "Miscellaneous," which is neither skilled nor professional labor, amounts to 38 per cent. It may be assumed that the same proportions hold good for the three years from 1886 to 1889, and it must be noted also that the detailed tables indicate that the number of persons without occupation increases in a slightly larger ratio than the rate of increase of the total immigration.

These figures give an idea of the general character of the foreign immigration into the United States during a long period of fourteen years. It is more important, however, to determine whether the immigration of this general character improves or deteriorates as

[1] Reprinted from Henry Cabot Lodge, "The Restriction of Immigration," *North American Review* 150, no. 11 (January 1891):27–36.

it increases. This can be ascertained best by examining the rate of increase in the immigration from the different countries from which it chiefly comes during the two periods of eight years each from 1874 to 1881 and from 1882 to 1889, respectively:

	Annual average 1874–1881	1882–1889	Percentage of difference	
France	6,064	4,885	19.4	Decrease
Norway	10,767	16,862	59.5	Increase
Great Britain and Ireland	86,649	145,461	67.8	"
Germany	76,416	135,052	76.7	"
Switzerland	4,159	7,831	88.3	"
Netherlands	2,535	4,847	91.2	"
Sweden	18,224	37,730	107.	"
Denmark	4,012	8,663	114.3	"
Austria	9,272	21,926	136.5	"
Belgium	847	2,023	138.8	"
Poland	1,691	4,498	166.	"
Italy	7,893	30,474	286.	"
Russia	5,430	21,567	297.	"
Hungary	2,273	13,101	476.4	"

These percentages of increase are interesting and deeply significant. The nations of Europe which chiefly contributed to the upbuilding of the original thirteen colonies were the English, the Scotch-Irish, so called, the Dutch, the Germans, and the Huguenot French. With the exception of the last they were practically all people of the same stock. During this century and until very recent years these same nations, with the addition of Ireland and the Scandinavian countries, have continued to furnish the chief component parts of the immigration which has helped to populate so rapidly the territory of the United States. Among all these people, with few exceptions, community of race or language, or both, has facilitated the work of assimilation. In the last ten years, however, as appears from the figures just given, new and wholly different elements have been introduced into our immigration, and—what is more important still—the rate of immigration of these new elements has risen with much greater rapidity than that of those which previously had furnished the bulk of the population of the country. The mass of immigration, absolutely speaking, continues, of course, to come from the United Kingdom and from Germany, but relatively the immigration from these two sources is declining rapidly in comparison with the immigration from Italy and from the Slavic countries of Russia, Poland, Hungary,* and Bohemia, the last of which appears under the head of Austria. Of the generally good character of the immigration from the United Kingdom, Germany, and the Scandinavian countries it is hardly necessary to speak; but I will quote a single sentence from the State Department report already referred to, in regard to the immigration from the United Kingdom and Germany:

"The diagrams show the remarkable predominance of the United Kingdom and Germany in supplying the United States

---

* The Hungarian immigration appears to be mainly Slavic, and not Magyar, and hence I have classified it with that of the Slavic countries.

with skilled labor, and also the fact that the Germans represent those industries that depend upon hand labor or the requirements of everyday life, while the English supply the mechanical element. While Germany sends blacksmiths, butchers, carpenters, coopers, saddlers, shoemakers, and tailors, the United Kingdom supplies miners, engineers, iron- and steel-workers, mechanics and artisans, weavers and spinners. This distinction is clearly marked and is certainly important."

Now as to the immigration from the other countries, which has been increasing so much faster than that to which we have been accustomed, and which we know from experience to be in the main valuable. Consul-General Jussen says in his report (1886) in regard to the Austrian immigration:

"The young men who want to escape military service, the ultra-socialist, the anarchist, the men who have lost all social and business footing here, the bankrupt, embezzler, and swindler, stop not to obtain permission of the government, and naturally the authorities have no sort of record here either as to the number or the place of destination of this class of emigrants. . . . The government would, as a matter of course, prohibit, if it could do so, the emigration of all young men subject to military duty, but it is quite natural that it feels no regret to get rid of the ultra-socialists and that it is quite willing the bankrupt and swindler should depart for foreign countries and that the paupers should find support away from home."

He also speaks as follows in regard to the Bohemian emigration, which forms a large part of that which is classed under the head of Austria:

"The labor and agricultural classes of Bohemia probably supply the greatest number of emigrants to the United States, and among the Bohemian industrial laborers some of the most violent ultra-socialists are to be found. The great majority of these Bohemian laborers, both of the industrial and agricultural class, are illiterate and ignorant in the extreme. They stand in great awe of the police authorities at home."

In regard to Hungarian emigration, Mr. Sterne, consul at Budapest, speaks (1886) as follows:

"I am of the opinion that with the present condition of the labor market in the United States there is no room there at present for this class of people. I even believe that under more favorable conditions in the United States these Slovacks are not a desirable acquisition for us to make, since they appear to have so many items in common with the Chinese. Like these, they are extremely frugal, the love of whiskey of the former being balanced by the opium habit of the latter. Their ambition lacks both in quality and quantity. Thus they will work similarly cheap as the Chinese, and will interfere with a civilized laborer's earning a 'white' laborer's wages."

The emigration from Italy comes largely from the southern provinces—from Naples and Sicily; a smaller proportion being drawn from the finer population of northern Italy. In regard to this Italian emigration, Mr. Alden, consul-general at Rome, says (1886):

"As to the habits and morals of the emigrants to the United States from the northern and central portions of Italy, both men and women are sober and industrious, and as a rule trustworthy and moral. They are generally strong, powerful workers, and capable of enduring great fatigue. A less favorable view may be taken of the emigrants from the southern districts and Sicily. These are the most illiterate parts of Italy, and in these districts brigandage was for many years extremely prevalent."

In regard to the emigration from Russia, Mr. Young, the consul-general, says (1886):

"The government of Russia does not encourage emigration. On the contrary, it prohibits all Russian subjects from leaving the empire of Russia, except Poles and Jews. . . . The Mennonites have emigrated perhaps more extensively than any other class of Russian subjects. . . . The lowest classes generally form the greater part of emigration."

Thus it is proved, first, that immigration to this country is increasing, and, second, that it is making its greatest relative increase from races most alien to the body of the American people and from the lowest and most illiterate classes among those races. In other words, it is apparent that, while our immigration is increasing, it is showing at the same time a marked tendency to deteriorate in character. . . .

In a word, the continued introduction into the labor market of four hundred thousand persons annually, half of whom have no occupation and most of whom represent the rudest form of labor, has a very great effect in reducing the rates of wages and disturbing the labor market. This, of course, is too obvious to need comment. Moreover, the shifting of the sources of the immigration is unfavorable, and is bringing to the country people whom it is very difficult to assimilate and who do not promise well for the standard of civilization in the United States—a matter as serious as the effect on the labor market.

The question, therefore, arises,—and there is no more important question before the American people,—What shall be done to protect our labor against this undue competition, and to guard our citizenship against an infusion which seems to threaten deterioration? We have the power, of course, to prohibit all immigration, or to limit the number of persons to be admitted to the country annually, or—which would have the same effect—to impose upon immigrants a heavy capitation tax. Such rough and stringent measures are certainly neither necessary nor desirable if we can overcome the difficulties and dangers of the situation by more moderate legislation. These methods, moreover, are indiscriminate; and what is to be desired, if possible, is restriction which shall at the same time discriminate. We demand now that immigrants shall not be paupers or diseased or criminals, but these and all other existing requirements are vague, and the methods provided for their enforcement

are still more indefinite and are perfectly ineffective. Any law, to be
of use, must require, in the first place, that immigrants shall bring
from their native country, from the United States consul or other
diplomatic representatives, an effective certificate that they are not
obnoxious to any of the existing laws of the United States. We
ought, in addition, to make our test still more definite by requiring
a medical certificate in order to exclude unsound and diseased persons. . . .

We ought also to insist that the consular certificate be given
only after careful inquiry and due proof, and we must make a further
definite test which will discriminate against illiteracy if we desire
any intelligent restriction or sifting of the total mass of immigration.
It is a truism to say that one of the greatest dangers to our free
government is ignorance. Every one knows this to be the case, and
that the danger can be overcome only by constant effort and vigilance. We spend millions annually in educating our children that
they may be fit to be citizens and rulers of the Republic. We are
ready to educate also the children who come to us from other countries; but it is not right to ask us to take annually a large body of
persons who are totally illiterate and who are for the most part beyond the age at which education can be imparted. We have the
right to exclude illiterate persons from our immigration, and this
test, combined with the others of a more general character, would in
all probability shut out a large part of the undesirable portion of
the present immigration. It would reduce in a discriminating manner the total of immigrants, and would thereby greatly benefit the
labor market and help to maintain the rate of American wages. At
the same time it would sift the immigrants who come to this country,
and would shut out in a very large measure those elements which
tend to lower the quality of American citizenship, and which now in
many cases gather in dangerous masses in the slums of our great
cities.

The arguments for restrictive immigration laws appeared to be
validated by two government investigations: The Dillingham Commission
Report of 1910 and the Report of the House Immigration Committee in
1922, both of which were instrumental in fostering the belief that the
new immigration was socially inferior to the older immigration. The
earlier report served as the foundation for the Quota Acts of the 1920's.
The following selection includes an explanation about the scope of the
Congressional inquiry and the Commission's conclusion that basic qualitative differences existed between the ethnic groups that made up Old
Immigration and New Immigration.

Plan and Scope of the Inquiry[2]

Briefly stated, the plan of work adopted by the Commission included a study of the sources of recent immigration in Europe, the
general character of incoming immigrants, the methods employed

[2] Reprinted from *Reports of the Immigration Commission,* vol. 1 (reprint ed., New
York: Arno Press, Inc., 1970), pp. 13–14, 42.

here and abroad to prevent the immigration of persons classed as undesirable in the United States immigration law, and finally a thorough investigation into the general status of the more recent immigrants as residents of the United States, and the effect of such immigration upon the institutions, industries, and people of this country. As above suggested, the chief basis of the Commission's work was the changed character of the immigration movement to the United States during the past twenty-five years.

During the fiscal year 1907, in which the Commission was created, a total of 1,285,349 immigrants were admitted to the United States. Of this number 1,207,619 were from Europe, including Turkey in Asia, and of these 979,661, or 81 percent, came from the southern and eastern countries, comprising Austria-Hungary, Bulgaria, Greece, Italy, Montenegro, Poland, Portugal, Roumania, Russia, Servia, Spain, Turkey in Europe, and Turkey in Asia.

Twenty five years earlier, in the fiscal year 1882, 648,186 European immigrants came to the United States, and of these only 84,973, or 13.1 per cent, came from the countries above enumerated, while 563,213, or 86.9 per cent, were from Belgium, Great Britain and Ireland, France, Germany, the Netherlands, Scandinavia, and Switzerland, which countries furnished about 95 per cent of the immigration movement from Europe to the United States between 1819 and 1883.

During the entire period for which statistics are available—July 1, 1819, to June 30, 1910—a total of 25,528,410 European immigrants, including 106,481 from Turkey in Asia, were admitted to the United States. Of these, 16,052,900, or 62.9 per cent, came from the northern and western countries enumerated, and 9,475,510, or 37.1 per cent, from southern and eastern Europe and Turkey in Asia. For convenience, the former movement will be referred to in the Commission's reports as the "old immigration" and the latter as the "new immigration." The old and the new immigration differ in many essentials. The former was, from the beginning, largely a movement of settlers who came from the most progressive sections of Europe for the purpose of making for themselves homes in the New World. They entered practically every line of activity in nearly every part of the country. Coming during a period of agricultural development, many of them entered agricultural pursuits, sometimes as independent farmers, but more often as farm laborers, who, nevertheless, as a rule soon became landowners. They formed an important part of the great movement toward the West during the last century, and as pioneers were most potent factors in the development of the territory between the Allegheny Mountains and the Pacific coast. They mingled freely with the native Americans and were quickly assimilated, although a large proportion of them, particularly in later years, belonged to non-English-speaking races. This natural bar to assimilation, however, was soon overcome by them, while the racial identity of their children was almost entirely lost and forgotten.

On the other hand, the new immigration has been largely a movement of unskilled laboring men who have come, in large part temporarily, from the less progressive and advanced countries of Europe in response to the call for industrial workers in the eastern and middle western States. They have almost entirely avoided agricultural pursuits, and in cities and industrial communities have congregated together in sections apart from native Americans and the older immigrants to such an extent that assimilation has been slow as compared to that of the earlier non-English-speaking races.

The new immigration as a class is far less intelligent than the old, approximately one-third of all those over 14 years of age when admitted being illiterate. Racially they are for the most part essentially unlike the British, German, and other peoples who came during the period prior to 1880, and generally speaking they are actuated in coming by different ideals, for the old immigration came to be a part of the country while the new, in a large measure, comes with the intention of profiting, in a pecuniary way, by the superior advantages of the new world and then returning to the old country.

The old immigration movement, which in earlier days was the subject of much discussion and the cause of no little apprehension among the people of the country, long ago became thoroughly merged into the population, and the old sources have contributed a comparatively small part of the recent immigrant tide. Consequently the Commission paid but little attention to the foreign-born element of the old immigrant class and directed its efforts almost entirely to an inquiry relative to the general status of the newer immigrants as residents of the United States.

Assimilation of Immigrants

It is difficult to define and still more difficult to correctly measure the tendency of newer immigrant races toward Americanization, or assimilation into the body of the American people. If, however, the tendency to acquire citizenship, to learn the English language, and to abandon native customs and standards of living may be considered as factors, it is found that many of the more recent immigrants are backward in this regard, while some others have made excellent progress. The absence of family life, which is so conspicuous among many southern and eastern Europeans in the United States, is undoubtedly the influence which most effectively retards assimilation. The great majority of some of these races are represented in the United States by single men or men whose wives and families are in their native country. It is a common practice for men of this class in industrial communities to live in boarding or rooming groups, and as they are also usually associated with each other in their work they do not come in contact with Americans, and consequently have little or no incentive to learn the English language, become acquainted with American institutions, or adopt American standards. In the case of families, however, the process of assimilation is usually much more rapid. The families as a rule live in much more wholesome surroundings, and are reached by more of the agencies which promote assimilation. The most potent influence in promoting the assimilation of the family is the children, who, through contact with American life in the schools, almost invariably act as the unconscious agents in the uplift of their parents. Moreover, as the children grow older and become wage earners, they usually enter some higher occupation than that of their fathers, and in such cases the Americanizing influence upon their parents continues until frequently the whole family is gradually led away from the old surroundings and old standards into those more nearly American. This influence of the children is potent among immigrants in the great cities, as well as in the smaller industrial centers.

Among the new immigration as a whole the tendency to become naturalized citizens, even among those who have been here five years or more, is not great, although much more pronounced in some races than in others. This result is influenced by language considerations and by the fact that naturalization is accomplished with greater difficulty than formerly, as the requirements are higher and expense greater, and that adequate facilities are not in all cases provided. Another reason is that many do not regard their stay here as permanent.

In recent years the work of promoting the welfare and assisting in the assimilation of recent immigrants has been inaugurated on a large scale by various religious and civic organizations. Until recently a great part of the efforts of this nature was carried on by organizations of the various races or peoples, but now the movement has been joined by organizations composed of all classes of citizens. In general this propaganda is in the main divorced from any semblance of proselytizing and is confined to practical efforts calculated to promote the well-being and advancement of the immigrant. Most of the societies lay particular stress upon influencing the immigrant to become acquainted with the duties and privileges of American citizenship and civilization. Teaching the English language and the primary branches of learning is a prominent feature in most of this work. It does not appear that the Federal Government can directly assist in this work, but where possible effort should be made to promote the activities of these organizations.

The following extract is from a book written by Oscar Handlin, a foremost student of American immigration. In his study, *Race and Nationality in American Life,* Handlin expands on the rationale (philosophy) underlying the Dillingham Commission report. The historical setting is vital to an understanding of the climate. Restrictionist intentions intensified in the 1917–1924 period, culminating in the end of unrestricted immigration. This was the result of multiple historical factors: the misgivings with which Yankee families of New England viewed the foreign-born, the concern for job security on the part of organized labor, and the unfavorable attitude toward immigration by substantial blocs of Southerners, Populists and Progressives. But a basic motivation behind restriction was the ethnic one: the desire to limit the influx of undesirable ethnic peoples.

One fundamental premise lay behind the immigration legislation of 1917–1924 and animated also the McCarran-Walter Act of 1952.[3] Embodied in the quota system, this premise held that the national origin of an immigrant was a reliable indication of his capacity for Americanization. It was averred, and science seemed to show, that some people, because of their racial or national constitution, were

[3] Reprinted from Oscar Handlin, *Race and Nationality in American Life* (Boston: Atlantic-Little, Brown, 1957), pp. 94–95.

more capable of becoming Americans than others. Furthermore, it was argued that the "old immigrants," who came to the United States before 1880, were drawn from the superior stocks of northern and western Europe, while those who came after that date were drawn from the inferior breeds of southern and eastern Europe.

There was a demonstrable connection between the diffusion of this assumption and the course of immigration legislation in the first quarter of the century. Those who argued in favor of a restrictionist policy did so not merely, perhaps not primarily, because they wished to reduce the total volume of immigration, but, more important, because they wished to eliminate the "new" while perpetuating the "old" immigration.

Nativism accelerated during and after World War I as the fear of cheap labor was augmented by the fear of radicalism and communism, the growing awareness of the changing character of immigration, and the hostility of nativistic groups expressed in anti-Semitic, anti-Catholic, and anti–new ethnic group drives. The political, intellectual, and social climate was, therefore, conducive to the triumph of Anglo-American supremacy, as it culminated in the most restrictive immigration policy in United States history—the quota systems. The most important of these laws was the National Origins Act of 1924, clearly an example of ethnic-motivated legislation. The act's provisions gave decided preference to northwestern European ethnic groups, while discriminating heavily against southern and eastern European nationalities. Asians and Africans were subject to virtual total exclusion. Thus of the maximum allowance of 165,000 immigrants annually (the western hemisphere was excluded), northwestern European peoples received 80 percent of the quota.

The fact that the act placed an end to unrestricted immigration was less important than the fact that the nation had by law adopted a policy of ethnic preference. Moreover, this policy would be adhered to for the next four decades.

The discriminatory intent of the act under the guise of immigration limitation is attacked in the excerpt below by Senator David I. Walsh of Massachusetts, the first United States senator of Irish immigrant parents.

Mr. President, the proposal to make the census of 1890, instead of that of 1910, the basis for the quota hereafter to be admitted, as advocated by many, is objectionable on many grounds.[4]

A few facts regarding the population census of 1890, as compared with the census of 1910, give practical assurance that a great American principle would be violated by the change proposed.

Two per cent of the alien inhabitants in 1890 would total about 160,000, whereas the same percentage in 1910 would number about 238,000. This represents a material reduction in the num-

[4] Reprinted from U.S., Congress, Senate, *Congressional Record*, 68th Cong., 1st sess., 1924, pp. 6355–6357.

ber of aliens to be admitted and indicates a tendency to further restrict the number of admissible immigrants.

The most important aspect of this question, however, is that such a change would inject into the law a very apparent discrimination against immigrants of certain nationalities. The census of 1890 shows that a large majority of our alien inhabitants were then natives of northern and western Europe, while the census of 1910 shows more nearly equal proportions from southern and eastern Europe. In 1890 about 87 per cent of our alien population were people from northern and western Europe, as compared with 56 per cent in 1910. Who can say that it would be fair to abandon a basis of calculation that is very close to an equal division between the races of northern and western Europe and the races of southern and eastern Europe and adopt a basis that will give the people of northern and western Europe 87 per cent of our immigration during the coming years?

Since we have said to the people of all nations, "We are going to admit only a certain percentages of your future immigrants," can we go further and add that to certain nationalities we shall extend preference? That is what the suggestion of the 1890 census basis means. It simply amounts to reducing and practically eliminating all emigration from southern and eastern Europe.

Whatever may be the surface for the change in data, it must be insisted that the true reason is social discrimination. An attempt is being made to slip by this proposal, which is aimed clearly and mercilessly at the Slav, the Latin, and the Jew, under the harmless guise of a change in the date of the census.

Mr. President, if I were convinced that the admission of immigrants to this country, however it might ease conditions abroad, could in the slightest degree imperil not merely the safety of our institutions, but the prospect of employment for our own laborers or of prosperity of the American people, I would advocate not lessening but preventing it. But because I believe the immigrants who cultivate the soil, such as those who have of recent years taken possession of the abandoned farms of New England, contribute to the welfare of the country as much as they derive from it, I am opposed to too rigidly restricting a source of benefit so important and valuable.

To everything that has been said concerning the admission of insane, diseased, depraved persons—persons against whom any objection can be made on the score of their capacity for citizenship—I most emphatically subscribe and support. We have set up stringent requirements to keep out the weak and incapacitated. We very properly require that the immigrant must possess an established good character, be of sound body, and that his political opinions must not be in conflict with those principles which underlie the stability of our Government. More than that we require—what is not imposed on an American citizen—the immigrant be able to read a language. What more desirable addition to our citizenship can be demanded than a man or woman meet all these requirements? If we do not rigidly and effectively enforce these requirements, it is our own not the immigrants' fault.

Mr. President, what is the real driving force behind the movement of basing the quota on the census of 1890? The peoples of the world will attribute it to our belief that the "Nordic" is a superior race. The world will assume that our Government considers the Italians, Greeks, Jews, Poles, and the Slavs inferior to the Nordics, congenitally as well as culturally. It is a dangerous assumption. Millions of people here in America will resent this slur upon their racial character. The vilification of whole races does not produce a very pleasant mental state in that part of our population who happen to be foreign born. Do we not realize that we are making for ourselves a greater national problem than ever before? Does the agitation provoked by the proposed law conduce to the early assimilation of the immigrant which you claim is your desideratum? . . .

Men and women, Mr. President, do not come 3,000 or 5,000 miles, suffering the utmost hardships of a trans-Atlantic voyage, parting oftentimes with the last penny in order to obtain passage, by a desire that is not worthy and commendable. Can there be a higher proof of devotion to the benefits and blessings of our country than that men and women to come under its blessings will take all the discomforts and risks of journeying to a country of whose language they are ignorant, to whose customs they are strangers, leaving their house and their fireside, often their most loved ones, and the associations of all the generations that preceded them?

Leave your places of comfort and visit the places where the immigrants are found in American life before you condemn them. Whose faces are those going up and down in the shafts that bring to the surface of the earth our mineral deposits? They are those of our immigrants. Stand at the mill gates and the exits of the sweatshops, where those commodities are manufactured that require the most exacting labor. Our immigrants are the "factory hands." Watch at the entrance of a savings bank in our industrial centers. The depositors most numerous in the lines are our immigrants. Whose children are those running in and out among the vehicles of the city streets, with no playground but the crowded and littered roadway in the midst of the cities' marts? They are our immigrants. Whose weary and careworn faces—mothers' faces—are leaning out over the fire escapes in the tenement rows trying to catch a breath of fresh air? They are our immigrants. Look in at the winter sessions of our evening schools. Who are the men and women, simply clad, with drawn countenances and calloused hands, seeking a knowledge of our language and the history of our country? They, too, are our immigrants.

The records, Mr. President, show that immigrants must seek employment where they can find it, and as they are without funds to travel any great distance, they are obliged to enter the mines and mills near the places of their arrival. We have made them the slaves of our industrial system. Our greed and not their self-seeking has directed them and sent them and their families into the factories, sweatshops, down into the depths of the earth and on the docks of our waterways, wherever there is lowly and fatiguing work.

In 1918, 58 per cent of the steel and iron workers were foreign born, 61 per cent of our packers' labor, 62 per cent of the bitumious miners and wool weavers, 69 per cent of the cotton-mill operators, 72 per cent of clothing shopmen, and 65 per cent of the sugar refiners' help came from abroad.

Mr. President, we have, I fear, often been the means of causing them to substitute the material for the spiritual. It is toil, toil, ceaseless toil, which we have offered them. The industrial master is their first and often their only teacher of Americanism. They soon learn his interest is not entirely altruistic.

Look about and observe more closely the conditions prevailing in the immigrant settlements, especially in the crowded districts of our large cities. What are the conditions in these areas? Overcrowded dark tenements, lack of sanitation, sunless and airless narrow streets. Does anyone for a minute believe that the immigrants choose to reside in these unattractive surroundings? They have no choice. It is true that they find there a kindred acquaintance willing to sympathize with them and if possible assist them, but they are there because they are forced into these districts.

With this knowledge of our neglect, of our indifference to the immigrant and his opportunities for assimilation and Americanization, how unfair, how injurious is the opprobrious language used in the references to him in the pages of the *Congressional Record* and the public discussion of this measure! They have been called mongrels, garbage, riffraff, anarchists, socialists, and Bolshevists. Every conceivable name that could be thought of has been used in describing these immigrants and their families whom we have forced into most unsatisfactory living and working conditions. Men and women who have come from the open fields of Europe, farmers and peasants who have lived in the sunshine and amid the song and laughter of their native surroundings, overnight have been forced into the conditions of living of which complaint is very properly made. Well you know we have done this, and we have done it regardless of their souls, regardless of their spiritual welfare. Let us be humane and just to the immigrant, and if we are we will in the future concern ourselves more about the living conditions of these foreigners rather than condemn and abuse them and close our ports to them. Let us think of them as human beings and less as undesirables.

Mr. President, our slight work of assimilation, let us frankly admit, has been haphazard and often misguided, yet the war proved, to the credit of our immigrants, that we were as closely united a country as many of the more homogeneous State of Europe; we attained without conscious effort results in assimilation that Germany with all her systematic efforts failed to attain. . . .

The theories of superior race value and selection that have accompanied the discussion of this question are humiliating and insulting. Do we fancy that the peoples and Governments of Italy, Poland, Hungary, Austria, Greece, or Rumania have no national pride?

What are the nationalities whose coming to America is chiefly curtailed by this arbitrary resort to the 1890 census? The Greeks, to whom civilization owes so much in the fields of literature, science, art, and government. The Italians, who from the day of early Roman history have contributed immensely to civilization along the lines of government, literature, art, music, and navigation, including the gift of the discoverer of America. The liberty-loving Poles, whose sacrifices and struggles for freedom have arrested the admiration of mankind and who saved all Europe from the Turks at Vienna scarcely two centuries ago, and who were once in the van of culture. The Jews, who contributed to the world literature, religion, standards of righteous conduct that can not be overvalued. . . .

Have we learned nothing from the earlier generations' mistaken notions about the Dutch, the French, the Irish, the Germans, and the Scandinavians, now an essential element in our assumed racial superiority? They were condemned and criticized by the earlier settlers, just as we are now undertaking to condemn the races from southern Europe. Have we forgotten that at the time of the Revolution one-fifth of the population of America could not speak the English language? Have we forgotten that more than one-half of the population of America at the time of the Revolution was not Anglo-Saxon?

Factors of all sorts enter into play in determining race values, and often an alien most desirable from one point of view is least so from another. But is not the whole concept in variance with fundamental American principles and policies?

The whole idea of relative race values is objectionable, unreasonable, and grossly offensive. Ever since Edmund Burke's famous saying it has been generally recognized that you can not draw an indictment against a whole nation.

Illiteracy and poverty may be high among the races from southern and eastern Europe, but these are not crimes. In the statistics of alcoholism, insanity, and disease, their racial inferiority does not hold. Considering their opportunities, these immigrants have done about as well as any other nationalities that have been here for the same length of time. All these races have brought with them a rich cargo of values, a keen sense of good workmanship, tireless industry, a remarkably sane and intelligent outlook upon life, a family solidarity, a simplicity of life, and a depth of spirituality that is most commendable.

Attempt to grade our aliens! Which race is to be rated "100 per cent American"? It is a shortsighted view which measures the desirability or undesirability of any group of aliens only by the rapidity or tardiness with which they forget their past spiritual connections and allow themselves to be rapidly molded into an undeterminate type which is vagued termed a "100 per cent American." . . .

Mr. President, what group of aliens failed to respond willingly and serve bravely when our country needed them? On the outskirts of this city, in the National Cemetery, within a few months we buried the body of an American soldier, born in Greece, who was acclaimed as one of the bravest of the brave, whose heroism in death was one of the thrilling and inspiring episodes of the recent war. And we are now, after such an illustration of patriotism—and it could be multiplied many times—to inform the Americans of Hellenic descent that they are among the undesirables.

Read the names upon the crosses in the American military cemeteries in France. Go there, you who are saying that certain races are undesirable, and read the names upon the graves of the poor lads who had neither father nor mother nor any other loved one to request that their bodies be interred in Arlington Cemetery. Read the names of these dead; read the names of those over whom

the poppies now grow, practically all of them foreign born—Poles,
Italians, Greeks, and Slavs—scarcely an Anglo-Saxon name among
America's brave dead now sleeping in France. . . .

The triumphant restrictionist policy of the 1920's continued into
the 1930's, as numerous bills were presented to Congress with the object
of further restricting immigration. Nativism increased as the economic
depression persisted. With few exceptions, the New Deal leadership
generally remained indifferent to the critical problem of immigration and
the plight of the immigrants. Vito Marcantonio, the Italian-American
congressman from East Harlem, New York, emerged as the leading
defender of the immigrants and fought to defeat punitive and restrictive
immigration measures. The following selection analyzes the relationships
of the New Deal, the immigrants, and Marcantonio. It is interesting to
note that although the pervasiveness of the Depression emphasized economic factors, ethnic considerations were not forgotten. Thus, proponents
of severe anti-alien policies usually came from the same ethnic groups
that had always been identified with nativism, while defenders of immigrants were usually found among representatives of new ethnic stock.

As with most previous depressions, the nineteen-thirties were years
of increasing restrictionist demands, even to the point of total cessation of immigration.[5] In 1935 the legislature of California proposed
the deportation of all unemployed aliens who had become public
charges; while the Oregon legislature called for registration of aliens.
Were these regional unfavorable attitudes toward the immigrants
really indicative of a national movement threatening their very
existence in America? Louis Adamic, the famous Yugoslav immigrant scholar, provides one of the more poignant reflections as he
mourned the ominous transition which had transformed Ellis Island
from the symbolic haven of hope to the chief deportation depot.
"No one of any influence in America today seems to want to raise
again the old 'welcome' sign." . . .
    If restrictionists did not completely succeed in obtaining
legislation further limiting immigration, they found more fertile
ground in striking at aliens already here; primarily those who had
entered the country illegally; but also those who had complied with
the law. In many ways, non-citizens were the most forgotten men of
the era. Americans as a whole regarded it a misfortune for so many
fellow-citizens to be afflicted with poverty born of unemployment,
but few were ready to show much sympathy for immigrants. This
delineation also applies to the Roosevelt Administration, which has
been generally regarded as exercising political sagacity when it
came to mirroring public opinion. What was most revealing about
this administration was that neither the President nor his associates
exerted anything approaching a strenuous effort on behalf of immigrants. The public record shows that they studiously avoided the

[5] Reprinted from Salvatore J. LaGumina, "The New Deal, the Immigrants, and Congressman Vito Marcantonio," The International Migration Review 4, no. 11 (Spring
1970):57–74.

subject in the mid-nineteen-thirties. The exceptions were Secretary of Labor Frances Perkins and her subordinate, Colonel Daniel C. MacCormack, Commissioner of Immigration and Naturalization, who had official jurisdiction in these matters.

For most Americans, worrying about American citizens was the extent of their responsibilities. This included even representatives of respected American organizations, such as the president of a family welfare society who recriminated heavily against uncontrolled immigration, maintaining that it "has been the means of spreading mass poverty which is far more permanent and causes far more suffering and hardships to individuals, [than] restrictive laws."

Accurately expressing the prevailing view, one newspaper wrote: "Existing immigration laws ought to be strengthened not weakened." The American Civil Liberties Union, when it came to immigration questions, found the "forces of reaction" more excessive than at any other time since World War I. It is against this backdrop that a burgeoning alien deportation controversy ensued in the Seventy-Fourth Congress.

One observer noted the determination of committee leaders who had already processed prohibitive immigration measures through their committees and on to a receptive Congress which believed "in restrictive measures at present for economic reasons, if for no other." The leading Congressional restrictionist, Congressman Martin Dies of Texas, blamed the whole Depression on immigration. "If we had refused admission to the 16,500,000 foreign-born who are living in this country today, we would have no unemployment problem to distress and harass us." This simplistic view of the economic effects of immigration was symptomatic of many Americans who assumed that the high rate of unemployment could be eliminated or significantly reduced by the simple expedient of deleting large numbers of aliens from the American economic picture. This assumption displayed a misunderstanding of the economic process and the role of immigrants as consumers. Even more important, it failed to consider the occupational diversity characterizing the American economic system in which numerous categories of job classifications rule out the transfer of workers from one industry or occupation to another.

Still there were other reasons accounting for anti-alien sentiment. Again Dies best expressed them. "There is no middle ground or compromise. Either we are for or against America. If we are for America, we must be for the exclusion of these new-seed immigrants and the deportation of those unlawfully here." Dies, a spokesman for 155 organizations and 150 congressmen, advocated a drastic reduction of all immigration and the deportation of six million aliens. One of his bills would deprive aliens of jobs which would ordinarily be filled by citizens, bar entry to those without relatives in the United States, deporting all those here illegally, and threaten those lawfully in the country with deportation if they did not rapidly attain their naturalization papers.

Against this vindictive mentality Marcantonio's voice emerged as one of the strongest in the House of Representatives on behalf of these foreigners. In many ways his defense of the aliens was in accord with the positions taken by other congressmen whose districts harbored large foreign-born populations, as well as their sons and daughters. . . .

Aware of his ethnic origin and of his association with Fiorello H. LaGuardia, who in his congressional tenure had proved a formidable defender of the immigrants, Marcantonio developed a strong interest in legislation affecting them. Besides, many of his constituents were Italo-Americans, who had a tendency to delay naturalization and were, therefore, in special need of protection. . . .

He criticized the Congress for its denigration of aliens. "I never thought that in the House of Representatives of the United States, good, patriotic Americans would dare talk disparagingly about any racial group in the United States where, after all, we are all of alien stock." Fervidly, he continued to remind them of thousands of immigrants who had fought and died for this nation in World War I. "They were good decent people then. Why are they not good decent people now?" Against this disgusting bigotry, "I cry shame." In this fashion the young Congressman helped gain approval of the stay of deportation resolution.

Other measures of a similar nature gained his support. One was the Sirovich Bill which sought to humanize the existing immigration law regarding separated families by granting privileged positions in the quota system to relatives of Americans. It acquired widespread Italo-American endorsement, including appeals for its support by Il Progresso Italo-Americano. It also produced a letter-writing campaign with Marcantonio the recipient of numerous communications, the most poignant of which was a telegram from thirty-three Italians detained on Ellis Island who pleaded: "We on bended knees pray to you who are of Italian descent and a representative of Italian-American citizens to visualize the untold hardships we martyrs of Italian parentage are forced to contend with." Despite hearings and expression of Administration support, the bill never reached the floor of Congress, which would seem to indicate its low priority with the Administration.

There is a close correlation between American immigration policy and the ethnic composition of the nation. Immigration laws, especially the quota acts, are among the most complicated and difficult to understand. Nevertheless, their discriminatory effects are obvious. In the following selection, Helen F. Eckerson states the purposes of the national origins plan.

The national-origins plan was to accomplish two purposes: (1) to reduce the volume of immigration by establishing a numerical limit for all countries except the designated countries in the Western Hemisphere and (2) to make automatic the selection of immigrants by nationalities by providing a fixed number of each nationality.[6] It was said to be nondiscriminatory since all nationalities were treated the same way. At the same time the underlying intention of the law—that is, to preserve the ethnic composition of the popula-

6 Reprinted from Helen F. Eckerson, "Immigration and National Origins," The Annals of the American Academy of Political and Social Science 367 (September 1966):7, 8.

tion of the United States through the selection of immigrants whose tradition, languages, and political systems were akin to those in this country—would be accomplished. . . .

When the national-origins quotas were finally proclaimed, it seemed that here was a scheme that would control immigration both in volume and in selectivity. It was held that most of those who would come would be those easily assimilable, and in the tradition of the American Dream.

Doubtless, the new Immigration Act of 1965 will have a dramatic effect on the United States. It is too early to forecast its total impact, but some early indicators point to such developments as a change in the ethnic character of immigration, the effect on our southern and northern neighbors in the Western Hemisphere, and the age of the immigrant population; indeed, further social, political, and economic implications can be deduced. Barbara M. Watson identifies and analyzes the major changes of the new immigration law in the selection that follows.

We are now in the second year after the first major change in immigration legislation and policy since 1924, and the experience of the first year may give us a glimpse of the shape of immigration of the future.[7]

Some of the changes wrought by the Act of October 3, 1965, come immediately to mind. Foremost, perhaps, is the sharp upsurge in immigration from Asia. The shift from northern Europe to southern Europe as a primary source of immigration has been equally significant. The increase in total volume of immigration is unmistakable and seemingly permanent, despite the recent imposition of a numerical limitation on immigration from the Western Hemisphere. Not least important among the changes is that the hemispheric limition had the initial effect of cutting immigration from Canada, one of our two closest neighbors, to approximately half the former level.

Looking more closely at each of these phenomena, we find first that there are at least two sources of the impetus toward more immigration from the East, both somewhat psychological. Demand for immigration is seemingly stimulated by the opportunity to immigrate. Thus when the former quotas of 100 (or so) per annum were abolished, the rate of petitioning to establish a preference status for relatives bounded upward. At the same time, the right extended to members of the professions to file petitions in their own behalf for third preference status, coupled with relatively limited professional petitions by Asians, most particularly Filipinos, Chinese, and Indians. As a result, total immigration from the former Asia-Pacific Triangle rose from 15,186 in fiscal year 1965 to 80,971 in fiscal year 1969.

It is noteworthy that this increase was not, in strictly numerical terms, at the expense of immigration from other parts of the Eastern Hemisphere. (Only the Western Hemisphere is defined in

[7] Reprinted from Barbara M. Watson, "Immigration Today," *The International Migration Review* 4, no. 12 (Summer 1970):47–51.

the Immigration and Nationality Act; we thus define administratively all the rest of the world as the Eastern Hemisphere.) The level of immigration from the rest of the Hemisphere (Europe, Africa, Oceania) remained static or rose slightly. Under prior law, however, upwards of one-third of allowable quota numbers were unused each year. Now the maximum ceiling is being reached annually and the difference is in Asian immigration.

There is, however, room for debate as to whether in specific categories (most particularly third preference) the predominance of Asian applicants is deterring immigration by others. For the moment, at least, the answer is "no." Despite the fact that 90% of the 17,000 third preference visa numbers were allocated to natives of just five Asian nations in fiscal year 1969, over 12,000 members of the professions, scientists and artists of exceptional ability, and kindred workers were admitted in that same year from Europe, Africa, and Oceania. These immigrants may have had a preference status based on relationship to a United States citizen or resident alien but it is likely that most were admitted in the nonpreference class. Because of a demand in excess of the 20,000 foreign state limitation by applicants in higher preferences, nonpreference visa numbers were not available for persons born in the Philippines (nor in China until the last month of the fiscal year). Therefore, although persons born in those foreign states were preempting most of the third preference visa numbers, they were contributing to the availability of nonpreference visa numbers for others.

By contrast, the altered pattern of immigration from Europe stems more from technical changes in the law than from psychological impetus. Previously, certain relatives of United States citizens and resident aliens were entitled to 50% of each country's quota. Now they are entitled to 74% of the overall ceiling of 170,000 for the Eastern Hemisphere. This was and is of immediate and continuing benefit to applicants from those countries in which family associations are very close and in which there has been a tradition of emigrating in family groups. Primary among those have been Italy, Greece, and Portugal, from each of which the level of immigration has multiplied since 1965. Conversely, immigrants from northern Europe have traditionally been those seeking enlarged opportunities, a chance for a new life in a new environment. Such intending immigrants must now compete for the reduced amount of visa numbers available for the third and sixth preference and nonpreference classes. In addition, they must obtain a certification from the Secretary of Labor to the effect they will not displace nor otherwise adversely affect American labor. Since, in many instances, this means they must have pre-arranged employment, this labor certification requirement at least delays immigration by such aliens, even if it does not totally deter it.

Given present conditions, there is no reason to expect the overall volume of immigration to change markedly. With the removal of such artificial barriers to demand itself (as well as to the satisfaction of demand) as the national quotas were, reaching the annual limitation for each hemisphere should be almost automatic each year. (This could always be off by a few numbers, of course, due to unexpected "returns" of numbers at end of June, such as happened in 1968 when "only" 169,945 of the 170,000 visa numbers were used.) The only expectable variants from the authorized total volume, however, would be in the levels of immediate relatives and of certain special immigrants.

The Western Hemisphere changes have been felt more sharply than some of the others, perhaps, because this is the first time in our history that immigration from our neighbors has been subject to a numerical limitation. There has thus been a certain element of shock (as distinct from surprise) from the results of the new system.

KEY QUESTIONS

1. Two United States Senators from Massachusetts present their views on immigration policy in this chapter. Summarize their views, and evaluate the reasons they used to justify their views.

2. What was the relationship of the Dillingham Commission Report of 1910 to the restrictive immigration policy of the 1920's?

3. Explain fully three reasons why "nativism" intensified in the decade preceding World War II.

4. What was unique about the Immigration Law of 1965?

5. Has there been any new development in the ethnic composition of the nation resulting from the 1965 Immigration Law? Explain.

12

Conclusion

The major concern of this book has been to promote an understanding of the texture of American life through the exploration of ethnicity. The variety of ethnic experiences, positive and negative, shows that this phenomenon has had remarkable staying power and that it promises to continue to play a significant role in American history. The assimilation process has not yet been completed among a number of prominent ethnic groups. Moreover, even among those groups supposedly long since assimilated, ethnic identifications persist, thereby rendering the "melting pot" concept dubious. Many qualified historians and social scientists have come to accept the mutuality of cultural pluralism and cultural unity as more reflective of American life. This might be expressed another way by saying that although American life manifests broad diversity, there is enough that is common ground about the American experience that readers of this volume can profitably explore the various dimensions of ethnic experiences. The documentary record of the peripheral American's experience in this country has a validity of its own.

To study the history of ethnicity in America is not only to study the past but necessarily to study the present, for ethnic America still lives, although modified and set in unfamiliar ecological and social backgrounds. Unfortunately, the recognition of the existence of this social force is often associated with a negative evaluation, such as the much-discussed white backlash of recent years. For the ethnics of the lower white middle class the times are particularly disturbing. Apparently threatened by nonwhite competition for the jobs, housing, political power, and other benefits they have only recently won, they are beset by other social problems. Their affluence is tenuous at best and is usually the result of the employment of both spouses, a development with far-reaching consequences regarding the redefinition of family roles and traditional values of ethnic group life. As a consequence, these Americans feel almost as powerless as do the poorest residents of the ghetto. If this is so, then it is a disservice to treat them in an idealized, almost nostalgic fashion. The approach to these ethnic groups, as to all ethnic groups in American society, should be based on sympathy and empathy—the only way to construct sound social policies.

We take the position that ethnicity persists as an important element in American society. Far from merging into a cultural homogeneity, groups in this country remain distinctive and visible as they meet many individual and social needs. Thus we live in the United States not solely as members of the entire American social structure but also as members of ethnic subsocieties, crisscrossed by social class. As a leading student put it, "Ethnic differences, even in the second half of the twentieth century, proved far more important to men than did differences in philosophy or economic system. Men who would not die for a premise or a dogma or a division of labor would more or less cheerfully die for a difference rooted in ethnic origins."[1]

In this concluding chapter an effort will be made to tie together the many threads of the cloth of ethnicity so as to place into proper perspective its role on the American scene. It will be interesting to note that the debate about ethnicity, the melting pot concept, and cultural pluralism has not ceased, although it has entered a new phase. Accordingly, selections covered in this chapter will include contemporary evaluations on the development of ethnic America. Like selections in earlier chapters they emanate from the full spectrum of American life: academic, literary, propagandistic, and social and political viewpoints, among others.

Is there an "ethnic American?" Can he be classified? Barbara Mikulski, a Polish-American, responds that there are over 40 million ethnic Americans who are urban, primarily from the working class, overtaxed, underrepresented, and exploited. American ethnics are neglected and ridiculed by bureaucrats, liberals, militants, and intellectuals. Ms. Mikulski vehemently states the case for the ethnic Americans in the article that follows.

> America is not a melting pot.[2] It is a sizzling cauldron for the ethnic American who feels that he has been politically extorted by both government and private enterprise. The ethnic American is sick of being stereotyped as a fascist and dullard by phoney white liberals, pseudo black militants and patronizing bureaucrats. He pays the bill for every major government program and gets nothing or little in the way of return. Tricked by the political rhetoric of the illusionary funding for black-oriented social programs, he turns his

[1] The American Jewish Committee, *The Reacting Americans* (New York: American Jewish Committee, 1968), p. 13.

[2] Reprinted from Barbara Mikulski, "The Myth of the Melting Pot," *Ethnos* 1 (August 1970) (Newsletter of the U.S. Catholic Conference Task Force on Urban Problems).

anger to race—when he himself is the victim of class prejudice. He has worked hard all of his life to become a "good American." He and his sons have fought on every battlefield—then he is made fun of because he likes the flag.

The Ethnic American is overtaxed and underserved at every level of government. He does not have fancy lawyers or expensive lobbyists getting him tax breaks on his income. Being a home owner he shoulders the rising property taxes—the major revenue source for the municipalities in which he lives. Yet he enjoys very little from these unfair and burdensome levies. Because of restrictive eligibility requirements linked either to income or "target areas," he gets no help from Federal programs. If he wants to buy in the "old neighborhood" he cannot get an FHA loan. One major illness in his family will wipe him out. When he needs a nursing home for an elderly parent, he finds that there are none that he can afford nor is he eligible for any financial assistance. His children tend to go to parochial schools which receive little in the way of government aid and for which he carries an extra burden. There is a general decline of community services for his neighborhood, e.g., zoning, libraries, recreation programs, sanitation, etc.

His income of $5,000 to $10,000 per year makes him "near poor." He is the victim of both inflation and anti-inflationary measures. He is the guy that is hurt by layoffs, tight money that chokes him with high interest rates for installment buying and home improvements. Manufacturers with their price fixing, shoddy merchandise and exorbitant repair bills are gouging him to death. When he complains about costs, he is told that it is the "high cost of labor" that is to blame. Yet he knows he is the "labor" and that in terms of real dollars he is going backwards.

The ethnic American also feels unappreciated for the contribution he makes to society. He resents the way the working-class is looked down upon. In many instances he is treated like the machine he operates or the pencil he pushes. He is tired of being treated like an object of production. The public and private institutions have made him frustrated by their lack of response to his needs. At present he feels powerless in his daily dealings with and efforts to change them.

Unfortunately, because of old prejudices and new fears, anger is generated against other minority groups rather than those who have power. What is needed is an alliance of white and black; white collar, blue collar, and no collar based on mutual need, interdependence and respect . . . an alliance to develop the strategy for a new kind of community organization and political participation.

In order to understand the developing polarization in American society, it would be well to examine the situation in New York City, where conflict has surfaced between the newcomers and the established groups. The current peripheral Americans, the blacks and Puerto Ricans, face the backlash from the white ethnics in the struggle for prestige and power. Arnold J. Bornfriend explores this conflict in New York City with special emphasis on tactics, strategies, and groupings in the following selection.

The newcomers, concerned primarily with poverty, welfare, housing, racial, community, and neighborhood problems largely black and Puerto Rican with some support from white socially conscious groups, face a series of dilemmas.[3] In contrast to the mature participants, most of their energies are directed at governmental agencies, for their goals can only be realized in the public sector. To survive they must win their demands or at least convince their constituencies of their immediate potential. . . .

To compensate for their low status and lack of influence, the newcomers, unlike the established groups, must rely on high pressure tactics—i.e., protests, confrontations, sit-ins, rent-strikes, demonstrations, nonnegotiable demands, and institutional shut-downs. . . .

The established groups have reacted to the mobilization of newcomers in different ways. Public-employee unions, ethnic groups, and others who feel most directly threatened by their demands may adopt similar tactics, producing an upward spiral of increasingly militant behavior. . . .

The following selection presents the response of the respected historian, Arthur Mann, to a paper written by Salvatore John LaGumina, "Case Studies of Ethnicity and Italo-American Politicians." Mann examines the persistence of ethnicity and stresses the value of continued study of the subject as a legitimate academic pursuit. Further, he compares white ethnic leaders with the black leaders of today and discovers many parallels.

Professor Mann provided a superb synthesis, encapsuling the numerous ideas that had been offered during the day.[4] He agreed completely with LaGumina's thesis of the persistency of ethnicity and suggested that LaGumina's paper serve as a model for future study in this area. Mann divided his comments in four areas:

First, he expanded on the persistency of ethnicity thesis, pointing out that historians are compelled to acknowledge it even when they decry it. Even more important is the awareness that ethnicity has always been a distinguishable trait in American society. Thus, prejudice against the Irish in Boston, or the Jews in New York City, or Mexican-Americans in San Diego, are continuing proofs of its role in American history. Italian-Americans are not the only people professing a special feeling for their place in American society. Indeed, every group feels itself important. Why does ethnicity persist? This is the kind of people we are. Between 1880 and 1930, over thirty million immigrants arrived in the United States, with over seventy percent of them settling east of the Mississippi River. For example, in 1910 over ninety percent of

[3] Reprinted with permission from the *Proceedings of the Academy of Political Science*, "Governing the City: Challenges and Options for New York," 29 (August 1969), 65–66.

[4] Reprinted from Arthur Mann's response to a paper written by Salvatore J. LaGumina, "Case Studies of Ethnicity and Italo-American Politicians," *Proceedings of the First Annual Conference of the American Italian Historical Association*, New York, 1968, pp. 33–35.

Chicago were either first or second generation Americans. But it would be a mistake to identify immigration with the East or the Middle West. A numerical majority of all the major cities in all the states were either immigrants or children of immigrants in 1910. Immigrant groups have gone through a curious evolution. Whereas many of the second-generation Americans deliberately rejected the culture, even the language of their parents, for fear of being rejected by American society, third-generation Americans are less sensitive to social ostracism. Many of them do not want to forget their past. They profess a nostalgia for their immigrant roots and are interested in studying it. The contemporary civil rights movement seems to intensify this interest because the movement is in essence a search for roots and fulfills the need for self-identification. . . .

The third area Mann considered was the character of political leadership. He found it fascinating as well as mysterious to note that Italian-American politicians, such as Fiorello LaGuardia, James Lanzetta and Vito Marcantonio, although possessing disparate styles and philosophies, and although representing different political parties, all were supported by the same electorate. Obviously, the element they shared in common was their Italian background. However, this experience led to different results. In the case of Lanzetta, it served to narrow his horizons, while with LaGuardia and Marcantonio it served to expand their outlook, as they became national reformers. Mann considered these reformers as the typical American reformers. "The only angry men in politics were ethnics." One does not expect an indignant Leverett Saltonstall or Henry Cabot Lodge to be in the vanguard of reform movements. Considering white southerners as a kind of ethnic group, Mann maintained that George Wallace can be regarded as an angry candidate from the right, since he reflects the views of a significant minority. Mann then likened the radical leaders of ethnic groups like Marcantonio with many of today's radical black leaders, maintaining that they were permitted their extremism because in both instances these politicians expressed their people's resentment against the establishment. They represented people who were looking at American society from the outside, rather than as valuable participants. Thus, in an effort to combat a sense of alienation and powerlessness, many Afro-Americans, although they might disagree with a Rap Brown or an Adam Clayton Powell, would support them because it brings to them a sense of pride and satisfaction that black Americans are expressing themselves and being heard. The leaders of the ethnic groups who expressed their views were angry toward the people standing in their way and they did seem like demagogues, but they used the only ways for those on the outside to express their sentiments.

At the age of fifty-eight, author John Steinbeck set out in search of America. Traveling in a small truck with his dog, Charley, he visited nearly forty states, becoming acquainted with an America he had never known. Having "found no strangers," despite the many ethnic elements extant, he concluded, "we are a nation, a new breed" and Americans "have more in common than they have apart." Sensing the paradox of ethnic pluralism, he nevertheless attempts to identify the American identity in the following brief but poetic paragraphs.

This monster of a land, this mightiest of nations, this spawn of the future, turns out to be the macrocosm of microcosm me.[5] If an Englishman or a Frenchman or an Italian should travel my route, see what I saw, hear what I heard, their stored pictures would be not only different from mine but equally different from one another. If other Americans reading this account should feel it true, that agreement would only mean that we are alike in our Americanness.

From start to finish I found no strangers. If I had, I might be able to report them objectively. But these are my people and this is my country. If I found matters to criticize and to deplore, they were tendencies equally present in myself. If I were to prepare one immaculately inspected generality it would be this: *For all of our enormous geographic range, for all of our sectionalism, for all of our interwoven breeds drawn from every part of the ethnic world, we are a nation, a new breed.* Americans are much more American than they are Northerners, Southerners, Westerners, or Easterners. And descendants of English, Irish, Italian, Jewish, German, Polish are essentially American. This is not patriotic whoop-de-do; it is carefully observed fact. California Chinese, Boston Irish, Wisconsin Germans, yes, and Alabama Negroes, *have more in common than they have apart.* And this is the more remarkable because it has happened so quickly. It is a fact that Americans from all sections and of all racial extractions are more alike than the Welsh are like the English, the Lancashireman like the Cockney, or for that matter the Lowland Scot like the Highlander. It is astonishing that this has happened in less than two hundred years and most of it in the last fifty. The American identity is an *exact and provable thing.* . . .

When I laid the ground plan of my journey, there were definite questions to which I wanted matching answers. It didn't seem to me that they were impossible questions. I suppose they could all be lumped into the single question: *"What are Americans like today?"*

In Europe it is a popular sport to describe what the Americans are like. Everyone seems to know. And we are equally happy in this game. How many times have I not heard one of my fellow countrymen, after a three-week tour of Europe, describe with certainty the nature of the French, the British, the Italians, the Germans, and above all the Russians? Traveling about, I early learned the difference between an American and the Americans. They are so far apart that they might be opposites. Often when a European has described the Americans with hostility and scorn he has turned to me and said, "Of course, I don't mean you. I am speaking of those others." It boils down to this: *the Americans, the British are that faceless clot you don't know, but a Frenchman or an Italian is your acquaintance and your friend.* He has none of the qualities your ignorance causes you to hate.

[5] From *Travels with Charley In Search of America* by John Steinbeck. Copyright © 1961, 1962 by The Curtis Publishing Co., Inc. Copyright © 1962 by John Steinbeck. Reprinted by permission of The Viking Press, Inc.

I had always considered this a kind of semantic deadfall, but moving about in my own country I am not at all sure that is so. Americans as I saw them and talked to them were indeed individuals, each one different from the others, but gradually *I began to feel that the Americans exist, that they really do have generalized characteristics regardless of their states, their social and financial status, their education, their religious, and their political convictions.* But if there is indeed an American image built of truth rather than reflecting either hostility or wishful thinking, *what is this image?* What does it look like? What does it do? If the same song, the same joke, the same style sweeps through all parts of the country at once, it must be that all Americans are alike in something. The fact that the same joke, the same style, has no effect in France or England or Italy makes this contention valid. *But the more I inspected this American image, the less sure I became of what it is.* It appeared to me increasingly paradoxical, and it has been my experience that when paradox crops up too often for comfort, it means that certain factors are missing in the equation. [Editor's Italics.]

The character of ethnicity emerges in the next selection, which analyzes the cultural impact of immigration in the United States. An extract from Maldwyn Allen Jones' standard study, *American Immigration,* summarizes the enduring quality of ethnic groups; yet Jones believes that the ethnic groups have transformed "their own identity in the larger American community."

Most difficult of all to assess is the cultural impact of immigration.[6] The commonest way of tackling the problem has been to compile lists of distinguished people of foreign birth or parentage as evidence of the "contribution" of various ethnic groups. Quite apart from the fact that this approach has led to exaggerated and absurd claims, any attempt to define cultural influences in this way is misconceived. For one thing, American culture is more than the sum of its parts; essentially a unit, it cannot be broken up into component parts, each of them attributable to particular groups of individuals. For another, such attempts to analyze "contribution" inevitably concentrate upon a comparatively small group of exceptional immigrants to the neglect of the great majority.

A more rewarding approach is one which attempts to examine the organized life of immigrants against the background of American culture as a whole. Each immigrant group, anxious to preserve traditional ways, at first endeavored to create a subculture of its own. In order to do so it was obliged to develop separate religious, educational, and benevolent institutions. But this step alone showed how strong was the pressure toward conformity with the existing American pattern, for these voluntary organizations, none of which had existed in Europe, adopted a common American form.

This tendency became increasingly evident with the passage of time. Even among first-generation immigrants only a proportion

[6] Reprinted from Maldwyn Allen Jones, *American Immigration,* pp. 316–319. Copyright © 1960 by the University of Chicago. By permission of the University of Chicago Press.

participated fully in the life of the group, and most of the second generation abandoned it altogether. Hence the only means whereby the old ways could survive was by being grafted onto the existing body of culture, a process necessarily involving the further modification of immigrant institutions. The immigrant press, for example, became in style and content indistinguishable from American newspapers generally, and immigrant schools and colleges likewise adapted themselves to a common mold.

It was in the immigrant churches, however, that the tendency toward accommodation was most clearly evident. It is true, of course, that many American religious denominations have retained their ethnic character; to this, indeed, the multiplicity of American sects is to be mainly attributed. In some cases the ethnic association is apparent from the name of the sect itself; the 1958 census of American religious bodies lists, among others, the Lithuanian and Polish National Catholic churches, the Finish Evangelical Lutheran Church, the Free Magyar Reformed Church, and the Albanian, Carpatho-Russian, Assyrian, Greek, Romanian, Russian, Serbian, Syrian, and Ukrainian Orthodox churches. No less ethnic in character are a number of churches whose names no longer indicate the fact; thus the Augustana Evangelical Lutheran Church is largely Swedish in membership, the Lutheran Free Church is Norwegian, and both the Evangelical Lutheran Church and the United Lutheran Church are German. Even churches founded in colonial days have not entirely lost their ethnic coloring: the Presbyterian Church is to some extent Scotch-Irish and Scottish, the Protestant Episcopal Church mainly English and the Reformed Churches are either Dutch or German.

Even so, these churches resemble each other, not only in having adopted the English language but in having taken on an American form of church life. Transplanted from Europe, where they had usually been part of the political structure, into the competitive American environment produced by the separation of church and state, the immigrant churches were forced to reorganize. Obliged to compete actively for members, they have become evangelical in tone and have tended to stress personal religious experience at the expense of dogma. Freed from a hierarcical control no less political than religious, they have embraced democratic forms of church government, usually involving lay representation. Shorn of their connection with the state, they have discarded their old political loyalties and have become avowedly non-political. In a word, they have been metamorphosed into characteristically American institutions.

This subtle yet profound type of alchemy provides the key not only to the immigrant contribution to American culture but also to the paradox of immigrant loyalties. To some observers there has been an element of contradiction in the fact that immigrants assert their American patriotism as members of separate groups. But the contradiction is only superficial. When Polish-Americans observe Pulaski Day, when Irish-Americans parade in honor of St. Patrick, when Italian-Americans gather to fete San Rocco or San Genaro, and even when Americans of Greek, Mexican, or Armenian origin celebrate the old country's independence day, they are merely asserting their cultural distinctiveness, merely seeking to make clear

their own identity in the larger American community. And even
while doing so, they rededicate themselves to the common national
ideals that bind them together.

In this way the immigrants have infused new meaning into
the national motto. To the Founding Fathers *e pluribus unum* meant
the fusion of thirteen separate states into a single political unit,
to the midtwentieth-century American it also denotes the unity that
has developed from the mingling of peoples diverse in origin but
sharing a common devotion to liberty, democracy, and tolerance.

What will be the future strength of ethnic subcultural identification? How can ethnic communality be properly juxtaposed in a society
which is vastly diverse and plural in design? In the selection that follows,
Milton M. Gordon examines pluralism, democratic values and long-range
goals for America. His conclusion: "Ethnic communality will not disappear in the foreseeable future and its legitimacy and rationale should be
recognized and respected." Additionally, the bonds that link all men
together should be encouraged in order to develop tolerant democratic
values.

Pluralism, Democratic Values, and Long-Range Goals for America:[7]
Our final remarks deal with the implications of our analysis of ethnic
communality and the assimilation process for long-range goals in
American social life with regard to intergroup relations. Into this
analysis we must interpolate, too, the significance of democratic
values as we understand them.

The struggle to eliminate racial and religious prejudice and
discrimination from American life—a struggle, the unequivocal
rightness of which, sociologically and ideologically, this volume
takes for granted—goes on against the underlying social reality of
ethnic communality tenaciously maintaining itself in an industrial
urbanized society. We have described the nature of this ethnic communality as basically, structural pluralism accompanied by an ever-
decreasing degree of cultural pluralism. The relationship of this
kind of a society to the problems inherent in attempting to eliminate
ethnic prejudice and discrimination have been discussed in the preceding pages. What, now, of the future? What are the viable goals
for America with regard to ethnic communality, given the desire to
eliminate or reduce prejudice and discrimination, the nature of
sociological realities, and commitment to the American democratic
value system?

The system of cultural pluralism (which ultimately depends
on structural pluralism) has frequently been described as "cultural
democracy," since it posits the right of ethnic groups in a democratic society to maintain their communal identity and their own
subcultural values. We have already argued that since ethnic communality rests principally on personal choices in primary group relations and private organizational affiliations, it falls well within the
scope of those areas of free choice guaranteed by democratic values.

[7] From *Assimilation in American Life* by Milton M. Gordon, pp. 262–65. Copyright ©
1964 by Oxford University Press, Inc. Reprinted by permission.

Reversing the coin, however, we must also point out that democratic values prescribe free choice not only for groups but also for individuals. That is, the individual, as he matures and reaches the age where rational decision is feasible, should be allowed to choose freely whether to remain within the boundaries of communality created by his birthright ethnic group, to branch out into multiple interethnic contacts, or even to change affiliation to that of another ethnic group should he wish to do so as a result of religious conversion, intermarriage, or simply private wish. If, to the contrary, the ethnic group places such heavy pressures on its birthright members to stay confined to ethnic communality that the individual who consciously wishes to "branch out" or "move away" feels intimidated or subject to major feelings of personal guilt and therefore remains ethnically enclosed, or moves but at considerable psychological cost, then we have, in effect, cultural democracy for groups but not for individuals. Realistically, it is probably impossible to have a socialization process for the child growing up in a particular ethnic group that does not involve some implicitly restrictive values; nevertheless, the magnitude and intensity of such restrictive norms must be kept within bounds if we are not to be left with a system which provides cultural democracy for groups but enforced ethnic enclosures for individuals.

Probably the vast majority of Americans, as revealed in their choices in primary group relations and organizational affiliations, desire ethnic communality, at least in essential outline. Their preferences are reinforced by the self-perpetuating pressures generated by the nature of subcommunity organizational life and by the demands and exhortations, grounded in ideological conviction, of their ethnic community leaders. As we have suggested, some individuals, as a result of their particular inclinations and perspectives, move out into an amorphously structured intellectual subcommunity which contains people of all ethnic backgrounds. All of these recurring processes are probably inevitable and basically irreversible. Thus the prognosis for America for a long time to come is that its informal social structure will consist of a series of ethnic subcommunities crisscrossed by social class, within which primary group relationships will tend to be confined, that secondary group relationships across ethnic group lines will take place in abundance as a result of the requirements of an urbanized industrial society, and that the intellectual subsociety will grow somewhat both in numbers and in institutional articulation as a result of the constant increase in the magnitude of higher education.

The major problem, then, is to keep ethnic separation in communal life from being so pronounced in itself that it threatens ethnic harmony, good group relations, and the spirit of basic good will which a democratic pluralistic society requires, and to keep it from spilling over into the civic arena of secondary relations to impinge on housing, jobs, politics, education, and other areas of functional activity where universalistic criteria of judgment and assignment are necessary and where the operation of ethnic considerations can only be disruptive and even disastrous. The attainment of this objective calls for good sense and reasonableness on the part of the average American citizen, regardless of ethnic background, and in addition to these qualities, a high degree of civic statesmanship on the part of ethnic communal leaders who will be tempted at times, out of their own convictions and enthusiasms, to emphasize ethnic exclusion and the demands in time and resources from their particular constituents which are likely to make for exclusion and separation, regardless of intent.

In sum, the basic long-range goal for Americans, with regard to ethnic communality, is fluidity and moderation within the context of equal civic rights for all, regardless of race, religion, or national background, and the option of democratic free choice for both groups and individuals. Ethnic communality will not disappear in the foreseeable future and its legitimacy and rationale should be recognized and respected. By the same token, the bonds that bind human beings together across the lines of ethnicity and the pathways on which people of diverse ethnic origin meet and mingle should be cherished and strengthened. In the last analysis, what is gravely required is a society in which one may say with equal pride and without internal disquietude at the juxtaposition: "I am a Jew, or a Catholic, or a Protestant, or a Negro, or an Indian, or an Oriental, or a Puerto Rican;" "I am an American;" and "I am a man."

KEY QUESTIONS

1. Do you agree with Barbara Mikulski's belief that America is not a melting pot? Explain your reasons.

2. Increasingly America's cities are becoming inhabited by large numbers of nonwhite ethnics. Elaborate on why you think they are or are not going through the same "Americanization" process that the pre–World War I immigrants experienced.

3. Professor Arthur Mann has stated, "The only angry men in politics were ethnics." Discuss the validity of this statement.

4. Define the following concepts: pluralism, assimilation.

5. Based upon your own experiences, has ethnicity played any role in your life? Explain.

Appendix

1. Proportion of Total Population Formed by Each Nationality: 1790.
2. White Population in 1790 by Nationality.
3. White and Black Population in 1790.
4. The American Indian Population.
5. Total and Negro Population: 1900, 1940, 1950, 1960, and 1966 to 1971.
6. United States Population by Race, Ethnic Origin, and Sex: March 1971.
7. Immigration to the United States 1820–1971.

Proportion of Total Population Formed by Each Nationality: 1790.

* Reprinted from U.S., Bureau of the Census, *A Century of Population Growth* (Washington, D.C.: Government Printing Office, 1909), p. 117.

White Population in 1790 by Nationality*

Nationality	Number	Percent
English	2,605,699	82.1
Scotch	221,562	7.0
Irish	61,534	1.9
Dutch	78,959	2.5
French	17,619	.6
German	176,407	5.6
Hebrew	1,243	1
All Other	9,421	.3
Total	3,172,444	100.0

[1] Less than 1/10 of 1 percent.

* Reprinted from Marion T. Bennett, *American Immigration Policies* (Washington, D.C.: Public Affairs Press, 1963), p. 298; and U.S., Census, *Century of Population Growth*, chap. 11.

White and Black Population in 1790†

	Number	Percent
White	3,172,444	80.73
Black	757,208	19.27
Total	3,929,652	100.00

† Reprinted from Bennett, *American Immgiration Policies,* p. 298; and U.S., Census, *Century of Population Growth,* chap. 11.

THE AMERICAN INDIAN POPULATION[1]

The 1970 Census revealed that the American Indian population increased more than 50% in the previous ten years. The figure of 791,839 was 258,248 over the 1960 population. The complete count of American Indians was not made before 1890 because the Indian population living on reservations or in the territories was not counted. The following figures cover the first official Census count up to the last:

1890	248,253
1900	237,196
1910	265,683
1920	244,437
1930	332,397
1940	333,929

[1] United States population figures based on the Official Census, 1890–1970, as found in *The World Almanac and Book of Facts 1974,* published for THE NEWS by Newspaper Enterprise Association, New York, 1973, p. 149.

1950	343,410
1960	523,591
1970	791,839

The final figures also reveal that 53% of the American Indian population lived in five states: Oklahoma, 97,731; Arizona, 95,812; California, 91,018; New Mexico, 72,788; and North Carolina, 43,387.

Total and Negro Population: 1900, 1940, 1950, 1960, and 1966 to 1971*
(Numbers in millions)

Year	Total	Negro	Percent Negro
1900[1]	76.0	8.8	12
1940[1]	131.7	12.9	10
1950[1]	150.7	15.0	10
1960	179.3	18.9	11
1966	195.0	21.2	11
1967	197.0	21.6	11
1968	198.9	21.9	11
1969	200.9	22.2	11
1970	203.2	22.6	11
1971	205.7	23.0	11

Note: Data are as of April 1 for each year. Data exclude Armed Forces overseas.
[1] Data exclude Alaska and Hawaii.

Source: U.S. Department of Commerce, Social and Economic Statistics Administration, Bureau of the Census.

* Reprinted from U.S., Bureau of the Census, "The Social and Economic Status of the Black Population in the United States, 1971," *Current Population Reports,* Series P–23, no. 42, p. 11.

**United States Population by Race, Ethnic Origin,
and Sex: March 1971***
(Numbers in thousands. Noninstitutional population)

Race and ethnic origin	Total	Male	Female	Percent distribution		
				Total	Male	Female
Total	202,848	98,420	104,428	100.0	100.0	100.0
RACE						
White	177,626	86,420	91,206	87.6	87.8	87.3
Negro	22,810	10,795	12,015	11.2	11.0	11.5
Other races	2,412	1,205	1,207	1.2	1.2	1.2
ETHNIC ORIGIN						
English, Scotch, Welsh	31,006	14,852	16,154	15.3	15.1	15.5
French	5,189	2,509	2,679	2.6	2.5	2.6
German	25,661	12,854	12,806	12.7	13.1	12.3
Irish	16,325	7,706	8,619	8.0	7.8	8.3
Italian	8,733	4,351	4,381	4.3	4.4	4.2
Polish	4,941	2,444	2,497	2.4	2.5	2.4
Russian	2,132	1,038	1,094	1.1	1.1	1.0
Spanish origin	8,956	4,419	4,539	4.4	4.5	4.3
Central or South American .	501	235	267	0.2	0.2	0.3
Cuban	626	313	313	0.3	0.3	0.3
Mexican	5,023	2,562	2,461	2.5	2.6	2.4
Puerto Rican	1,450	655	795	0.7	0.7	0.7
Other Spanish origin	1,356	654	703	0.7	0.7	0.7
Other ethnic origin[1]	84,689	40,655	44,035	41.7	41.3	42.2
Not reported	15,216	7,593	7,623	7.5	7.7	7.3

[1] Includes about 20 million Negroes, as well as many persons reporting more than one origin.

* Reprinted from U.S., Bureau of the Census, "Selected Characteristics of Persons and Families of Mexican, Puerto Rican, and Other Spanish Origin: March 1971," *Current Population Reports*, Series P–20, no. 224, p. 3.

Immigration to the United States*
1820–1971

[From 1820 to 1867, figures represent alien passengers arrived; from 1868 through 1891 and 1895 through 1897, immigrant aliens arrived; from 1892 through 1894 and 1898 to the present time, immigrant aliens admitted.]

Year	Number of persons	Year	Number of persons	Year	Number of persons	Year	Number of persons
1820–1971¹	45,533,116	1861–1870	2,314,824	1901–1910	8,795,386	1941–1950	1,035,039
1820	8,385	1861	91,918	1901	487,918	1941	51,776
1821–1830	143,439	1862	91,985	1902	648,743	1942	28,781
1821	9,127	1863	176,282	1903	857,046	1943	23,725
1822	6,911	1864	193,418	1904	812,870	1944	28,551
1823	6,354	1865	248,120	1905	1,026,499	1945	38,119
1824	7,912	1866	318,568	1906	1,100,735	1946	108,721
1825	10,199	1867	315,722	1907	1,285,349	1947	147,292
1826	10,837	1868	138,840	1908	782,870	1948	170,570
1827	18,875	1869	352,768	1909	751,786	1949	188,317
1828	27,382	1870	387,203	1910	1,041,570	1950	249,187
1829	22,520	1871–1880	2,812,191	1911–1920	5,735,811	1951–1960	2,515,479
1830	23,322	1871	321,350	1911	878,587	1951	205,717
1831–1840	570,125	1872	404,806	1912	838,172	1952	265,520
1831	22,633	1873	459,803	1913	1,197,892	1953	170,434
1832	60,482	1874	313,339	1914	1,218,480	1954	208,177
1833	58,640	1875	227,498	1915	326,700	1955	237,790
1834	65,365	1876	169,986	1916	298,826	1956	321,625
1835	45,374	1877	141,857	1917	295,403	1957	326,867
1836	76,242	1878	138,469	1918	110,618	1958	253,265
1837	79,340	1879	177,826	1919	141,132	1959	260,686
1838	38,914				430,001	1960	265,398
1839	68,069						

1841–1850	1,713,251	1881–1890	5,246,613	1921–1930	4,107,209
1841	80,289	1881	669,431	1921	805,228
1842	104,565	1882	788,992	1922	309,556
1843	52,496	1883	603,322	1923	522,919
1844	78,615	1884	518,592	1924	706,896
1845	114,371	1885	395,346	1925	294,314
1846	154,416	1886	334,203	1926	304,488
1847	234,968	1887	490,109	1927	335,175
1848	226,527	1888	546,889	1928	307,255
1849	297,024	1889	444,427	1929	279,678
1850	369,980	1890	455,302	1930	241,700
1851–1860	2,598,214	1891–1900	3,687,564	1931–1940	528,431
1851	379,466	1891	560,319	1931	97,139
1852	371,603	1892	579,663	1932	35,576
1853	368,645	1893	439,730	1933	23,068
1854	427,833	1894	285,631	1934	29,470
1855	200,877	1895	258,536	1935	34,956
1856	200,436	1896	343,267	1936	36,329
1857	251,306	1897	230,832	1937	50,244
1858	123,126	1898	229,299	1938	67,895
1859	121,282	1899	311,715	1939	82,998
1860	153,640	1900	448,572	1940	70,756

1961–1970	3,321,677
1961	271,344
1962	283,763
1963	306,260
1964	292,248
1965	296,697
1966	323,040
1967	361,972
1968	454,448
1969	358,579
1970	373,326
1971	370,478

[1] Since July 1, 1868, the data is for fiscal years ending June 30. Prior to fiscal year 1869, the periods covered are as follows: from 1820–1831 and 1843–1849, the years ended on September 30; 1832—1843 covers 9 months; from 1832–1842 and 1850–1867, the years ended on December 31 —1832 and 1850 cover 15 months. For 1868, the period ended on June 30 and covers 6 months.

* U.S., Department of Justice Immigration and Naturalization Service, *1971 Annual Report, Immigration and Naturalization Service* (Washington, D.C.: U.S. Government Printing Office, 1971), p. 25.

Bibliography

CHAPTER 1

Greene, Arnold W. *Sociology*. 4th edition. New York: McGraw-Hill, 1964.

Handlin, Oscar. *This Was America*. New York: Harper & Row, 1964.

Kallen, Horace. *Culture and Democracy in the United States*. New York: Liveright, 1924.

Noel, Donald L. "A Theory of the Origin of Ethnic Stratification." *Social Problems* 16 (Fall, 1968).

Novak, Michael. *The Rise of the Unmeltable Ethnics*. New York: Macmillan, 1972.

Parenti, Michael. "Ethnic Politics and Ethnic Identification." *American Political Science Review* 61 (September, 1967).

The Reacting Americans. New York: American Jewish Congress, 1969.

Schweiker, Richard S. "Ethnic Studies: Toward a New Pluralism in America." In *Pieces of a Dream*, edited by Michael Wenk, Silvan M. Tomasi, and Geno Baroni. New York: The Center for Migration Studies, 1972.

CHAPTER 2

Abbott, Edith. *Historical Aspects of the Immigration Problem*. Chicago: University of Chicago Press, 1926.

Bradford, William. *Of Plymouth Plantation 1620–1647*. Reprint. Edited by Samuel Eliot Morison. New York: Alfred A. Knopf, Inc., 1952.

Colton, Calvin. *Manual for Emigrants to America*. Reprint. New York: Arno Press, 1969.

Catlin, George. *Letters and Notes of the Manners, Customs, and Conditions of the North American Indians*. Vol. 1. London, 1841. Reprint. New York: Dover Publications, 1973.

Conway, Alan. *The Welsh in America*. Minneapolis: University of Minnesota Press, 1961.

de Tocqueville, Alexis. *Democracy in America*. Reprint. New York: Alfred A. Knopf, Inc., 1961.

Donaldson, Gordon. *The Scots Overseas*. London: Robert Hale, 1966.

Dunaway, W. F. *The Scotch-Irish of Colonial Pennsylvania*. Chapel Hill: 1944.

Eddis, William. *Letters from America, Historical and Descriptive, Comprising Occurrences from 1769 to 1770 inclusive*. London: 1772.

Faust, Albert B. *The German Element in the United States*. Vol. 1. 1909. Reprint. New York: Arno Press, 1969.

Ford, Henry Jones. *The Scotch-Irish in America*. Reprint. New York: Arno Press, 1969.

Gibson, Florence Elizabeth. *The Attitudes of the New York Irish toward State and National Affairs, 1848–1892*. New York: Columbia University Press, 1954.

Goodwin, Maud Wilder, ed. *Historic New York*. Vol. 2. Reprint. Port Washington: Ira J. Friedman, 1969.

Handlin, Oscar, ed. *This Was America*. New York: Harper & Row, 1964.

Hartmann, Edward G. *Americans from Wales*. Boston: The Christopher Publishing House, 1967.

Hirsch, Arthur Henry. *The Huguenots of Colonial South Carolina*. Hamden, Conn.: The Shoe String Press, 1962.

Hoff, Rhoda. *American Immigrants*. New York: Henry Z. Walck, 1969.

Irving, Washington. *The Sketchbook*. Philadelphia: Henry Altemus, 1895.

Katz, William L. *Eyewitness: The Negro in American History*. New York: Pitman Publishing Co., 1967.

Kraus, Michael. *Immigration, The American Mosaic: From Pilgrims to Modern Refugees*. New York: Litton Educational Publishing, Inc., 1966.

Larabee, Leonard W., ed. *The Papers of Benjamin Franklin*. Vol. 4. New Haven: Yale University Press, 1961.

Leach, Douglas Edward. *Flintlock and Tomahawk, New England in King Philip's War*. New York: W. W. Norton & Company, Inc., 1958.

Lucas, Henry S. *Dutch Immigrant Memoirs and Selected Writings*. Vol. 1. Seattle: University of Washington, 1955.

MaGuire, John Francis. *The Irish in America*. 1868. Reprint. New York: Arno Press, 1969.

Mittleberger, Gottlieb. *Journey to Pennsylvania in the Year 1750 and Return to Germany in the Year 1754*. Edited and translated by Oscar Handlin and John Clive. Cambridge, MA: Harvard University Press, 1960.

Mulder, Arnold. *Americans from Holland*. Philadelphia: J. P. Lippincott Company, 1947.

Northup, Solomon. *Twelve Years a Slave*. Edited by Sue Eakin and Joseph Logsdon. Baton Rouge: Louisiana State University Press, 1968.

Osofsky, Gilbert, ed. *Puttin' On Ole Massa, The Slave Narratives of Henry Bibb, William Wells Brown, and Solomon Northup*. New York: Harper & Row, 1969.

Schrier, A. *Ireland and the American Emigration, 1850–1900*. New York: Russell & Russell, 1970.

Wabeke, B. H. *Dutch Immigration to North America, 1824–1860*. New York: 1944.

Walker, Mack. *Germany and the Emigration, 1816–1885.* Cambridge, MA: Harvard University Press, 1964.

Weld, Ralph Foster. *Brooklyn Village, 1816–1834.* New York, 1938. Reprint. New York: AMS Press, 1970.

Wood, Ralph, ed. *The Pennsylvania Germans.* Princeton: 1942.

Woodham-Smith, C. *The Great Hunger—Ireland, 1845–1849.* New York: 1902.

CHAPTER 3

Abbott, Edith. *Immigration, Select Documents and Case Records.* Chicago: University of Chicago Press, 1924.

Adams, William F. *Ireland and the Irish Emigration to the New World from 1815 to the Famine.* 1932.

Babcock, K. C. "The Scandinavian Element in the American Population." *The American Historical Review* 16 (1911).

Barthold, Richard. *From Steerage to Congress, Reminiscences and Reflections.* Philadelphia: Dorrance and Co., Inc., 1930.

Benson, Adolph B., and Hedin, Naboth, eds. *Swedes in America.* New Haven: Yale University Press, 1938.

Berthoff, Rowland Toppan. *British Immigrants in Industrial America, 1790–1950.* Cambridge, MA: Harvard University Press, 1953.

Blegen, Theodore G. *Land of Their Choice.* Minneapolis: University of Minnesota Press, 1955.

————. *Norwegian Migration to America, 1825–1860.* Northfield, Minnesota: Norwegian-American Historical Association, 1931.

Hansen, Marcus Lee. *The Mingling of the Canadian and American People.* New Haven: 1950.

Hawgood, John A. *The Tragedy of German America.* New York: G. P. Putnam and Sons, 1940.

Johnson, Stanley C. *A History of Emigration from the United Kingdom to North America.* London: 1913.

Larson, Lawrence Marcellus. *The Log Book of a Young Immigrant.* Northfield, Minn.: Norwegian-American Historical Association, 1939.

MacDonugh, Oliver. "Irish Overseas Emigration During the Famine." In *The Great Famine,* edited by R. D. Edwards and T. D. Williams.

MaGuire, John Francis. *The Irish in America.* 1868. Reprint. New York: Arno Press, 1969.

O'Connor, Richard. *The German Americans, An Informal History.* Boston: Little, Brown and Co., 1968.

Osland, Birger. *A Long Pull from Stavanger, The Reminiscences of a Norwegian Immigrant.* Northfield, Minn.: Norwegian-American Historical Society, 1945.

Qualey, C. C. *Norwegian Settlements in the United States.* Northfield, Minn.: Norwegian-American Historical Society, 1938.

Riis, Jacob A. *The Making of an American.* New York: Macmillan, 1901. Reprint. Edited by Roy Lubove. New York: Harper, 1966.

Rolvaag, Ole. *Giants in the Earth.* New York: Harper and Row, 1927.

Schurz, Carl. *The Reminiscences of Carl Schurz.* Vol. 3. New York: The McClure Co., 1908.

Unonius, Gustav. *A Pioneer in Northwest America, 1841–1858.* Vol. 2. Minneapolis: University of Minnesota Press, 1960.

Wittke, Carl. *German-Americans and the World War.* Columbus: 1936.

Wright, Tobert L. *Swedish Emigrant Ballads.* Lincoln, Nebraska: University of Nebraska, 1965.

Works Progress Administration. *The Swedes and Finns in New Jersey.* Bayonne, N.J.: 1938.

CHAPTER 4

Buaken, Iris B. "You Can't Marry A Filipino." *Commonweal* 41 (1945): 534–537.

Buaken, Manuel. *I Have Lived with the American People.* Caldwell, Idaho: The Caxton Printers, 1948.

Coolidge, Mary Roberts. *Chinese Immigration.* New York: Arno Press, 1969.

Daniels, Roger. *The Politics of Prejudice.* New York: Atheneum, 1968.

Girdner, Audrie, and Loftis, Anne. *The Great Betrayal.* London: Macmillan, 1969.

Hosokawa, Bill. *Nisei, The Quiet Americans.* New York: William Morrow, 1969.

Kawakami, Kiyoshi Karl. *The Real Japanese Question.* New York: Macmillan, 1920.

Kitagawa, Daisuke. *Issei and Nisei, The Internment Years.* New York: The Seabury Press, 1967.

Kitano, Harry H. L. *Japanese Americans.* Englewood Cliffs, N.J.: Prentice-Hall, 1969.

Lasker, Bruno. *Filipino Immigration.* Chicago: University of Chicago Press, 1931.

Miller, Stuart Creighton. *The Unwelcome Immigrant, The American Image of the Chinese, 1785–1882.* Berkeley, CA: University of California Press, 1969.

Park, No-Yong. *An Oriental View of American Civilization.* Boston: Hale, Cushman, and Flint, 1934.

Spicer, Edward H.; Hansen, Asael T.; Luomala, Katherine; and Opler, Marvin K. *Impounded People, Japanese-Americans in Relocation Centers.* Tucson: The University of Arizona Press, 1969.

Sung, Betty Lee. *Mountain of Gold.* New York: Macmillan, 1967.

Thomas, Dorothy Swaine, and Nishimoto, Richard S. *The Spoilage, Japanese American Evacuation and Resettlement.* Berkeley, CA: University of California Press, 1969.

War Relocation Authority. "A Nisei Who Said 'No.'" *Community Analysis Notes* 1 (January 15, 1944): 1–9.

———. "Nisei Report on Their Adjustment to Tule Lake." *Community Analysis Notes* 7 (December 20, 1944): 1–3.

CHAPTER 5

Balch, Emily G. *Our Slavic Fellow Citizens.* 1910. Reprint. New York: Arno Press, 1970.

Capek, Thomas. *The Czechs (Bohemians) in America: A Study of Their National, Cultural, Political, Social, Economic and Religious Life.* 1920. Reprint. New York: Arno Press, 1969.

Davis, Jerome. *The Russian Immigrant.* 1922. Reprint. New York: Arno Press, 1969.

Fox, Paul. *The Poles in America.* 1922. Reprint. New York: Arno Press, 1970.

Halich, Wasyl. *Ukrainians in the United States.* 1937. Reprint. New York: Arno Press, 1970.

Kutak, Robert I. *The Story of a Bohemian-American Village: A Study of Social Persistence and Change.* 1933. Reprint. New York: Arno Press, 1970.

Miller, Kenneth D. *The Czechoslovaks in America.* New York: Doran, 1922.

Roberts, Peter. *The New Immigration: A Study of the Industrial and Social Life of Southeastern Europeans in America.* 1914. Reprint. New York: Arno Press, 1970.

Sheridan, Frank J. *Italian, Slavic and Hungarian Unskilled Laborers in the United States.* 1907. Reprint. New York: Jerome S. Ozer, 1971.

Thomas, William I. and Znaniecki, Florian. *The Polish Peasant in Europe and America.* 5 vols. 1920. Reprint (5 vols. in 1). New York: Dover Publications, 1958.

Warne, Frank J. *The Slav Invasion and the Mine Workers: A Study in Immigration.* 1913. Reprint. New York: Jerome S. Ozer, 1971.

CHAPTER 6

Cahan, Abraham. *The Rise of David Levensky.* New York: Harper and Row, 1960.

Davis, Jerome. *The Russians and Ruthenians in America.* New York: George H. Doran Co., 1922.

Gold, Michael. *Jews Without Money.* New York: Liveright Publishers, 1930.

Goldstein, Sidney. *Jewish Americans: Three Generations in a Jewish Community.* Englewood Cliffs, NJ: Prentice-Hall, 1968.

Halich, Wasyl. *Ukrainians in the United States.* Chicago: University of Chicago Press, 1937.

James, E. J., ed. *The Immigrant Jew in America.* New York: 1907.

Joseph, Samuel. *Jewish Immigration to the United States from 1881 to 1910.* New York: Columbia University Press, 1914.

Kezierska, Anzia. *Children of Loneliness.* New York: Funk and Wagnalls Co., 1923.

Leibbrandt, George. "The Emigration of the German Mennonites from Russia to the United States and Canada, 1873–1880." Part Two. *The Mennonite Quarterly Review* 7 (1933): 36–37.

United Hebrew Charities. *Twentieth Annual Report.* New York: 1886.

Wischnitzer, Mark. *Visas to Freedom.* Cleveland: World Publishing Co., 1956.

CHAPTER 7

Covello, Leonard. *Social Background of the Italo-American School Child* Leiden, Netherlands: E. J. Brill, 1967.

DeConde, Alexander. *Half Bitter, Half Sweet, An Excursion into Italian American History*. New York: Charles Scribner's Sons, 1971.

Engel, Madeline, and Tomasi, Sylvan M. *The Italian Experience in the United States*. New York: Center for Migration Studies, 1971.

Fairchild, Henry P. *Greek Immigration to the United States*. New Haven: Yale University Press, 1921.

Felici, Ecilio. *Father to the Immigrants, Life of John Baptist Scalabrini*. New York: P. J. Kenedy and Sons, 1955.

First Annual Report with Constitution and By-laws of the Syrian Society of the City of New York. New York: May, 1893.

Foerster, Robert F. *Italian Emigration of Our Times*. Cambridge, MA: Harvard University Press, 1924.

Hitti, Philip K. *The Syrians in America*. New York: George H. Doran, 1924.

Iorizzo, Luciano J., and Mondello, Salvatore. *The Italian Americans*. New York: Twayne Publishers, 1971.

Leder, Hans Howard. "Cultural Persistence in a Portuguese-American Community." Doctoral thesis, Stanford University, 1968.

Neff, Alixa. "Belief in the Evil Eye Among the Christian Syrian-Lebanese in America." *Journal of American Folklore* (January 1965): 46–47.

Rolle, Andrew F. *The Immigrant Upraised*. Norman, Oklahoma: University of Oklahoma Press, 1966.

Saloutos, Theodore. *The Greeks in the United States*. Cambridge, MA: Harvard University Press, 1964.

———. *They Remember America, The Story of the Repatriated Greek-Americans*. Berkeley, CA: University of California Press, 1956.

Schiavo, Giovanni. *Italians in Chicago*. Chicago: Italian American Publishing Company, 1928.

———. *The Italians in Missouri*. Chicago: Italian American Publishing Company, 1929.

Taft, Donald. *Two Portuguese Communities in New England*. New York: Arno Press, 1969.

Xenides, J. P. *The Greeks in America*. New York: George H. Doran Co., 1922.

CHAPTER 8

Barrett, S. M., ed. *Geronimo, His Own Story*. (Introduction and Notes by Frederick W. Turner.) New York: E. P. Dutton, 1970.

Brown, Dee. *Bury My Heart at Wounded Knee*. New York: Holt, Rinehart and Winston, 1970.

Chaput, Donald. "Some Repatriement Dilemmas." *The Canadian Historical Review* 49:4 (1968): 400–412.

Debo, Angie. *A History of the Indians of the United States*. Norman, Oklahoma: University of Oklahoma Press, 1970.

Forbes, Jack. *Hearing Before the United States Commission on Civil Rights*. Hearing held in San Antonio, Texas, December 9-14, 1968. Washington, D.C.: Government Printing Office, 1968, pp. 25–31.

Gamio, Manuel. *Mexican Immigration to the United States*. Chicago: University of Chicago Press, 1930.

Grebler, Leo; Moore, Joan W.; and Guzman, Ralph C. *The Mexican-American Peoples, The Nation's Second Largest Minority.* New York: The Free Press, 1970.

Ham, Edward E. "French Patterns in Quebec and New England." *The New England Quarterly* (December, 1945): 435–447.

Howard, John R., ed. *Awakening Minorities.* Chicago: Aldine, 1970.

McWilliams, Carey. *North from Mexico.* New York: Greenwood Press, 1968.

Meier, Matt S., and Rivera, Feliciano. *The Chicanos.* New York: Hill and Wang, 1972.

Moore, Joan W. and Cuellar, Alfredo. *Mexican Americans.* Englewood Cliffs: Prentice-Hall, 1970.

Moquin, Wayne, and Van Doren, Charles, eds. *A Documentary History of the Mexican Americans.* New York: Praeger, 1971.

Nava, Julian. *Mexican Americans: Past, Present, and Future.* New York: American Book Company, 1969.

Stillwell, Hart. "The Wetback Tide." *Common Ground* 9 (1949): 3–14.

Vogt, Evon. "The Acculturation of American Indians." *The Annals of the Academy of Political and Social Sciences* 311 (1957): 137–146.

Wessel, Bessie Bloom. *An Ethnic Survey of Woonsocket, Rhode Island.* New York: Arno Press, 1970.

CHAPTER 9

Alexander, Tom. "Those Amazing Cuban Emigres." *Fortune Magazine* 74 (1966): 144–149.

Glazer, Nathan, and Moynihan, Daniel Patrick. *Beyond the Melting Pot.* Cambridge, MA: The MIT Press, 1963.

Holbrook, Sabra. *The American West Indies.* New York: Meredith Press, 1969.

Lewis, Gordon K. *Puerto Rico, Freedom and Power in the Caribbean.* New York: Harper and Row, 1963.

Lewis, Oscar. *La Vida.* New York: Random House, 1965.

Portes, Alejandro. "Dilemmas of a Golden Exile: Integration of Cuban Refugee Families in Milwaukee." *American Sociological Review* 34 (1969): 505–518.

Pousner, Michael. "Haitians: The Invisible Minority." *New York Daily News,* January 11, 1971, p. 32.

Rand, Christopher. *The Puerto Ricans.* New York: Oxford University Press, 1958.

Senior, Clarence. *The Puerto Ricans, Strangers—Then Neighbors.* Chicago: Quadrangle Books, 1965.

Thomas, Piri. *Down These Mean Streets.* New York: The New American Library, 1967.

Wakefield, Dan. *Island in the City.* Boston: Houghton-Mifflin, 1959.

CHAPTER 10

Breitman, George, ed. *Malcolm X Speaks.* New York: Grove Press, 1965.

Carmichael, Stokely, and Hamilton, Charles V. *Black Power: The Politics of Liberation in America.* New York: Random House, 1967.

Clark, Kenneth B. "Sex, Status, and Underemployment of the Negro Male." In *Employment, Race and Poverty*, edited by Arthur M. Ross and Herbert Hill. New York: Harcourt, Brace and World, 1967.

Ellison, Ralph. *The Invisible Man*. New York: The New American Library, 1952.

King, Martin Luther, Jr. "Letter from Birmingham City Jail." In *Black on Black*, edited by Arnold Adoff. New York: Macmillan, 1968.

Lomax, Louis. *The Negro Revolt*. New York: Harper and Row, 1962.

Mebane, Mary E. "Daddy Wasn't a Numbers Runner." *The New York Times*, February 18, 1971, p. 35.

Pinkney, Alphonso. *Black Americans*. Englewood Cliffs, NJ: Prentice-Hall, 1969.

Randolph, A. Philip. "March on Washington Movement Presents Program for the Negro." In *What the Negro Wants*, edited by Rayford W. Logan. Chapel Hill: University of North Carolina Press, 1944.

Snellings, Roland. "Sunrise." In *Black Fire*, edited by LeRoi Jones and Roy Neal. New York: Morrow, 1968.

Wilkins, Roy. "Integration." *Ebony* 25 (1970): 54–60.

CHAPTER 11

Committee on the Judiciary, U.S. House of Representatives. *Immigration and Nationality Act, With Amendments and Notes on Related Laws*. 5th edition. Washington, D.C.: Government Printing Office, 1966.

"Controversy Over U.S. Immigration Policy." *Congressional Digest* (May, 1965).

Eckerson, Helen F. "Immigration and National Origins." *Annals of the American Academy of Political and Social Sciences* 366 (1966): 5–15.

Grant, Madison. *The Passing of the Great Race*. New York: Charles Scribner's Sons, 1921.

Handlin, Oscar. *Race and Nationality in American Life*. Boston: Little, Brown and Co., 1957.

LaGumina, Salvatore J. "The New Deal, the Immigrants, and Congressman Vito Marcantonio." *The International Migration Review* 4:11 (1970): 57–74.

Lodge, Henry Cabot. "The Restriction of Immigration." *North American Review* 152 (1891): 27–36.

———. *Reports of the Immigration Commission*. Vol. 1. Reprint. New York: Arno Press, 1970.

Walsh, David I. *Congressional Record*. 68th Congress, 1st Session (April 15, 1924): 6355–6357.

Watson, Barbara M. "Immigration Today." *The International Migration Review* 4 (1970): 47–51.

CHAPTER 12

Bornfriend, Arnold J. "Political Parties and Pressure Groups." *Governing the City, Proceedings of the Academy of Political Science* 29 (1969): 55–67.

Fairchild, Henry Pratt. *The Melting Pot Mistake*. Boston: Little, Brown and Co., 1926.

Gordon, Milton M. *Assimilation in American Life*. New York: Oxford University Press, 1964.

Huthmaker, J. Joseph. *A Nation of Newcomers: Ethnic Minority Groups in American History*. New York: Delacorte Press, 1967.

Jones, Maldwyn Allen. *American Immigration*. Chicago: University of Chicago Press, 1960.

Mann, Arthur. "Response to LaGumina Paper." *Ethnicity in American Political Life—the Italian American Experience, Proceedings of the First Annual Italian American Historical Association* (1968): 33–35.

Mikulski, Barbara. "The Myth of the Melting Pot." *Ethnos* (Newsletter) 1:2 (1970).

Steinbeck, John. *Travels with Charley*. New York: Bantam, 1963.